WORD DANCE

WORD DANCE

THE LANGUAGE OF NATIVE AMERICAN CULTURE

Carl Waldman

PEN-AND-INK DRAWINGS BY

Molly Braun

Facts On File, Inc.

AN INFOBASE HOLDINGS COMPANY

For Brant

Word Dance: The language of Native American culture

Copyright © 1994 by Carl Waldman
Drawings copyright © 1994 by Molly Braun

Facts On File, Inc.
11 Penn Plaza
New York, NY 10001

Library of Congress Cataloging-in-Publication Data

Waldman, Carl.
Word dance : the language of native American culture / Carl Waldman ; pen-and-ink drawings
by Molly Braun.
    p. cm.
Includes bibliographical references.
ISBN 0-8160-2834-6
ISBN 0-8160-3494-X (pbk)
1. Indians of North America—Dictionaries. I. Braun, Molly. II. Title.
E76.2.W36   1994
970.004'97'003—dc20   94–10311

Text design by Catherine Rincon Hyman
Jacket design by Carla Wiese
Printed in the United States of America

MP VC 10 9 8 7 6 5 4 3 2

This book is printed on acid-free paper.

CONTENTS

INTRODUCTION

The language pertaining to Native American cultural studies is a unique challenge, encompassing a broad range of subject areas—history, anthropology, sociology, archaeology, geology, geography, linguistics, technology, architecture, art, religion, mythology, musicology, biology, and botany. Different fields of study have different vocabularies. Terms also vary from age to age, and from text to text, within the same field of study. Moreover, many words encountered in Indian studies are from native dialects or from foreign languages; many have more than one spelling.

Word Dance is designed as a short-entry study aid and companion volume for students pursuing many aspects of American Indian cultural studies. Since language usage and word definitions are central to it, the book is closest in form to a glossary or dictionary. But *Word Dance* also resembles an encyclopedia in that entries discuss how a term or concept relates specifically to Native American culture and history.

In a single-volume word book of limited length for generalized cultural studies, it is difficult deciding what *not* to include. Some terms—many of which are familiar but might not be properly understood—are given individual entries; examples include "wampum" and "wigwam." Other terms come up again and again in readings on Native Americans and are obvious choices, such as "medicine bundle" and "potlatch." Some well-known terms have to be explained in the context of Indian studies, such as "clan" and "slavery." But after a certain point, arbitrariness comes into play. For instance, a book such as this cannot be all-inclusive in regard to recorded tribal ceremonies. But some, such as the "Sun Dance" and "Vision Quest," are cited often in writings on Indians. Others struck this author as representative or fascinating. Such is the case with the names of legendary beings; this book lists many names most frequently encountered, along with a representative number of others. Some animals and plants serving as food staples are included; others are cited because they carry with them intriguing mythology. Some natural phenomena are included because they are difficult terms; or because they relate to archaeological studies; or because they have a noteworthy connection to Indian history or legends. And so on.

Because of the vastness of the material, a single-volume book such as this has to have an internal logic that becomes a system of study and supplies a kind of outline of Indian culture. For example, *Word Dance* utilizes a system of culture areas common to many scholars, but not to all; tribal entries are cross-referenced to them. (A "culture area" is a cartographic classification based on geography and customs.)

Although *Word Dance* is by design a companion to Native American cultural studies, it has application in historical studies as well. Some historical concepts are defined and discussed in broad terms. One can look up "activism" but not particular activist organizations; one can look up "warfare" but not a particular battle. Certain events and places that have taken on broad cultural and symbolic implications have been included, such as the "Trail of Tears," "Sand Creek," "Little Bighorn," and "Wounded Knee." Although the book does not list archaeological sites, it does list certain prehistoric cultures. Nor is *Word Dance* a "who was who." It does not contain entries for people other than legendary beings, but some individuals are mentioned within the entries, as in the case of founders of certain religions. In addition, since one cannot study either American Indian culture or history without knowing the past and present locations of tribes, the tribal entries include some dates of migration.

Word Dance is weighted toward native peoples of North America, that is, the part of North America comprising the present-day United States and Canada, with many North American peoples, cultures, languages, and tribes listed. Some bands (or subtribes) have their own entries if they are discussed frequently as a distinct group, or if they exist as tribal entities today. Other tribes, especially extinct groupings, are listed under language families (groupings of similar languages). Yet the level of organization for Central American and South American Indians, other than a few exceptions, stops at language families. Moreover, North American Indian lifeways covered also outnumber South American Indian ones, but what might be called a starter list is provided for the latter.

Word Dance is not a dictionary of Indian languages, although many of the terms listed are derived from them. In order to help the researcher locate native terms, many of them are listed under their translations. Those included may serve as a sampling of the richness of Indian culture as expressed in language and spark interest in the hundreds of surviving Native American languages (before it's too late). A categorical appendix and a tribal index give additional windows into the material. A bibliography of books on general titles, with a section on Indian languages as well as additional bibliographies, will help in further studies.

As a glossary, *Word Dance* is of course alphabetically arranged. The book utilizes the letter-by-letter alphabetizing method as opposed to the word-by-word method, i.e., two words are treated as one ("Blackfoot" coming before "Black Legs Ceremony").

Cross-references (in small capital letters) are designed to increase accessibility and are used to aid in understanding. But commonly known and repeated terms that have their own entry in this book, such as "Native American" or "tool," are not always cross-referenced. Relevant cross-references not mentioned in the text are listed parenthetically at the end of the entries.

Headings are singular unless the words are used only in the plural. But within the entry, terms are sometimes cross-referenced as they appear in plural. For example, the cross-reference might say "Mohawks," but the actual headword is "Mohawk."

Entry headings that are from a native or foreign language are italicized. In some instances, such as "powwow," a word is used often enough in English so that italicization is not necessary. Proper names, even from an Indian word, are not italicized, such as the names of legendary beings. Spoken expressions and in some cases dated historical terms are indicated by quotation marks.

After the heading, alternate spellings as well as synonyms are listed. Commonly encountered alternate spellings (i.e., "tipi") have their own headings as well and are cross-referenced to the main spelling (i.e., "tepee"). Some acronyms ("BIA") are also included. Some terms appear in Indian studies as two words without a hyphen, with a hyphen, or as one word. This author tended to select the single-word form, i.e., "sandpainting." As for native language terms, differing dialectal versions of the same term are sometimes, but not always, given. In each tribal entry, language families (or language isolates) are cited, along with culture areas, historical and present-day locations, and, if known, etymologies of tribal names. Many more alternate tribal names and spellings exist than are included in this book.

With regard to capitalization, there is inconsistency among writers. Some capitalize "manitou," for instance, and some do not; some capitalize "culture" in "Anasazi Culture," or "period" in "Paleolithic period," and others do not. While consistent choices have been made herein, the reader might encounter other usage elsewhere.

An additional challenge has been the question of tense. Indian studies involve the past as well as the present, with some terms applying to the past, some to the present, and some to both. So tenses shift accordingly. Yet their usage is not absolute. For instance, some crafts more relevant to early Indian studies, such as the "flaking" of stone points, might be discussed in the past tense although they are still practiced today in order to preserve traditions.

It is hoped that *Word Dance* will serve as an accessible reference tool, helping students and researchers understand particular terms. It is also hoped that it will impart an overview of Indian culture and language, inspiring and facilitating further studies of the Native American legacy and worldview.

Abenaki (Abnaki, Abenaqui, Wabanaki) An ALGONQUIAN-speaking tribe of the NORTHEAST CULTURE AREA, located in present-day Maine and eastern New Hampshire. The Amaseconti, Arosaguntacook, Missiassik, Norridgewock, Ossipee, Pequawket, Rocameca, Sokoki, and Wawenoc subtribes were part of the Abenaki Confederacy, along with the MALECITE, MICMAC, PASSAMAQUODDY, PENOBSCOT, and PENNACOOK tribes. By the early 1700s, many bands had moved to Quebec. In addition to the Passamaquoddies, Penobscots, and Pennacooks, the following groups maintain tribal identity: the St. Francis/Sokoki Band of Abenakis in Swanton, Vermont; the Abenaki Indian Village in Lake George, New York; and the Abenakis of Becancour and of Odanak in Quebec. *Abenaki* or *Wabanaki* means "those living at the sunrise," "people of the dawn," or "easterners" in Algonquian.

Abitibi (Abittibi, Abittibbe, Abitiwinne) A subtribe of the ALGONKIN Indians, located on Abitibi Lake in present-day Ontario. Two contemporary Canadian bands that use the Abitibi tribal name, living near Matheson, Ontario and Amos, Quebec, have CHIPPEWA and CREE ancestry as well. *Abitibi* means "halfway across lake" in Algonquian.

Abnaki See ABENAKI.

aboriginal Originating in a particular place, as in "aboriginal peoples." "Autochthonous" is a synonym, as in "autochthonous flora or fauna." The noun form aborigine, a primary inhabitant of a region, is more often applied to the earliest inhabitants of Australia than to NATIVE AMERICANS. (See also INDIGENOUS; NATIVE PEOPLES.)

abrader A tool used to shape, smooth, or polish a material by friction. GRINDSTONES and WHETSTONES are types of abrasive stones or abrading implements.

Absarokee See CROW (Absarokee).

absolute dating The dating of ancient materials by means of an independent technique with a fixed time scale, such as DENDROCHRONOLOGY or RADIOCARBON DATING, as opposed to RELATIVE DATING.

acculturation The transfer of cultural elements between societies, especially the modification of a subordinate CULTURE through contact with a dominant one. (See also ASSIMILATION; CULTURAL DISPOSSESSION; DETRIBALIZATION.)

Achomawi (Achomawe, Achumawi, Pit River) A PALAIHNIHAN-speaking tribe of the CALIFORNIA CULTURE AREA, located on the Pit River between the Warner Range and Mount Shasta and Mount Lassen in present-day California. Descendants, known as Pit River Indians, hold the following rancherias (reservations) in California: Alturas, Big Bend, Likely, Lookout, Montgomery Creek, Roaring Creek; they share Round Valley, Susanville, and X L rancherias with other tribes. Achomawi is derived from the Palaihnihan word for river.

Acolapissa See MUSKOGEAN.

Acoma Pueblo See KERES.

acorn The nut of the oak treee (genus *Querchus*) was a staple of CALIFORNIA INDIANS, who made acorn soup and acorn meal. Indians collected acorns in the fall from oak trees, then removed the kernels from the shell, and dried them in the sun. To make the meal, the kernels were cracked, then ground with a stone MORTAR AND PESTLE. Because of the acorn's bitterness, a finely woven basket was used after soaking as a strainer to leach out the tannin. The meal could be boiled into a soup or mush, baked into a bread, or stored dry for future use.

activism Political and social action or involvement, sometimes militant; used especially in reference to the political philosophy and methods of 20th-century Indian individuals ("activists") and their organizations, such as the American Indian Movement (AIM), founded in 1968. (See also FISH-IN; INDIAN RIGHTS; ORGANIZATION; RESISTANCE; WATER RIGHTS.)

Acuera See TIMUCUA.

Adai See CADDOAN.

adaptation Change in behavior of an individual or group to a new cultural situation or new physical environment.

Adena Culture A cultural tradition of related archaeological sites in eastern North America, lasting from approximately 700 B.C. to A.D. 400 and perhaps even later, peaking in about 100 B.C. The name Adena comes from an estate near Chillicothe, Ohio, where a large MOUND stands. Adena MOUNDBUILDERS also built earthworks in territory in present-day Kentucky, West Virginia, Indiana, and Pennsylvania, primarily along the Ohio River Valley. More than 200 Adena sites have been located. Adena trade goods have been found farther to the east at sites in New York, Vermont, New Jersey, Delaware, and Maryland. Most of the Adena earthworks were burial mounds. Others were effigy mounds with symbolic shapes, such as the Great Serpent Mound near present-day Peebles, Ohio. The Adena Indians lived in permanent villages of WATTLE-AND-DAUB and THATCH houses. They were primarily hunter-gatherers, although they might have grown sunflowers and pumpkins for food and cultivated tobacco

for smoking rituals. It is theorized that some among them were the ancestors of the Indians of the HOPEWELL CULTURE, who came to displace them, starting about 100 B.C. Or perhaps the Hopewell Indians were outsiders who invaded Adena territory.

adobe A wet clay mixture, either sundried into bricks or applied wet as a mortar to hold stones together; straw is sometimes added to the mud for strength. Adobe was used by SOUTHWEST INDIANS in PUEBLO architecture. The word adobe comes from the Spanish *adobar*, meaning "to plaster." "Puddled adobe" refers to an adobe mixture that is applied wet to a wall or floor as a finish coat. (See also PISÉ.)

adoption The taking of a new member into a family, clan, band, or tribe, and granting him or her equal status (as opposed to SLAVERY). Tribes had different rules governing adoption and the resulting KINSHIP. People who might have been adopted include: offspring of deceased relatives; CAPTIVES; families, clans, bands, and villages; and possibly even entire tribes, as in the case of the IROQUOIS LEAGUE admitting the TUSCARORAS in the early 18th century.

adz (adze) A cutting, scraping, planing, or gouging tool, mainly for woodwork, with an arched axlike blade at right angles to the handle. Adz blades were made from stone, bone, shell, copper, or, in post-Contact times, iron. The wood often was charred by fire before an adz was used.

affinal A relation by marriage. An affinal relative is someone who traces a relationship to another through at least one marital link. An affinal marriage is with an in-law. Levirate marriage (the marriage of a woman to her deceased husband's brother) and a sororate marriage (the marriage of a man to his wife's sister) are types of affinal marriages. "Affine" is a noun, indicating a relative by marriage or an in-law.

afterworld   The land or realm of the dead. Many Indian tribes have detailed descriptions of the place GHOSTS or SOULS inhabit in the afterlife. For PLAINS INDIANS and PLATEAU INDIANS, the afterworld was often in the West. Some tribes, such as the PAI-UTES, regarded the Milky Way as the Road of the Dead. In post-Contact times, some Indians accepted the Christian concept of heaven and hell. The concept of a HAPPY HUNTING GROUND is an oversimplification by non-Indians. (See also SPIRIT WORLD.)

agamous   A random pattern of marriage among social groups, i.e., neither ENDOGA-MOUS or EXOGAMOUS. The term is also used for the absence or nonrecognition of marriage within a cultural group. "Agamy" is the noun form.

agave (maguey)   A genus *(Agave)* of flowering plants with fleshy leaves clustered at the base; also called maguey. The century plant or American aloe *(A. americana)* grows in the American Southwest. MESCAL is a liquor distilled from certain species (especially *A. atrovirens.*) PULQUE is a fermented milky beverage also made from agave. Sisal *(A. sisalana)* is cultivated for its stiff fiber to make rope.

agent   See INDIAN AGENT.

agriculture   See FARMING.

Ahantchuyuk   See KALAPUYAN.

Ahtena (Ahtna, Atna, Copper, Yellowknife)   An ATHAPASCAN-speaking tribe of the SUB-ARCTIC CULTURE AREA, located on the Copper River in present-day Alaska. Two contemporary Ahtena bands, Copper Center and Gulkana, are incorporated as Ahtna, Inc. Both the Ahtenas and TATSANOTTINES have been referred to as Copper Indians and Yellowknife Indians. *Ahtena* means "ice people" in Athapascan.

Ais   See MUSKOGEAN.

Akokisa   See ATAKAPA.

akubua   A hallucinogenic snuff made from the resin of the *Virola calophylla* tree and used by SOUTH AMERICAN INDIANS of the rain forest.

Akwaala   See YUMAN.

Akwesasne   See MOHAWK.

Alabama (Alibamu)   A MUSKOGEAN-speaking tribe of the SOUTHEAST CULTURE AREA, located on the upper Alabama River in present-day Alabama. Some bands also lived in northern Florida. The Alabamas were part of the Creek Confederacy. After 1763, many of them migrated to present-day Louisiana and eventually Texas; their descendants now share the Alabama-Coushatta Reservation in Polk County with COUSHATTA Indians. Other tribal members were forced by whites to move to the IN-DIAN TERRITORY (present-day Oklahoma) with the CREEKS. Still others joined the SEMINOLES in Florida. *Alabama* possibly means "to camp" or "weed gatherer" in Muskogean.

alabaster   A dense, fine-grained variety of calcite, called Mexican onyx, but not a true onyx; also, a variety of gypsum. Both types of alabaster are often white and translucent. MESOAMERICAN INDIANS used the calcite variety for carvings of effigy figures. North American Indians also quarried and carved it; they used the gypsum variety for whitening leather and feathers.

alcoholic beverage   Many agricultural Indians made a variety of beers and wines from cultivated and wild plants, using the process of FERMENTATION. In post-Contact times, whites used hard liquor, i.e., distilled beverages, as a trade item. White officials also commonly used it as a negotiating ploy to induce tribal representatives to cede lands. Alcoholism has been a persistent problem in many native communities, and many reservations are now "dry." (See also BALCHE; CHICHA; MESCAL; PERSIMMON; PULQUE; TESGUINO.)

Aleut (Aleyut) An ESKIMO-ALEUT-speaking tribe (or people) of the ARCTIC CULTURE AREA, located on the Aleutian Islands, the Shumagin Islands, and the western Alaska Peninsula. Subdivisions include the Atka on the Near, Rat, and Andreanof islands; and the Unalaska on the Fox and Shumagin islands and the Alaska Peninsula. The majority of Aleuts now live on the Alaskan mainland. The native-run Aleut Corporation, centered in Anchorage, Alaska, oversees 13 Aleut villages; Koniag, Inc., centered in Kodiak, oversees seven Aleut villages; the Bristol Bay Native Corporation, centered in Dillingham, oversees 24 villages, both Aleut and INUIT; and Chugach Natives, Inc., centered in Anchorage oversees four villages, both Aleut and ATHAPASCAN. *Aleut* possibly means "islands." The Aleut native name is *Unagagen*, meaning "those of the seaside."

Algonkin (Algonquin) An ALGONQUIAN-speaking tribe of the NORTHEAST CULTURE AREA located on the Ottawa River and its northern tributaries in present-day Ontario and Quebec. (The ABITIBI band of Algonkins is classified as part of the SUBARCTIC CULTURE AREA.) A band known as Algonquin of Golden Lake now holds reserve lands in Ontario; the Barrière Lake, Grand Lac Victoria, Kipawa, Lac Simon, Long Point, Obedjiwan, River Desert, Timiscaming, and Wolf Lake bands hold reserve lands in Quebec. *Algonkin* possibly means "at the place of spearing fish or eels"; it was originally applied to one band, the Weskarini, that lived on the Gastineau River, but came to be applied to other bands as well and eventually to an entire language family.

Algonquian (Algonquin, Algonkian, Algonkin) A language family and subdivision of the MACRO-ALGONQUIAN phylum comprising dialects spoken by Indians of the NORTHEAST CULTURE AREA, among them the ABENAKI, ALGONKIN, Amikwa (Otter), CHIPPEWA, Chowanoc, CONOY, Coree (probably Algonquian), FOX, HATTERAS, ILLINOIS, KICKAPOO, Kitchigami, LENNI-LENAPE (Delaware), Machapunga, MAHICAN, MALECITE, MASSACHUSET, Mattabesec, MENOMINEE, MIAMI, MICMAC, MOHEGAN, MONTAUK, Moratok, NANTICOKE, NARRAGANSET, Nauset, NIANTIC, NIPISSING, NIPMUC, Noquet, OTTAWA, Pamlico, PASSAMAQUODDY, PENNACOOK, PENOBSCOT, PEQUOT, Pocomtuc, POTAWATOMI, POWHATAN, Quinnipiac, SAC, SECOTAN, SHAWNEE, WAMPANOAG, WAPPINGER, and Weapemeoc (probably Algonquian) tribes; of the GREAT PLAINS CULTURE AREA, among them the ARAPAHO, BLACKFOOT, CHEYENNE, and GROS VENTRE tribes; and of the SUBARCTIC CULTURE AREA, among them the CREE, MONTAGNAIS, and NASKAPI tribes. The Algonquian-speaking tribes, especially those of New England, are often referred to generally as Algonquians.

Alibamu See ALABAMA.

Alliklik See UTO-AZTECAN.

"all my relations" See MITAKUYE OYASIN.

allotment A policy of the U.S. federal government, starting with the General Allotment Act (Dawes Act) of 1887 and lasting until the Indian Reorganization Act (IRA) of 1934. Under the policies of allotment, tribally held Indian lands were broken up and distributed to individuals in 160-acre parcels to encourage private farming and further the process of ASSIMILATION. A large portion of lands held by Indians in the INDIAN TERRITORY (Oklahoma) were allotted. Due to allotment, many Native Americans eventually lost their land.

alpaca See LLAMA.

Alsea (Alcea, Alseya, Alsi) A YAKONAN-speaking tribe of the NORTHWEST COAST CULTURE AREA, located on the Alsea River in present-day Oregon. Alsea descendants live on the Siletz Reservation near Siletz,

Oregon, with other Yakonan-speaking as well as KUSAN-speaking tribes.

altar   A structure or object before or on which ceremonies are enacted. Incense is commonly burned and OFFERINGS are made at altars while prayers are spoken. Altars might be a fire, a pile of rocks, or a BUFFALO SKULL; or they might be an elaborate structure of stone and wood and other materials. Objects to be used in a ceremony at the altar (altar ceremony) have a specific arrangement (altar display). In some instances, altars symbolize the earth. The term altar also has been applied to the bowl of the CALUMET, or SACRED PIPE. (See also SHRINE.)

Amacano   See MUSKOGEAN.

amber   A fossilized vegetable resin, found especially in alluvial soils. Translucent brownish yellow or orange and able to take a high polish, amber has been traditionally valued for beads and other ornaments.

American Arctic-Paleo-Siberian   A phylum of language stocks, including the ESKIMO-ALEUT family in North America and Greenland as well as the CHUKCHI-KAM-CHATKAN family in Siberia.

American Indian   A term referring to the native peoples of the Americas, the long form of "INDIAN." In the United States, its usage is still widespread, although "NATIVE AMERICAN" is becoming just as prevalent. In Canada, "Indian" and "NATIVE" are most widely used. "North American Indian" is sometimes used to refer to native peoples north of Mexico.

American Indian Movement (AIM)   See ACTIVISM; ORGANIZATION; URBAN INDIANS; WOUNDED KNEE.

Amerind   The term Amerind was invented by anthropologist and linguist John Wesley Powell in 1899 from the first syllables of "American" and "Indian," as a substitute for "INDIAN". Although adopted by some scholars, it never gained widespread use. "Amerindian" is a variation.

Amikwa   See ALGONQUIAN.

amulet   An object thought to contain supernatural power and often worn around the neck as a charm against evil, injury, or disease. (See also CHARMSTONE; FETISH; TALISMAN.)

Anasazi Culture   A cultural tradition in the American Southwest, lasting from about 100 B.C. to A.D. 1300. The Anasazi core area was the Four Corners region, where present-day Colorado, Utah, Arizona, and New Mexico meet. Anasazi development can be divided into two distinct phases: the Basket Maker period from about 100 B.C. to A.D. 700, during which Anasazi peoples lived in PITHOUSES and learned to weave containers and sandals from plant matter, such as straw, vines, and rushes, and refined their skills in agriculture and pottery; the second phase, the Pueblo period, starting about A.D. 700, during which the Anasazis kept the underground dwellings as ceremonial structures (KIVAS), but also built aboveground ADOBE structures known as PUEBLOS. Anasazi Indians built their early pueblos on top of mesas. By about A.D. 1150, Anasazi Indians had evacuated most of their mesatop villages and, until about 1300, built their pueblos as CLIFF-DWELLINGS, which offered protection against invaders. During the Pueblo phase of Anasazi Culture, sometimes referred to as "the Golden Age," the Anasazis used IRRIGATION techniques to increase their agricultural output and support large village populations. Cultural influences spread to Indians of the MOGOLLON CULTURE and HOHOKAM CULTURE. It is not known for certain how Anasazi Culture declined. From 1276 to 1299, a prolonged drought struck the Southwest. A contributing factor might have been invasions by ATHAPASCANS from the north, the ancestors of the APACHES and NAVAJOS. Or perhaps the various pueblos began fighting among themselves for food. The depletion of the wood supply also might have caused Anasazi peoples to move. Anasazis were probably the ancestors of the HOPIS and other PUEBLO INDIANS. *Anasazi* means "ancient ones" in the Navajo dialect of Athapascan.

ancestor (forefather, progenitor) One from whom a person is descended. In many Native American traditions, LEGENDARY BEINGS are considered ancestors, or MYTHICAL ANCESTORS. "Ancestral" is the adjective form. "Ancestor spirit" and "ancestral spirit" are synonyms for "GHOST."

anchor stone A stone attached to a line and used to keep a boat in place. In some cases, the stone had an encircling groove to fasten the line. The artifact could double as a grooved AX. Prehistoric anchor stones have been found throughout the Americas.

ancient Indians See PREHISTORIC INDIANS.

Andaste See SUSQUEHANNOCK.

Andean-Equatorial A phylum of language stocks, including the ARAUCANIAN-CHON, ARAWAKAN, JIVAROAN, QUECHUAMARAN, TIMOTEAN, TUPI-GUARANI, ZAMUCOAN, and ZAPAROAN families.

angakok (angakuk) The INUIT term in various dialects of the ESKIMO-ALEUT language for "SHAMAN."

Anglo-American Americans whose ancestry and language are English. The term is used especially in historical discussions of the American Southwest to distinguish from MEXICAN-AMERICANS.

animal See CATEGORICAL APPENDIX, "ANIMALS."

animal husbandry See DOMESTICATION OF ANIMALS.

Animal People In a general sense in Indian mythology, all animals other than people. Many tribes, such as the NAVAJOS, considered the original Animal People deities who talked and from whom animals are descended. The Bird People and the Fish People are sometimes distinguished from the Animal People. Particular species also are commonly referred to as "people," i.e., Bear People or Snake People.

animism The belief that natural phenomena and inanimate objects possess souls and personalities. "Animistic" is the adjective form. (See also PANTHEISM; SHAMANISM.)

Anishinabe See CHIPPEWA.

anklet An ornament worn around the ankle, or between the ankle and knee. In some cases, anklets with attached BELLS are worn as rhythm instruments in dancing.

annealing A process of tempering in METALWORK, by first heating then cooling. Some metals, such as silver, are cooled suddenly by quenching in water. Copper and others are cooled slowly. Annealing supposedly toughens metal by reducing brittleness.

Annikadel One of two supreme deities of the ACHOMAWI Indians, grandson of the other supreme deity Tikado Hedache, the World's Heart. Since Annikadel's undersides are blue, no one looking up can see him against the sky. All that is seen is a glint of light. When the First People (the original animals) were transformed into animals on earth, Annikadel became a lizard to the Real People (human beings) with a blue throat and sides (one of the iguanid lizards of the genus *Sceloporus*). Annikadel is compared to Christ, and Tikado Hedache to the Christian God, the Father.

annuity A yearly payment in the form of money, goods, or services to a tribe, as compensation for land or resources, based on a TREATY or some other agreement.

antelope See PRONGHORN.

anthropology The study of humankind. Anthropology encompasses the physical, racial, social, and cultural origins, development, and characteristics of human beings. The science of anthropology can broadly be subdivided into physical anthropology and cultural anthropology. (See also ARCHAEOLOGY; DEMOGRAPHY; ETHNOGRAPHY; ETHNOLOGY; LINGUISTICS; SOCIOLOGY.)

anthropomorphism The attribution of human characteristics to objects. The adjective "anthropomorphic" is used in discussions of artwork in which elements of the human figure are given to nonhuman objects. (See also ZOOMORPHISM.)

antler work See HORN AND ANTLER WORK.

anvil A tool with a hard surface on which to hammer and shape some other object, commonly used in stonework and metalwork. A boulder or a piece of rock might have served as an anvil for Indians. In post-Contact times, pieces of iron also were utilized.

Apache An ATHAPASCAN-speaking tribe of the SOUTHWEST CULTURE AREA, located in present-day southern Arizona and New Mexico, western Texas, and southeastern Colorado, and ranging into present-day northern Mexico. The various groupings of Apaches are based on linguistic associations, although the names are geographically and historically derived: APACHE PEAKS; ARAVAIPA; CHIRICAHUA; CIBECUE; GILENOS; JICARILLA; KIOWA-APACHE; LIPAN; MESCALERO; MIMBRENO; MOGOLLON; PINAL; SAN CARLOS; TONTO; WARM SPRINGS; and WHITE MOUNTAIN. Apache descendants hold the following reservations: Camp Verde (with YAVAPAIS) in Yavapai County, Arizona; Fort Apache in Apache, Gila, and Navajo counties, Arizona; Fort McDowell (with MOJAVES and Yavapais) in Maricopa County, Arizona; San Carlos in Gila and Graham counties, Arizona; Jicarilla in Rio Arriba and Sandoval counties, New Mexico; and Mescalero in Otero County, New Mexico. The Fort Sill Apache Tribe of Oklahoma, centered in Anadarko, also maintains tribal identity. *Apache* or *apachu* probably means "enemy," originally the ZUNI name for the NAVAJOS. The Apache native name is *Tineh* (or Tinneh, Tinde, Dini, Inde, N'de), meaning "the people."

Apache fiddle An instrument of the APACHE Indians in post-Contact times, consisting of a sound box made from a YUCCA

Apache fiddle

stalk and painted with designs plus a single string of sinew hair attached to a tuning peg. The Apache fiddle is played with a bow of wood and sinew or wood and horse hair. The instrument is probably derived from the MUSICAL BOW.

Apache Peaks A subtribe of the APACHE Indians (part of the SAN CARLOS grouping), located in the Apache Mountains, northeast of present-day Globe, Arizona.

Apalachee A MUSKOGEAN-speaking tribe of the SOUTHEAST CULTURE AREA, located near present-day Tallahassee, Florida, near Apalachee Bay. One band lived for a time on Mobile Bay in present-day Alabama. After 1764, some Apalachee bands migrated into Louisiana, settling on the Red River, but they eventually lost their tribal identity. Other Apalachees joined the CREEKS. *Apalachee* is thought to mean "people on the other side" in the CHOCTAW dialect of Muskogean.

Apalachicola See CREEK; MUSKOGEAN.

Appaloosa A breed of HORSE having a mottled hide, vertically striped hooves, and eyes showing a lot of white. The NEZ PERCE and PALOUSE Indians first developed the breed; *Appaloosa* is derived from the latter tribal name.

"apple" (Indian apple) A derogatory expression for an Indian who emulates whites and aspires to a non-Indian life-style, as in "red on the outside, white on the inside."

appliqué A technique of EMBROIDERY in which pieces of one material are applied to another, as in QUILLWORK or RIBBONWORK. Also, the practice of affixing shapes on the surface of pottery or to inlaying materials into woodwork.

apron A loose-hanging garment, attached at the waist, worn by both men and women over other garments. (In Indian studies, the term is not associated with cooking, as in common usage.) Aprons worn by men are sometimes referred to as kilts. Indians of various tribes, especially in the warmer climates, wore aprons front and back with no other clothing underneath; they resembled BREECHCLOTHS but were unattached between the legs. (See also DANCE APRON.)

aqueduct A conduit for conveying water from a remote source, usually by gravity. MESOAMERICAN INDIANS and the INCAS engineered stone aqueducts for household water as well as for IRRIGATION. The canals of the HOHOKAM CULTURE are also sometimes referred to as aqueducts.

Aranama See COAHUILTECAN.

Arapaho (Arapahoe) An ALGONQUIAN-speaking tribe of the GREAT PLAINS CULTURE AREA, probably once living in the Red River region of present-day Minnesota and North Dakota as one people with the GROS VENTRES. These Algonquians are thought to have migrated westward to the headwaters of the Missouri River sometime in the 1700s, possibly as far as present-day Montana. The group subdivided, with the Gros Ventres heading north and the Arapahos south. At some point in the 1800s, the Arapahos again divided into the Northern Arapahos and the Southern Arapahos: The northern branch settled on the North Platte River in present-day Wyoming; the southern, on the Arkansas River in present-day Colorado. Northern Arapahos share the Wind River Reservation near Riverton, Wyoming with the SHOSHONES; Southern Arapahos are part of the Cheyenne-Arapaho, sharing trust lands near Concho, Oklahoma with the CHEYENNES. *Arapaho* is possibly derived from *tirapihu*, meaning "trader" in the PAWNEE dialect of CADDOAN. The Arapaho native name is *Inuna-ina*, meaning "our people."

Araucanian-Chon A language family and subdivision of the ANDEAN-EQUATORIAL phylum comprising dialects spoken by

SOUTH AMERICAN INDIANS, including the Araucanian, Chono, Ono, Puelche, Tehuelche, and Yahgan tribes of present-day Argentina and southern Chile, and others.

Aravaipa (Arivaipa) A subtribe of the APACHE Indians (part of the SAN CARLOS grouping). The Aravaipas once lived in present-day south-central Arizona on Aravaipa Creek between the San Pedro Creek and Aravaipa Mountains. They now live on the San Carlos and Fort Apache reservations in Arizona with other Apache groups. *Aravaipa* means "girls" in the PIMA dialect of UTO-AZTECAN.

Arawak (Taino) An ARAWAKAN-speaking tribe of the CIRCUM-CARIBBEAN CULTURE AREA and of South America, located in the West Indies, including the Greater Antilles (present-day Cuba, Dominican Republic, Haiti, Jamaica, and Puerto Rico), the Bahamas, and Trinidad. The Arawaks of the West Indies are known as Taino. Arawakan-speaking peoples also live in northern South America as far south as Paraguay. In pre-Contact times, the Arawaks migrated northward from South America onto the Caribbean islands; the CARIB Indians drove them north from the Lesser Antilles. Christopher Columbus had contact with the Arawaks and referred to them as Indians, the first such usage. After the Spanish took over and settled their homelands, the Arawaks died out through disease and slavery. Those who survived lost their Indian identity through intermarriage with the colonists. No pure Arawaks remain in the West Indies. Surviving Arawakan-speaking peoples live along the Amazon River in Brazil.

Arawakan A language family and subdivision of the ANDEAN-EQUATORIAL phylum comprising dialects spoken by Indians of the CIRCUM-CARIBBEAN CULTURE AREA, including the ARAWAK (Taino) tribe of the West Indies as well as by SOUTH AMERICAN INDIANS, including the Baure, Mojo, and Paressi tribes of present-day eastern Bolivia; the Campa tribe of present-day Peru; the

Chane and Guana tribes of present-day Paraguay; the Guayape tribe of present-day Colombia; the Palicur tribe of present-day northern Brazil; and others.

arbor A shade structure. SOUTHEAST INDIANS built open-sided POST-AND-BEAM arbors; PLAINS INDIANS constructed BENT-FRAME ones covered with brush. The Spanish referred to the arbors of SOUTHWEST INDIANS as RAMADAS.

archaeological site A location of former habitation or use by humans, including ruins of dwellings or other structures, burials, artifacts, and refuse piles, as indicated through the methods of ARCHAEOLOGY. (See also TYPE SITE.)

archaeology (archeology) The recovery, reconstruction, and study of material evidence remaining from early peoples and cultures in order to determine their ways of life. An archaeologist practices this discipline.

Archaic Indians (Foraging Indians) PRE-HISTORIC INDIANS of the ARCHAIC PERIOD. Archaic Indians had a more varied economy than the earlier PALEO-INDIANS. With the big game now extinct, they hunted and trapped the species of mammals known today; they fished in rivers and lakes; and they gathered a variety of edible wild plants. Archaic Indians are sometimes referred to as Foraging Indians because of their varied diet. A wider variety of tools and utensils and a number of key inventions distinguish the Archaic Indians from Paleo-Indians: They wove plant materials into clothing and baskets; they used baskets and hide containers to store food; they placed heated stones into stone pots to make boiling water (STONE-BOILING); they constructed boats; and they domesticated the dog. Another cultural trait typical of Archaic Indians was the shaping of materials into ornaments and ceremonial objects. They also had elaborate burials. Among the various Archaic traditions are the COCHISE CULTURE, DESERT

CULTURE, OLD COPPER CULTURE, OLD CORDILLERAN CULTURE, and RED PAINT CULTURE.

Archaic period   A prehistoric cultural period in North America equivalent to the Neolithic period. The end of the PLEISTOCENE epoch marked the beginning of the current geologic period called the Recent or Holocene epoch. With the melting of the glaciers, the PALEOLITHIC PERIOD evolved into the Archaic period (about 8000 B.C.–1000 B.C.), and PALEO-INDIANS gradually gave way to ARCHAIC INDIANS. The Archaic period is sometimes referred to as the Foraging period. (Some scholars define the transitional period in North America between the Paleolithic period and the Archaic period—when the glaciers were melting—as the WATERSHED AGE, placing the beginning of the Archaic period at about 5000 B.C.)

archery   The use of a BOW and ARROW, especially for sport. Competitive games in archery for accuracy and distance served as training for skill in HUNTING and WAR.

architecture   The art and science of making buildings and related structures. (See also CATEGORICAL APPENDIX, "HOUSES AND ARCHITECTURE"; DWELLING; HOUSE; SHELTER.)

Arctic Culture Area   The geographical and cultural region extending west to east from the Aleutian Islands in Alaska to Labrador in Canada, some 5,000 miles, and north to south from the Arctic Ocean to the northern timberline. Although most of this CULTURE AREA lies in present-day northern Alaska and northern Canada, it also includes territory in Siberia (part of Russia) to the west as well as in Greenland (part of the kingdom of Denmark) to the east. It touches on three oceans: the Arctic, Pacific, and Atlantic. The Arctic environment is called the TUNDRA, most of which consists of treeless, rolling plains, with little vegetation other than mosses, lichens, and stunted shrubs. In the west are the northern reaches of the Rockies. The Arctic has long, cold winters with few hours of sunlight. Arctic precipitation is light; gale-force winds stir up what surface snow exists, forming snowdrifts. Only the surface ice thaws during the short summer; the subsoil remains in a state of PERMAFROST. Water does not drain, but forms numerous lakes and ponds along with mud and rising fog. The Arctic Ocean, frozen in wintertime, breaks up into drift ice during the summer thaw. Wildlife in the Arctic includes: SEA MAMMALS, such as WHALES, walruses, seals, and sea lions; saltwater and freshwater fish; seagulls and other birds; polar BEARS; and CARIBOU. In certain locations on the tundra in the summertime, RABBITS, rodents, and OWLS provided subsistence for ARCTIC PEOPLES—the INUITS (Eskimos) and ALEUTS—who migrated when necessary to obtain food. The Inuits traditionally lived in IGLOOS; in stone, log, and sod homes; or in TENTS of driftwood poles and caribou hide. The primary dwelling of the Aleuts was the BARABARA.

Arctic Peoples   The people inhabiting the ARCTIC CULTURE AREA, i.e., INUITS (Eskimos) and ALEUTS, speaking dialects of the ESKIMO-ALEUT language family. Arctic inhabitants came later to North America than other native peoples, traveling from Siberia in boats, starting about 3000 B.C. They are generally shorter and broader than other Native Americans, with rounder faces, lighter skin, and epicanthic eye folds (the small fold of skin covering the inner corner of their eyes that is typical of Asian peoples). The Inuits and Aleuts are referred to as natives more often than as Indians.

argillite   See SLATE.

Arikara   (Aricara, Arikaree, Ree, Ricaree) A CADDOAN-speaking tribe of the GREAT PLAINS CULTURE AREA, located on the upper Missouri River in present-day North Dakota near the South Dakota border and ranging into present-day eastern Montana. (Arikaras had split off from the PAWNEES earlier in pre-Contact times, becoming the northernmost Caddoans.) The SIOUAN-speaking HIDATSAS and MANDANS were their neighbors. The Three Affiliated Tribes now share the Fort Berthold Reservation near New Town, North Dakota. *Arikara* is thought to mean "horn" in Caddoan, in reference to the male custom of wearing two upright bones in the hair.

Arkansas   See QUAPAW.

armor   Native American armor protecting the body was made of twined wooden rods or slats as well as overlapping plates of bone, ivory, and, in post-Contact times, iron. Coats and leggings of hardened hide or quilted cloth also were utilized. The wooden variety was found especially among the TLINGITS and other NORTHWEST COAST INDIANS. The COMANCHES had leather armor for their horses. Woven cotton or other fibers an inch thick were used by the AZTECS. Some among the SOUTH AMERICAN INDIANS also had hide and fiber armor. HELMETS are a kind of armor. "Body armor" is sometimes distinguished from "parrying armor," i.e., the SHIELD.

arrow   A straight, thin projectile, designed to be shot from a BOW and used in HUNTING and WAR. An arrow consists of an ARROWHEAD, ARROW SHAFT, ARROW FEATHERS, and a nock (notch) for fitting onto the BOWSTRING. "Fire-arrow," "flaming arrow," and "burning arrow" all refer to arrows used to set fires in warfare. Arrows are carried in a QUIVER. Some arrows were made for ceremonial purposes as a kind of PRAYER STICK. In Native American religion, arrows symbolize a oneness with animals in life and death; the ZUNI Indians traditionally tie arrows to the backs of their bear FE-

TISHES. Arrows also are associated in legends with LIGHTNING. (See also ARCHERY.)

arrow feather   A feather attached to the rear of the ARROW SHAFT to assure a straight flight, when the ARROW is shot from a BOW. Some arrows had two feathers; others, three. Eagles or wild turkeys provided the feathers of choice.

arrow game   Any game played with ARROWS apart from ARCHERY. In one such widespread game, a player tossed an arrow on the ground, and other players tried to throw their own arrows across it.

arrowhead   The striking tip of an ARROW, removable from the ARROW SHAFT; made of flint and other types of stone as well as wood, bone, horn, antler, shell, copper, and, in post-Contact times, iron. Some arrowheads are blunt rather than sharp, intended for stunning game. Others have shoulders or barbs, designed to stay in the wound. The terms POINT or PROJECTILE POINT are more generalized than "arrowhead," referring to the head of a SPEAR, DART, and HARPOON as well as that of an arrow. Archaeologists use points to determine and define cultures.

arrow release   The method of holding the nock (notch) of an ARROW on a BOWSTRING. There are four main types of arrow release: primary release, in which the arrow and bowstring are held between the ball of a thumb and the side of the forefinger; secondary release, the same as the primary release except that the middle and third fingers are laid inside the string; tertiary release, in which the arrow is held between the thumb and the tips of the forefinger and middle finger; and the Eskimo or Mediterranean release, in which the string is pulled

Sioux arrow

by the tips of the forefinger, middle finger, and third finger, with the arrow between the first two (and without the thumb).

arrow shaft The long, narrow stem or body of an ARROW, usually made out of wood but also from reed or cane. In addition to the main shaft, some arrows had a foreshaft, a piece of heavy wood, bone, or ivory for holding the ARROWHEAD. At the other end of the main shaft, ARROW FEATHERS are usually attached next to a nock (notch) that fits to the BOWSTRING. Arrow shafts were sometimes painted. PLAINS INDIANS cut grooves in the shaft, called lightning marks, to keep the wood from warping, to assure accurate flight, and to serve as a blood gutter, which facilitated the flow of blood on striking prey. An arrow-shaft wrench (arrow-shaft straightener) is a device for straightening an arrow shaft, consisting of a hole pierced in stone, bone, ivory, or antler; a circular hook crafted out of these materials; or a groove in these materials. The shaft is pulled though the hole, hook, or groove, in order to plane it evenly.

art See ARTS AND CRAFTS; FINE ART.

articulate mask (articulated mask, transformational mask) A MASK, typical of the NORTHWEST COAST INDIANS, with movable parts. In some cases, the different sections are controlled by strings.

artifact Any object made by humans. Houses, boats, and clothing are artifacts by definition, but the term typically refers to tools, weapons, ornaments, or pottery.

artifact density A formula for the number of artifacts in an archaeological site—the number of total artifacts divided by the area in which they were found. For example, 23 POTSHERDS found in an area of 10 square meters gives an artifact density of 2.3 per square meter.

arts and crafts ARTIFACTS made for utilitarian as well as ceremonial, symbolic, or aesthetic purposes. Since many Indian artifacts display great workmanship, design, detail, and expressiveness, separating the two concepts of "art" and "craft" is often difficult. The term FINE ART is usually applied to modern-day works created for primarily an aesthetic purpose, even if traditional techniques are used. At contemporary FESTIVALS or POWWOWS, many of the crafts on display are also now considered fine art. (See also CATEGORICAL APPENDIX, "ARTS AND CRAFTS.")

aryballos (aryballus) A POTTERY flask or bottle, typical of the INCAS, having a globular body, one or two handles, a short neck, and a flared lip.

ashpile The remains of a fire—indicating the earlier presence of humans—or a trash area, where ashes were dumped from the hearth along with other trash.

ash-splint See SPLINT.

asi A conical, WATTLE-AND-DAUB winter house of the CHEROKEES, with a FIREPIT in the center.

assemblage A collection of ARTIFACTS from a single ARCHAEOLOGICAL SITE or a subunit of finds from a particular site. (See also COMPLEX.)

assimilation A late 19th and early 20th century policy of the U.S. and Canadian governments calling for the rejection of the Indian and tribal way of life and ADAPTATION of dominant Euroamerican cultural traits. The assimilation policy emphasized the adoption of a farming way of life, the conversion to Christianity, the wearing of Euroamerican-style clothing, and forced attendance in white-run BOARDING SCHOOLS. It also was known as the civilization program. (See also ACCULTURATION; CULTURAL DISPOSSESSION; DETRIBALIZATION.)

Assiniboine (Assiniboin, Assineboine, Stoney) A SIOUAN-speaking tribe of the

GREAT PLAINS CULTURE AREA. It is thought that the Assiniboines were originally one people with the YANKTONAI subtribe of SIOUX, living near Lake Superior in present-day northern Minnesota and southwestern Ontario. In the 1600s, the Assiniboines migrated westward onto the Northern Plains, settling west of Lake Winnipeg in present-day Manitoba, with some bands continuing on to the Assiniboine and Saskatchewan rivers in present-day Saskatchewan and north of the Milk and Missouri rivers in present-day Montana. Assiniboines share the Fort Belknap Reservation near Harlem, Montana, with the GROS VENTRES and the Fort Peck Reservation near Poplar, Montana with the Sioux. In Saskatchewan, the Mosquito Grizzly Bear's Head band also maintains tribal identity; other Assiniboines (also in Manitoba) share reserve lands with the Sioux, CHIPPEWAS, and CREES. *Assiniboine* is from the Chippewa term in ALGONQUIAN for "one who cooks with stones," in reference to STONE-BOILING.

Atakapa (Attacapa, Akokisa) A MACRO-ALGONQUIAN-speaking (Atakapa or Atakapan isolate) tribe of the SOUTHEAST CULTURE AREA, located along the Louisiana and Texas coasts from Vermillion Bayou to Trinity Bay. The Opelousas and possibly the Deadose Indians spoke a similar dialect. It is not known what became of the Atakapas in the 19th century. *Atakapa* means "man-eater" in the CHOCTAW dialect of MUSKOGEAN, because of their reported CANNIBALISM. Their native name was *Yuk'hiti ishak*, probably meaning "the people."

Atfalati See KALAPUYAN.

Athabasca A subtribe of the CHIPEWYAN Indians, located on Athabasca Lake in present-day Northwest Territories. Their name, from which ATHAPASCAN is derived, means "grass (or reeds) here and there."

Athapascan (Athabascan) A language family comprising dialects spoken by Indi-

ans of the SUBARCTIC CULTURE AREA, including the AHTENA, ATHABASCA, BEAVER (Tsattine), CARRIER, CHILCOTIN, CHIPEWYAN, DOGRIB, HARE, HAN, INGALIK, KOYUKON, KUTCHIN, NABESNA, NAHANE, SEKANI, SLAVE, TANAINA, TANANA, TATSANOTTINE, TSETSAUT, TUTCHONE tribes; of the SOUTHWEST CULTURE AREA, among them the APACHE and NAVAJO tribes; of the CALIFORNIA CULTURE AREA, among them the Bear River, CAHTO, Chilula, HOOPA, Lassik, Mattole, Nongatl, Sinkyone, TOLOWA, WAILAKI, and Whilkut tribes; of the NORTHWEST COAST CULTURE AREA, among them the CHASTACOSTA, CHETCO, Clatskanie, Dakubetede, Kwalhioqua, Mishikhwutmetunne, TALTUSHTUNTUDE, TUTUTNI, and UMPQUA tribes; of the PLATEAU CULTURE AREA, among them the Stuwihamuk tribe; and of the GREAT PLAINS CULTURE AREA, among them the KIOWA-APACHE and SARCEE tribes. The Athapascan language family is a subdivision of the NADENE phylum. The native peoples of Alaska and western Canada, as distinct from INUITS and ALEUTS, often are referred to generally as Athapascans.

atlantes (Atlantean figure) An architectural support in the form of a human figure or half-figure, typical of the TOLTECS. The term is derived from the Greek *Atlantes*, plural of *Atlas*. A caryatid is a supporting column in the shape of a human female figure, derived from the Greek *karyatides*.

atlatl (atl atl, dart-thrower, dart sling, spear-thrower, throwing stick, throwing board) A throwing stick that increases the leverage of the human arm. Atlatls were made from sticks usually about 16 to 20 inches long, with hide finger-loops for a firm grasp, stone weights for balance, and spurs and grooves to hold spear or dart shafts. They were invented in the PALEOLITHIC PERIOD and used throughout the Americas before the BOW and ARROW. The AZTECS and INCAS continued to use them as weapons even after the advent of the bow and arrow. *Atlatl* is a NAHUATL word. (See also BANNERSTONE.)

Atsina See GROS VENTRE.

Atsugewi See PALAIHNIHAN.

Attiwandaronk See NEUTRAL.

Avanyu A serpent figure appearing on the POTTERY of the PUEBLO INDIANS, especially among the TEWAS; also referred to as water serpent, feathered-water-serpent, and horned-water-serpent. The serpent's protruding tongue is thought to symbolize lightning.

Avoyel See MUSKOGEAN.

awl A pointed tool for making holes in hide, wood, and fiber; often used as a punch. Awls were made from flint, wood, bone, horn, ivory, and plant thorns. In post-Contact times, iron was utilized for the point. A splinter awl is made from a splintered section of bone. Awls were often stored in wood, bone, or metal sheaths. (See also BODKIN.)

ax (axe) A sharp tool used in chopping and crushing. An ax's cutting edge, unlike that of an ADZ, is in line with the handle. Early axes had heads of stone, or sometimes shell or copper, and wooden handles. Some axes had double blades. The term grooved ax refers to an ax head with encircling groove for securing a handle. An ungrooved ax is another name for a CELT. The term fist ax or hand ax refers to an ax head held in the hand without a handle. A HATCHET is a small ax held in one hand. In post-Contact times, European iron axes, trade axes, replaced stone axes.

ayorama (ayuqnaq) An INUIT expression in the ESKIMO-ALEUT language, meaning "it can't be helped" or "life is like that," or literally "because I am helpless."

Aztec (Mexica, Mexicano, Mexitin) A NAHUATL-speaking people of the MESOAMERICAN CULTURE AREA, located in the Valley of Mexico in what is now central Mexico. Aztec tradition holds that they were one of the Chichimec tribes, originally living as nomadic hunters and known as Mexicas. They probably migrated into the Valley of Mexico from the highlands to the north about A.D. 1168. Scholars theorize that some were farmers and military aides to the TOLTECS. With the Toltec Empire in a state of decay, the Mexicas competed with other peoples for territory; their warriors, armed with bows and long arrows, found work as mercenaries in the armies of local cities. In 1325, they founded two villages of their own on swampy islets in Lake Texcoco known as Tenochtitlan and Tlatelolco. The inhabitants of Tenochtitlan, who called themselves Tenochas, conquered those of Tlatelolco and eventually formed an alliance with the Alochuas. Tenochtitlan rapidly expanded; the Tenochas created new land to farm and build on by making CHINAMPAS. They began calling themselves *Aztec*, after Aztlan, the legendary "white place." In the following years, Tenochtitlan, the site of present-day Mexico City, grew to a city of hundreds of stone buildings, interconnected by canals, with about 300,000 inhabitants. The Aztecs launched military campaigns against surrounding peoples from the Gulf of Mexico to the Pacific Ocean. Through conquest, the Aztec Empire came to comprise 5 million people; the Aztecs created a tributary economy, imposing taxes on their subjects. In Aztec society, an emperor, or Chief of Men, was selected by the nobles, who each ruled a section of the city. PRIESTS also wielded great power. The next most influential social classes were the war chiefs and wealthy merchants. Beneath them were common soldiers, craftsmen, and farmers; then a propertyless group of unskilled laborers; and, below them, the slaves. Aztec clothing revealed social status, as did houses. The Chief of Men and the wealthiest noblemen had two-story multiroomed palaces, with stone walls and log and plaster roofs. Less wealthy noblemen and merchants had one-story dwellings. Commoners lived in small huts, usually only one room, made from clay bricks or from pole frames and plant stems packed with clay (WATTLE-AND-DAUB). The Spanish defeated the Aztec armies in 1521. Aztec descendants still live in the Valley of Mexico, many still speaking Nahuatl. The Spanish form of "Aztec" is *Azteca*.

Aztec-Tanoan A phylum of language stocks, including the KIOWA-TANOAN and UTO-AZTECAN families.

▲ B ▲

babiche A thong or strip, made of de-haired rawhide, sinew, or gut, used in SLEDS, TOBOGGANS, SNOWSHOES, BAGS, NETS, and other objects for binding and webbing. "Babiche" is probably from the MICMAC dialect of ALGONQUIAN, passed to English via French. (See also SHAGANAPPI.)

bacheeitch The CROW word for "chief" in SIOUAN, literally "good man."

bag A CONTAINER, made from a supple material, such as leather, hair, bark, or fiber, used for transportation, gathering, and storage. A saddlebag is one type of bag. A bag is usually larger than a POUCH, except in the case of a PIPE BAG or TOBACCO BAG. (See also BANDOLIER BAG; MOSS-BAG.)

baidarka (baidarra) An ALEUT boat, similar to the KAYAK of the INUITS, having oiled walrus or seal skins stretched over a light wooden frame. *Baidarkas* were short, with the bow curved upward and the stern squared off; bows were sometimes shaped like a bird's open beak. There were usually two cockpits, the rear one for the paddler and the front one for the harpooner.

baking stone A term applied generally to a variety of stones used in the baking process, such as slabs placed over a fireplace to make bread by PUEBLO INDIANS; but also applied specifically to a class of prehistoric stone artifacts used by CALIFORNIA INDIANS. These latter baking stones, usually made of SOAPSTONE—and typically less than a foot long and about an inch thick—were lightly hollowed out on one side and rounded on the other, with a hole at one end to aid in handling when hot. (See also BOILING STONE; *PIKI*.)

balche A drink, typical of the MAYAS, made of fermented honey.

baleen (whalebone) The horny growth on the upper jaw of certain WHALES, which serves as a strainer in collecting plankton and other minute food from the sea. About two to 12 feet long, light and flexible but strong, usually black but sometimes white or greenish, baleen has been valued by native peoples for making tools and ceremonial objects. Also inaccurately called whalebone.

ball-court An ancient playing field, sometimes sunken and sometimes paved, common in the MESOAMERICAN CULTURE AREA, where games were played with a RUBBER ball. The ball-courts of the AZTECS, where TLACHTLI was played, were I-shaped or T-shaped and surrounded by vertical walls. In CREEK towns and those of other SOUTHEAST INDIANS, open spaces about 250 yards long were strewn with sand for their BALL-GAMES, such as CHUNKEY (chunkey yards).

ball-game (ball play) Any game or sport using a ball or disk. Various ball-games were played throughout the Americas. It is

Aleut baidarka

thought that the OLMECS originated the highly ritualized version of the MESOAMERICAN CULTURE AREA. (See also BALL-COURT; CHUNKEY; DOUBLE-BALL; HANDBALL; JUGGLING; KICKBALL; LACROSSE; PILLMA; SHINNY; SINGLE POLE BALL-GAME; TLACHTLI.)

balsa   A type of raft or boat made with bulrushes, especially TULE, tied in bundles in a cylindrical shape, usually between 10 and 15 feet long. The bundles would become waterlogged after a period of use but would dry out in the sun. For the most part, balsas were poled rather than paddled. Typical of the POMOS and YOKUTS as well as other CALIFORNIA INDIANS and some GREAT BASIN INDIANS and SOUTHWEST INDIANS; also found in Central and South America. "Balsa" is of Spanish derivation, meaning "raft" or "float."

banco   A benchlike shelf along the inside wall of a KIVA or PITHOUSE. *Banco* is Spanish for "bench" or "seat."

band   A subdivision or SUBTRIBE of an Indian TRIBE, often consisting of an extended family, i.e., sets of nuclear families living, traveling, and obtaining food together. A band is therefore the smallest type of politically independent, self-contained group other than a family. A tribe or even subtribe might be made up of several bands. Historically, the word band is used when a part of a tribe breaks off from the main group under a new leader. In Canada, different self-governing groups, although sharing the same tribal descent, are referred to as "bands."

(See also CATEGORICAL APPENDIX, "TRIBES, BANDS, PEOPLES, LANGUAGES, and CULTURES"; CLAN.)

bandolier (bandoleer)   A broad belt worn over the shoulder, across the breast, and under the arm, from which articles, such as ammunition, are suspended.

bandolier bag (bandolier pouch, friendship bag)   A type of BAG or pouch worn by men in the style of a BANDOLIER; usually made of deerskin, wool, or muslin, and decorated with quillwork, beadwork, or embroidery. Typical of NORTHEAST INDIANS.

bani   An ARAPAHO word in ALGONQUIAN for "my comrade," when a boy addresses another boy. The equivalent term for girls is *bisa*.

bannerstone (birdstone, butterfly stone)   A polished stone artifact, often in a bannerlike, winged bird, or butterfly shape. Bannerstones were possibly used as counterweights on ATLATLS or SPEARS, or as the heads of ceremonial STAFFS.

Bannock   (Snake)   A UTO-AZTECAN-speaking tribe of the GREAT BASIN CULTURE AREA, located in present-day southeastern Idaho and western Wyoming. Starting in the early 1700s, after they had acquired horses, Bannocks ranged into parts of present-day Colorado, Utah, Montana, and Oregon as well. Bannocks share the Fort Hall Reservation near Fort Hall, Idaho, with SHOSHONES. The tribal spelling of their name is *Bana'kwut*.

Yokuts balsa

barabara (barabora) A large communal house of the ALEUTS and some INUIT bands; a kind of PITHOUSE. A square pit, about two-feet deep, is lined with planks that extend above the surface; planks and poles—often driftwood or whale ribs—are used to form a roof, which is covered with sod, except over a SMOKEHOLE. The door faces east. The word *barabara* is of Russian derivation.

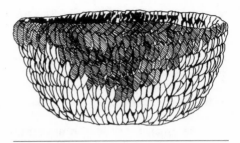

Apache basket

bar-gorget A polished stone bar, usually with one or two holes, and thought to be worn suspended around the neck as a GORGET. Some similar artifacts are classified more generally as bar amulets. (See also PERFORATED STONE.)

bark craft The act, process, or resulting artifact of work in tree bark, or the general use of tree bark as a resource. Bark has been used traditionally in the making of coverings for boats and houses as well as in the crafting of containers and other utensils. BIRCHBARK and ELM BARK have been highly valued for coverings. CEDAR bark is supple enough to be made into strips that can be twisted into string and textiles to be woven into baskets, mats, blankets, and clothing. Various types of bark also provided sources of food, medicine, dye, and poison. Willow bark was used in the smoking mixture *KINNIKINNICK*. (See also BAST; FIBER CRAFT; WOODWORK.)

basalt A hard dense igneous rock, black or dark gray in color, and used extensively for tools and utensils. Outcroppings in the American West are referred to as lava beds. The OLMECS sculpted enormous basalt heads.

basic culture A CULTURE providing a base of themes and influences, adopted by succeeding cultures.

basket A container made of interwoven material, such as grasses, rushes, twigs, wood splints, roots, or bark. Baskets were traditionally used in numerous applications, especially the carrying, processing, and storing of food. (See also BASKETRY; DEGIKUP; KIAHA; WINNOWING BASKET.)

basketry (basket-making, basketwork) The process or technique of making BASKETS, a TEXTILE art. There are two main types of baskets; in woven baskets, a coarse WARP serves as a foundation through which a WEFT (woof) is interwoven; in coiled baskets, coils are built up in a spiral and attached together with ties. FEATHERS and BEADS are added to baskets for decoration. (See also BRAIDWORK; CHECKERBOARD; COILING; FIBER CRAFT; SPLINT; WEAVING; WICKER.)

bas-relief (low relief) A sculptural projection that varies little in relief from its background.

bast (bass) Any of certain strong woody fibers obtained from plants, such as flax and hemp, or from the inner bark of trees. Bast is used in BASKETRY and to make CORDAGE.

baton See STAFF.

bayeta A kind of baize or flannel of English manufacture, traded to the Indians by the Spanish (or any similar woven material of commercial yarn). The SOUTHWEST INDIANS unraveled bayeta and used the yarn along with native wools in their WEAVING. The bayeta period refers to a period of NAVAJO weaving, about 1800 to 1880. A Spanish word.

Bayogoula See MUSKOGEAN.

bayou   A tributary to a lake, river, or bay in the south-central part of the United States, typically marshy. A Louisiana French-derived word from the CHOCTAW word *bayuk* in MUSKOGEAN.

bead   A small, globular piece of some material, such as stone, clay, copper, wood, seed, bone, horn, shell, or quill, used for stringing. The Europeans introduced glass and porcelain beads, called European beads, to Indians. (See also BEADWORK; PONY BEADS; WAMPUM.)

beadwork   The act, process, or resulting artifact of work with BEADS, in particular as stitched on clothing, bags, and other items. Beadwork commonly replaced SHELLWORK and QUILLWORK among Indians after Europeans brought glass and porcelain beads to the Americas (although some shellwork is referred to as beadwork). Beadwork designs have ornamental as well as symbolic and ceremonial purposes. (See also HESHI; WAMPUM.)

bean   Any number of plants of the genus *Phaseolus*. Beans, including the runner bean (*P. coccineus*), tepary bean (*P. acutifolius*), lima bean (*P. limensis*), and common bean (*P. vulgaris*), were cultivated by native peoples throughout the Americas. The screw bean is a variety of MESQUITE. In IROQUOIS tradition, CORN, beans, and SQUASH are the THREE SISTERS. (See also SUCCOTASH.)

bear   Any of various animals of the family Ursidae. Native Americans hunted black bears, brown bears, grizzly bears, and polar bears for meat, fur, skin, and fat. The NASKAPIS called the bear *nemocu'm*, meaning "grandfather" in Algonquian. Among many native peoples, the bear held an honored place in mythology because of its power and mystery, and was often associated with HEALING. They ate bears in a communal meal honoring the kinship between humans and Grandfather Bear, the Master of the Mountain. (See also BEAR-CLAW NECKLACE; BEAR DOCTOR; NANUK.)

bear-claw necklace   An ornament made from the claws of a bear, typical of PLAINS INDIANS. Bear claws were especially valued as TROPHIES and AMULETS.

Bear Doctor   A SHAMAN whose GUARDIAN SPIRIT is the bear. The term is associated with CALIFORNIA INDIANS.

Bear River   See ATHAPASCAN.

beaver   Large aquatic rodents of the genus *Castor*, with thick fur, a broad flat hairless tail, webbed hind feet for swimming, and hard incisor teeth suited for cutting trees to make dams. Beavers were believed by Indians to have human traits because of their industriousness and their lodges, which resemble WIGWAMS. Beaver teeth were prized as amulets and for making cutting tools or weapons. Some tribes ate beaver meat. The popularity of beaver fur in Europe led to the development and resulting economics of the FUR TRADE and the depletion of the animal throughout much of North America.

Beaver   (Tsattine) An ATHAPASCAN-speaking tribe of the SUBARCTIC CULTURE AREA, located on the prairies south of the Peace River and east of the Rocky Mountains in present-day Alberta. The Beaver Indians were formerly one people with the SEKANIS, who migrated westward, and the SARCEES, who migrated southward. The Boyer River, Heart Lake, and Horse Lake bands maintain tribal identity in Alberta, as do the Blueberry River, Doig River, and West Moberly bands in British Columbia. Their native name, *Tsattine*, means "those who live among beavers" in Athapascan.

bec   See FLAKE.

bed   See FURNITURE; HAMMOCK.

beer   See ALCOHOLIC BEVERAGES.

Begging Dance   (Beggars' Dance) A dance ceremony of the BLACKFEET, SIOUX, and CHIPPEWAS in which the CREATOR is asked to inspire the well-off to contribute food and objects to the needy.

bell   Bells probably evolved among Indian peoples from clay and shell RATTLES. Copper bells with stone strikers have been found at archaeological sites, especially among SOUTHWEST INDIANS and SOUTHEAST INDIANS, probably European trade items via MESOAMERICA. Contemporary Indians wear bells on their legs and ankles (ANKLETS) for dancing. (See also TINKLER.)

Bella Bella (Bellabella, Heiltsuk, Heiltsuq) A subtribe of the HEILTSUK Indians, located on Milbank Sound in present-day British Columbia. The name is a native corruption of *Milbank*, taken back into English. Their own tribal name, *Heiltsuk*, is applied to Indians of a number of other subtribes as well and to a language dialect. Bella Bellas live on their ancestral homeland with other Heiltsuks.

Bella Coola (Bellacoola) A SALISHAN-speaking tribe of the NORTHWEST COAST CULTURE AREA, located on Bella Coola River, Dean River, Dean Channel, North Bentinck Arm, and South Bentinck Arm in present-day British Columbia. The Bella Coolas are the northernmost of the Salishan peoples. The Bella Coola band maintains tribal identity on its ancestral homeland in British Columbia.

belt   A band or strip of leather or cloth worn around the waist to support clothing, bags, tools, or weapons, or as decoration. Indians wore belts to support BREECHCLOTHS as well as for ceremonial purposes. Traditionally they have been decorated with quillwork and beadwork. The NAVAJOS are known for their CONCHA belts, which have silver ornaments shaped like shells. (See also BANDOLIER; SASH; WAMPUM.)

bent-frame   An architectural term for a type of construction in which saplings are set into the ground, then bent over and tied together, forming a domed shape, as in a WICKIUP or WIGWAM. Other basic types of Native American construction are COMPRESSION SHELL and POST-AND-BEAM.

Beothuk   A Beothukan-speaking (language isolate, probably of the MACRO-ALGONQUIAN phylum) tribe of the SUBARCTIC CULTURE AREA, located on the island of Newfoundland, part of the present-day Newfoundland province. The Beothuks were pushed to the northern part of the island by the MICMACS, allies of the French. By the 1700s, they were extinct as a tribal identity; some survivors settled among the NASKAPIS. The last Beothuk on record died in 1829. "Beothuk" possibly means "human being." The Micmacs referred to the Beothuks as *Macquaejeet*, for "red man," in reference to their practice of painting their bodies with red OCHER, possibly the derivation of the term REDSKIN.

berdache   A man living as a woman, doing women's work, and participating in women's ceremonies. Berdaches often performed a spiritual role, belonging to MEDICINE SOCIETIES. The PLAINS INDIANS, SOUTHWEST INDIANS, and other groups thought berdaches were chosen by the CREATOR for their contribution to the tribe. The term is derived from a Persian word *bardaj*, for "slave" or "kept boy," via the French *bardache* or the Spanish *bardaje*. Tribes had varying names: CROW, *bate* in SIOUAN; HOPI, *hova* in UTO-AZTECAN; KERES, *kokwimu* in Keresan; SHOSHONE, *dubas* in Uto-Aztecan; SIOUX (Lakota), *winktan* in Siouan; and ZUNI, *ihamana* in PENUTIAN.

Beringia (Bering land bridge, Bering Strait land bridge)   During the PLEISTOCENE, so much of the earth's water was locked up in GLACIERS that the oceans were lower and more land was exposed. Where there is now water between Alaska and Siberia (eastern Russia), known as the Bering Strait, there was once land about 1,000 miles wide. Present-day islands were mountaintops. Scholars refer to this once-exposed landmass as the Bering Strait land bridge or Beringia. Animals could have migrated across this now-submerged land, including the now-extinct MAMMOTHS and MASTODONS as well as longhorn BUFFALO and SABER-TOOTHED TIGERS. The big-game hunters who depended on these animals for food could have followed them out of Asia to North America. The exact time the first bands of PALEO-INDIANS arrived in North America is not known; most scholars have estimated 10,000 B.C. It is commonly believed that about 12,000 years ago a passable southern route had opened through the glaciers along the present-day border of British Columbia; about 11,200 years ago the people of the CLOVIS CULTURE had settled at a freshwater pond in present-day New Mexico; and about 11,000 years ago Clovis people had reached Tierra del Fuego at the southern tip of South America. But other scholars, based on more recent archaeological findings, date the migration as much earlier, perhaps during other interglacial periods, or interstadials. In any case, Asian migration to North America probably happened over many thousands of years in many waves of small bands.

Bering Strait land bridge See BERINGIA.

berry A variety of small, edible fleshy fruits, such as the blueberry, cranberry, and mulberry. Native Americans gathered berries wild; it has been reported that the INCAS cultivated blackberries, raspberries, and strawberries. Dried berries were a trade item. Different types of berries were also valued as DYES. Many tribes have FIRST FOOD CEREMONIES surrounding the ripening of berries.

BIA See BUREAU OF INDIAN AFFAIRS.

Bidai See TUNICAN.

big-game hunting The hunting by PALEO-INDIANS of extinct mammals, such as longhorn BUFFALO, MAMMOTHS, MAST-

ODONS, and SABER-TOOTHED TIGERS. Spears, ATLATLS, and stamping techniques were used. The term is sometimes capitalized to define a culture, i.e., the Big Game-Hunting Tradition or Culture.

Big Head Religion See BOLE-MARU RELIGION.

Bighouse Ceremony (Ga'mwij, Ga-muing, Ga'mwin) A 12-day ceremony of the LENNI LENAPE (Delaware) Indians for the purpose of renewal and tribal unity and good fortune. The rituals involve a log structure, referred to as the Big House (*Xijwika'on*) and symbolizing the universe, as well as the lighting of a new sacred fire. Some bands made offerings to Misinghalikun, the Guardian of the Game.

bilineal descent See DESCENT.

bilocal (bilocal residence, ambilocal) The residence after marriage among or near the family of either the wife or husband, or shifting between both, as opposed to a UNILOCAL residence.

Biloxi A SIOUAN-speaking tribe of the SOUTHEAST CULTURE AREA, located on the lower Pascagoula River in present-day Mississippi. The Biloxis later moved to Louisiana along the Red River. They now share the Tunica-Biloxi Indian Reservation near Marksville, Louisiana, with TUNICAS. The Biloxi native name is *Taneks haya*, meaning "first people."

bingo A modern-day game in which numbers are drawn and called out; players place markers on their cards accordingly, trying to form a straight line and spell the word B-I-N-G-O. The game resembles traditional Indian GUESSING GAMES. A number of tribes have opened bingo halls on their reservations to create tribal revenue. (See also GAMBLING.)

birchbark The bark of the birch tree (genus *Betula*), valued as a resource by WOOD-

LAND INDIANS—in particular the ALGONQUIANS—who used it to cover boats and houses and for containers and as a writing surface for PICTOGRAPHS. (See also BARK CRAFT; CANOE; DECOY; *MOCUCK*; WIGWAM.)

bird The bird, any vertebrate of the class Aves, was hunted by Native Americans for food and for its FEATHERS. In many tribal mythologies, birds are associated with the spirit world. The LENNI LENAPE (Delaware) word for "bird" in ALGONQUIAN is *tscholens*; a "little bird" is *tscholentit*. (See also CROW; EAGLE; FEATHERWORK; HAWK; MAGPIE; OWL; PARROT; QUETZAL; RAVEN; TURKEY.)

birdstone See BANNERSTONE.

birth See CHILDBIRTH; RITE OF PASSAGE.

bison See BUFFALO.

Black Drink (Carolina Tea) A tea of the SOUTHEAST INDIANS, made from a variety of ingredients, usually including yaupon (*Ilex vomitoria*) or other hollies, such as *Ilex cassine*, plus TOBACCO and other plants. The drink is an emetic, purgative, and diuretic, and was imbibed for ritual PURIFICATION, as in the GREEN CORN CEREMONY. The CREEK name in MUSKOGEAN for the drink is *assi-luputski*. British traders called the tea "Black Drink" because of its color.

Blackfeet Sioux See SIHASAPA.

Blackfoot (Blackfeet; Siksika) An ALGONQUIAN-speaking tribe of the GREAT PLAINS CULTURE AREA, located from the North Saskatchewan River in present-day Alberta to the upper Missouri in present-day Montana. The Blackfoot proper, or Siksika bands, lived the farthest north; then the BLOOD bands in the middle; and the PIEGAN bands to the south. Along with the GROS VENTRE and SARCEE tribes, they made up an alliance known as the Blackfoot Confederacy. In Montana, Blackfeet (mostly of Pie-gan ancestry) now hold the Blackfeet Reservation in Glacier and Pondera counties; in Alberta, the Blackfoot band near Gleichen, the Blood band near Standoff, and the Piegan band near Brocket have reserves. *Siksika* means "black feet" in Algonquian, in reference to black moccasins.

Black Legs Dance (T'ow-kow-ghat) A dance of the KIOWA Indians, which originated as a ceremony of the Black Legs Warrior Society or Black Leggings Society. The members of this MILITARY SOCIETY painted their legs black before battle because of an 1830 incident in which a war party returned home with blackened legs after having survived a fire trap. Black Leg dancers re-create movements from battle.

blackware Any type of black POTTERY, such as black-on-black (or black matte). Blackware, typical of the TEWA Indians of the Santa Clara and San Ildefonso pueblos, is made from the same red clay used to make REDWARE; the blackening results from low temperatures and low oxygen in FIRING.

bladder dart A type of HARPOON, typical of the INUITS, used in hunting sea mammals. An inflated seal bladder FLOAT serves as a drag and a marker when the harpoon's detachable barbed point is embedded in the prey. (See also SEALING DART.)

Bladder Festival A five-day renewal ceremony of Alaskan INUITS. In preparation, the men make new tools and compose new songs; the women make new clothing. The bladders of sea mammals are inflated, painted, and hung in the KASHIM, where various rituals, including SWEATING, are held for PURIFICATION.

blade Generally, the flat-edged, sharpened cutting part of a tool or weapon. Specifically, a long, narrow, parallel-sided FLAKE, also called a lamellar flake. An end blade is a blade attached to the end of a handle; a side blade is attached to the side of a handle. A microblade is a small blade, less than an inch and a half in length. (See also BLADE AND CORE.)

blade and core   A technique of percussion FLAKING used to produce a long, narrow flake with parallel sides from a specially prepared stone nodule. A bone chisel or punch is struck with a HAMMERSTONE to chip a BLADE from the CORE.

blank   A stone POINT or blade in an unfinished stage, partially worked to the shape and size of the intended tool.

blanket   A large covering, woven from hair, fur, feathers, bark, cotton, wool, or other fibers. Indians traditionally have used blankets for a variety of purposes; as bed coverings; as the bed itself; as clothing; as rugs; as hangings for decoration, doors, partitions, and sunshades; as platforms for drying; as cradles and containers; as saddles; and as a means of sending SMOKE SIGNALS. Blanket designs have symbolic meanings. Blankets also became a trade item between whites and Indians. (See also BLANKET INDIAN; BUTTON BLANKET; CHIEF'S BLANKET; CHILKAT BLANKET; EYE DAZZLER; HUDSON'S BAY BLANKET; NAVAJO BLANKET; SERAPE.)

"Blanket Indian"   A term-applied in the late 19th century to those Native Americans who resisted ASSIMILATION and refused to dress in non-Indian ways.

blind   A concealment, such as a screen made from brush, used in the hunting of birds, especially waterfowl. Typical of CALIFORNIA INDIANS.

Blood (Kainah)   A subtribe of the BLACKFOOT Indians, located in southern Alberta south of present-day Calgary and ranging into present-day western Saskatchewan and northern Montana. A Canadian band known as Blood is now centered at Standoff, Alberta. The Blood native name, *Kainah*, means "many chiefs" in Algonquian.

bloodletting   The act of intentional bleeding for medicinal purposes; usually performed on a patient in an effort to reduce localized pain. (See also SCARIFICATION; SUCKING DOCTOR.)

blowgun   A weapon consisting of a tube through which darts or clay or stone pellets are discharged by blowing. The tube is made from a hollowed-out cane, reed, or shaft of wood; the darts, from splints or stems sharpened at one end and with thistledown, cotton, or feathers. Typical of SOUTH AMERICAN INDIANS, some of whom poison the darts, especially with CURARE. SOUTHEAST INDIANS used blowguns for hunting and not warfare. Among EASTERN INDIANS in general, blowguns also were crafted as toys.

"bluecoat"   An Indian name for U.S. soldiers, especially for the cavalry.

boarding school   A school where Indian children were sent to live, furthering the policies of ASSIMILATION in the late 19th and early 20th centuries. The Carlisle Indian School in Carlisle, Pennsylvania, founded in 1879 for Indians from all over the United States, is the most famous of the former Indian boarding schools. Its founder,

Cherokee blowgun

Richard Henry Pratt, believed that boarding schools should be far from reservations. (See also INDIAN SCHOOL.)

boat See CATEGORICAL APPENDIX, "TRANSPORTATION."

boatstone A prehistoric stone artifact in the shape of a boat, the purpose of which is unknown. The perforations and grooves in some boatstones indicate the use of a cord, enabling suspension from the neck as TALISMANS. Others might have been used as AT-LATL weights, similar to BANNERSTONES. Found in eastern North America.

bodkin See NEEDLE.

body-painting See PAINT; PAINTING.

boiling stone (cooking ball) Fist-size stones heated by fire and dropped in containers to boil and cook food. The process is called STONE-BOILING. (See also BAKING STONE.)

Bois Brulés See METIS.

bola A hunting weapon, typical of SOUTH AMERICAN INDIANS (such as INCA warriors), consisting of two or more weights (stone, bone, antler, or ivory) tied on thongs that are attached to a longer line. When thrown, bolas entangle the legs of mammals or wings of birds. The INUITS also used bolas consisting of bone or ivory blocks attached to rawhide (or sinew) cords, with handles made of grass stems or feathers.

Bole-Maru Religion A religious revitalization movement of the PATWINS, POMOS, MAIDUS, and other tribes of north-central California in the late 19th century. It had elements of the DREAMER RELIGION (an alternate name of Bole-Maru) and the GHOST DANCE RELIGION, drawing on traditional as well as Christian beliefs, with revelations from dreams playing a central role. Dances included the Bole or Maru Dance, the Bole-Hesi Dance, and the Ball Dance.

Bole is a Patwin word in the PENUTIAN language; *maru* is a Pomo word in HOKAN; both refer to the dreams of SHAMANS. The Big Head Religion, with devotees among CAHTOS, Lassiks, SHASTAS, WAILAKIS, WINTUNS, and YUKIS, is thought to be an offshoot of the Bole-Maru movement; in this variety, dancers wore large headdresses.

bonework (bone carving) The act, process, or resulting artifact of work in animal and human bones. Bone was used for tools as well as for ceremonial objects. Antlers, tusks, hoofs, beaks, and teeth also were used for similar carvings. (See also HORN AND ANTLER WORK; SHELLWORK.)

booger mask A carved mask of the CHEROKEES, used in what was called the Booger Dance. Booger masks have exaggerated features and expressions, they often represent

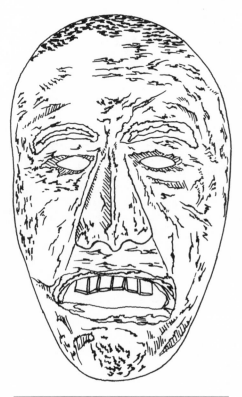

Cherokee booger mask

white people as well as animals. The names of the masks are often comical and obscene. In the Booger Dance, the behavior of enemies and strangers, usually whites, is represented and ridiculed. The term booger is derived from the same European root as *boogie* in "boogieman" ("bogeyman").

boot INUITS and ALEUTS traditionally wore fur-lined boots, the Inuit variety known as MUKLUKS. Other Native Americans had hide boots for rugged terrain. Some MOCCASINS covering part of the leg also might be called boots. SOUTH AMERICAN INDIANS, MESOAMERICAN INDIANS, and CIRCUM-CARIBBEAN INDIANS used RUBBER to waterproof footwear, which can be called the first rubber boots.

boreal Pertaining to the northern and mountainous regions of North America, Greenland, and Central America, where there are coniferous forests and the mean temperature does not exceed 64.4 degrees Fahrenheit. The SUBARCTIC CULTURE AREA is boreal. "Boreal" also is sometimes used synonymously with northern, thus referring to Arctic lands as well.

"Boston" Because the city of Boston in Massachusetts was a port city and a center of trade, its name became synonymous with "America" among many tribes. *Bostoon* is the MICMAC name for the United States in their ALGONQUIAN dialect. In the CHINOOK JARGON, "Boston" translates as "America." "Boston Charley" is a MODOC personal name.

bow A weapon made from a curved strip of wood, bone, or horn, strung with a BOWSTRING and used to shoot ARROWS. The parts of the bow are called the back, the belly, and the grip, with two wings and nocks (notches), plus the string. The four major types of Native American bows are: a self-bow, made from a single piece of wood; a compound bow, made from several layers of material, lashed or glued together; a sinew-wrapped bow, wrapped with SINEW from end to end for elasticity; and a sinew-backed or reinforced bow, with a strip of sinew or hide glued and lashed to the back. Some bows have a bow brace, a shaped piece of bone or antler, lashed or pegged to the bow's belly for strengthening. Chosen woods for bows were osage orange, ironwood, cedar, hickory, white ash, dogwood, and mulberry. Bows used from horseback were usually shorter than other bows. By about A.D. 500, the bow and arrow had replaced the ATLATL in North America. By about A.D. 1000, it was also used by MESOAMERICAN INDIANS. (See also ARCHERY; DRILL; MUSICAL BOW; PELLET-BOW; SINEW TWISTER.)

bow and arrow See ARROW; BOW.

bow drill See DRILL.

bowguard (wristguard) A device worn on the wrist to protect the skin from the snap of the released BOWSTRING, when shooting a BOW and ARROW. Bowguards usually were made of hide and sometimes decorated, often, in post-Contact times, with a silver plaque. Sometimes they were worn as wristlets. The NAVAJO word in ATHAPASCAN for "bowguard" is *ketoh*.

bowl Native Americans made concave vessels from stone, especially SOAPSTONE, pottery, bone, shell, skin, wood, bark, and

Crow bow

gourds. They used bowls for gathering, winnowing, drying, cooking, and serving food as well as in ceremonies and games.

bowl game   See DICE.

Bow Priesthood   See PRIESTHOOD OF THE BOW.

bowstring   The string on a BOW that, when pulled, bends the bow and pushes the ARROW. One end is tied to a nock (notch) on one wing of the bow, while the other end is looped and slipped up to the other wing, creating tension. Bowstrings usually are made from rawhide, sinew, gut, or twisted vegetable fiber.

box   Native Americans traditionally have crafted boxes out of wood, bark, bone, ivory, hide, and quill, with intricate symbolic carvings. They are used for storage, especially of ceremonial items, as well as other applications, such as DRUMS. (See also CHEST.)

braidwork   The act, process, or resulting artifact of WEAVING with three or more strands. Braidwork, or braiding, is used as a HAIRSTYLE. In BASKETRY, the term refers to the sewed binding edge on the rim of a basket.

"brave"   A term used in historical writings for WARRIOR. It probably was first applied by the Spanish in the phrase *Indios bravos*, in reference to the fierceness the Indians demonstrated in battle. Certain tribes had phrases translating as "having a brave or courageous time," i.e., a time of danger and hardship.

brave song   See DEATH SONG.

bread   See FRY BREAD; INDIAN BREAD; LEAF BREAD; *PIKI*; TORTILLA.

breastplate   (pectoral) An ornament or protective covering worn over the chest. PLAINS INDIANS made breastplates out of HAIR PIPES.

Breath of Life   (Breath-of-Life)   The breathing of the universe, which makes life possible; the life force. For many tribes, the Breath of Life is associated with the wind. Rituals surrounding the Breath of Life include inhaling the first light of day and giving blessing by exhaling. DANCE has been referred to as the Breath of Life made visible. The SACRED PIPE is associated with the concept. The ZUNI name for the Breath of Life in Penutian is *mili*. (See also SPIRIT.)

breechcloth   (breechclout, loincloth)   An article of clothing, folded over a belt and drawn between the legs, to cover the loins in front and back; made from animal skin, woven cloth, or some other material, such as Spanish moss. Typically worn by men, sometimes along with LEGGINGS and an APRON.

"broken promises"   A phrase used by contemporary Indians in reference to the repeated pattern of TREATY violations by federal, state, or provincial governments. Many tribes have filed legal LAND CLAIMS based on treaties that were ignored by whites soon after their signing. (See also ACTIVISM; INDIAN RIGHTS.)

Brotherton Indians   A band of MAHICAN Indians as well as other ALGONQUIANS from the MOHEGAN, MONTAUK, NARRAGANSET, PEQUOT, and WAPPINGER tribes. In 1788, these displaced peoples settled on land in Oneida County, New York. In the 1830s, they migrated to Wisconsin with the ONEIDA Indians. A group of Raritan and other LENNI LENAPE (Delaware) Indians also used the name Brotherton for their reservation in Burlington County, New Jersey. They too eventually migrated to Wisconsin. A group, centered in Arbor Vitae, Wisconsin, is still known as Brotherton.

browband   See FRONTLET.

brujo   (bruja)   The Spanish word for SORCERER, applied to Indian SHAMANS; a *bruja* is a WITCH. "*Brujo*" is also used in reference to a sculpted male figurine, made by ancient Indians of the Cauca Valley of present-day Colombia.

Brule (Sicangu, Sitchanxu) A subtribe of the TETON division of the SIOUX Indians, located on the upper Missouri River near the White River in present-day South Dakota and ranging throughout the Northern Plains, especially in present-day North Dakota, Montana, Wyoming, and Nebraska. *Brulé* is French for "burned," a translation of the SIOUAN *Sicangu*, meaning "burnt thighs."

buckskin See DEERSKIN.

buffalo (American bison, bison) A dark-brown, hoofed mammal (*Bison bison*) with a shaggy mane, a large hump, and short curved horns. American bison or bison is the proper term, and buffalo the popular one. *Pte* is a SIOUAN name for the animal. Buffalo once ranged over much of North America; their primary habitat, however, was the prairies and plains west of the Mississippi River and east of the Rocky Mountains from Canada into Texas. The buffalo was essential to the PLAINS INDIANS for food and basic materials. Native Americans made TEPEE coverings, SHIELDS, TRAVOIS platforms, PARFLECHES, ROBES and other clothing from the skins, either in rawhide form or softened into leather; thread and rope from sinews or buffalo hair; various tools from bones, including sled runners from ribs; RATTLES and other ceremonial objects from hooves, horns, and skulls; and fuel for fire from buffalo chips. The Indians' nomadic way of life revolved around the migration of herds. Tribal hunts were conducted in late spring and summer; small hunting parties went out in winter. The horse was used in most post-Contact buffalo-hunting. The near extinction of the buffalo in the late 1800s by white hunters affected the course of Plains Indian history. Many tribes had Buffalo Dances and other ceremonies honoring the buffalo. The rare white buffalo, celebrated in Native American mythology, is an albino. The longhorn buffalo, or bighorn bison, is a now-extinct animal hunted by PALEO-INDIANS. (See also BUFFALO ROBE; BUFFALO SKULL.)

Buffalo Calf Pipe (chanumpa) The SACRED PIPE of the SIOUX (Lakota). According to legend, it was given to the tribe by WHITE BUFFALO WOMAN.

buffalo robe A ROBE made of BUFFALO furs, typical of PLAINS INDIANS. Such robes were used as BLANKETS and MATS as well as wraps. Although women rarely decorated their own robes, they often embroidered those worn by men. Men also painted their own robes, showing TOTEMS and deeds. Different ways of gathering them around the body became personal statements.

buffalo skull The bleached skull of the BUFFALO, painted symbolically and stuffed with prairie grass, and serving as a sacred object during the SUN DANCE of the PLAINS INDIANS.

bullboat A circular, cup-shape boat, made from hide (often a whole buffalo skin), stretched over a willow frame and sealed with animal fat and ashes. Typical of the Indians of the upper Missouri River, especially the ARIKARAS, HIDATSAS, and MAN-

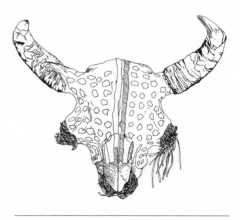

Sioux Sun Dance buffalo skull

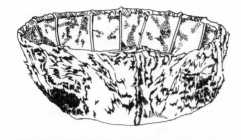

Hidatsa bullboat

DANS. A bullboat was light enough to carry on one's back.

bullroarer (rhombus, whizzer, whizzing stick, lightning stick) An instrument consisting of a small wooden slat that produces a rhythmic roar when spun on a cord; used to call people together and in religious rites, such as RAINMAKING. Some native peoples believed bullroarers made the call of the THUNDERBIRD. They also were used as toys in some tribes.

bundle burial A type of secondary BURIAL in which dried bones are tied or wrapped together randomly and reinterred.

Bureau of Indian Affairs (BIA) The agency of the U.S. federal government that handles Indian issues, formed in 1824 as part of the War Department and made a subsidiary of the Department of the Interior in 1849. The BIA originally managed trade with Indian tribes and supervised reservation life; its mandate during the late 19th century was one of ASSIMILATION. It now manages federal programs and controls the transfer of federal funds to tribes, with a supposed mandate of tribal SELF-DETERMI-NATION. A commissioner of Indian Affairs, appointed by the president and under the secretary of the interior, supervises the BIA from a central office in Washington, D.C. In addition to the central office, area offices are in charge of a number of agencies, which in turn are responsible for one or more reservations, depending on reservation size.

burial (interment, inhumation) The word burial is sometimes applied specifically to the placing of a dead body in the earth or to a dug GRAVE itself. In Indian studies, the term also is used in reference to many different ways of disposal as well as associated mortuary customs, thus sometimes including the concept of a funeral and related practices, such as MOURNING. A primary burial is the direct interment of a corpse after death; a secondary burial is the reburial of a corpse, often in dismembered form, or with the bones cleaned. An extended burial is one in which the corpse lies stretched out in the grave. In a flexed burial, the corpse lies in a fetal position, with the legs drawn up to the chin and the arms folded. (See also BUNDLE BURIAL; CAIRN BURIAL; CA-NOE BURIAL; CAVE; CIST; CREMATION; GRAVE GOODS; GRAVEHOUSE; HOUSE BURIAL; MOUND; MUMMY; NECROPOLIS; OSSUARY; SCAFFOLD BURIAL; TREE BURIAL; URN BURIAL.)

burial mound See MOUND.

burin (graver) A tool with a narrow blade and small angled edge or a sharp point, resembling a CHISEL, used to engrave or carve hard materials, such as stone, bone, antler, or ivory.

"bury the hatchet" An expression meaning "to make peace." It is thought to have been derived from the custom of lighting a PIPE-TOMAHAWK, with its blade stuck in the ground, at peace-making ceremonies.

busk See GREEN CORN CEREMONY; *PUSKITA.*

bustle An attachment to clothing on the hind side, typically of feathers, for wearing in dances, as in bustle dancing. Some tribes wore shields as bustle, such as the sun shield of the HOPIS. In the GRASS DANCE, the bustle is a tail of braided grass.

butterfly stone   See BANNERSTONE.

button   In post-Contact times, SOUTH-WEST INDIANS and other peoples used buttons, often in silver, as ornaments, decorating clothing, blankets, and pouches. (See also BUTTON BLANKET.)

button blanket   A type of BLANKET with a red cloth border made by NORTHWEST COAST INDIANS in which Chinese mother-of-pearl BUTTONS are attached in an animal shape on the blue background of European trade blankets.

▲ C ▲

cacao See CHOCOLATE.

cache A place to hide food and possessions—such as under rocks, in hollow tree trunks, or in prepared and sealed holes—for protection from animals as well as enemies. The word, of French derivation, also is used in the verb form, indicating the act of hiding supplies. In archaeology, "cache" is a technical term for a deposit of artifacts, often accompanying a BURIAL.

cacique (cazique) A CHIEF or HEADMAN. Cacique is from the ARAWAKAN term *kassequa*, applied by the Spanish to the rulers of various CIRCUM-CARIBBEAN INDIANS, MESOAMERICAN INDIANS, and SOUTH AMERICAN INDIANS. The term also was passed via the Spanish to the PUEBLO INDIANS, some of whom use it to refer to a supreme PRIEST or the religious leader of a MOIETY.

Caddo A CADDOAN-speaking tribe of the SOUTHEAST CULTURE AREA, located from the Red River Valley in present-day Louisiana to the Brazos River Valley in present-day Texas, including part of what is now southern Arkansas. Those who became known historically as the Caddo Indians included bands of the Hasinai, Kadohadacho, and Natchitoches confederacies. The Adai and Eyeish Indians eventually merged with them. In 1859, the Caddos were placed on reservation in the Indian Territory. Caddos now jointly share trust lands near Anadarko, Oklahoma (the name of the city is derived from one of the Hasinai bands), with the WICHITAS and LENNI LENAPES (Delawares). *Kadohadacha*, from which *Caddo* is derived, means "real chiefs" in Caddoan.

Caddoan A language family and subdivision of the MACRO-SIOUAN phylum comprising dialects spoken by Indians of the GREAT PLAINS CULTURE AREA, among them the ARIKARA, Kichai, PAWNEE, TAWAKONI, Waco, WICHITA, and Yskani tribes; and Indians of the SOUTHEAST CULTURE AREA, among them the Adai, CADDO, and Eyeish tribes.

Cahto (Kato) An ATHAPASCAN-speaking tribe of the CALIFORNIA CULTURE AREA, located on the upper South Fork of the Eel River. Cahtos share the Laytonville Reservation in Mendocino County with a group of POMO INDIANS. *Cahto* or *Kato* is the Pomo word for "lake."

Cahuilla (Coahuila, Kawia) A UTO-AZTECAN-speaking tribe of the CALIFORNIA CULTURE AREA, located in present-day southern California. The subdivision known as Desert Cahuillas lived at the northern end of the Colorado Desert; the Mountain Cahuillas lived in the mountains south of San Jacinto Peak; and the Western or Pass Cahuillas lived in Palm Springs Canyon. Some of the Cahuillas were missionized by the Spanish, becoming known as MISSION INDIANS, but most resisted successfully. Tribal identity is preserved on the Agua Caliente, Augustine, Cabazon, Cahuilla, Morongo, Ramona, Santa Rosa, and Torres-Martinez reservations in Riverside County, California.

cairn A pile of stones, rounded or conical. Carefully laid rock piles have been found throughout the Americas. Their exact purpose is unknown; they possibly served as SHRINES or markers. (See also CAIRN BURIAL.)

cairn burial A BURIAL in which the body is placed in a pit, then covered with stones.

Calapooya See KALAPUYA.

calendar Native Americans used differing means to record the passage of time, among them PICTOGRAPHS on hide, notches on CALENDAR STICKS, and knots tied in strings, such as on *QUIPUS*. The MESOAMERICAN INDIANS had highly developed calendar systems, often carved in stone, based on astronomy (the MAYA calendar was accurate to the day for a period of 374,400 years), as well as painted on codices. Most tribes divided the day into four periods—the rising of the sun, noon, the setting of the sun, and midnight; and the year into moons—either 12, 12 and a half, or 13, with the month beginning on a new MOON. Native Americans also determined time by the cyclical movement of the stars and the changing of seasons. Until post-Contact times, Indians used a tribal or natural event to define their individual ages. (See also CALENDAR STONE; CARDINAL POINTS; CODEX; KIOWA CALENDAR; TIME CYCLE; WINTER COUNT.)

calendar stick A wooden stick with incisions and notches representing tribal history, typical of the PAPAGOS and PIMAS. Those tribes had "Calendar-Stick Men" who, by feeling the notches on the sticks, could recite historical and mythological events.

calendar stone A stone carved as a calendar. In 1790, what is known as the Aztec Calendar Stone was found in ruins under Mexico City: 13 feet in diameter, it symbolizes the sun and depicts in PICTOGRAPHS the history of AZTEC civilization.

caliche A pavementlike layer under the surface of much of the desert in the American Southwest; a crust or hard soil layer of calcium carbonate. Ancient Indians of the region, such as those of the HOHOKAM CULTURE, dug their PITHOUSES as deep as the caliche, which served as a floor.

California Culture Area A geographical and cultural region corresponding roughly to present-day California but also including the Lower California Peninsula, which is part of Mexico (Baja California). To the east, the mountain range known as the Sierra Nevada provides a natural barrier. The smaller Coast Range also runs north-south. Between the two mountain ranges, in the heart of the CULTURE AREA, is the Great California Valley, formed by the San Joaquin and Sacramento rivers and their tributaries. The northern uplands receive the greatest amount of precipitation, mostly in winter, resulting in tall forests. The southern region is much drier. Near the California-Arizona border is the Mojave Desert. In Mexico, most of the coastal lowlands—especially along the Gulf of California—are also desert country. The region offered up many wild plant foods and game to CALIFORNIA INDIANS, who prospered and grew to high population levels as hunter-gatherers without farming, their only cultivated crop being TOBACCO. The dietary staple of California Indians was the ACORN; other wild plant foods included berries, nuts, seeds, greens, roots, bulbs, and tubers. Native peoples also ate insects, picking grubs and caterpillars off plants, then boiling them with salt, and driving grasshoppers into pits, then roasting them. To catch DEER, California Indians journeyed into the hill country to hunt with bows and arrows; they also herded them into CORRALS. RABBITS were much more common throughout the culture area; Indians hunted them with bows and arrows and clubs as well as traps and snares. Waterfowl also provided meat; Indians shot arrows at them from BLINDS or bagged them from boats with nets. California Indians fished with hooks and lines, spears, nets, and WEIRS. Along the seashore and in tidal basins, they also gathered SHELLFISH, and they caught seals and sea otters. The most typical house throughout the culture area was conical, about eight feet in diameter at the base; it was constructed from poles covered with brush, grass, reeds, or mats of TULE. Other kinds of dwellings included domed earth-covered PITHOUSES and LEAN-TOS of bark slabs. In the north, some tribes built wooden PLANK HOUSES. Most of the California houses served as single-family dwellings, but some were communal or ceremonial.

California Indians Inhabitants of the CALIFORNIA CULTURE AREA. The main language groupings are the HOKAN and PENUTIAN language phyla, and the UTO-AZTECAN language family. There were other language families spoken as well: ALGONQUIAN, ATHAPASCAN, YUKIAN, and YUMAN. Other tribes of the California Culture Area were located in Baja California, part of present-day Mexico; the Yuman-speaking Cochimis held the most territory. California peoples were not made up of true tribes, but rather groups of interrelated villages, sometimes referred to as TRIBELETS.

calumet (Grand Pipe, Sacred Pipe, medicine pipe, peace pipe, sacred pipe) A PIPE having special ceremonial significance for a tribe. Calumets typically had intricately carved bowls of stone, antler, or bone, and long wooden (often ash or sumac) or reed stems, decorated with quills, beads, feathers, fur, and horsehair. The PIPESTONE QUARRY in Minnesota was the main source of red PIPESTONE (catlinite). SOAPSTONE was another favored stone. "Calumet" is a French-derived word from the Latin *calamus*, for "reed" or "cane." With regard to the other terms used by non-Indians, "medicine pipe" and "sacred pipe" are more accurate than "peace pipe," since calumets traditionally have been used in a variety of ceremonies, such as preparation for war, as well as peacemaking. (For many tribes, white feathers symbolized peace and red feathers, war.) Typical of GREATS LAKES INDIANS and PLAINS INDIANS, especially east of the Missouri River. (See also SACRED PIPE.)

Calumet Dance (Pipe Dance) A dance, typical of NORTHEAST INDIANS and PLAINS INDIANS, performed with a pipestem or feathered wand in each hand.

Calusa (Caloosa) A tribe of the SOUTHEAST CULTURE AREA, probably MUSKOGEAN-speaking, located on the west coast of present-day Florida, from Tampa Bay to the Florida Keys, and inland as far as Lake Okeechobee. Some Calusas possibly migrated to Cuba in 1763. The Muspa band stayed behind and is thought to have merged with the SEMINOLES.

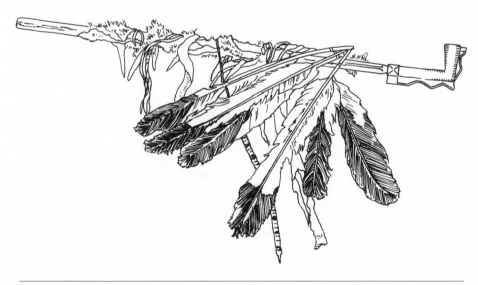

Menominee calumet

camas (camass, cammass, kamass, quamash, quamish) A plant of the genus *Camassia*, especially *C. quamash*, having blue or white flowers and edible bulbs. Found on the western slopes of the Rocky Mountains, camas root was a staple of northern GREAT BASIN INDIANS and PLATEAU INDIANS. It also was called *pomme blanche* (white apple) and *pommes des prairies* (apple of the prairies) by early French traders, as well as wild hyacinth by English-speaking settlers. The derivation of the word camas is from CHINOOK JARGON based on the NOOTKA word *chamas*, for "sweet" or "pleasant to the taste."

camp (encampment) A temporary place of abode. Native Americans camped for hunting, fishing, gathering, warfare, and visiting. In some instances, Indians slept under the open sky, but they also used LEAN-TOS, TEPEES, WICKIUPS, WIGWAMS, and other portable or easily erected shelters. For PLAINS INDIANS following BUFFALO herds, camping was the norm since most bands did not have permanent village sites. "Base camp" refers to the main camp of a nomadic people. (See also TOWN; VILLAGE.)

camp circle (tepee circle) A circular formation of TEPEES indicating political status and kinship among tribal members. A camp circle of the PLAINS INDIANS usually had a diameter of about a quarter of a mile. The circle was actually concentric circles of three or four lines.

camp crier An individual in an encampment who conveyed news from lodge to lodge; he also solicited problems of tribal members and shaped prayer songs on their behalf. Camp criers were typical of PLAINS INDIANS. The SIOUAN (Lakota) word for camp crier is *eyepaha*.

campfire See FIRE.

cannibalism (anthropophagy) Among American Indians, the eating of human flesh was generally ceremonial (ritual cannibalism) and based on the belief that one could absorb an enemy's strength and courage by ingestion. Some instances of cannibalism were for survival in times of famine. The practice was more common in South America than in North America. Where food was seasonally scarce and cannibalism a temptation, such as in the SUBARCTIC CULTURE AREA, some tribes developed strong TABOOS against it. The word "cannibal" derives from the tribal name CARIB. (See HAMATSA DANCE; WINDIGO.)

canoe A slender boat with pointed ends, propelled by paddles. The term canoe usually is applied to a frame boat with bark covering, but it also is used for DUGOUTS, carved from a single log, as in "dugout canoe." The most famous canoes are the BIRCHBARK canoes, widespread east of the Mississippi River, especially among NORTHEAST INDIANS and SUBARCTIC INDIANS; they were light enough for easy PORTAGES and drew little water, making them suitable for shallow lakes, rivers, and streams. ALGONQUIAN peoples crafted them with a framework of spruce wood and a covering of birchbark, tied together and sealed with melted PITCH. Size varied from the small river canoes for one or two people, to the large lake canoes that could hold eight or ten. Bow shape varied from tribe to tribe. The IROQUOIS used ELM BARK instead of birch. Some among the PLATEAU INDIANS

Penobscot birchbark canoe

were known to use pine bark. The Yakutat band of TLINGIT Indians had what is called an ice canoe (actually a dugout), with a knoblike projection above the waterline for breaking up ice floes.

canoe burial A type of BURIAL, typical of NORTHWEST COAST INDIANS, in which corpses were placed in CANOES, or more accurately DUGOUTS, on posts or in the forks of trees.

cape See CLOAK; ROBE.

Cape Fear See SIOUAN.

Capote A subtribe of the UTE Indians, located in present-day northwestern New Mexico. Capotes hold the Southern Ute Reservation near Ignacio, Colorado, with the MOUACHE band. *Capote* means "mountain people" in UTO-AZTECAN.

captive The taking of prisoners in war and their subsequent treatment served as a tribal catharsis. Tribes had varying rituals involving captives, such as RUNNING THE GAUNTLET. Some tribes turned prisoners over to women seeking vengeance for loss of their own family members. Captives often were adopted into tribes to fill the places of those who had died to help assure the tribe's survival. Women and children were more likely to be spared. (See also CAPTIVITY NARRATIVE; SLAVERY.)

captivity narrative Stories by white CAPTIVES telling of their experiences among Indians. Such accounts became popular with the publication of Mary Rowlandson's diary *A Narrative of the Captivity and Restoration of Mrs. Mary Rowlandson* (1682), about living with the NARRAGANSETS in 1676 during King Philip's War.

carbon-14 dating See RADIOCARBON DATING.

cardinal points The four principal directions — north, south, east, and west — used in the placement of dwellings, altars, ceremonial logs in a fire, etc., as well as their relevance in the movement of the sun, moon, and stars and the marking of time. The SIOUX refer to the cardinal points as Four Directions or Four Winds. In one of their ceremonies, a SHAMAN calls on the power of the Four Winds, i.e., the power over space, to bring the spirit of a deceased relative for a visitation. The CHEYENNES believed that Four Sacred Persons guarded the four directions, which they defined as northeast, northwest, southeast, and southwest. The MAYAS and other peoples believed in six directions, the four cardinal points plus up and down or above and below (the zenith and the nadir), a cubic representation of the universe. In many cultures, varying colors — referred to as directional colors — were associated with the cardinal points.

Carib (Cariba, Caniba, Calina, Galibi, Kalibi, Karina) A CARIBAN-speaking tribe of the CIRCUM-CARIBBEAN CULTURE AREA, located on the Lesser Antilles of the West Indies. Caribs also lived in northern South America in present-day Venezuela, Guyana, Surinam, French Guiana, and Brazil. Warlike and practicing ritual CANNIBALISM, they migrated northward out of present-day Brazil onto the Lesser Antilles (possibly about A.D. 1400), driving out the ARAWAKS. Carib men typically married Arawak women. The Caribs were virtually exterminated by the Spanish, except for a number on the island of Dominica, a group that settled in Guatemala, and other Cariban-speaking tribes of northern South America. *Carib* is the ARAWAK name meaning "strong men" and the origin of the work "cannibal."

Cariban A language family and subdivision of the GE-PANO-CARIB phylum comprising dialects spoken by Indians of the CIRCUM-CARIBBEAN CULTURE AREA, among them the CARIB tribe of the West Indies and northern South America; by other SOUTH AMERICAN INDIANS, among them the Arara, Arma, Calamari, Camaracoto, Makiritare (So'to), Motilon, and

Quimbaya tribes of northern South America; and by the Yagua of present-day Peru.

caribou The American reindeer, *Rangifer tarandus*. The two main North American species are the woodland caribou (*R. caribou*) and the smaller, barren-ground caribou (*R. arcticus*). The caribou was a source of food and hide for many SUBARCTIC INDIANS and ARCTIC INDIANS, who followed the large herds, much as PLAINS INDIANS followed their staple, the BUFFALO. The skins of an Asian species of reindeer were traded across the Bering Strait. "Caribou" is a French corruption of an ALGONQUIAN term, probably from the MICMAC *khalibu*, for "pawer" or "scratcher."

Caribou See TUTCHONE.

Carrier (Takulli) An ATHAPASCAN-speaking tribe of the SUBARCTIC CULTURE AREA, located on the upper tributaries of the Fraser River in present-day British Columbia. A number of bands hold reserves in their ancestral homeland. The name Carrier was derived from the custom of widows carrying the ashes of deceased husbands for three years; the alternate name *Tukulli*, used by other Athapascans for the Carrier Indians, means "people who go upon the water."

carrying capacity The capacity of a region's ecosystem to support a human community; measured in population density.

carrying strap See TUMPLINE.

carving See BONEWORK; HORN AND ANTLER WORK; SCULPTURE; STONEWORK; WOODWORK.

caryatid See ATLANTES.

Cascade Culture See OLD CORDILLERAN CULTURE.

cassava (manioc, yuca) Any of several tropical plants of the genus *Manihot*, with a large starchy root; used to make flour, soup, and alcoholic beverages by CIRCUM-CARIBBEAN INDIANS and SOUTH AMERICAN INDIANS of the tropics and now used to make tapioca. "Cassava" and the alternate name "yuca" (originally for the root of the plant, not to be confused with YUCCA) are ARAWAKAN words; the alternate "manioc" is a TUPI-GUARANI word. Bitter cassava (*M. utilissima*) is most often used in making bread; sweet cassava (*M. dulcis*) is used as a table vegetable and fodder.

caste system (class structure) Social and political organization, typical of the INCAS, MESOAMERICAN INDIANS, and SOUTHEAST INDIANS, in which classes of society are hereditary, determining rank or professions. (See also HEREDITARY TITLE.)

catastrophe A break in the CONTINUITY of an archaeological record, indicating sudden and extreme change in a culture.

Catawba A SIOUAN-speaking tribe of the SOUTHEAST CULTURE AREA, located in York and Lancaster counties in present-day South Carolina and near the Catawba River in present-day southern North Carolina. (Some scholars consider their language an isolate of the MACRO-SIOUAN phylum and not part of the Siouan family.) Many other Siouan-speaking Indians of the region, such as the Cheraw, Congaree, Eno, PEE DEE, and Wateree tribes, merged with them, as possibly did the Keyauwee, Santee, Sewee, Sissipahaw, and Sugeree tribes. The Catawba Indian Tribe operates out of Rock Hill, South Carolina.

category A set of objects, cultural traits, or people classed together because of common features.

Cathlamet See CHINOOKAN.

Cathlapotle See CHINOOKAN.

catlinite See PIPESTONE.

cat's cradle The weaving of patterns of string on the fingers. One currently well-known pattern resembles a kind of cradle, but there were many others. For Native Americans, the patterns had symbolic and ceremonial purposes. The NAVAJOS and ZUNIS associate their designs with the web-spinning of the spider.

cattail (reed mace) Any of several marsh plants of the genus *Typha*, especially *T. latifolia*, having long flat leaves and a cylindrical head of tiny brown flowers. The terms cattail and TULE are sometimes used interchangeably; the latter more accurately refers to similar bulrushes of the genus *Scirpus*.

Caughnawaga See MOHAWK.

cave Indian peoples used caves for shelter, storage, and burials. The term cavern refers to a large cave; the term rock shelter usually refers to a shallow cave or a rock overhang. Caves are important archaeologically for their preservation of prehistoric artifacts. (See also CLIFF-DWELLING.)

Cayuga An IROQUOIAN-speaking tribe of the NORTHEAST CULTURE AREA, located in the Finger Lakes region, especially about Cayuga Lake, in present-day New York. The Cayugas are part of the IROQUOIS LEAGUE. They now hold the Cayuga Nation Reservation near Versailles, New York; others are part of the Six Nations of the Grand River band, centered in Oshweken, Ontario. In Iroquoian, CAYUGA means "place where locusts were taken out."

Cayuse A PENUTIAN-speaking (Cayuse isolate) tribe of the PLATEAU CULTURE AREA, located on the upper Wallawalla, Umatilla, and Grande Ronde rivers (tributaries of the Columbia), from the Blue Mountains to the Deschutes River, in present-day northeastern Oregon and southeastern Washington. Cayuse Indians share the Umatilla Reservation in Umatilla County, Oregon, with UMATILLAS and WALLAWALLAS. The Cayuse language was formerly grouped with that of the Molalas in a family known as Waiilatpuan.

"cayuse pony" An Indian pony. Whites applied this term to horses because the CAYUSE Indians were known as skilled breeders and traders.

cedar Any of several coniferous evergreen trees of different genera, depending on the location and continent. The name comes from the genus *Cedrus*, located in the Near East. In North America, three varieties are found: the genera *Chamaecyparis* (white cedar); *Thuja* (*T. plicata* is the western red cedar); and *Juniperus* (JUNIPER). The genus *Cedrela* is found in Mexico and tropical America. The tree often is used for ritual purposes, the wood as incense and the boughs for CEREMONIAL HOUSES. NORTHWEST COAST INDIANS made PLANK HOUSES, TOTEM POLES, and DUGOUTS from cedar. The berries have been used for medicinal purposes, and the needles were made into an ash paste for fixing dyes.

celt (ungrooved ax) A stone or metal tool, used for cutting and scraping in WOODWORK, that is shaped like a CHISEL but with

stone celt

a wider blade. Celts usually were made by grinding rather than FLAKING. Although celts, unlike the heads of AXES, have no groove for attachment to a handle, some are thought to have been inserted in a cavity in a piece of wood or antler, or wrapped at one end in rawhide. Some celts served a ceremonial purpose.

cenote   A natural underground water hole. Of Spanish derivation, originally from the MAYAN word *conot*, "cenote" describes the natural wells of the Yucatan peninsula used in irrigation.

ceramic   A product made of clay and similar materials from FIRING, in particular POTTERY, but also brick, glass, enamel, and cements. "Ceramics" can also refer to the art and technology of the same.

ceremonial center   A complex of buildings, such as TEMPLES, used for religious purposes and typical of MESAOMERICAN INDIANS and the INCAS. Few permanent residents other than perhaps priests and their servants lived at ceremonial centers.

ceremonial house   (ceremonial lodge)   A structure used for religious purposes and sometimes for civic and social purposes as well. (See also COUNCIL HOUSE; *KASHIM*; KIVA; MEDICINE LODGE; SMOKE HOUSE; *VAHKI*.)

ceremonial object   See SACRED OBJECT.

ceremonial runner   An individual who ran from village to village to convey information. He held a position of authority within the tribe and was believed to have spiritual powers, such as controlling the weather. The FOX Indian term in ALGONQUIAN is *a'ckapawa*.

ceremonial society   See SECRET SOCIETY.

ceremony   Although the term ceremony is sometimes used interchangeably with "RITUAL" and "rite," a ceremony implies a broader grouping; i.e., it makes more sense to say a ceremony has rituals or rites than vice-versa. The adjective form ceremonial is also sometimes used as a noun. (See also BURIAL; DANCE; FESTIVAL; POTLATCH; POWWOW; RELIGION; RITE OF PASSAGE.)

Chac Mool   (Chac, Chac-Mool, Chacmool, Chac-Mol)   The MAYA god of rain, thunder, lightning, and wind. He also symbolizes fertility and sometimes is referred to as "the reclining god," based on reclining stone figures in Mexico and the Yucatan. He is the equivalent of the TOLTEC and AZTEC god TLALOC, the Huastec god Tajin, and the Zapotec god Cocijo.

chairman   The elected head of a tribal COUNCIL, as mandated by the Indian Reorganization Act of 1934.

Chakchiuma   See MUSKOGEAN.

chalcedony   A variety of QUARTZ, translucent to transparent, with a waxy luster and black impurities; used for FLAKING. Agate, jasper, bloodstone, and onyx, showing variegated coloring, are kinds of chalcedony. FLINT and CHERT also are sometimes grouped under this heading because they are of the quartz family.

Changing Woman   See HOLY PEOPLE.

chant   A vocal expression or recitation of words, usually in a monotonous, rhythmic voice, with a number of syllables or words for each tone. The act of chanting is religious for Native Americans. Used as a noun or a verb. The terms call chant and chantway also are used. (See also SONG.)

chapayeka   A spiritual being in YAQUI tradition, derived from native as well as Christian beliefs. The chapayekas symbolize evil as enemies of Christ. In Yaqui ceremonies, many of which correspond to the Christian calendar, chapayeka masks of painted hide or paper cover the entire head. The behavior of the chapayeka IMPERSONATORS is typically comical. (See also CLOWN; PASCOLA.)

charm See AMULET; CHARMSTONE; FE-
TISH; TALISMAN.

charmstone A stone carried or worn as
an AMULET or TALISMAN.

Chastacosta (Chasta-Costa, Chasta) An
ATHAPASCAN-speaking tribe of the NORTH-
WEST COAST CULTURE AREA, located on
the Rogue River near its junction with the
Illinois River in present-day Oregon. In the
mid-1800s, tribal members were settled with
other tribes on the Siletz Reservation near
Siletz, Oregon.

Chatot See MUSKOGEAN.

Chawasha See TUNICAN.

checkerboard In BASKETRY, the simplest
weave, an over-one-under-one pattern.

Chehalis A SALISHAN-speaking tribe of
the NORTHWEST COAST CULTURE AREA,
located on the lower Chehalis River near
Grays Bay in present-day Washington. The
Chehalis later held what had been CHINOOK
territory around Willapa Bay. The Upper
Chehalis, or the Kwaiailk, came to be defined as those bands living north of the
Satsop River, and the Lower Chehalis, as
those to the south. The Chehalis tribe holds
the Chehalis Reservation near Oakville,
Washington, along with Chinook, Clatsop,
and COWLITZ Indians, and the Shoalwater
Reservation near Tokeland with the Chinook and QUINAULT tribes. *Chehalis* is
thought to mean "sand" in Salishan.

Chehaw See CHIAHA.

Chelamela See KALAPUYAN.

Chelan See SALISHAN.

Chelkona (Tcirkwena, Season Dance, Skip-
ping Dance, Winter Rain Dance) A fertility and RAINMAKING ceremony of the
PAPAGO Indians, performed by children.

Chemehuevi A UTO-AZTECAN-speaking
tribe of the GREAT BASIN CULTURE AREA,
related linguistically to the PAIUTE Indians.
The Chemehuevis once lived in the eastern
Mojave Desert in present-day California
and later in the Chemehuevi Valley along
the Colorado River. They hold the Chemehuevi Reservation in San Bernardino
County, California, and they share the Colorado River Reservation in Yuma County,
Arizona, and San Bernardino and Riverside
counties, California, with the MOJAVES. The
tribe's native name is *Nuwu,* meaning
"people."

Chepenafa See KALAPUYAN.

Cheraw See SIOUAN.

Cherokee An IROQUOIAN-speaking tribe
of the SOUTHEAST CULTURE AREA, located
in the mountains and valleys of the southern
Appalachian chain, including the Great
Smoky Mountains of present-day western
North Carolina, the Blue Ridge of present-
day western Virginia, and the Great Valley
of present-day Tennessee. The Cherokees
also lived in the Appalachian high country
of present-day South Carolina and Georgia,
as far south as present-day northern Alabama. In the early 1800s, some Cherokee
bands migrated to Arkansas and Texas. The
majority of Cherokees were relocated to the
INDIAN TERRITORY in the 1830s on the
TRAIL OF TEARS. Descendants, known as
Western Cherokees, hold trust lands near
Tahlequah, Oklahoma. Eastern Cherokees
hold the Cherokee Reservation near Cherokee, North Carolina. In North Carolina, a
band known as the Cherokee Indian Tribe
of Robeson and Adjoining Counties and a
band known as the Cherokee Indians of
Hoke City maintain tribal identity. In Alabama, the following bands are active: Cherokees of Jackson City, Cherokees of
Northeast Alabama, Cherokees of Southeast
Alabama, Echota Cherokee Tribe of Alabama, and United Cherokee Tribe of Alabama. In Georgia, the following bands exist:
Cherokee Indians of Georgia, Georgia

Tribe of Eastern Cherokees, Southeastern Cherokee Confederacy. In Tennessee, there is the Red Clay Inter-Tribal Indian Band of Southeastern Cherokee Confederacy; in Florida, the Tuscola United Cherokee Tribe of Florida and Alabama; in Missouri, the Northern Cherokee Tribe of Missouri; and in Oregon, the Northwest Cherokee Wolf Band of Southeastern Cherokee Confederacy. *Cherokee* possibly is derived from the CREEK word in MUSKOGEAN, *tciloki,* meaning "people of the different speech," or from the LENNI LENAPE (Delaware) name for them, *Talligewi* or *Tsalagi.* The Cherokee native name is *Ani Yunwiya,* or "real people."

Cherokee alphabet A SYLLABARY of the CHEROKEE language, invented by the Cherokee Indian Sequoyah in the early 1800s so the language could be written.

chert A kind of rock, cryptocrystalline silica or fibrous CHALCEDONY; dense and glassy and often often purplish in color. Like FLINT, chert was a favored stone for FLAKING into tools or spear and arrow POINTS. (See also QUARTZ.)

chest NORTHWEST COAST INDIANS carved large wooden boxes with intricate and symmetrical designs in BAS-RELIEF. The HAIDAS are known for their elaborate chests.

Chetco (Chetkoe) An ATHAPASCAN-speaking tribe of the NORTHWEST COAST CULTURE AREA, located on the lower Chetco River in present-day Oregon. In 1853, the Chetcos were settled on the Siletz Reservation, where their numbers dwindled. A group centered in Brookings, Oregon, maintains the tribal name, which means "close to the mouth of the stream" in Athapascan.

Cheyenne (Tsistsistas, Dzitsistas) An ALGONQUIAN-speaking tribe of the GREAT PLAINS CULTURE AREA. The Cheyennes originally lived among other Algonquians in present-day Minnesota. After 1680, they crossed the Minnesota River and migrated westward into present-day North and South Dakota, settling along the Missouri River. In the early 1800s, they pushed westward along the Cheyenne River, a tributary of the Missouri, into the Black Hills. During this period, they were joined by the Sutaio (Suhtaio) Indians, who became one of the 10 bands in the Cheyenne CAMP CIRCLE. The SIOUX Indians pushed the Cheyennes farther south to the North Platte River in present-day eastern Wyoming and western Nebraska. In about 1832, the Cheyennes separated into two groups: one, which became known to whites as the Northern Cheyennes, stayed on the upper Platte, ranging as far north as southern Montana; the other, known as the Southern Cheyennes, migrated south to the upper Arkansas River in present-day eastern Colorado and western Kansas. The Northern Cheyennes became allies of the Sioux and Northern ARAPAHOS; the Southern Cheyennes were allies of the Southern Arapahos, COMANCHES, and KIOWAS. Northern Cheyennes now hold the Northern Cheyenne Reservation near Lame Deer, Montana; Southern Cheyennes share trust lands near Concho, Oklahoma, with Arapahos. *Cheyenne* is derived from *Shyela,* a SIOUAN name for the tribe, meaning "red talkers" or "people of different speech." The Cheyenne native name is *Tsistsistas,* for "beautiful people" or "our people."

Chiaha (Chehaw) A MUSKOGEAN-speaking tribe of the SOUTHEAST CULTURE AREA, once having bands in present-day Georgia, Tennessee, and South Carolina. The Chiahas were part of the Creek Confederacy. Some of them may have migrated to Florida, becoming MICCOSUKEES; others were relocated to the INDIAN TERRITORY with the CREEKS. Their name resembles the CHOCTAW and ALABAMA word for "high" in Muskogean, perhaps referring to mountains.

Chibchan A language family and subdivision of the MACRO-CHIBCHAN phylum comprising dialects spoken by Indians of the CIRCUM-CARIBBEAN CULTURE AREA, among them the Cuna, Guaymi, Guetar, and Miskito (Mosquito) tribes of present-day Nicaragua, Costa Rica, and Panama; as well as by SOUTH AMERICAN INDIANS, including the Cara and Chibcha (Muisca) of present-day Columbia. Some Chibchan dialects have survived in those regions.

chicha A kind of beer, typical of the INCAS, made from chewed CORN, CASSAVA, or other plants.

Chickahominy A subtribe of the POWHATAN Indians, located on the Chickahominy River in present-day Virginia. Descendants, centered around Providence Forge, Virginia, still use the Chickahominy name, possibly meaning "hominy people" or "cleared place" in ALGONQUIAN.

Chickasaw A MUSKOGEAN-speaking tribe of the SOUTHEAST CULTURE AREA, located in present-day northern Mississippi, especially Pontotoc and Union counties. The tribe also claimed much of present-day western Kentucky and Tennessee as hunting territory. Bands also lived in Alabama, South Carolina, and Georgia during the 1700s. The Chickasaws were relocated to the INDIAN TERRITORY in the 1830s. They hold trust lands near Ardmore, Oklahoma.

Chickasaw trade language See MOBILIAN TRADE LANGUAGE.

chickee A kind of house, typical of the SEMINOLES, raised on stilts or piles and open on four sides, with a wooden platform and THATCH roof; usually about three or four feet above the ground and about nine feet wide by 16 feet long. The Seminoles build chickees from products of the PALMETTO tree, using the trunks for foundation and framing, the leaves for thatch, and the fibers for lashing. Other tribes once also constructed raised houses, using wooden posts or mounds of earth or shells to stay above water or swampy ground, or to level

Seminole chickee

a structure on the side of a hill. These, like chickees, are classified under the general headings of platform houses or pile dwellings.

chief A person of high authority within a TRIBE, BAND, or CLAN; a traditional Indian leader. The term varies in meaning among tribes. Some tribes have more than one chief: "war chief" indicates a leader in war; "peace chiefs" or "civil chiefs" lead in peacetime. In some tribes, a chief is a hereditary position; in others, chiefs are chosen through merit, often by a COUNCIL. The term HEADMAN is sometimes used interchangeably with chief. Europeans used the term head chief especially in reference to the leaders of confederacies, as well as the term king or emperor, although chiefs rarely had absolute power. Contemporary Indians consider the term derogatory when used by non-Indians in reference to an Indian who is not a true chief. (See also CACIQUE; CHAIRMAN; CHIEFDOM; GRAND SACHEM; GREAT SUN; SACHEM; SAGAMORE.)

chiefdom A TRIBE in which a CHIEF has absolute power over other tribal members, such as in legal and religious affairs and property. The term pertains especially to SOUTHEAST INDIANS.

chief's blanket (chief blanket) A name applied to NAVAJO BLANKETS, popular in the 19th century, worn over the shoulders in such a way that the longer dimension extended from side to side rather than top to bottom. Their use spread to PLAINS INDIANS. The earliest blankets were striped; block designs were later added to the stripes, and then triangles.

Chilcotin An ATHAPASCAN-speaking tribe of the SUBARCTIC CULTURE AREA, located on the Chilcotin River in present-day British Columbia. The Chilcotins hold reserves in their ancestral homeland. *Chilcotin* means "people of young man's river" in Athapascan.

childbirth In order to ensure the well-being of mothers and children, different tribes had varying rituals before, during, and following the act of bearing children, such as the COUVADE. There were also many TABOOS surrounding pregnancy, such as that of the KWAKIUTLS against handling injured animals. Women continued to work through their pregnancies and in many tribes gave birth unassisted in a kneeling position, sometimes returning to work the next day. In other tribes, SHAMANS and midwives helped in the birth. Women took herbs to facilitate birth and healing.

childhood name The name bestowed at birth. Among PLAINS INDIANS and peoples of other regions as well, the childhood name was changed at the time of passage to adulthood in a special NAMING CEREMONY; a DREAM NAME might then be used.

child life An anthropological term for tribal customs with regard to children and infants, activities of children and "child-rearing." Children generally had great social freedom within the tribe; they were expected to learn by example and behave accordingly. Indian children have been disciplined by verbal statements, including humor, ridicule, advice, tales, and legends. Physical punishment was rare, though at times supernatural sanctions were threatened. (See also DOLL; GAME; JOKING RELATIVE; TOY.)

chili (chile, chilli) The fruit of several varieties of the plant *Capsicum frutescens*, the source of the condiment cayenne or red pepper. *Chili* is a NAHUATL word.

Chilkat A subtribe of the TLINGIT Indians, with villages at the head of Lynn Canal and on Chilkat River in present-day Alaska. The Chilkats became widely known for the manufacture of CHILKAT BLANKETS. Their name is thought to mean "storehouses for salmon."

Chilkat blanket A ceremonial BLANKET named after the CHILKAT band of TLINGITS and made by them as well as by other Tlingit bands and by TSIMSHIANS. The blankets were crafted from cedar-bark fiber and mountain-goat or mountain-sheep hair. Some of the yarn spun from wool was left white; the rest was dyed black, blue green, or yellow. Over a period of about a year and a half, women wove the yarn into intricate totemic designs and animal forms, with special meaning for families and clans. The resulting blankets were about six feet long with a straight edge at the top and an uneven bottom edge, about two feet wide at the ends and three feet wide in the middle. There were long fringes on the side and bottom but none along the top edge.

Chilliwack See COWICHAN.

Chilluckittequaw See CHINOOKAN.

Chilula See ATHAPASCAN.

Chimakuan A language family of undetermined phylum affiliation comprising dialects spoken by the CHIMAKUM and QUILEUTE tribes of the NORTHWEST COAST CULTURE AREA.

Chimakum (Chemakum) A CHIMAKUAN-speaking tribe of the NORTHWEST COAST

CULTURE AREA, located on the peninsula between Hood's Canal and Port Townsend in present-day Washington. The Chimakums are related linguistically to the QUILEUTES. In 1855, they were placed on the Skokomish Reservation near Shelton with SKOKOMISH Indians, where their numbers dwindled and they lost their tribal identity.

Chimariko See HOKAN.

Chimmesyan See TSIMSHIAN.

chinampa An artificial island made by piling silt and plant matter on wickerwork baskets in shallow lakes, often used as a vegetable garden. The AZTECS constructed *chinampas* on Lake Texcoco to create additional land for the city of Tenochtitlan. A Spanish word, from the NAHUATL *chinamitl*, meaning "garden in the water."

Chinantecan A language family and subdivision of the OTO-MANGUEAN phylum comprising dialects spoken by Indians of the MESOAMERICAN CULTURE AREA, including the Chinantec tribe of what is now central Mexico.

chinking An architectural term for any materials, such as mud or grass, used to fill cracks between logs. The term chinks refers to the cracks themselves (i.e., one fills in "chinks" with "chinking," or, in the verb form, one "chinks" the cracks).

Chinook (Tchinouk) A CHINOOKAN-speaking tribe of the NORTHWEST COAST CULTURE AREA, located on the north side of the Columbia River from its mouth to Grays Bay. Three groups maintain tribal identity: the Chinook Indian Tribe, centered in Chinook, Washington; the Chinook Tribe, in Oakland, Oregon; and the Tchinouk Indians, in Klamath Falls, Oregon. Other Chinooks share the Shoalwater Reservation in Pacific County with CHEHALIS and QUINAULT Indians.

Chinookan A language family and subdivision of the PENUTIAN phylum comprising dialects spoken by the Cathlamet, Cathlapotle, Chilluckittequaw, CHINOOK, Clackamas, Clatsop, Clowwewalla, Multomah, Skilloot, Wasco, Watlala, and Wishram tribes of the NORTHWEST COAST CULTURE AREA.

Chinook Jargon (Oregon Jargon, Oregon trade language) A dialect combining CHINOOKAN, SALISHAN, WAKASHAN, and other Native American dialects along with English, French, and perhaps Russian. Originally an intertribal lingua franca used by NORTHWEST COAST INDIANS and PLATEAU INDIANS, it began incorporating European words in about 1810 with the Oregon FUR TRADE.

chinook wind Warm winds in the western United States and Canada. Fur traders in the Pacific Northwest trading post of Astoria first applied the term to a warm, moist southwest wind blowing from the direction of the CHINOOK village. It later referred to a warm, dry westerly wind descending from the eastern slopes of the Rocky Mountains as well as to any wind raising temperatures in winter.

chip (spall) A small waste piece of stone in FLAKING; also called a FLAKE.

Chipayu-Uru A language family and subdivision of the PENUTIAN phylum comprising dialects spoken by the Chipayu and Uru tribes of present-day Bolivia.

Chipewyan An ATHAPASCAN-speaking tribe of the SUBARCTIC CULTURE AREA, located north of the Churchill River between Great Slave Lake and Hudson Bay, in present-day northern Saskatchewan, Manitoba, Alberta, and southern Northwest Territories. A number of Chipewyan bands hold tracts of reserve lands throughout their ancestral homeland. *Chipewyan* is a CREE term in ALGONQUIAN, meaning "pointed skins," in reference to the shape of their shirts. (See also ATHABASCA.)

Chippewa (Chippeway, Ojibway, Ojibwa, Ojibwe, Otchipwe, Anishinabe, Anishinabeg) An ALGONQUIAN-speaking tribe of the NORTHEAST CULTURE AREA (southern bands); the SUBARCTIC CULTURE AREA (northern bands); and the GREAT PLAINS CULTURE AREA (Plains Chippewa). The Chippewas' closest linguistic relatives are the OTTAWAS and POTAWATOMIS. Their most populous location was around Lakes Superior and Huron in present-day Minnesota, Wisconsin, Michigan, and Ontario, but they spread into surrounding areas, south of the Great Lakes and as far west as Manitoba and North Dakota. In Michigan, Chippewas now hold the Bay Mills, Grand Traverse, Isabella, L'Anse, Sault Ste. Marie reservations; in Minnesota, the Fond du Lac, Grand Portage, Leech Lake, Mille Lacs, Nett Lake, Red Lake, and White Earth reservations; in Montana, the Rocky Boy's Reservation (with CREES); in North Dakota, Ojibwa of the Red River and Turtle Mountain reservations; in Wisconsin, the Bad River, Lac Courte Oreilles, Lac du Flambeau, Red Cliff, St. Croix, and Sokaogon Chippewa reservations. In Manitoba, Ontario, and Saskatchewan, tribal members hold numerous tracts. In Michigan, there also are tribal groups known as the Consolidated Bahwetig Ojibwas and Mackinac Tribe and the Lac Vieux Desert Band of Superior Chippewa Indian Tribe; in Montana, the Little Shell Tribe of Chippewa Indians and the Swan Creek and Black River Chippewas; and in North Dakota, the Christian Pembina Chippewa Tribe. *Chippewa* (and the alternate spelling *Ojibway* prevalent in Canada) possibly means "to roast until puckered up" in Algonquian, in reference to the puckered seams in moccasins; or possibly "those who make pictographs." The Chippewa native name is *Anishinabe*, for "first men." An alternate tribal name, *Saulteaux*, was originally applied to the Chippewas living near the falls at Sault Ste. Marie. (See also MISSISAUGA; NIPISSING.)

Chiricahua   A subtribe of the APACHE Indians, originally living in the Chiricahua Mountains in present-day southeastern Arizona, but ranging into New Mexico and northern Mexico as well. The Chiricahua-Mescalero group includes the MESCALERO and GILENOS divisions; the Gilenos include the Chiricahua, MIMBRENO, MOGOLLON, and WARM SPRINGS bands. The Chiricahuas were settled on the Fort Apache and San Carlos reservations in Arizona and the Fort Sill Reservation in Oklahoma. *Chiricahua* means "great mountain" in ATHAPASCAN.

chisel   A tool with a narrow, beveled blade for cutting and shaping; made from stone, bone, antler, and, in post-Contact times, steel. It is often used with a HAMMER in woodwork, stonework, and bonework. A cold chisel is made of hardened steel and used for cutting cold metal, as in silverwork. (See also GOUGE.)

Chitimacha   A   MACRO-ALGONQUIAN-speaking (Chitimacha or Chitimachan isolate) tribe of the SOUTHEAST CULTURE AREA, located on Grand River, Grand Lake, and the lower Bayou La Teche in present-day Louisiana. Tribal members hold the Chitimacha Reservation in Saint Mary Parish, Louisiana. *Chitimacha* means "they possess cooking vessels" in the CHOCTAW dialect of MUSKOGEAN.

chocolate   The food obtained from grinding the bean of the cacao tree (*Theobroma cacao*), roasted without shell or germ; developed by the AZTECS. "Chocolate" is derived from the NAHUATL word *chocolatl*. "Cacao" and "cocoa" are also Nahuatl-derived, from *cachuatl*.

Choctaw   A MUSKOGEAN-speaking tribe of the SOUTHEAST CULTURE AREA, located in present-day southeastern Mississippi, with some bands in present-day Alabama, Georgia, and Louisiana. The majority of Choctaws were relocated to the INDIAN TERRITORY in the 1830s. The Choctaw Nation of Oklahoma holds trust lands near Durant, Oklahoma. Other descendants have rights to the Mississippi Choctaw Reservation near Philadelphia, Mississippi. The Apache-Choctaw Indian Community of Ebarb, the Clifton-Choctaws, the Jena Band of Choctaws, and the Louisiana Band of Choctaws maintain tribal identity in Louisiana. The Mowa Band of Choctaw Indians operates out of McIntosh, Alabama. The meaning of Choctaw is uncertain, although it might have been from the Indian name of the Pearl River, *Hachha*. The Chickasaws called them *Pansh Falaia*, meaning "long hairs"; the French called them *Têtes Plates*, meaning "flat heads" because of their custom of HEAD DEFORMATION.

Chopunnish See NEZ PERCE.

Chorotegan See MANGUEAN.

Choula See MUSKOGEAN.

Chowanoc See ALGONQUIAN.

Chowchilla See MIWOK; YOKUTS.

Christian Indians See MISSION INDIANS; PRAYING INDIANS.

chronology The historical order of events, objects, or archaeological sites. Some tribes had assigned individuals to record tribal history in order of occurrence.

Chukchi-Kamchatkan (Chukotian) A language family comprising dialects spoken by native peoples of Siberia, part of the AMERICAN ARCTIC-PALEO-SIBERIAN phylum and related to the dialects of the ESKIMO-ALEUT family.

Chukotian See CHUKCHI-KAMCHATKAN.

chullpa (chulpa) A cylindrical or square burial tower erected in stone or ADOBE by the pre-INCA inhabitants of present-day Peru and Bolivia. The term also refers to a spirit of death among the QUECHUA-speaking Indians.

Chumash (Santa Barbara) A CHUMASH-AN-speaking tribe of the CALIFORNIA CULTURE AREA, located near present-day Santa Barbara, California, as well as on the three closest Channel Islands. Those tribal members missionized by the Spanish became known to whites as MISSION INDIANS. Descendants hold the Santa Ynez Reservation in Santa Barbara County, California. *Chumash* was originally applied to the Santa Rosa Island Chumashans.

Chumashan A language family and subdivision of the HOKAN phylum comprising dialects spoken by the bands of the CHUMASH tribe of the CALIFORNIA CULTURE AREA.

Chungichnish Religion (Chinigchinix, Chinginix, Chingichngish, Chungicgnishm Cult) A religion of CALIFORNIA INDIANS in the southern part of the state, among the DIEGUENO, Gabrielino, and LUISENO tribes. It is not known for certain when it was founded; it may have begun after Indians began dying from European diseases brought to the region by early explorers. Chungichnish is the name of a deity who had human form and after death ascended into a spiritual realm, like the Christian Jesus. An angry god, he demands adherence to secret rituals. Some Chungichnish ceremonies involve the use of the hallucinogen JIMSONWEED. The principal ritual is the *Pames*, also known as the Eagle Ceremony.

chunkey (chunky, chunkee, wheel-and-stick) A game or sport played with a stone disk or ring and a pole having a crook at one end. The object is to throw the pole and trap the disk (sometimes referred to as a CHUNKEY STONE) in its crook. Typical of

SOUTHEAST INDIANS, especially the CREEKS, who had special chunkey yards strewn with sand. Chunkey also was played and perhaps invented by Indians of the MISSISSIPPIAN CULTURE.

chunkey stone The name given to a variety of DISCOIDS, symmetrical stones from about one to eight inches in diameter, mostly found east of the Mississippi River. Some, but probably not all, were used in the game of CHUNKEY; the stones most likely served some other unknown purpose. Many chunkey stones were polished with holes in the center.

Cibecue A subtribe of the SAN CARLOS division of APACHE Indians, consisting of the Canyon Creek, Carrizo, and Cibecue bands present-day in Gila and Navajo counties, Arizona.

circle An important symbol for many Native American tribes, representing that which is connected, never-ending, and all-embracing. The circle is found in art and design, in dance formations, and in dwelling shapes. (See also CAMP CIRCLE; MEDICINE WHEEL; SACRED HOOP; SACRED SHIELD; TIME CYCLE.)

Sioux quillwork circle

Circum-Caribbean Culture Area A cultural and geographical region comprising the West Indies and coastal Colombia and Venezuela as well as western Honduras, Costa Rica, Nicaragua, and Panama in Central America. The Caribbean and Central American environment, predominantly tropical rain forest, warm all year with plentiful rain, resembles that of South America, and the CIRCUM-CARIBBEAN INDIANS were to a large extent under the sphere of influence of SOUTH AMERICAN INDIANS. The West Indies, an archipelago in the Caribbean Sea, also are known as the Antilles and are subdivided north to south into the Bahama Islands; the Greater Antilles (including Cuba, Jamaica, Haiti-Dominican Republic, and Puerto Rico); and the Lesser Antilles (including the Leeward Islands, the Windward Islands, Barbados, and Trinidad-Tobago). The northern islands, the Bahama group, are low and flat and covered with grass or trees. Cuba also consists mostly of lowlands, except at the southeastern end, which has mountains. All the other Caribbean islands to the south are high islands. Hispaniola (Haiti and the Dominican Republic), Jamaica, and Puerto Rico of the Greater Antilles have mountain ranges running through them. The Central American part of the CULTURE AREA is also mountainous. A primary route of migration to the Caribbean islands was northward from South America along the Antilles chain. People of this region were farmers as well as hunter-gatherers. The most important crops were CASSAVA, CORN, SWEET POTATOES, peanuts, peppers, COTTON, and TOBACCO. The palm tree, both the trunk and leaves, served as the primary building material for both rectangular and circular buildings. The dominant form of social organization was the CHIEFDOM—autonomous bands united politically and religiously under a CACIQUE with social classes. The Indians of the region hunted a variety of animals and birds. The HUTIA was a main source of meat in the West Indies. Hunters used clubs as well as SPEARS, BOWS and

ARROWS, and BLOWGUNS. They also drove hutias into CORRALS with TORCHES and trained DOGS. The ARAWAKS also kept PARROTS. Most of the fishing was from DUGOUTS, with spears, NETS, and FISHHOOKS and lines.

Circum-Caribbean Indians Peoples of the CIRCUM-CARIBBEAN CULTURE AREA. They spoke languages of the GE-PANO-CARIB and ANDEAN-EQUATORIAL phyla in the West Indies and languages of the AZTEC-TANOAN, MACRO-CHIBCHAN, and OTO-MANGUEAN phyla in Central America. (See also ARAWAK; CARIB.)

cire perdue (lost wax) A technique of casting METALWORK. A clay model is covered in wax, then coated with an outer layer of clay and charcoal. Heat causes the wax to melt, forming a space between the two ceramic layers. Molten metal is then poured into the space. After drying, the clay is removed. For a solid object, the model can be shaped of wax, then covered in clay; the molten metal takes the shape of the wax core, and the outer clay is removed after drying. *Cire perdue* is French for "lost wax."

cist An oval or circular pit, roofed and often slab-lined, used for storage of food and other items. Cists also were sometimes used in BURIALS.

city-state A city, and its surrounding territory, with a government independent from other cities. Used in reference to population centers of the MESOAMERICAN CULTURE AREA as well as of the INCAS and related cultures. Some MOUNDBUILDERS also lived in what might be called city-states.

civilization The term ancient civilizations is used for American Indian societies with a high degree of social complexity, having CASTE SYSTEMS and being centralized in cities or CITY-STATES, such as the OLMEC, TOLTEC, MAYA, AZTEC, TEOTIHUACAN, and INCA cultures. Yet "civilization" also is used as a synonym of CULTURE. Therefore, it can be said that all tribes, with their rules of social interaction, consist of civilizations. (See also FIVE CIVILIZED TRIBES.)

Clackamas See CHINOOKAN.

Clallam (Klallam, Sklallam, Tlallam) A SALISHAN-speaking tribe of the NORTHWEST COAST CULTURE AREA, located on the south side of the Strait of Juan de Fuca, between Port Discovery and the Hoko River, in present-day Washington. In 1855, tribal members were granted rights to a small reservation with SKOKOMISH Indians but resisted settling there. Eventually they were granted territory in their ancestral homeland near Port Angeles, Washington, under the Indian Reorganization Act of 1934. In 1936, the Port Gamble Reservation was established; in 1968, the Lower Elwha Klallam Reservation was granted trust status. Another group, the Jamestown Band of Clallam Indians, has its headquarters at Sequim, Washington. *Clallam* means "strong people" in Salishan.

clan A multigenerational social group within a TRIBE, made up of several FAMILIES that trace descent in either the male or female line ("patriclan" or "matriclan," i.e., a PATRILINEAL clan or MATRILINEAL clan) from a common, sometimes mythical, ancestor. Because clan members consider themselves related, marriage within the clan typically is prohibited; a clan is therefore an EXOGAMOUS group of people. In many tribes, clans control LAND, CEREMONIES, and TOTEMS. A "clan-segment" is a portion of a clan, such as several patrilineal families living separately from the main group. Some scholars define a clan as matrilineal to distinguish it from the patrilineal GENS. The term sept, originally applied to social groupings in ancient Ireland, is sometimes used synonymously with clan. (See also CLAN ANIMAL; CLAN EMBLEM; CLAN MOTHER; MOIETY; PHRATRY; SIB.)

clan animal The animal TOTEM and protector of a CLAN. Clan members believe that they have a special relationship with the clan animal and manifest some of its traits. Bear Clan members, for example, often are associated with HEALING because of the animal's perceived power.

clan emblem   A symbol of a real or legendary being, from whom a CLAN traces descent. (See also CLAN ANIMAL; CREST.)

Clan Mother   The elder female head of a CLAN among MATRILINEAL peoples, such as the IROQUOIS.

clapper   A percussion instrument typical of CALIFORNIA INDIANS and NORTHWEST COAST INDIANS made from a split stick, which creates a clapping noise when waved.

Classic period   A stage of cultural development in MESOAMERICA, often divided into the Preclassic, Classic, and Postclassic periods. The Preclassic lasted from about 1000 B.C. to A.D. 300. The OLMECS reached their cultural peak during this period. (The term FORMATIVE PERIOD is sometimes used synonymously with Preclassic; in the study of PREHISTORIC INDIANS to the north of Mesoamerica, however, the Formative period is defined as lasting through the Classic period as well as the Postclassic period.) The Classic period proper lasted from about A.D. 300 to 900, during which time the MAYAS, the Zapotecs, and the city of Teotihuacan flourished. The Postclassic period is the stage of cultural development in Mesoamerica from about A.D. 900 to 1500, during which time the TOLTECS, Mixtecs, and AZTECS were dominant.

Clatskanie   See ATHAPASCAN.

Clatsop   See CHINOOKAN.

clay   See CERAMIC; POTTERY.

Clayoquot   A subtribe of the NOOTKA Indians, located on Meares Island and Torfino Inlet in present-day British Columbia. A Nootka band with headquarters at Torfino still uses the Clayoquot name.

Clear Lake   See POMO.

cliff dweller   See ANASAZI CULTURE; CLIFF-DWELLING; SINAGUA CULTURE.

cliff-dwelling   A dwelling along the walls of cliffs and canyons. The term usually refers to more than one home and apartmentlike living. Modification of natural caves and ledges was common through digging and the adding of stone or ADOBE walls. Wooden ladders provided access. Cliff-dwellings offered protection from marauders, who could not attack from above. Crops were grown on the tops of mesas and on canyon floors. Indians of the ANASAZI CULTURE and the SINAGUA CULTURE lived in cliff-dwellings.

cloak   A loose outer garment, usually sleeveless and worn hanging from the shoulders; often ceremonial. The term mantle is sometimes applied to cloaks, as in the feather mantle typical of the NATCHEZ. "Mantle" sometimes applies to a type of cloak worn around the torso, under one arm, and over the opposite shoulder, typical of PUEBLO INDIAN women. The term cape also is used, usually in reference to a garment fastened at the neck. (See also BLANKET; MATCHCOAT; ROBE.)

cloth   See TEXTILE.

clothing   See CATEGORICAL APPENDIX, "CLOTHING, COVERINGS, AND ADORNMENT."

Clovis Culture (Llano Culture)   A cultural tradition of the PALEOLITHIC PERIOD, lasting from before 10,000 B.C. to 8000 B.C. The Clovis culture is named after the Clovis site in New Mexico, but Clovis POINTS have been found all over the Americas, usually with MAMMOTH and MASTODON bones. They were one and a half to five inches long

Clovis point

in the shape of a leaf, with FLUTING along the base on both sides.

clown (sacred clown) In many tribal religions, clown figures, i.e., people representing spiritual beings who act comically, outrageously, and blasphemously, are considered sacred, imparting special wisdom. Among some peoples, they are thought to have HEALING powers. PUEBLO INDIAN clowns have been called delight-makers; others have been called contraries. The ARAPAHOS have Crazy Dancers; the CAHUILLAS have Funny Men; and the KWAKIUTLS have Fool Dancers. (See also CHAPAYEKA; CONTRARY WARRIOR; GALAXY SOCIETY; *HEYOKA*; KOSHARE; KOYEMSHI; KWERANA; MASSAUM CEREMONY; MUDHEAD; TACHUKTU.)

Clowwewalla See CHINOOKAN.

club See SECRET SOCIETY; SODALITY.

club (cudgel) Weapons made of wood and bone, some with a stone, bone, or antler head. (See also HAMMER; HUNTING CLUB; STAFF; TOMAHAWK; WARCLUB.)

Coahuiltecan A HOKAN-speaking tribe (Coahuiltec or Coahuiltecan isolate) of the SOUTHWEST CULTURE AREA, located on both sides of the lower Rio Grande in present-day Texas and Coahuila, Mexico. The Coahuiltecans were actually a number of politically distinct tribes related linguistically. The Aranamas of the Gulf Coast of present-day Texas probably spoke the same language. Although some of their descendants may survive in Mexico, they no longer speak their native language.

coati (coatimondi, coatimundi) Any of a number of omnivorous mammals of the genus *Nasua*, about one foot tall and with a two-foot-long body. The snouts are slender and flexible, and the sometimes two-and-a-half-foot tails are ringed. Coatis are found mostly in the South American and Central American tropics, but species also are found as far north as the American Southwest. They are related to the raccoon. Among certain tribes, the coati's hip bone, ground and mixed with a liquid, is considered a powerful aphrodisiac. The word was passed to English via Portuguese, originally from the TUPI-GUARANI word for "belt-nosed."

coca Any of the South American shrubs of the genus *Erythroxylon*, especially *E. coca*. The leaves are chewed by SOUTH AMERICAN INDIANS as a stimulant. The chemical substance known as cocaine is extracted from the coca leaf. Among the INCAS, only the nobility were allowed to chew coca; they held their supply in a pouch known as a *chuspa*.

Cochise Culture A cultural tradition of ARCHAIC INDIANS in present-day southeastern Arizona and southwestern New Mexico, evolving out of the DESERT CULTURE. The Cochise complex lasted from about 7000 to 500 B.C. Cochise Indians hunted many different kinds of small mammals, such as deer, antelope, and rabbits; they also foraged for snakes, lizards, insects, and edible wild plants. Archaeologists have found many Cochise MANOS and METATES for grinding food. Another important find among Cochise remains is the first evidence of agriculture north of Mexico: in Bat Cave, New Mexico, archaeologists found dried-up cobs of corn from a cultivated species of the plant dating from about 3500 B.C. Yet agriculture did not become common in the region until centuries later, about A.D. 100, during the FORMATIVE PERIOD. The name of the Cochise culture is taken from the 19th-century APACHE chief.

Cochiti Pueblo See KERES.

Cocopah (Cocopa, Kwikapa) A YUMAN-speaking tribe of the SOUTHWEST CULTURE AREA, located at the mouth of the Colorado River in present-day Arizona. In the late 1760s, the Cocopahs lived with the MARICOPAS and YUMAS. After the groups broke apart, the Yumas were left with a reservation known as Cocopah. The Cocopah proper were settled among MOJAVES and CHEMEHUEVIS on the Colorado River Reservation, where they lost their tribal identity.

Code of Handsome Lake See LONGHOUSE RELIGION.

code talker An Indian who used his native language to convey battlefield messages by radio for the military. In World War I, CHOCTAW Indians became the first code talkers. In World War II, the Choctaws again served in Europe, as did the COMANCHES, for the army's Signal Corps; the NAVAJOS served in the marines in the Pacific. Their codes were never deciphered by the Germans or Japanese.

codex (pl., codices) A manuscript volume, in particular an ancient one. The AZTECS, MAYAS, Mixtecs, and other MESOAMERICAN INDIANS painted pictures along with HIEROGLYPHIC symbols on deerskin, cotton, and sisal paper, treated with lime. Some were astronomical CALENDARS; others, historical narratives. Few codices survived the Spanish occupation of Mexico and Central America.

Coeur d'Alene (Skitswish) A SALISHAN-speaking tribe of the PLATEAU CULTURE AREA, located on the Spokane, Coeur d'Alene, and St. Joe rivers and on Coeur d'Alene Lake in present-day northern Idaho and eastern Washington. Tribal members hold the Coeur d'Alene Reservation in Benewah and Kootenai counties, Washington. *Coeur d'Alene*, French for "awl heart" or "pointed heart," refers to a trader.

cognate An anthropological term, indicating relation by birth, and a linguistic term, indicating a relation in origin. "Cognate" is either an adjective or noun. As a noun, it is sometimes used to mean "cognate word." "Cognatic" is another adjective form. Cognatic tribe refers to a TRIBE in which membership is based on familial connections.

coiling A technique of making both POTTERY and BASKETRY. In pottery, ropelike coils of clay are built up from the bottom of the pot. The indentations are then smoothed over to form the inner and outer walls. Sometimes the ridges and depressions are left, creating a scalloped effect after FIRING (corrugated pottery). In basketry, coils are spiraled upward and sewed together with a flexible WEFT.

coin silver See SILVER.

cold-hammering The shaping of metals in METALWORK without heating.

college See INDIAN COLLEGE.

Columbia (Sinkiuse, Sinkiuse-Columbia, Moses) A SALISHAN-speaking tribe of the PLATEAU CULTURE AREA, located on the east side of the Columbia River near Point Eaton in what is now central Washington. The Columbias formerly lived on the Columbia Reservation but were forced to settle on the Colville Reservation with other Salishans in 1884. They are now known as the Moses band after a famous leader.

Columbian exchange The transfer of knowledge, technologies, peoples, plants, animals, and diseases between the Americas and Europe (and by extension the rest of the world) during and after the voyages of Christopher Columbus. The term is used in contemporary writings to avoid Eurocentricism, indicating that while European knowledge was being carried to the Americas by explorers and settlers, Native American knowledge, such as the domestication of corn, potatoes, and tomatoes was being diffused to the rest of the world. (See also ETHNOCENTRIC.)

Colville A SALISHAN-speaking tribe of the PLATEAU CULTURE AREA, located on the Colville and Columbia rivers near Kettle Falls in present-day Washington. The tribe has shared the Colville Reservation near Nespelem, Washington, with other Inland Salishans since 1872. The tribal name is derived from Fort Colville, a post established by the Hudson's Bay Company at Kettle Falls in 1825; other Salishans called them *Skuyelpi*. (See also COLUMBIA; LAKE; METHOW; OKANAGAN; PALOUSE; SANPOIL.)

comal A flat dish of stone or pottery on which TORTILLAS are cooked. A Spanish word, from the NAHUATL *comalli*.

Comanche (Snakes) A UTO-AZTECAN-speaking tribe of the GREAT PLAINS CULTURE AREA. In the 1600s, the Comanches probably separated from the SHOSHONES in territory that is now Wyoming and migrated southward along the eastern Rocky Mountains, settling in northwestern Texas by the mid-1700s and also ranging into western Oklahoma, southwestern Kansas, eastern New Mexico, southeastern Colorado, and northern Mexico. Comanche subtribes include the following: Kewatsana; Kotsai; Kwahadie (Kwahari, Kotsoteka); Motsai; Nokoni (Nocoan, Detsanayuka); Pagatsu; Penateka (Penande); Pohoi; Tanima (Tenawa, Tenahwit); Wasaih; and Yamparika (Ditsakana, Widyu, Yapa). Comanches hold trust lands near Anadarko, Oklahoma. *Com-anche* is thought to be derived from the UTE name *Komon'teia*, meaning "one who wants to fight me" in Uto-Aztecan. The Comanche native name is *Nermurnuh* (*Nemene, Nimenim, Numa*) for "people" or "true human beings."

comanchero A Spanish-American trader of horses and mules among the PLAINS INDIANS, especially the COMANCHES in present-day Texas and Oklahoma, during the 1800s.

commerce See TRADE.

Commissioner of Indian Affairs See BUREAU OF INDIAN AFFAIRS.

Comox A SALISHAN-speaking tribe of the NORTHWEST COAST CULTURE AREA, located on the east coast of Vancouver Island in present-day British Columbia, including both sides of Discovery Passage. The Comox, Homalco, and Klahoose bands live on their ancestral homeland.

complex An ASSEMBLAGE of related items, in particular artifact types or cultural traits, which help scholars define a culture and its time span.

composite tribe A change of culture within a tribe, resulting in a new way of life shared with other tribes, such as the Plains tribes whose diverse customs merged into a single nomadic way of life. (See also PAN-INDIAN.)

compression shell A self-supporting roof structure in which individual parts, such as ice blocks in an IGLOO or ADOBE and stone bricks in a PUEBLO, distribute loads in all directions. BENT-FRAME and POST-AND-BEAM are the other basic types of Indian construction.

concha (concho) A silver plaque or disk, round or oval in shape; used as ornaments on belts and other clothing by SOUTHWEST INDIANS in post-Contact times.

cone Prehistoric conical polished stone artifacts often made of HEMATITE. Found generally east of the Mississippi River, cones were perhaps part of a SHAMAN's kit or a game.

Conestoga See SUSQUENHANNOCK.

confederacy (confederation, alliance, league) A political union of two or more TRIBES, often for military purposes. (See also IROQUOIS LEAGUE.)

Congaree See SIOUAN.

conjuring lodge See SHAKING TENT.

Conoy (Ganaway, Ganawese, Piscataway) An ALGONQUIAN-speaking tribe of the NORTHEAST CULTURE AREA, located between the Potomac River and the western shore of the Chesapeake in present-day Maryland. Some Conoys perhaps lived along the Kanawha River (the name of which resembles their tribal name) in present-day West Virginia. By the mid-1700s, tribal members were living among the NANTICOKES and SUSQUEHANNOCKS. Many eventually migrated north and merged with the LENNI LENAPES (Delawares) and MAHICANS. Two contemporary groups use the alternative tribal name *Piscataway*, also a former village name: the Piscataway Indian tribe, centered in Waldorf, Maryland, and the Piscataway-Conoy Confederacy and Sub-Tribe, centered in Indian Head.

conquistador Spanish word for "conqueror," referring to Spanish explorers and soldiers who invaded Indian lands and subjugated Indian peoples.

consanguinity A relationship by blood. Consanguine, consanguineous, or consanguineal relatives trace relationship to one another on the basis of biological DESCENT. (See also SIB.)

Contact (contact) A term used to describe the first meetings between Indian peoples and Europeans or Euroamericans and subsequent cultural changes among both sets of people. "Pre-Contact" (sometimes "precontact" or "pre-contact") refers to the period of time before Indians met whites (synonymous with PRE-COLUMBIAN). "Post-Contact" ("postcontact" or "post-contact") refers to the period of time after Indians had established communication and trade with whites. Contact for one tribe might have come at a different time than for another, although the team is also applied generally. (See also PREHISTORY.)

container (receptacle) An object for holding possessions, food, and liquids. One also sees the terms beaker, case, cup, pot, goblet, kettle, mug, pitcher, sheath, urn, vase, vessel, and water bottle (or canteen). (See also CATEGORICAL APPENDIX, "CONTAINERS.")

continuity The indication of gradual development of a culture, as opposed to CATASTROPHE.

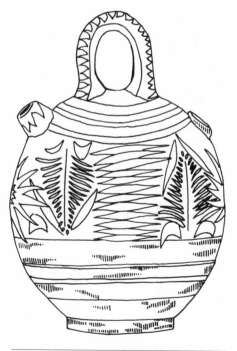

Southwest Indian pottery canteen

contrary warrior   An individual belonging to a MILITARY SOCIETY, whose members ritually say or act out the opposite of what is meant or expected; typical of PLAINS INDIANS.

cooking   The process of preparing food for eating, especially by applying heat, as in roasting, broiling, baking, boiling, frying, etc. (See also BAKING STONE; BOILING STONE; FIRE; FOOD PREPARATION AND PRESERVATION; OVEN.)

cooking ball   See BOILING STONE.

coontie (coonti, coontia, koontie)   Any of several tough woody plants of the genus *Zamia*, the starchy roots and half-buried stems of which are edible. A SEMINOLE-derived word; *kunti* is the name of the flour or bread made from the roots of the plant in MUSKOGEAN.

Coos (Kus, Kusa)   A KUSAN-speaking tribe of the NORTHWEST COAST CULTURE AREA, located on Coos River and Coos Bay in present-day Oregon. Descendants were settled on the Siletz Reservation after 1855 with YAKONAN-speaking tribes, their tribal headquarters at Siletz, Oregon. Another group, the Confederated Tribes of Coos, Lower Umpqua and Siuslaw Indians, operates out of Coos Bay, Oregon. (See also KUITSH; SIUSLAW.)

Coosa   A tribe of the SOUTHEAST CULTURE AREA, probably MUSKOGEAN-speaking, located at the mouth of the Edisto River and on the Coosawhatchie and Ashley rivers in present-day South Carolina. The Coosas, and possibly the CUSABOS to the east on the coast with whom they are sometimes classified, merged with the CATAWBAS. *Coosa* or *Kusa* also is used for one of the subtribes of the CREEK Indians, taken from a town name.

Copalis   See SALISHAN.

copalli   A resin of recent or fossil origin, aromatic and brittle, obtained from various tropical trees. The AZTECS used it for INCENSE. The modern term, derived from NAHUATL, is copal, which is now used in making varnishes and plastics.

Copehan   See WINTUN.

copper   A metal of a reddish color, malleable and ductile. Copper nuggets were found in abundance near Lake Superior as well as in smaller deposits elsewhere; ARCHAIC INDIANS learned to hammer the nuggets into tools, weapons, and ornaments, some of them from sheet copper. Raw copper and copper artifacts came to be valuable trade items. For the NORTHWEST COAST INDIANS, copper symbolized the light of heaven and the wealth of the sea. (See also MINING; OLD COPPER CULTURE.)

Copper (Indians)   See AHTENA; TATSANOTTINE.

corbeled arch (corbel arch, corbeled vault, corbel vault)   An arch between two parallel walls; the inner faces of each wall are built in overlapping courses until the two walls connect and are bridged with capstones. The MAYAS built corbeled or corbel arches.

cordage   Rope, string, or cords, especially the rigging of boats. Cordage is sometimes used specifically for ties of plant fiber or hide for securing a frame in architecture. (See also BABICHE; NETTING; ROPE; *SHAGANAPPI*.)

cord-marked pottery   POTTERY having designs on its exterior wall made by pressing or stamping with a cord-wrapped paddle before FIRING. (See also PADDLING.)

core   A piece of FLINT, CHERT, OBSIDIAN, or other stone from which FLAKES have been struck, leaving an approximate cylinder in shape with fluted sides; sometimes called polyhedral core. A prepared core is a piece of stone designed so that the shape of the flakes or BLADES can be controlled. Cores are generally considered leftover material from STONEWORK, but some of them perhaps served a purpose of their own, such as working bone or antler. A microcore is the small core resulting from shaping microblades. (See also BLADE AND CORE; FLUTING.)

Coree See ALGONQUIAN.

corn (Indian corn, maize) A cereal grass and staple crop of many tribes with an edible seed (*Zea mays*). The term maize comes to English via the Spanish *maiz*, originally from the ARAWAKAN word *marise*, *maysi*, or *mahiz*. Corn is thought to have been cultivated by native farmers from the grasses *Euchloena mexicana* of southern Mexico and *E. luxurians* of Guatemala. It was the first plant to be domesticated in the Americas. The plant and food became central to the religious life of agricultural tribes and was celebrated in a variety of festivals. Perfect ears of corn were kept as fetishes. Some Indians refer to it as Mother Corn, Giver of Life, or a variation of the same. In post-Contact times, corn became a food crop elsewhere in the world. (See also *CHICHA*; CORN COB; CORN DANCE; CORNHUSK; CORNMEAL; HOMINY; LEAF BREAD; MILPA; *PIKI*; *PINOLE*; POD CORN; POPCORN; ROCK-AHOMINY; SAGAMITE; SAMP; SOFKI; SUCCO-TASH; *TESGUINO*; THREE SISTERS.)

corn cob The central part of an ear of CORN, on which the kernels grow. Native Americans utilized corn cobs as fuel, especially for smoking meat and hide, as well as for scrubbing brushes and scratchers, stoppers in containers, the ends of dance wands, the bodies of dolls, and more. (See also CORNHUSK DOLL.)

Corn Dance With CORN being a staple of Native American agriculture, many tribes had fertility dances or ceremonies surrounding it, known by several names. (See also GREEN CORN CEREMONY.)

cornhusk The dry outer covering of ears of CORN. The husks traditionally have been valued by Native Americans as a resource for kindling and to wrap food for cooking

as well as in the making of cordage, bedding, mats, baskets, pouches, quivers, rattles, moccasins, ankle bands, balls, dolls, masks, and other artifacts. (See also CORNHUSK DOLL; HUSK FACE SOCIETY; HUSKING PIN.)

cornhusk doll A doll made from CORN, typical of the IROQUOIS. In some cases, the husk is used for both the body and clothing; the cob sometimes is used for the body. Ash splints, leather, cloth, feathers, or beadwork sometimes were added. Black yarn is often used for hair.

cornmeal (corn meal, Indian meal) Ground CORN used in food preparation. Some native peoples, such as the PUEBLO INDIANS, considered cornmeal to be sacred and sprinkled it as an OFFERING. The KERES Indians call it *petana*.

corral An enclosure for trapping and confining animals. American Indians drove animals into stone, wood, or brush corrals in communal hunts.

Cosmic Pillar See COSMIC TREE.

Cosmic Tree In various tribal traditions, trees are considered to have their roots in the ground (the underworld), their trunk in the domain of humans, and their leaves in the sky world, or SPIRIT WORLD. The concept has been translated as Cosmic Tree or World Tree, sometimes believed to be a particular tree. Some tribes have symbolic representations of trees—the SACRED POLE, for example—around which ceremonies are conducted. The central HOUSEPOST in some Native American dwellings is considered sacred and has been translated as Cosmic Pillar and Earth Naval. (See also TREE OF LIFE.)

cosmology A system of beliefs dealing with the origin and order of the universe. In some cosmological studies, the realms of the soul and the spirit are considered along with the physical realm. "Cosmogony" is used synonymously with "cosmology"; the former, however, is applied more accurately to a particular theory of the evolution of the universe. In many Native American cosmologies, reality is viewed as a succession of worlds, each with its own deities. (See also CARDINAL POINTS; WORLDVIEW.)

Costanoan (Costanos) A MIWOK-COSTANOAN-speaking tribe of the CALIFORNIA CULTURE AREA, located on the coast of present-day California between San Francisco Bay and Point Sur. The Costanoans were missionized by the Spanish, becoming known as MISSION INDIANS. They dwindled and became extinct by the early 1900s. Their name is from the Spanish *Costanos*, meaning "coast people."

cotton Any of various plants of the genus *Gossypium*, harvested wild and cultivated for the soft, white fiber surrounding the seeds, or the fibers themselves, used in the making of TEXTILES. Differing strains of cotton grow all over the world and are utilized by many different peoples. SOUTH AMERICAN INDIANS, MESOAMERICAN INDIANS, and SOUTHWEST INDIANS, especially the HOPIS, used cotton.

cougar See PUMA.

council A gathering of tribal leaders for discussion of plans. Many tribes had councils of peace CHIEFS, who made decisions concerning internal issues and relations with other peoples. The Council of Forty-Four of the CHEYENNE Indians, for example, had a head priest-chief, known as the Sweet Medicine Chief, plus four sacred chiefs and 39 ordinary chiefs representing different bands. Every year the IROQUOIS LEAGUE has traditionally held a Great Council of 50 chiefs, representing the Six Nations. The term also is used for a modern-day tribal council whose members are elected, the leader being a CHAIRMAN rather than a hereditary chief. (See also POWWOW.)

council house A structure used for a civic, social, or ceremonial purpose. One also sees the terms council tepee and council lodge. (See also CEREMONIAL HOUSE; *KASHIM*; KIVA.)

counting For calculation by number, most Native Americans used either a decimal (intervals of 10) or vigesimal (intervals of 20) numeral system, based on the number of fingers and toes. The MAYAS, however, used a system of counting that allowed them to write figures up to 1,280,000,000 and had a sign for zero (500 years before the Hindus also invented one). (See also CALENDAR; *QUIPU*.)

coup An act of bravery in battle for PLAINS INDIANS. Warriors earned a differ-

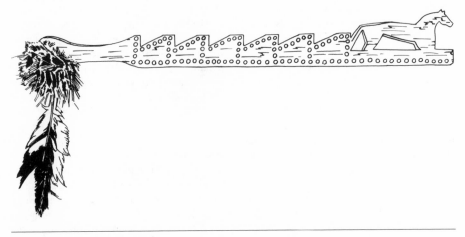

Arapaho ceremonial coup stick

ent number of coup for specific deeds, such as touching an enemy while he was alive with the hand, butt of a weapon, or COUP STICK; killing an enemy; SCALPING an enemy; touching a dead enemy; stealing an enemy's horse; or touching an enemy's tepee. "Counting coup" refers to the public and ceremonial recitation of deeds of valor. *Coup* is a French-derived word for "blow" or "stroke."

coup stick A stick used by PLAINS INDIANS to touch a live enemy in warfare and thus count a COUP, and for ceremonial purposes. Coup sticks were usually bent at one end and decorated with fur.

coureur de bois A fur trader of French descent who worked independently of the large trading companies and lived much of the time with Indians. Literally, French for "runner of the woods." (See also FUR TRADE; VOYAGEUR.)

courtship Tribes had a number of wooing, or courting, customs, such as special SONGS and love charms. (See also FLAGEOLET.)

Coushatta (Koasati, Shati) A MUSKOGEAN-speaking tribe of the SOUTHEAST CULTURE AREA, located south of the junction of the Coosa and Tallapoosa rivers in present-day Alabama. In the late 1700s, part of the tribe settled on the Red River in present-day Louisiana; some continued westward into Texas and lived among ALABAMAS, who also had migrated there. Like the Alabamas, the Coushattas were part of the Creek Confederacy. Many of this latter group eventually returned to Louisiana. Coushattas now live in both states; some hold the Coushatta Reservation near Coushatta, Louisiana; others share the Alabama-Coushatta Reservation in Polk County, Texas, with the Alabamas. At least one band joined the SEMINOLES in Florida; others migrated to the INDIAN TERRITORY (present-day Oklahoma) with the CREEKS. *Coushatta* possibly means "white cane" in Muskogean.

couvade A custom, typical of SOUTH AMERICAN INDIANS, in which a father goes into seclusion immediately preceding or during CHILDBIRTH, in some cases ritually imitating the delivery.

cowboy A hired hand who rode horses to drive cattle to pasture and water, protect them from wild animals and thieves, round cattle up, and drive them to the railheads from where they were shipped to the East. Most cattle trails out of Texas were northward through the INDIAN TERRITORY and other Indian lands, at times leading to conflict. But "cowboys and Indians," i.e., cowboys fighting Indians, was probably less frequent than cowboys fighting sheepherders or farmers, and certainly less common than cavalrymen fighting Indians. Cowboys adopted many Indian customs, including animal and plant foods, deerskin clothing, horsehair ropes, buffalo chips as fuel, reading SIGN, and the "war whoop" used when celebrating their leisure time in cow towns.

Cowichan A SALISHAN-speaking tribe of the NORTHWEST COAST CULTURE AREA, located on the southeast coast of Vancouver Island and on the lower Fraser River in present-day British Columbia. Those Cowichans on the lower Fraser, such as the Chilliwack band, are sometimes classified separately under the name Stalo (or Halkomelem). A number of Cowichan bands hold reserve lands in British Columbia.

Cowlitz A SALISHAN-speaking tribe of the NORTHWEST COAST CULTURE AREA, located on the Cowlitz River in present-day Washington. (The SAHAPTIN-speaking Taidnapams are sometimes referred to as Upper Cowlitz.) The Cowlitz were placed on the Chehalis Reservation with CHEHALIS Indians and on the Puyallup Reservation with other Salishan peoples. A group centered in Tacoma, Washington, still uses the tribal name.

coyote (prairie wolf, brush wolf) A small wolflike mammal of the dog family, *Canis latrans*, ranging north to Alaska, east to the

Great Lakes, and south to Central America. Coyote skin was valued by PLAINS INDIANS for making QUIVERS. Because of their nocturnal, elusive, and adaptive behavior, coyotes are part of many Native American legends. When capitalized, Coyote is a TRICKSTER figure, also referred to as Old Man by SOUTHWEST INDIANS. Coyote is also depicted in contemporary writings and paintings as a symbol for tribal self-determination. The word coyote came to English via the Spanish, originally from the NAHU-ATL *coyotl*.

Coyotera See WHITE MOUNTAIN.

cradleboard (papoose board, papoose frame, baby carrier) A carrier for babies,

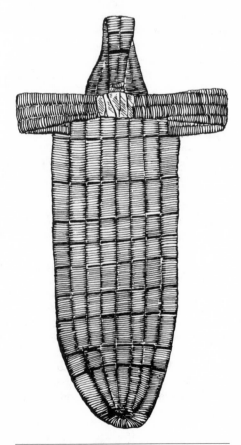

Hopi wicker cradleboard

which was held in hand, worn on the back, supported on the head, hung on a horse, or propped up. Cradleboards were made from a wood, hide, or wickerwork frame, with a variety of coverings, such as skin, bark, mats, or basketry, plus a soft material for a pillow and lining, such as fur or feathers. They were decorated with quills and beads and, sometimes notched to show the number of children who had used them; AMULETS and RATTLES were hung from them. Children were laced in the cradleboards, often by means of BABICHE, during much of their first year. EASTERN INDIAN cradleboards were typically carved in relief and painted; PLAINS INDIAN cradleboards had studded slats and beaded deerskin pouches. (See also MOSS-BAG.)

craft See ARTS AND CRAFTS.

crazing (crackling) In POTTERY, a pattern of fine cracks in the SLIP or GLAZE, resulting from the uneven shrinkage of underlying clay during a FIRING.

creation story (creation myth, emergence myth, genesis story) A tribal legend, recounting the origin of the tribe. In some accounts, people emerge from one dying world into another as part of a TIME CYCLE.

Creator (Great Creator, Life Giver, Maker, Earthmaker) A translation of various Indian names for the personification of the creative force in the universe. Many Indian legends begin with the Creator, who passes special knowledge or sacred objects to the tribe's CULTURE HERO. The following were some of the many names for the Creator: Acahadadea (CROW); Awonawilona (ZUNI); GITCHEE MANITOU (ALGONQUIAN); Maheo (CHEYENNE); Sus-sustinako (KERES); Tabaldak (ABENAKI); Taiowa (HOPI); Tam Apo (SHOSHONE); Ussen (APACHE); WAKAN TANKA (SIOUX); and Yoka (CHEROKEE). (See also GREAT SPIRIT.)

Cree An ALGONQUIAN-speaking tribe of the SUBARCTIC CULTURE AREA (Swampy

Cree and Woodland Cree) and the GREAT PLAINS CULTURE AREA (Plains Cree), located from James Bay to the Saskatchewan River in present-day Quebec, Ontario, Manitoba, and Saskatchewan. The Swampy Cree (Maskegon) lived in the wet north country south of Hudson Bay; the Western Wood Cree, in the forests northwest of Lake Winnipeg in northern Saskatchewan; the Eastern Wood Cree, in Quebec (such as the MISTASSINI and Tête de Boule); and the Plains Cree, in southern Saskatchewan. Many Cree bands hold reserve lands throughout their ancestral homeland in Canada. Crees also share the Rocky Boy's Reservation near Box Elder, Montana with the CHIPPEWAS. *Cree* is the shortened form of *Kristinaux*, a French derivation of *Kenistenoag*, their native name.

Creek (Muskogee) A MUSKOGEAN-speaking tribe of the SOUTHEAST CULTURE AREA, located in present-day Georgia and Alabama as well as in present-day northern Florida, eastern Louisiana, southern Tennessee, and southwestern South Carolina. The Creeks sometimes are classified as the Upper Creeks on the Coosa and Tallapoosa rivers, and the Lower Creeks on the lower Chattahoochee and Ocmulgee rivers. Bands (or towns) include Abihka, Atasi, COOSA, Coweta, EUFAULA, Fus-hatchee, Hilibi, Holiwahali, Kan-hatki, Kasihta, Kealedji, Kolomi, Okchai, Pakana, Tukabahchee, Wakoki, and Wiwohka. What is known as the Creek Confederacy was an alliance of tribes, including the various bands of the Creeks (Muskogees), as well as those of the ALABAMA, Apalachicola, CHIAHA, COUS-HATTA, HITCHITI, Muklasa, Okmulgee, Osochi, Pawokti, Sawokli, Tawasa, Tuskegee, and YUCHI tribes, a total of more than 50 towns in all. Many Creeks were relocated to the INDIAN TERRITORY in the 1830s. Their descendants hold trust lands near Okmulgee, Oklahoma. A band known as the Lower Creek Muskogee Tribe East of the Mississippi, centered in Cairo, Georgia, also maintains tribal identity. (See RED STICK; WHITE STICK.)

cremation Disposal of a corpse through burning. (See also BURIAL; URN BURIAL.)

crest A heraldic symbol—often the image of a legendary being or animal representing a family or CLAN—used especially in reference to NORTHWEST COAST INDIANS. (See also CLAN EMBLEM; TOTEM.)

Croatan (Croatoan) An Indian village on an island of the same name, probably where Cape Lookout is situated, on the coast of present-day Carteret County, North Carolina; and a name associated with the Roanoke Colony of 1587, because it was carved in a tree in the "Croatoan" spelling by one of the missing colonists. It has been theorized that the original Croatan Indians were actually the HATTERAS. "Croatan Indians" also was applied by North Carolina officials in 1885 to Indians living especially in Robeson County; in 1911, they were designated "Robeson County Indians"; in 1953, they took the name LUMBEE.

crop See FARMING.

cross The SYMBOL formed by the intersection of two (or sometimes more, as in a "double-barred cross") straight lines is common design in Indian arts, perhaps representing the CARDINAL POINTS. (See also SWASTIKA.)

cross dating Dating a culture by the comparison of one or more artifact types, unique to a period of time, to those found in other locations and cultures. A type of RELATIVE DATING.

crow Any of several oscine birds of the genus *Corvus*, especially *C. brachyrhynchos* of North America, having glossy black feathers and a raucous call. The crow is the sacred bird of the GHOST DANCE RELIGION. The ARAPAHO word for it in ALGONQUIAN is *ho*. (See also RAVEN.)

Crow (Absarokee, Absaroke, Abasroka, Absaroki, Absaraka, Kite) A SIOUAN-speaking tribe of the GREAT PLAINS CULTURE AREA. It is thought that sometime in the 1700s, the Crows split off from the HIDATSAS of the upper Missouri in present-day North Dakota and migrated upriver to the Yellowstone River and its tributaries in present-day southern Montana and northern Wyoming. The Mountain Crows lived near the Bighorn Mountains; the River Crows lived in the valleys of the Little Bighorn and Powder rivers. Crows now hold the Crow Reservation in Big Horn, Yellowstone, and Treasure counties of Montana. Their native name *Absarokee* means "children of the long-beaked bird" or "bird people," leading to the French name *Gens des Corbeaux* and the English name Crow.

crusting Hunting on snow when the crust of the snow supports a human's weight but not that of a large animal.

cry house A ceremonial funeral structure of the YUMA and COCOPAH Indians. In addition to mourning and cremation ceremonies, annual memorials are held there.

cult See RELIGION; SECRET SOCIETY.

cultivation See FARMING.

cultural diffusion The passing of cultural traits from one people or region to another through migration, trade, invasion, or some other interaction.

cultural dispossession The suppression of the lifeways of a subordinate culture by a dominant one, either because of settlement patterns and resulting trade and contacts or by governmental policy, such as in the case of ASSIMILATION and TERMINATION. (See also ACCULTURATION; DETRIBALIZATION; DISPLACEMENT.)

cultural evolutionism An approach to anthropological studies in which the development of a particular culture is viewed as a pattern of progression toward societal

complexity. (See also CULTURAL RELATIVISM.)

cultural relativism An approach to anthropological studies in which the development of a particular culture is viewed as unique to that culture and can be understood only in the framework of its own customs. (See also CULTURAL RELATIVISM.)

cultural trait (culture trait, custom) A custom or characteristic of a particular culture or society. "Lifeways," "folkways," and "mores" are synonyms of the plural form.

culture The learned customs characteristic of a given people. Culture includes behavior and beliefs, as found in institutions and rituals, as well as material objects, such as tools, clothing, and art. The term culture also is used in reference to particular societies or communities. In archaeology, the term also can refer to a cluster of diagnostic characteristics. (See also BASIC CULTURE; CATEGORICAL APPENDIX, "TRIBES, BANDS, PEOPLES, LANGUAGES, AND CULTURES"; CULTURAL TRAIT; CULTURE AREA; CULTURE SEQUENCE; CULTURE STAGE; TRADITION.)

culture area A geographical region where different Indian tribes had similar ways of life. In Indian studies, culture areas make up a classification system based on geography and lifeways. The habitat—i.e., the type of geography, climate, and wildlife—affected the way native peoples lived: what foods they ate, what materials they used for shelter and clothing, and how they viewed the world. (See also CATEGORICAL APPENDIX, "TRIBES, BANDS, PEOPLES, LANGUAGES, AND CULTURES.")

culture hero A legendary figure, thought to have supernatural powers and usually considered a tribal ancestor. In many traditions, culture heroes live after the creation of the world but before that of people; they passed down knowledge and objects essential to survival and do battle with a people's enemies. Some are represented with animal characteristics. (See also LEGENDARY BEING; MYTHICAL ANCESTOR.)

culture sequence The development of a group of people through a number of CULTURE STAGES.

culture stage The lifeways of a group of people at a given time. The PALEOLITHIC PERIOD, ARCHAIC PERIOD, FORMATIVE PERIOD, CLASSIC PERIOD, and HISTORIC PERIOD are all culture stages used in the study of Native American peoples and cultures, based on food acquisition, technologies, and settlement patterns.

cup-and-ball See RING-AND-PIN.

cupstone (nutstone) A rock with one or several depressions carved into its surface, in some cases on both sides. Cupstones may have been used for holding nuts to crack, hence the alternate name nutstone. Another theory is that they were used as a mortar in grinding paint. (See also MORTAR AND PESTLE.)

curare (curari, urari) A poison derived from tropical plants of the genus *Strychnos*, especially *S. toxifera*, as well as from plants of the genus *Chondodendron*, the root of the pareira, and frog poisons. It was applied to arrowpoints and blowgun darts by SOUTH AMERICAN INDIANS; also used medicinally as a muscle relaxant. "Curare" is of TUPI-GUARANI origin, passed to Spanish, Portuguese, and English.

curative song See SONG.

curing The term curing is used both for FOOD PREPARATION AND PRESERVATION and for HEALING the sick. (See also JERKY; MEDICINE; SMOKING.)

curing society See MEDICINE SOCIETY.

Cusabo A MUSKOGEAN-speaking tribe of the SOUTHEAST CULTURE AREA, located in present-day southern South Carolina, between Charleston Harbor and the Savannah River. Subtribes include Ashepoo, Combabee, EDISTO, Escamacu, Etiwaw, Kiawaw, Stono, Wando, and Wimbee. The COOSAS, living inland from the Cusabos, are sometimes grouped with them. The Cusabos possibly merged with either the CATAWBAS or CREEKS.

custom See CULTURAL TRAIT; CULTURE.

.D.

dagger See KNIFE.

Dakota See SANTEE (DAKOTA); SIOUX.

Dakubetede See ATHAPASCAN.

dance For Native Americans, rhythmic motion to music has symbolic meaning and is an element of CEREMONIES with a variety of purposes, such as preparing for hunting or warfare, celebrating a harvest or a victory, or celebrating a rite of passage, such as marriage. Certain ceremonies, or entire religions, that have a number of dances and other rituals are known by the name of a particular dance. Some dances are performed by groups, either men or women or both, or by children; others by an individual. Tribes, clans, or SECRET SOCIETIES might have their own dances and regalia. Although many dances have been lost, some still are performed today at religious ceremonies and POWWOWS. Many traditional Native American dance steps accompany particular SONGS. One movement common to most tribes is the toe-heel step, with the toes of one foot brought down first, then the heel. Another is the stomp step, with the heel and ball of the foot raised and brought down with force, followed by hopping twice on the toes of both feet. A third is the drag step, with the toes of one foot touching the ground first, then dragged backward, followed by a downward motion of the heel. In the canoe step, the whole foot hits the ground, followed by the toes tapping three times. Variations include shuffling, gliding, hopping, and leaping motions. The individual can bring his or her own particular attitude to a dance. (See also CATEGORICAL APPENDIX, "RELIGION AND RITUAL.")

dance apron A ceremonial garment decorated with TOTEMS and worn in DANCES; typical of NORTHWEST COAST INDIANS.

dance society See SECRET SOCIETY.

dancing See DANCE.

da neho An IROQUOIAN phrase for "it is finished," traditionally used to end stories among SENECAS and other IROQUOIS.

danzantes Dancers carved in stone, usually in BAS-RELIEF, showing, it is believed, figures on their way to be executed or sacrificed; typical of MESOAMERICAN INDIANS in particular at the site of the city of Monte Alban in present-day Mexico. A Spanish word.

dart A pointed projectile similar to but shorter than an arrow. (See ATLATL; BLADDER DART; BLOWGUN; SEALING DART.)

dart-thrower See ATLATL.

Dasylirion See SOTOL.

datura See JIMSONWEED.

daub See WATTLE-AND-DAUB.

deacon See FAITHKEEPER.

deadfall A hunting trap in which a heavy object, such as a log or stone, is set up to fall on prey when triggered, disabling or killing it. (See also PITFALL.)

Deadose See ATAKAPA.

death See BURIAL; DEATH SONG; RITE OF PASSAGE.

Death Cult See SOUTHERN CULT.

death song (brave song) A song sung in the face of death, in battle or during injury or illness.

decoy An object, place, or act used to attract animals in hunting, or to trick an enemy in warfare. GREAT BASIN INDIANS crafted duck decoys out of buoyant TULE reeds, which they covered with paint or feathers. False deer heads were worn, the folds of the neck of the deerskin drawn over the shoulders. Similar disguises were used for other animals. Auditory decoys included whistling to imitate the sound of a bird or striking antlers together to create the sound of fighting bucks in the rutting season; birchbark calls might attract a moose or caribou; leaves or reeds held in the hands could be used to imitate the cry of a fawn in order to attract the mother.

deer Any of various hoofed ruminant mammals of the family Cervidae. The white-tailed deer was found in woodlands throughout the present-day southern Canada, United States, Central America, and northern South America; the mule deer ranged from the plains westward; and the black-tailed deer along the Pacific Coast. Indians made use of the entire deer: meat for food; hide for clothing and containers; antler and bone for tools and ornaments; hair from tail for embroidery; sinew for

Archaic Indian split-twig deer effigy

bindings; hoofs for glue and to make rattles; dewclaws (extra toes) for decorations on belts and anklets; paunch and bladder for bags; and brain and liver for dressing hides. Many tribes had Deer Dances, honoring the spirit of the deer and requesting good hunting. Contemporary Indians still hunt the whitetail. (See also CARIBOU; DEERSKIN; ELK; MOOSE; PRONGHORN.)

deerskin (buckskin) Leather made from deerhide. Deerskin was a preferred material for clothing; fringed jackets and skirts are still a prevalent symbol of Indian culture.

deer-toe game See RING-AND-PIN.

deflector An upright stone placed on the floor of a KIVA or PITHOUSE, between the doorway and the tunnel or ventilator shaft, in order to keep air currents away from the fire.

degikup A type of BASKET made by the WASHOE Indians, having a spherelike shape and small MOUTH. Originally used in ceremonies, *degikups* became valued collectibles among non-Indians in the late 1800s.

degyagomga The KIOWA word for "every living creature" in KIOWA-TANOAN.

deity See CREATOR; LEGENDARY BEING; SPIRITUAL BEING.

Delaware See LENNI LENAPE.

delight-maker See CLOWN.

demography The statistical study of human POPULATION, especially size, distribution, and MIGRATIONS.

dendrochronology The study of the annual growth of tree rings preserved in wood samples to determine the age of wood and chronological order of artifacts. A technique of ABSOLUTE DATING.

dentalium (pl., dentalia) A slender univalve shellfish found on the west coasts of Vancouver Island and Queen Charlotte Islands (*Dentalium pretisosum*), and the name of the shell itself, also called the money-tooth shell. Dentalia were strung on strings as money or as decoration on clothing. The NORTHWEST COAST INDIANS used dentalia in commerce; the shells became widespread in western North America. In the CHINOOK JARGON, dentalia were called *hiaqua*.

Department of Indian Affairs and Northern Department (DIAND) The Canadian equivalent of the BUREAU OF INDIAN AFFAIRS. Following Canadian Confederation in the British North America Act of 1867, Canada shaped its administrative machinery for the Department of Indian Affairs in the Indian Act of 1868 and in the subsequent Indian Acts of 1876 and 1951. DIAND is also referred to as the Indian Affairs Department.

descent A connection to ancestors through a series of parent-child relationships. In unilineal descent (unilateral or unilinear), kinship is determined through a single line of descent, i.e., either PATRILINEAL or MATRILINEAL descent. In bilineal descent (bilateral or bilinear), kinship is determined from both the father's and mother's side. (See also ANCESTOR; CLAN; CONSANGUINITY; FAMILY; KINSHIP.)

Desert Culture A cultural tradition of ARCHAIC INDIANS in the Great Basin region of what is now Utah, Nevada, and Arizona, lasting from about 9000 to 1000 B.C. At Danger Cave in Utah, archaeologists have found the first example of basketry in North America. They also have found grinding stones to prepare seeds and traps made of twine to capture small game. (See also COCHISE CULTURE.)

detribalization The governmental policy of breaking up political and economic tribal systems in order to accomplish ASSIMILATION. The ALLOTMENT policy was a means of detribalization in the 19th and 20th cen-

turies; and the TERMINATION policy, in the 1950s and 1960s.

dew cloth (tepee liner) A lining, usually of hide and later of canvas, inside TEPEES. Attached to the tepee's pole, the dew cloth keeps rain from dripping on sleeping areas, provides insulation, and creates an upward draft for funneling out smoke through the SMOKEHOLE. Dew cloths are sometimes painted, especially with scenes of family exploits.

diagnostician A Navajo, either a man or woman, who determines the causes of diseases by means of HAND-TREMBLING or STARGAZING. After diagnosis, he or she makes recommendations as to the proper HEALING ceremonies and as to PRACTITIONERS who can conduct them.

dialect A variation of a LANGUAGE, different from other dialects of the same language in vocabulary, grammar, or pronunciation. In Indian linguistic studies, the categories, from most localized to most generalized, are dialect, language, LANGUAGE FAMILY, and LANGUAGE PHYLUM.

dibble See DIGGING STICK.

dice A GAME of chance played in differing forms by various tribes. Numbered or marked objects, such as pieces of stone, bone, shell, wood, reed, or fruit seeds, are tossed and counted. One variety, sometimes called bowl game, involves small cubes of bone or ivory, or seeds or pits, tossed in a BOWL or BASKET. In the IROQUOIS peach bowl game (also called peach stone game), played by opposing sides of a LONGHOUSE, six peach stones are ground down and blackened on one side and tossed in a bowl; the goal is to have five or six sides of one color showing; participants often wager articles of clothing. In another version, played by PUEBLO INDIANS and sometimes referred to as *PATOLLI*, or stick dice game, sticks with varying designs are tossed. Dice games are often part of harvest and renewal ceremonies.

Diegueno A name applied to various YU-MAN-speaking tribes, among them the Kamias (Tipais) of present-day southern California and northern Baja California, after they had been missionized by the Spanish at San Diego, from where the name comes. The following reservations in San Diego County, California, are held by Dieguenos: Barona, Campo, Capitan Grande, Cuyapaipe, Inaja-Cosmit, Jamul, La Posta, Manzanita, Mesa Grande, San Pasqual, Santa Ysabel, Sycuan, and Viejas. (See also MISSION INDIANS.)

Digger Indians (Root-diggers) A name applied by whites to a band of Southern PAIUTES, the Nuanuints (or Uainuints), living in the vicinity of present-day St. George in southwest Utah, because of their means of finding food by digging for roots, reptiles, and insects. The name came to be applied to other tribes of the GREAT BASIN CULTURE AREA.

digging stick (dibble) A stick carved to a point, used to cultivate soil and make seed holes in farming and to dig for roots and insects in gathering. Stones (perhaps RINGSTONES) probably were added to one end for balance.

Dineh See NAVAJO.

discoid (disk, discoidal) A disk-shape stone artifact, the purpose of which is unknown. Those found in the Southeast have been called CHUNKEY STONES. The adjective discoidal is also used as a noun. (See also FLINT DISK.)

disease In the traditional Indian view, sickness is related to spiritual causes. Although practical solutions might have been obvious for wounds or minor illnesses, MEDICINE MEN depended on ceremonies in addition to herbal remedies in much HEALING. Infectious diseases carried to native populations by Europeans influenced the course of post-Contact Indian history. It is estimated that tribal populations declined by about 10 percent from Indian-white warfare but by about 25 to 50 percent from infectious diseases. Smallpox proved the most deadly because it would return to the same populations in epidemic proportions time and again, but measles, scarlet fever, typhoid, typhus, diptheria, influenza, chicken-pox, and diptheria also ravaged Indian peoples. Contemporary Native American are known to have the poorest health care of any ethnic group: respiratory disease, heart disease, tuberculosis, high blood pressure, diabetes, and other diseases continue to take their toll.

disguise See DECOY.

dish Among native peoples, dishes generally were not used for individual portions, since there was more often a communal pot or platter, but they were used for condiments. As with other containers, dishes were made from a variety of materials, including stone, wood, bark, shell, rawhide, pottery, basketry, and gourds.

displacement The loss of LAND. The word refers to depopulation from DISEASE and WARFARE; LAND CESSIONS from warfare and subsequent TREATIES; the forced REMOVAL from ancestral lands and onto RESERVATIONS; and governmental policies of RELOCATION to cities. CULTURAL DISPOSSESSION went hand and hand with displacement, since Native Americans had economic and spiritual ties to their homelands.

dispute settlement A society's recognized way of resolving conflict between individuals and groups. A SONG FIGHT is a type of dispute settlement, as can be WRESTLING.

djibai A CHIPPEWA word in ALGONQUIAN for a spirit or ghost other than *MANITOU*.

dog The domesticated carnivorous mammal (*Canis familiaris*), kept by Native Americans for companionship, hunting, and hauling (pulling a TRAVOIS or SLED). Dogs, one of the few domesticated animals in the Americas in prehistoric times, probably are derived from the northern WOLF (*Canis lupis*). Dog remains from the Jaguar Cave in the Birch Creek Valley, Idaho, date to about 8400 B.C. Indians of some tribes ate dogs, but usually as part of a CEREMONY; some tribes offered dogs as SACRIFICES. The dog was the totem of the DOG SOLDIERS. (See also HUSKY; MALAMUTE.)

Dogrib (Thlingchadinne) An ATHAPASCAN-speaking tribe of the SUBARCTIC CULTURE AREA, located between Great Bear Lake and Great Slave Lake in the present-day Northwest Territories. The Dog Rib Rae band has its tribal headquarters at Fort Rae. The Dogrib native name, *Thlingchadinne*, translates as "dog-flank people"; Dogrib legend has it that the tribe originated from the union of a TLINGIT sorcerer, who was part dog and part man, with a woman.

Dog Soldiers (Dog Men, Hotamitaneo, Hotamitanui) A MILITARY SOCIETY of the Southern CHEYENNES, the members of which drew power from dogs (as well as from horses). Although it started as a SODALITY or club, it began functioning as a BAND, with members and families living and traveling together during the PLAINS INDIAN wars. Other warrior sodalities of the Cheyennes include the Bow String, Elk, Fox, and Shield societies. "Dog Face," military slang for an "infantry man," is perhaps derived from the Dog Soldiers.

doll Among Native Americans, toys representing humans or LEGENDARY BEINGS sometimes served educational and ceremonial functions as well. They were made from a variety of materials, including wood, stone, bone, hair, clay, hide, leaves, stems, corn cobs, rags, and dough. (See also CORNHUSK DOLL; KACHINA DOLL; SEMINOLE DOLL.)

domestication of animals The raising and taming of animals. "Animal husbandry" refers to the raising of livestock for food and other resources, such as leather or wool. (See also DOG; HORSE; LLAMA; PARROT; SHEEP; TURKEY.)

domestication of plants See CATEGORICAL APPENDIX, "PLANTS"; FARMING.

double A life force believed to exist at the center of an individual. In contemporary mysticism, the double refers to the astral body. In Native American tradition, a double is closer in meaning to a SOUL or SPIRIT.

Iroquois cornhusk doll

double-ball A sport similar to LACROSSE, in which a curved stick is used to throw two balls attached by a thong; played especially by women throughout much of North America. (See also SHINNY.)

drama A ceremony consisting of SONGS, DANCE, STORYTELLING, and ORATORY in various combinations, with roles acted out by participants wearing costumes and masks. The drama usually represents tribal history and LEGENDS. Sometimes called ritual drama.

dream Many Native Americans believed that dreams, i.e., thoughts, images, and emotions occurring during certain stages of sleep, were spirits communicating to them and guiding them. Animals appearing in dreams were considered especially significant. In Indian studies, the term dream is often used synonymously with VISION, or a vision can occur during a dream. Some tribes traditionally have believed that certain individuals can obtain knowledge, diagnose the sick, or predict the future through their dreams; the IROQUOIS call them Dreamers. (See also DREAM CATCHER; DREAM DANCE; DREAMER RELIGION; DREAM NAME.)

Dream Catcher An object with webbing inside a circle and a hole in the middle of the webbing, made of various combinations of wood (typically red willow for the loop), hide, sinew, feathers, beads, and stones, designed to be hung in a lodge near bedding. According to legend, the Dream Catcher catches all dreams, good and bad. Bad dreams are trapped in the web until dawn and burn up; good dreams find their way to the hole in the center and flow into the feathers, where they stay until dreamed another night. Dream catchers are typical of NORTHEAST INDIANS and PLAINS INDIANS.

Dream Dance A religious revitalization movement of the KLAMATHS and MODOCS, involving the power of dreams and visions of the dead. One of the founders was the Modoc shaman Doctor George, who drew

Iroquois Dream Catcher

on the GHOST DANCE and EARTH LODGE RELIGION. The religion was practiced only for a short time in Oregon in the early 20th century. The name Dream Dance also is used for the DRUM RELIGION of western GREAT LAKES INDIANS.

Dreamer Religion A religious revitalization movement of PLATEAU INDIANS. In the 1850s, the Wanapam shaman Smohalla claimed he had visited the Spirit World and had returned to preach the resurgence of the aboriginal way of life, free from white influences, such as alcohol and agriculture. Drawing on teachings of the WASHANI RELIGION and WASHAT DANCE, Smohalla established ceremonial music and dancing to induce meditation. He also predicted the resurrection of all ancestral spirits to rid the world of white oppressors. Smohalla claimed that the truth came to him through dreams, and he is sometimes referred to as a dreamer-prophet. His oratory was known as "Shouting Mountain."

dream name A name derived from a DREAM or VISION QUEST. (See also CHILD-HOOD NAME.)

dress PLAINS INDIAN women sewed two deer or elk skins together to fashion dresses. Some had a third poncholike yoke piece attached. SOUTHWEST INDIAN women fashioned dresses out of a single rectangular piece of cotton cloth, tied over the right shoulder and angling under the left arm. (See also SKIRT.)

drift voyage An unintentional transoceanic journey by boat or raft between continents. Based on the extensive sea travel over the centuries for fishing and trading, plus the strong westward ocean current in the South Atlantic, westward current north of the equator in the Pacific, and eastward current in the North Pacific, it is theorized that some drift voyages occurred. Scholars have used cultural similarities of artifacts to make their case for drift voyages. Thor Heyerdahl in his 20th century *Kon-Tiki* voyage from Peru to the Tuamotu Islands and in his *Ra* voyage from Morocco to Barbados demonstrated that small wooden or reed crafts could make ocean crossings. There is no conclusive archaeological evidence of such early transoceanic contacts, however.

driftwood Wood floating on or washed ashore by water. Native Americans, especially those living in areas when wood was scarce, such as the INUITS, used driftwood for tent poles and for traditional carving of masks and other objects. In post-Contact times, some wood was salvaged from shipwrecks.

drill (borer) A tool with a pointed and sometimes beveled end for boring holes. Grasses, bristles, and quills were used for perforating soft materials. AWLS of stone, wood, or bone, rotated back and forth between the hands, were used for hard materials. A bow drill (drill bow) is a borer, operated by twisting the string of a bow around the drill stick and moving the bow

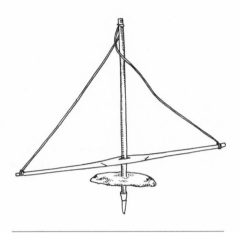

Inuit pump drill

back and forth. A pump drill, typical of the INUITS and PUEBLO INDIANS in post-Contact times, has a shaft, crosspiece, thongs, and a disk of stone, pottery, or wood; the disk is used to wind the thong and the crosspiece is used to push downward, thus moving the shaft. Pump drills sometimes also were utilized as FIRE DRILLS. The similar strap drill, typical of the Inuits and ALEUTS, has a headpiece on the drill stick for holding in the teeth while a thong wrapped around the shaft is pulled back and forth; bone or teeth handles on each end of the thong help maintain a good grip.

drought A long period of weather without rainfall, potentially leading to famine, migrations, and cultural demise.

drum A musical instrument consisting of a hollow, usually cylindrical wooden body with a tightly stretched animal skin or stomach head, which produces a booming or tapping sound when struck by the hand or a stick. Some drums are single headed; others are double headed, i.e., with both ends of the body covered. Many are decorated with combinations of carvings, paint, fur, or feathers. The sound of the drum can be altered by wetting it with water or holding it before a fire. Certain large drums are designed to be played by several persons.

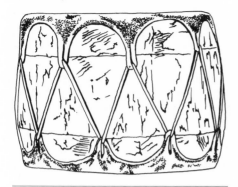

Pueblo Indian drum

among native peoples, were organized around the playing of sacred drums and the passing of sacred knowledge from one tribe to another.

drying The preservation of meat, fish, fruit, or vegetables by extracting the moisture. The term drying is used to refer to slow drying in sunlight, as opposed to SMOKING. Indians crafted drying racks to hold the food. Drying is a process in FOOD PREPARATION AND PRESERVATION.

dry-painting See SANDPAINTING.

duck tablet A prehistoric artifact of wood, bone, or copper in the stylized shape of a duck, found especially in the Southeast. Duck tablets were probably ceremonial objects. (See also BANNERSTONE.)

Another type of drum is a hollowed-out log. Some NORTHWEST COAST INDIANS and CALIFORNIA INDIANS traditionally used box drums with square bodies. Individuals as well as tribes, clans, or other groups might own a drum, which often was named. Drums are used in DANCES and other ceremonies and are considered sacred. The word drum also is used as a verb. The phrase host drum is used at intertribal POWWOWS to designate the tribe that brings the communal drum. (See also FOOT DRUM; TEPONATZLI; WATER DRUM.)

Drum Religion (Drum Dance, Dream Dance) A religious revitalization movement that began among the SANTEE (Dakota) subdivision of SIOUX in about 1880 and spread to other Indians in the western Great Lakes region, such as the CHIPPEWA, FOX, KICKAPOO, MENOMINEE, POTAWATOMI, and WINNEBAGO tribes. The rituals of this religion, which encouraged unity

dugout (dugout canoe) A type of boat, made by hollowing out a log. Small dugouts were typical of SOUTHEAST INDIANS and CALIFORNIA INDIANS. Some NORTHEAST INDIANS made boats in this fashion as well, along with birchbark CANOES. The seaworthy dugouts of the NORTHWEST COAST INDIANS were made from giant cedar logs, some nearly 100 feet long, painted with symbolic designs. High bows and sterns were attached to the hull with cedar pegs and ropes. An alternate term, pirogue, is of French derivation via the Spanish *piragua* and originally from the CARIBAN *piraguas*.

Duwamish (Duamish, Dwamish, Dwahmish) A SALISHAN-speaking tribe of the

Haida dugout

NORTHWEST COAST CULTURE AREA, located on the Duwamish River and on Lake Washington near present-day Seattle, Washington. Tribal members hold the Tulalip Reservation in Snohomish County, Washington with SNOHOMISH Indians and other tribes; another group, the Duwamish Tribe, maintains headquarters in Seattle. The part-Duwamish, part-SUQUAMISH chief Seattle gave the city its name.

dwelling A place of abode. "Dwelling" is a more general term than HOUSE; sometimes used interchangeably with SHELTER. (See also CATEGORICAL APPENDIX, "HOUSES AND ARCHITECTURE LODGE.")

dye A substance used to color material through soaking and staining. Native Americans made dyes from a variety of organic sources, such as berries, roots, bark, lichens, minerals, and insects (red cochineal dye) to color clothing, baskets, and other objects; some PLAINS INDIANS dyed their horses' manes and tails. Although it can apply to the coloring in dyes, the term PIGMENT is more often used in reference to the coloring in PAINT. (See also TIE-DYE.)

eagle Any of large birds of prey of the family Accipitridae, having long broad wings, keen vision, and a hooked bill. Because of the eagle's size, strength, and grace, it has been revered in American Indian tradition, with many tribes having eagle deities and representing them symbolically in artwork. In SIOUX tradition, for example, eagles control the weather. The THUNDERBIRD of NORTHWEST COAST INDIANS is depicted as an eagle. Eagle feathers have been considered sacred and are used on headdresses, shirts, and shields as well as a number of ceremonial objects, such as CALUMETS, TOTEM POLES, and PRAYER STICKS. Eagle bones, especially from the upper wing, also have been prized and used in WHISTLES and SUCKING TUBES; and eagle talons have been used as AMULETS. U.S. officials who chose the eagle as the nation's logo were aware of the symbolic value Native Americans placed on the bird. Indians commonly hunted eagles from inside a covered pit, with bait at its edge. (See EXPLOIT FEATHERS.)

eagle-bone whistle See EAGLE; WHISTLE.

Eagle Dance A ceremony invoking the spirit of the EAGLE to gain its power. The Eagle Dance is one of the animal dances of PUEBLO INDIANS; it also formerly was a war and peace ceremony of the IROQUOIS, which evolved into a healing ceremony. Other tribes also honor the eagle in dance.

eagle headdress See EAGLE; WARBONNET.

earplug See EARSPOOL.

earring See EARSPOOL; JEWELRY.

earspool (earplug) An ornament, often spool-shaped, worn in a perforation in the ear lobe.

earthenware See POTTERY.

earthlodge A large dome-shape dwelling, about 40 feet in diameter, having a log frame

Mandan earthlodge

(constructed in two series of posts and cross-beams), covered with branches, often willow, or brush mats, then packed with mud or sod. Earthlodges had central FIREPITS with SMOKEHOLES and are typical of the ARIKARAS, HIDATSAS, MANDANS, OSAGES, PAWNEES, and PONCAS.

Earth Lodge Religion A religious revitalization movement of northern California and southern Oregon tribes, which evolved out of the GHOST DANCE RELIGION, with similar predictions of the end of the world and a return of ancestors. It was founded about 1872, probably among the PATWINS and WINTUNS, and spread to the ACHOMAWIS, SHASTAS, SILETZ, and others. Among the POMOS, it became known as the Warm House Dance. The Earth Lodge Religion influenced the later DREAM DANCE of the KLAMATHS and MODOCS.

earthwork Any construction made primarily of earth and stone, such as permanent and temporary MOUNDS, enclosures, and embankments. The term can be used interchangeably with mound, except in a military application; i.e., "earthwork" would be used for a fortification or bulwark.

Eastern Indians A general term applied historically to those tribes east of the Mississippi River; sometimes referred to as WOODLAND INDIANS. Many of the eastern tribes were relocated westward with the policies of REMOVAL. (See also NORTHEAST INDIANS; SOUTHEAST INDIANS.)

Edisto A subtribe of the CUSABO Indians, located on the lower Edisto River in present-day South Carolina. A group centered at Ridgeville, South Carolina, known as the Four Holes Indian Organization, maintains its Edisto identity.

effigy A representation of a person or animal. The term is applied to sculptured images in stone, free-standing or carved on monuments or on other smaller stonework; to painted or drawn images; to POTTERY images; to images on PIPES; to DOLL figures; and to MOUNDS.

effigy mound See MOUND.

elder (tribal elder) In many tribes, old people were respected as teachers, the purveyors of tribal history and lore. They often served as shamans and as the leaders of SECRET SOCIETIES. Some served in political and civic functions as well. As survivors, they were respected for their advice on the best path for the tribe in times of hardship. It was widely believed that nearness to death made elders honest. The YOKUTS called an elder *modo'o* in their PENUTIAN language; the SHOSHONES used the term *muatupu* in UTO-AZTECAN; the oldest member of the KWAKIUTL tribe was known as *watsiti* in WAKASHAN. (See also GRANDFATHER; GRANDMOTHER.)

elk (American elk, wapiti) A large North American DEER, *Cervus canadensis*. The alternate name, *wapiti*, is an ALGONQUIAN term of the SHAWNEE dialect, meaning "white rump." Once found in large herds throughout much of North America, the elk is now confined to northern regions. The animal was a valued source of food and clothing to many Indian peoples. The horn and teeth were generally prized for ornaments. Some tribes, such as the CROWS, made BOWS from the horns.

elke A LENNI LENAPE (Delaware) expression of joy in ALGONQUIAN, meaning "great!" or "wonderful!" The opposite word is *ekesa*, meaning "terrible!" or "for shame!"

elm bark The bark of the elm tree (genus *Ulmus*). The IROQUOIS Indians used elm-bark slabs for the wall and roof coverings in horizontal overlapping rows on their LONGHOUSES. Some ALGONQUIAN peoples used elm bark to cover their WIGWAMS. The Iroquois used it to cover their canoes: The thick, scabrous bark also enabled them to use CANOES as barricades or as ladders. Various tribes shaped pieces of elm bark into TOBOGGANS, RATTLES, and CONTAINERS. The fibrous inner bark was woven into coverings for beds, floors, and doors. It also had medicinal purposes—slippery elm, as the herb is known, aids in bleeding lungs and other ailments. (See also BARK CRAFT.)

emblem   See CLAN EMBLEM.

embroidery   The art or process of creating a design with needle and thread on cloth or leather; also, the embroidered work itself. Embroidery was a means of pictorial expression among native peoples. In South America, LLAMA wool and COTTON were used to make designs. In North America during pre-Contact times, embroidery was restricted to QUILLWORK, a type of APPLIQUÉ.

emergence myth   See CREATION STORY.

encomienda   A Spanish term for an estate granted by Spanish kings, i.e., a royal land grant, part of the HACIENDA system. The term also refers historically to a grant of Indian peoples for their tribute or labor. In 1512, the Spanish Law of Burgos established the *encomienda* system under which a number of Indians were provided as laborers along with granted lands, a policy that amounted to legalized enslavement. Male Indians were required to work nine months yearly in return for entry into Spanish society. The *encomenderos* (those people holding *encomiendas*)—generally CONQUISTADORS and officials—thus obtained labor for their mining, ranching, farming, and public works. The clergy favored the policy, believing it would lead to native conversion to Catholicism. The royalty favored it because, in exchange for tributary labor, the *encomendero* would pay the crown a head tax on each Indian as well as finance his indoctrination. The word *encomienda* is derived from the Spanish *encomendar*, meaning "to entrust." The REPARTIMIENTO system replaced the *encomienda* system in 1542.

endogamous   An anthropological term describing a custom or rule requiring marriage within a defined social group, such as a TRIBE or CLAN. "Endogamy" is the noun form; also called in-marriage. (See also AGAMOUS; EXOGAMOUS.)

engraving   The act, process, or resulting artifact of cutting or scratching into a material, such as stone, wood, bark, bone, antler, ivory, pottery, copper, gold, and silver. American Indians traditionally have carved abstract designs as well as PICTOGRAPHS. Incising is the technique of decorating POTTERY by cutting a design in the SLIP with a sharp tool, before or after FIRING. (See also ETCHING; SCRIMSHAW.)

Eno   See SIOUAN.

epidemic   See DISEASE.

Erie   An IROQUOIAN-speaking tribe of the NORTHEAST CULTURE AREA, located in present-day northern Ohio, northwestern Pennsylvania, and western New York. The Eries were defeated by tribes of the IROQUOIS LEAGUE, in particular the neighboring SENECAS, who absorbed Erie captives. *Erie* means "long tail" in Iroquoian, in reference to the panther; the Eries also were known as the Cat Nation.

Eskimo   See INUIT.

Eskimo-Aleut   (Eskaleutian, Eskimaleut, Eskimauan, Eskimoan)   A language family and subdivision of the AMERICAN ARCTIC-PALEO-SIBERIAN phylum comprising dialects spoken by peoples of the ARCTIC CULTURE AREA, including bands of the INUIT and ALEUT peoples.

Esselen   See HOKAN.

Etchaottine   See SLAVE.

Etchemin   See MALECITE.

Hohokam acid-etched shell

etching   The act, process, or resulting artifact of making a design on metal or glass with acid. The Indians of the HOHOKAM CULTURE were probably the first people in the world to practice the art. They covered shells with acid-resistant pitch from trees, carved designs on the pitch, then soaked the shells in an acid solution made from fermented SAGUARO. On removing the coating, a design was etched in the shell's surface. In post-Contact times, INUITS have practiced etching. The term also is used synonymously with ENGRAVING.

ethnobotany   The study of plant remains and their comparative use by different peoples.

ethnocentric   The belief in the inherent superiority of one's own culture and the tendency to view another group in terms of one's own. It is ethnocentric or Eurocentric when Europeans assume that their form of progress and land development is superior to traditional Indian views and use of land. "Ethnocentricism" and "Eurocentricism" are the noun forms.

ethnography   The branch of cultural AN-THROPOLOGY that studies the origin and relationships of races and cultures; sometimes used interchangeably with ETHNOL-OGY, but ethnography is restricted to the purely descriptive study of peoples and races, with an emphasis on FIELDWORK, while ethnology involves comparative cross-cultural study and analytical classification.

ethnology   The branch of cultural AN-THROPOLOGY that studies and classifies races and peoples, including their origin, distribution, relationships, and shared and distinct characteristics. (See also ETHNOG-RAPHY.)

Eufaula (Eufala)   A subtribe of the CREEK Indians, located on or near the Tallapoosa River in present-day Alabama and later on the Chattahoochee River in present-day Georgia. Several different Creek towns had the name Eufaula in the course of the band's history. The Eufaulas were the first Creeks to establish a settlement in Florida, north of Tampa Bay, in 1761; their descendants along with those of other MUSKOGEANS became known as SEMINOLES.

Euroamerican (Euro-American)   A person from Europe living in the Americas or a person born in the Americas of European ancestry—i.e., a non-Indian of European ancestry. The term is used synonymously with WHITE in some historical or sociological writings.

Eurocentric   See ETHNOCENTRIC.

excavation   The removal of material, such as earth and stone, from above and around ancient remains. "Back dirt" is the earth removed. "Excavation" sometimes is used synonymously with ARCHAEOLOGICAL SITE.

excising   A technique in POTTERY in which deep grooves or fields are carved into the surface to create recessed designs.

exogamous A custom or rule requiring marriage outside a defined social group, such as a TRIBE or CLAN. "Exogamy" is the noun form; also called out-marriage. (See also AGAMOUS; ENDOGAMOUS.)

exploit feather A FEATHER, especially on a HEADDRESS, indicating an act of bravery in war. (See also COUP.)

explorer An explorer of the Americas can be defined as the first known non-Indian, or among the first non-Indians, to reach a particular tribe's land. Explorers came from a variety of vocational backgrounds: Some were simply adventurers; others were navigators, conquerors, colonizers, missionaries, military personnel, whalers, hunters, trappers, traders, scholars, writers, and artists. In numerous instances, Indians enabled the explorers to survive and succeed in their goals, providing food and shelter and acting as guides. Much of what is known about early Indian history before white settlement comes from the writings of explorers.

extended family See FAMILY.

eyayeye (eyehe, eyaheya, eyaheeye, eyeheeye, eye, eyeyeyeye, eyayo, hayeye, haeyeye, yeye) An exclamation without meaning used to fill in measures in the songs of the GHOST DANCE by the SIOUX, ARAPAHOS, CHEYENNES, and other Indians.

Eye Dazzler A type of NAVAJO BLANKET with bright colors and geometric designs, woven from dyed commercial yarns beginning in the 1890s.

Eyeish See CADDOAN.

.F.

Faces of the Forest In IROQUOIS tradition, forest spirits who control disease and inform people in dreams to carve FALSE FACES on trees.

face-painting See PAINT; PAINTING.

fair An exhibition and sale of products, such as food and arts and crafts. (See also FEAST; FESTIVAL; FIESTA; INDIAN MARKET; POWWOW.)

faithkeeper (deacon) A person responsible for administrative duties of the LONG-HOUSE RELIGION of the IROQUOIS, including scheduling, finances, and arranging burials. Each longhouse MOIETY has a male and female faithkeeper. Among the Iroquois living in Canada, the term deacon is used. The phrase keeper of the faith is used to refer to people with religious duties in other tribes. (See also PREACHER.)

False Face A wooden mask worn by a member of the False Face Society of the IROQUOIS to frighten away spirits that cause illness. The masks, representing the forest spirits known as FACES OF THE FOREST, are carved on a living tree; while they are cut out, there is a ceremony of prayer and the offering of tobacco. The False Face Society is a MEDICINE SOCIETY; both men and women can join, instructed to do so in a dream or healed by the society's ceremonies; women, however, do not wear the masks. A False Face Dance or series of dances is performed alone or at other ceremonies, such as the MIDWINTER CEREMONY, to heal the sick.

family The "family," or the basic social unit or grouping of people, has different meanings for different tribes. A nuclear family, i.e., a father, mother, and one or more children, might be included in the concept, as might an extended family, i.e., additional wives, grandparents, and adopted children. Rules governing marriage, birth, death, adoption, and the taking of captives all play a part in determining KINSHIP. CLANS and BANDS also can be considered extended families.

Fancy Dance A type of dancing in which performers use steps from a variety of

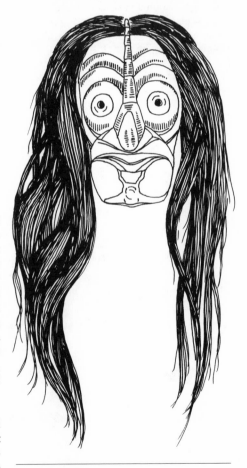

Iroquois False Face

dances with no fixed pattern. The Fancy Dance evolved among the PLAINS INDIANS out of the GRASS DANCE and spread to other tribes. Fancy Dancers, wearing elaborate and colorful costumes, participate in contest dances at modern-day POWWOWS. (See also STRAIGHT DANCE.)

farming (agriculture, horticulture) The cultivation of plants dates back as early as 7000 B.C. in the Americas. Cultivated beans, peppers, pumpkins, and gourds have been discovered in a dry cave in the MESOAMERICAN CULTURE AREA. The earliest cultivated strain of corn ever found, also in Mesoamerica, dates back to about 4000 B.C. Farming allowed the development of cities, because a large number of people could live in a small area and still have a regular food supply. In some tribes, such as those of the IROQUOIS LEAGUE, the women did the majority of the farming other than clearing the fields. IROQUOIS women also owned the crops. The term agriculture often is used to indicate the use of draft animals or heavy equipment in farming. The adjective "agricultural" sometimes is used synonymously with "agrarian." The term horticulture sometimes is used synonymously with "farming," especially with hand tools, but more often refers to the growth of plants for ornamental purposes. The DOMESTICATION OF ANIMALS is sometimes included in the concept of farming. (See also CATEGORICAL APPENDIX, "PLANTS.")

fast For Native Americans, abstaining from food or water, or fasting, was primarily a spiritual discipline in religious ceremonies and RITES OF PASSAGE, and was used for PURIFICATION and to induce VISIONS. In times of food shortage, group fasting helped assure a tribe's survival. Contemporary Indian activists might fast for political reasons.

feast A celebration in which food is eaten in abundance. Feasting was part of many different ceremonies, such as in THANKSGIVING after successful harvesting and hunt-

ing and in GIVEAWAYS. (See also FEAST DAY; FESTIVAL; POTLATCH; POWWOW.)

Feast Day Among the PUEBLO INDIANS and Indians of Latin America, a Feast Day is a commemorative festival honoring a particular Catholic saint, i.e., a "saint's day," with both Christian and native ritual, such as the TABLITA dance, and feasting.

Feast to the Dead (Feast for the Dead) Many native peoples had ceremonies with feasting that honored deceased tribal members. The INUIT and ALEUT versions also are referred to as Memorial Feasts; the IROQUOIS name of the ceremony is *Ohgiwe* (*Okiwe, Okiweh*); the Alaska ATHAPASCAN name is *Hi'o* and is sometimes called Stick Dance.

feather See FEATHERWORK.

Feather Dance Dances involving the ceremonial use of feathers are common to native peoples. The name is a translation of the KIOWA *Awh-mai-goon-gah* in the KIOWA-TANOAN language, their version of the GHOST DANCE; it also is called *Manposotiguan*, for "dance with clasped hands." The IROQUOIS Feather Dance is part of the LONGHOUSE RELIGION. Some contemporary tribes hold special Feather Dances to sanctify an eagle feather that has fallen to the ground accidentally during another dance. (See also FEATHER RELIGION.)

Feathered Serpent See QUETZALCOATL.

Feather Religion (Feather Cult, Feather Dance, Pom Pom Shakers, Waskliki, Spinning Religion) A religious revitalization movement of the PLATEAU INDIANS, founded by the KLICKITAT shaman Jake Hunt in 1904 and practiced for about 10 years. The religion drew on elements of both the earlier INDIAN SHAKER RELIGION and WASHANI RELIGION. Sacred eagle feathers were used in ceremonies, one of which involved ritual spinning, hence the alternate name, "Spinning Religion."

Zuni snake fetish

featherwork The act, process, or resulting artifact of work with bird feathers. Feathers were used for practical purposes, as in ARROW FEATHERS; symbolic purposes, as in EXPLOIT FEATHERS; and ceremonial purposes, as in PRAYER FEATHERS and PRAYER STICKS. They also were added to artifacts as decoration. Certain birds were considered sacred, and their feathers especially valued, such as those from the wings of EAGLES and the tails of wild TURKEYS and QUETZALS. Native Americans cut birdskins and feathers into strips and wove them into clothing and blankets. The quills and barbs sometimes were used in QUILLWORK. Down was utilized for padding and insulation.

federal Indian policy (federal policy) The governmental policy of the United States with regard to Native Americans and tribal groups. The policy has evolved through a number of stages from the American Revolution to the present. (See ALLOTMENT; ASSIMILATION; BUREAU OF INDIAN AFFAIRS; FEDERAL RECOGNITION; RESERVATION; SELF-DETERMINATION; TERMINATION.)

federal recognition The product of a trust relationship between an Indian tribe and the United States government, known as the Federal Acknowledgment Process. Federally recognized tribes, or those with TRUST STATUS, are entitled to special governmental programs. More than 300 tribal groups are now recognized by the U.S. government; more than 130 are seeking recognition.

Fernandeno See MISSION INDIANS; UTO-AZTECAN.

festival A celebration, marked by ceremonies, performances, feasting, or other observances, in many instances occurring at a particular time of year and involving religious themes. (See also FAIR; FEAST; FIESTA; POWWOW.)

fetish An object believed to have supernatural power; sometimes natural in form, sometimes carved. Since Indian peoples have regarded inanimate objects as having SPIRITS, possessing them is thought to bring power and protection to an individual. In Indian studies, the term fetish often is used interchangeably with AMULET or TALISMAN; in general use, however, it has taken on the connotation of excessive reverence or attention. Carved animal objects of the ZUNIS are known specifically as fetishes. Native Americans generally favor the term SACRED OBJECT. "Fetishism" is the belief in or worship of fetishes. (See also PRESTIGE ITEM.)

fetish bundle See MEDICINE BUNDLE.

fiber craft The act, process, or resulting artifact of work in fiber, the elongated, thick-walled cells that give support to plant tissue, i.e., stems, leaves, and inner bark. American Indians use fiber in the making of containers, clothing, furniture, and other artifacts. (See also BARK CRAFT; BASKETRY; BAST; CORDAGE; COTTON; WATAP; WEAVING.)

fieldwork Research done on site, as opposed to that done in a classroom or laboratory. "Participant observation" is a kind of fieldwork, conducted through living within a culture and taking part in everyday life while recording lifeways. (See also IN-FORMANT.)

fiesta A religious celebration in Spanish-speaking countries, in many instances a saint's day in the Catholic religion. Fiestas combine Spanish and Indian ritual, art, and pageantry and include feasting. (See also FEAST; FEAST DAY; PAHKO.)

figurine (statuette) A small sculpture. In Indian studies, the term usually refers to a human figure made out of POTTERY.

fine art Works created primarily for beauty rather than utility. The term is usually applied to PAINTING, SCULPTURE, and other "visual arts"; but sometimes also to ARCHITECTURE, DANCE, DRAMA, LITERATURE, and MUSIC. Many so-called Native American ARTS AND CRAFTS, both traditional and modern, can be classified as fine art.

fire American Indians burned fuel for light, heat, cooking, tool-making, protection from animals, hunting, warfare, and ritual. The communal fire traditionally has been a central place in a village or camp for socializing and ceremonies. Fire has been considered a mysterious power in Native American religions, and it is sometimes referred to as the Sacred Fire. The lighting of a new Sacred Fire is part of the GREEN CORN CEREMONY of SOUTHEAST INDIANS. The NAVAJOS have a Fire Dance, as do other tribes. Fire also serves as a political symbol: The IROQUOIS LEAGUE kept the Grand Council Fire burning continually, a symbol of the enduring alliance of the Six Nations, at Onondaga, the central village of the Six Nations. (See also FIRE-DRIVE; FIRE-MAKING; FIREPIT; FIRING; FOOD PREPARATION AND PRESERVATION; SWEATING.)

firearm (gun) During the colonial period, guns and gun powder were valued trade items. Tribes that had a supply of firearms had the upper hand over traditional ene-

mies. While BOWS and ARROWS could be more effective than muzzle-loading rifles, since a warrior could fire a number of arrows before a rifle was reloaded, guns induced fear in the early post-Contact years and led to such native names as "medicine iron." Breech-loading rifles, six-chambered revolvers, and repeating rifles further altered the nature of warfare and hunting in the 19th century, becoming essential tools for Indians as well as the white armies sent against them. Cannons also determined the outcome of many battles between Indians and whites.

fire drill A device for FIRE-MAKING in which one stick (the drill stick) is twirled rapidly in a hole of another piece of wood (the hearth stick), creating enough friction to ignite wood powder or other vegetable material. Pump DRILLS were used as fire drills by some tribes.

fire-drive A cooperative hunt in which fires are started to force game toward hunters or off a cliff.

fire-making There were two main techniques for starting FIRES among Indian peoples before the introduction of matches: percussive friction between FLINT and PYRITE (the latter eventually replaced by steel) and rotary friction between pieces of wood. Wood powder, twigs, bark strips, shredded grass, fungi, or other combustible vegetable materials served as tinder. (See also FIRE DRILL; FIRE-DRIVE; FIREPIT; LAMP; TORCH.)

firepit (hearth) A hole dug to hold a fire; located near or inside many different kinds of Indian dwellings and ceremonial structures. (See also SMOKEHOLE.)

firing The exposure of POTTERY to intense heat to harden it. In traditional firing, called ground firing or dung firing, pots are protected with pottery fragments or pieces of scrap metal, then surrounded with dung chips, which are set on fire. In KILN firing, the pots are baked in a gas or electric KILN.

first food ceremony A celebration surrounding the first seasonal harvesting of a wild plant or crop or capture of game. The term also can be applied to the rituals surrounding the first catch in the career of a young hunter. First food ceremonies have been referred to as first fruit ceremonies, first catch ceremonies, first salmon rites, or THANKSGIVING. The Acorn Feast of CALIFORNIA INDIANS is an example of a first food ceremony, as is the Cranberry Day of the WAMPANOAGS. The IROQUOIS Indians have in their traditional ceremonial calendar a Maple Festival, Raspberry Ceremony, Strawberry Festival, and Blackberry Ceremony. A HARVEST FESTIVAL or "harvest dance" can be considered a type of first food ceremony.

First Laugh A ceremony of the NAVAJOS, in which a newborn infant is kept in a CRADLEBOARD and watched until he or she laughs for the first time, indicating birth as a social being. The person who makes the child laugh then sponsors a celebration.

fish Vertebrates of the superclass Pisces were a staple food, especially of NORTHWEST COAST INDIANS and PLATEAU INDIANS. Some tribes refer to fish as Children of the River. (See also FISHING; SALMON; SHELLFISH.)

fishhook A curved and pointed device designed to fasten to a line in FISHING, made from stone, bone, ivory, shell, wood, or copper. American Indian hooks included a gorge, a spike of bone or wood, sharpened at both ends and attached to a line in the center (also used to capture birds and other game); a spike set in the end of a shaft; a plain hook; a hook with a barb; and a snap hook, the ends of which are held apart by a peg and released onto the fish's mouth when it takes the bait.

fish-in A type of civil disobedience in which Native American activists fish in waters forbidden by federal or state governments in order to demonstrate treaty rights, the traditional way of life, and economic necessities. The first fish-in took place in Washington State in 1964, sponsored by the National Indian Youth Council, when members of various tribes fished the Columbia River following the building of a dam at the Dalles. (See also WATER RIGHTS.)

fishing Native American fished for food with their bare hands; with SPEARS and HARPOONS; with BOWS and ARROWS; with CLUBS and sticks split at the end for "pinching"; with lines, including SETLINES, SINKERS, and FISHHOOKS; with TRAPS and NETS; and with POISONS. In addition to standing in the water, on the shore, on rocks, or on ice, Indians fished from boats and platforms. (See also SALMON; SEINE; WEIR; WHALING.)

Five Civilized Tribes A term used for the CHEROKEE, CHICKASAW, CHOCTAW, CREEK, and SEMINOLE tribes, starting in the mid-1800s. Although it came into widespread use after the tribes had been relocated to the INDIAN TERRITORY west of the Mississippi, it was their adaptation of white lifeways in their ancestral homelands of the Southeast that led to the name. Before removal westward, many tribes owned agricultural plantations and lived in log cabins and frame houses and kept black slaves. Factions of the Cherokees and Creeks also had developed governments under written constitutions with an executive branch, judicial and legislative branch, plus a public school system. (The Cherokee Indian Sequoyah also had devised a written alphabet for his people—the CHEROKEE ALPHABET—and his people published a newspaper with it.) The tribes continued to try to function as sovereign nations in the Indian Territory, but the federal government undermined their power through the ALLOTMENT policy.

Five Nations See IROQUOIS LEAGUE.

flageolet (flute) A flutelike wind instrument having several holes on the front and

Sioux flageolet

back for finger and thumbs and capable of making several different tones; sometimes called a courting flute, since in many tribes flageolets were played by young men during courtship. Unlike a flageolet, a WHISTLE is capable of making only a single note. (See also FLUTE CEREMONY.)

flake The thin, flat pieces of stone removed from a stone artifact during FLAKING, leaving a CORE. Some flakes are waste matter or CHIPS (spalls). Others are large enough to be used as tools (flakeknives) or placed in a handle as a kind of SCRAPER. A channel flake is the waste flake resulting from the creation of FLUTING on a FLUTED POINT; a guide flake is one of the small flakes removed from the base of the stone to prepare the size of the flute before the removal of the channel flake. A bec is a flake modified to form a single-pointed projection at one end.

flaked tool (flaked stone tool, chipped stone tool) Any tool made by the process of FLAKING.

flaker (flaking tool) An implement of bone, antler, wood, or stone used to chip FLAKES from a stone.

flaking (knapping, chipping) Removing FLAKES of stone, usually from chunks of FLINT, CHERT, or OBSIDIAN, in order to shape tools or POINTS. In percussion flaking, the chips are removed by striking with a tool known as a flaking tool or FLAKER. In pressure flaking, the chips are removed by applying pressure with a softer tool, usually of bone or antler. A combination of both techniques often was used to shape a stone ARTIFACT, with a certain amount of pressure retouch, i.e., sharpening, edging, or re-edging a tool. "Parallel flaking" refers to a process in which the flake scars, i.e., the ridges and valleys, end up approximately even and parallel. "Ripple flaking" refers to a process in which the resulting surface has wavy lines. The artifacts created by the various methods are known generally as FLAKED TOOLS or chipped stone tools. A biface is an artifact worked both front and back with uniform sides. The flakes removed in making bifaced artifacts are known as biface thinning flakes. (See also BLADE AND CORE.)

flaking tool See FLAKER.

Flathead (Salish) A SALISHAN-speaking tribe of the PLATEAU CULTURE AREA, located in present-day western Montana, centered around Flathead Lake. Tribal members share the Flathead Reservation near Dixon, Montana, with other Salishans and KOOTENAY Indians. The name Flathead derives from their not practicing HEAD DEFORMATION, which created a sloping crown, as did Coast Salishans.

Flat Pipe (Seicha) A sacred object, or PALLADIUM, of the GROS VENTRE Indians (the Feathered Pipe is another), which, according to legend, was given to the people by Earthmaker.

flesher A type of SCRAPER, usually made of stone or bone, for cleaning flesh and fat

Archaic Indian flaked tool

from animal SKINS, and for food preparation.

flint A kind of hard, smooth stone, gray to brown or black, that can be worked into tools and points through FLAKING; a variety of QUARTZ. Other stones, such as CHERT and types of CHALCEDONY, are sometimes grouped with flint. The plural, "flints," is applied to all flaked and chipped stone tools and weapons. (See also FIRE-MAKING; FLINT DISK; FLINTSTONE.)

flint disk Platelike objects, a kind of DISCOID, circular or elliptical, three to eight inches in diameter, made by the technique of FLAKING from FLINT or other flintlike stones. They are found east of the Mississippi River, their purpose unknown.

flintstone An artifact made out of FLINT.

float A device that remains on the surface of water without sinking. Some tribes designed SEINES using floats to keep them vertical in the water. The INUITS made inflated seal bladder floats to attach to HARPOONS in hunting sea mammals. (See also BLADDER DART.)

flute See FLAGEOLET; WHISTLE.

Flute Ceremony A RAINMAKING ceremony of the HOPI Indians, held in the summertime every other year by each pueblo, sponsored by the Blue Flute Society and Gray Flute Society; it alternates with the SNAKE DANCE.

fluted point A bifaced, leaf-shaped POINT with a groove or channel extending from the base toward the tip on one or both faces. The FLUTING is made by the removal of a channel flake. The fluting probably was designed to fit onto a shaft and to facilitate deep penetration of an animal and increase the flow of blood. (See also CLOVIS CULTURE; FLAKE; FOLSOM CULTURE.)

fluting Grooves or channels in POINTS. (See also FLUTED POINT.)

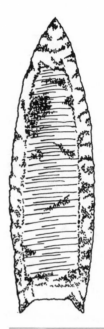

Folsom point

Folsom Culture A cultural tradition of the PALEOLITHIC PERIOD, lasting from about 9500 B.C. to 7000 B.C. While the Folsom culture is named after the Folsom TYPE SITE in New Mexico, evidence of Folsom hunters has been found in much of North America, especially on the Great Plains along with the remains of longhorn BUFFALO. The Folsom POINTS, three-quarters of an inch to three inches long, lanceolate in shape, were unique in that they had FLUTING on both sides running almost the entire length. It was during the Folsom period that Indians first used spear-throwing devices called ATLATLS.

food See CATEGORICAL APPENDIX, "FOOD PRODUCTION"; COOKING; FARMING; FISHING; FOOD PREPARATION AND PRESERVATION; HUNTING.

food preparation and preservation The preparation of food after hunting, gathering, or farming. The term encompasses separating, hulling, shelling, grinding, pounding, skinning, boning, CURING (through drying or smoking and "salting") as well as COOKING.

football A GAME in which one must kick a ball upward and keep it in the air as long as possible. The term sometimes refers to Indian KICKBALL.

foot drum A DRUM, typical of NORTHWEST COAST INDIANS, CALIFORNIA INDIANS, and SOUTHWEST INDIANS, played with the feet. Designs include a plank over a pit in the floor, hollowed-out logs, and hollowed-out masonry.

footprint sculpture A representation of a human, animal, or legendary being in a soft material such as sandstone. Footprints also were represented in PICTOGRAPHS.

footwear See BOOT; MOCCASIN; SANDAL.

foraging The seeking of food or supplies. The term can be used synonymously with HUNTING-GATHERING of all animals and wild plants but more often is applied to the gathering or collecting of wild plants, insects, and small animals such as lizards.

Foraging period See ARCHAIC PERIOD.

Formative Indians PREHISTORIC INDIANS of the FORMATIVE PERIOD. North American prehistory is usually defined as the PALEOLITHIC PERIOD, ARCHAIC PERIOD, and Formative period. During the Formative, from about 1000 B.C. to A.D. 1500, Indian life among agricultural tribes north of Mexico reached a high degree of organization and artistic expression: East of the Mississippi River were the MOUNDBUILDERS of the ADENA CULTURE, HOPEWELL CULTURE, and MISSISSIPPIAN CULTURE; west of the Mississippi in the Southwest were the peoples of the MOGOLLON CULTURE, HOHOKAM CULTURE, and ANASAZI CULTURE. There were other cultures, also characterized by agriculture, domesticated

animals, village life, houses, trade, pottery, weaving, basketry, the bow and arrow, refined craftsmanship, and elaborate religious ceremonies. Many cultural traits typical of Formative Indians were developed during the Archaic period or before: Indians in present-day Mexico cultivated plants as early as about 7000 B.C.; Indians north of Mexico farmed as early as about 3500 B.C. But agriculture and other typical Formative lifeways became widespread among Native North Americans only after about 1000 B.C.

Formative period A period of prehistory, lasting from about 1000 B.C. to A.D. 1500. What usually is called the Formative period in North America corresponds to the Preclassic period, CLASSIC PERIOD, and Postclassic period in MESOAMERICA.

fossil Any impression or trace of an animal or plant from a past geological era. A fossil beach, no longer next to water, is a shoreline of an earlier age. (See also PALEONTOLOGY.)

Four Directions See CARDINAL POINTS.

Fox (Mesquakie, Mesquaki, Outagamie, Outagami) An ALGONQUIAN-speaking tribe of the NORTHEAST CULTURE AREA, located on Lake Winnebago and the Fox River, and later on the Wisconsin River, in present-day Wisconsin. The Foxes are related linguistically to the SACS and KICKAPOOS. In the late 1700s, they occupied lands in present-day Illinois near their allies, the Sacs, against the ILLINOIS. In the early 1800s, they also occupied lands in present-day Iowa. Some Fox bands were relocated to present-day Kansas and then to Oklahoma; others stayed in or returned to Iowa. The Sac and Fox Tribe holds trust lands near Shawnee, Oklahoma; other Sacs and Foxes hold the Sac and Fox Reservation near Tama, Iowa. The name Fox is derived from the Algonquian *wagosh*, or "red fox," originally the name of a clan. The Fox native name is *Meshkwakikug* or *Mesquakie*, meaning "red-earth people." In their Algonquian dialect, the CHIPPEWAS called them *Outaga-mie*, meaning "people of the other shore."

Fremont Culture   A cultural tradition of the Great Basin, starting about A.D. 400. Although the center of this culture was located in present-day Utah, some scholars consider it to be a Southwest tradition with influences of the ANASAZI CULTURE, perhaps even an offshoot. Some Fremont village sites were abandoned by about A.D. 950; only a few remained after about A.D. 1300. It is not known whether Fremont peoples were ancestral to some among the GREAT BASIN INDIANS.

French Indians   Indian tribes allied with the French in colonial times. The ALGONQUIAN-speaking tribes of the Great Lakes and Maine, with the CHIPPEWAS and ABENAKIS being the most powerful, were for the most part allies of the French against the English in the French and Indian Wars of 1689 to 1763.

fresco   An art or method of painting on wet plaster by pressing in PIGMENTS ground and dissolved in water; or the resulting work itself.   MESOAMERICAN INDIANS made frescos.

Fresh Water   See TIMUCUA.

frontier   A region at the edge or just beyond a particular country's settled area, where flora and fauna exist in their relatively natural state. The term frontier typically is used for the lands beyond white settlement, in itself an ETHNOCENTRIC concept. To Europeans and their descendants, lands uninhabited by whites seemed wild. Yet for Native Americans, their homelands were not a frontier; from their vantage point, the frontier might be said to have extended onto lands appropriated and altered by whites. The term frontier remained in official use among whites until 1890, at which time the Federal Census Bureau announced it could no longer designate a contiguous frontier line beyond white settlement on its map of

the United States, as it had at the start of previous decades.

frontier painter   (frontier artist)   An individual who traveled among Indian tribes in the 19th century to record their images through drawings and paintings. Many artists sketched their subjects in the field and finished painting them in the studio. George Catlin is the most famous of the frontier painters; he was active in the mid-1800s.

frontier photographer   An individual who traveled among Indian peoples in the late 19th and early 20th century to record their images through photography, such as Edward Curtis.

frontlet   An ornament or band (browband) worn on the forehead; a type of HEADDRESS. NORTHWEST COAST INDIANS carved frontlets symbolizing CLAN EMBLEMS out of wood, painted them, and inlaid them with pieces of shell, copper, or, in post-Contact times, mirrors. The INUITS wore decorated pieces of ivory as ceremonial frontlets.

fry bread   (squaw bread)   Bread prepared by dropping dough in hot oil; usually it is shaped flat and round and it puffs up when cooked. When made by SOUTHEAST INDIANS with CORNMEAL, it is known as pone bread. At modern-day POWWOWS, fry bread is served with butter, sugar, or jam, as a part of "Navajo tacos."

funeral   See BURIAL.

fur   The thick coat of hair covering an animal, or a dressed animal PELT. (See also FUR TRADE; SKIN-DRESSING.)

furniture   Indian peoples used mats, ROBES, and BLANKETS as seats, bedding, screens, and for serving food. Sometimes wooden or wicker frames were built to hold the above. Down, bark, and moss were used to stuff pillows. Stones also were used as tables and chairs. IROQUOIS Indians had bunkbeds in their LONGHOUSES. INUITS had stone LAMPS. CHESTS, BASKETS, and other CONTAINERS were used for storage. Possessions also were hung from TEPEE poles and from other HOUSEPOSTS or beams. (See also HAMMOCK.)

fur trade Indians bartered FURS for European trade goods, including iron tools, cloth, glass beads, firearms, and alcoholic beverages. The demand for furs was a driving factor in the European development of the North American colonies. The French, Dutch, English, Russians, and, to a lesser extent, the Spanish developed an economy around the export of furs to Europe. Some tribes became partners in the enterprise: The HURONS acted as middlemen in trade with the French; it is thought that the IROQUOIS invaded Huron territory in the mid-1600s to keep up their own supply of beaver PELTS with the Dutch, then English. The ALEUTS were forced to participate in the Russian venture by the taking of their families hostage. Fur companies, such as the Hudson's Bay Company, the North West Company, the Russian-American Company, the American Fur Company, and the Missouri Fur Company, were chartered to exploit this resource; much of the non-Indian exploration of the Canadian and American West in the late 19th and early 20th centuries resulted from the fur trade. Some tribes consistently resisted the incursions onto their lands by traders, hunters, and trappers and the establishment of trading posts; the TLINGITS battled the Russians in Alaska; the BLACKFOOT Indians fought the MOUNTAIN MEN on the Northern Plains. The world fur market remained vital until about 1840, when the beaver hat went out of style in Europe. (See also COUREUR DE BOIS; *PROMYSHLENNIKI*; *SWANNEKEN*; VOYAGEUR.)

.G.

Gabrielino See MISSION INDIANS; UTO-AZTECAN.

Galaxy Society (Galaxy Fraternity, Neweekwe, Newekwe) A MEDICINE SOCIETY of the ZUNI Indians that attempts to cure the sick by acting like CLOWNS and releasing worries.

galena A blue-gray mineral with a metallic luster, the principal ore of lead. Prized for ceremonial purposes, it has been found in its raw form at MOUNDBUILDER sites.

Galice See TALTUSHTUNTUDE.

gambling A traditional activity of Native Americans in a variety of games, such as DICE, GUESSING GAMES, and RACING. In contemporary Indian America, some tribes have used their sovereign, tax-exempt status to open gambling casinos on reservations. (See also BINGO.)

game A term that can be used interchangeably with SPORT, but "games" are not necessarily athletic and can involve GAMBLING or the use of TOYS as well. For many American Indians, games have traditionally had symbolic and ceremonial meaning. According to some traditions, deities play games with humans; human affairs thus resemble a game of chance. "Game" also refers to animals hunted for food or sport. (See also BALL-GAME; CATEGORICAL APPENDIX, "GAMES, SPORTS, AND TOYS"; GUESSING GAME; SONG FIGHT; TOY.)

game of straw See GUESSING GAME.

gaming piece An artifact or natural object used in a GAME.

gan (Mountain Spirit) A spiritual being in APACHE tradition, a Mountain Spirit. According to legend, the gans brought agriculture to the people and are the guardians of wildlife. They are honored in the MOUNTAIN SPIRIT DANCE. The gans are the equivalent of the YEI of the NAVAJOS.

gathering See FORAGING; HUNTING-GATHERING.

Ge A language family and subdivision of the GE-PANO-CARIB phylum comprising dialects spoken by SOUTH AMERICAN INDIANS, including the Bororo, Botocudo, Caingang, Canella, Cayapo, Shavante, and Sherente tribes of present-day central and southern Brazil; the Manasi tribe of present-day eastern Bolivia; and others.

genesis story See CREATION STORY.

genizaro A New Mexican Indian who has adopted a Mexican way of life, often the descendant of Indians captured by the Spanish and raised Hispanic.

gens (pl., gentes) An anthropological term for an intertribal EXOGAMOUS, PATRILINEAL grouping. Some scholars have defined a gens as patrilineal and a CLAN as MATRILINEAL, but "clan" is now more commonly applied to groups with both types of lineage. The name of the gens is referred to as the gentile name.

geology The study of the earth and its rocks, including structure, origin, and history. Geological studies are relevant to ARCHAEOLOGY.

Ge-Pano-Carib A phylum of language stocks, including the CARIBAN, GE, GUAY-CURUAN, and PANOAN families.

German silver (nickel silver, white brass) An alloy of COPPER, nickel, and zinc. In the 19th century, PLAINS INDIANS began using German silver in place of true SILVER to make jewelry.

ghost Different tribes have had varying beliefs and customs concerning ghosts, i.e., ancestor spirits. PLAINS INDIANS and PLATEAU INDIANS, for example, traditionally believed in a world of ghosts in the distant west beyond a river that must be crossed by canoe. The IROQUOIS believed that dead warriors accompanied live warriors into battle. The FLATHEADS have perceived ghosts as GUARDIAN SPIRITS. Some PUEBLO INDIANS associate ghosts with OWLS. The NAVAJOS believe that ghosts interact with people and are dangerous if their pattern is disturbed; in their tradition, not following the proper burial routine or continuing to use the house of a deceased person can lead to "ghost infection." Because of their fear of ghosts rising from the dead, the Navajos, unlike most other western tribes, rejected the GHOST DANCE RELIGION. (See also DOUBLE; SOUL; SPIRIT.)

Ghost Dance A name applied to different religious revitalization movements. Some scholars distinguish between a Ghost Dance of 1870, founded by the PAIUTE prophet Wodziwob, and the later derivative Ghost Dance of 1889–90, often called the GHOST DANCE RELIGION. The earlier Ghost Dance also influenced the BOLE-MARU RELIGION and its offshoot the Big Head Religion, as well as the DREAM DANCE and EARTH LODGE RELIGION. Ghost Dances all called for a return to traditional, pre-Contact ways of life and honored the native dead while predicting their resurrection.

Ghost Dance Religion (Spirit Dance, Ghost Dance Religion) A religious revitalization movement of the Far West and Great Plains that grew out of earlier religions' GHOST DANCE traditions. It was founded by Wovoka (Jack Wilson), a Paiute and son of the visionary Tavibo. Following a visionary experience on January 1, 1889 during an eclipse of the sun, Wovoka predicted that the world would soon end, then come alive again. Indians, including the dead from past ages, would inherit a regenerated earth filled with lush prairie grasses and herds of buffalo. To earn this new reality, Indians had to live in harmony and avoid the ways of whites, especially alcohol. Rituals in the Ghost Dance Religion included meditation, prayers, chanting, and Ghost Dancing. While dancing, participants supposedly could catch a glimpse of the world-to-be. The movement spread throughout the West, especially among the SIOUX, leading up to the massacre of Indians by white soldiers at WOUNDED KNEE in 1890. (See also GHOST SHIRT.)

Ghost Keeping Ceremony (Wanagi yuhapi) The rituals surrounding the SIOUX (Lakota) custom of a family's keeping the soul of a deceased person in a symbolic ghost bundle for as much as a year. After ritual purification has been completed, the soul is released to the SPIRIT WORLD.

Ghost Shirt A ceremonial SHIRT worn by Ghost Dancers of the GHOST DANCE

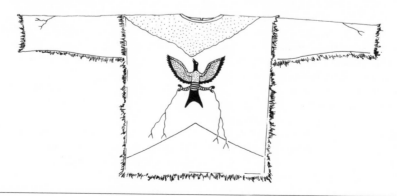

Sioux Ghost Shirt

RELIGION. The SIOUX probably first conceived of the shirts, which supposedly could stop bullets. ARAPAHOS and other PLAINS INDIANS made this particular custom part of their interpretation of the religious movement.

gifting See GIVEAWAY; POTLATCH.

Gilenos (Gila, Xila) A subtribe of the APACHE Indians, part of the larger Chiricahua-Mescalero grouping. The Gilenos or Gila division includes the CHIRICAHUA, MIMBRENO, MOGOLLON, and WARM SPRINGS bands. The name is taken from the Gila River in Arizona. (See also MESCALERO.)

Gitchee Manitou (Gitche Manitou, Kitchi Manito) The Supreme Being, CREATOR, or GREAT SPIRIT in CHIPPEWA tradition. Other ALGONQUIANS have variations in spelling. The ABENAKI version is "Ktsi Nwaska." (See also MANITOU; WAKAN TANKA.)

Gitksan (Kitksan) A PENUTIAN-speaking (Tsimshian or Chimmesyan isolate) tribe of the NORTHWEST COAST CULTURE AREA, located on the upper Skeena River in present-day British Columbia. The Gitskans are related linguistically to the TSIMSHIANS and NISGA'AS. The Gitanmaax, Gitwangak, Glen Voowell, Hagwilget, and Kitwancool bands hold reserves in British Columbia. *Gitkskan* means "people of Ksian (Skeena) River" in Penutian.

giveaway A ceremony involving gifting, the custom of sharing property or making some other personal sacrifice to honor the recipient and earn prestige for the giver. The giver (or givers, such as an entire family) acknowledges acceptance of responsibilities. The term giveaway appears especially in studies of PLAINS INDIANS. *Otu'han* is the SIOUAN (Lakota) ceremony. (See also POTLATCH.)

glacier A mass of ice, accumulating when snowfall in the winter exceeds summer melt-

ing; the ice moves slowly, descending from mountains (valley glaciers) or outward from centers of accumulation (continental glaciers). "Glacial" is the adjective form, as in a "glacial lake," formed by a glacier. "Glaciation" refers to glacial action. (See also PLEISTOCENE.)

glaze (enamel) A coating added to POTTERY before FIRING, consisting of minerals that melt in high temperatures, then resolidify to create a vitreous surface. The term glaze can refer to any glassy surface that results from polishing. (See also SLIP.)

glottochronology (lexicostatistics) The classification of language vocabularies and what they reveal with regard to linguistic origin and divergence.

glue Native Americans used a variety of materials to create adhesives, including tree resins, animal neck muscles and horns, and fish glands. (See also PITCH.)

Gluskap (Gluscap, Gluskabe, Gluskabi, Glooskap, Gloskap, Koluscap, Kloskap, The Liar) A CULTURE HERO, TRICKSTER figure, and creative force in ABENAKI tradition; the twin brother of Malsum, the Wolf. "Gluskap" is the most common version of the name among northern members of the Abenaki Confederacy, such as the MALECITES and MICMACS. "Gluskabi" is the equivalent figure among the more southern members, the PASSAMAQUODDDIES and PENOBSCOTS. (See also MANEBOZHO.)

glyph A carved PICTOGRAPH, either incised or in relief, as found in stone. Also used specifically for a unit of MAYA writing.

glyph writing See GLYPH; PETROGLYPH; PICTOGRAPH; TERRAGLYPH.

god See CATEGORICAL APPENDIX, "SPIRITS AND LEGENDARY BEINGS"; LEGENDARY BEING; SPIRITUAL BEING.

goggles A device worn over the head to shade the eyes. In addition to hats with visors, the INUITS fashioned wood and ivory goggles with one or two narrow slits to block out the sun's glare reflected from snow (snow goggles) and from the ocean.

gold MESOAMERICAN INDIANS, CIRCUM-CARIBBEAN, and SOUTH AMERICAN INDIANS used gold, a precious metal, in the making of ceremonial objects and ornaments. (See also GOLD RUSH; GOLDWORK; MINING.)

gold rush Historically, gold rushes — such as the California Gold Rush of 1848–49 and the Colorado (Pikes Peak) Gold Rush of 1858–59 — have meant the displacement and cultural dispossession of native peoples. Gold strikes brought numerous settlers and migrants to Indian lands.

goldwork The act, process, or resulting artifact of work in GOLD. Goldwork was typical of MESOAMERICAN INDIANS and SOUTH AMERICAN INDIANS, especially the INCAS of present-day Peru and the Indians of present-day Colombia. Objects found north of Mexico probably were trade items from Middle and South America or bounty from Spanish ships that were wrecked on their return journeys to Europe carrying gold stolen from native peoples. A goldworker also is called a goldsmith. (See also MISE EN COULEUR; *TUMBAGA*.)

gorge See FISHHOOK.

gorgerin A shell disk typical of MOUND-BUILDERS of the MISSISSIPPIAN CULTURE, with engraved or cut-out designs; about four to eight inches in diameter with two holes, indicating use as a pendant. (See also RUNTEE.)

gorget An ornamental plaque, tablet, or piece of armor worn over the throat (and sometimes the chest, in those instances making the term synonymous with BREAST-PLATE). Some gorgets were perforated and suspended by a string, i.e., types of PEN-DANTS; others were attached to clothing. Shell, sheet copper, and, to a lesser extent, stone were preferred materials for gorgets,

which were often elaborately carved. Typical of MOUNDBUILDERS. (See also BAR-GORGET.)

Goshute (Goshiute, Gosiute) A subtribe of the SHOSHONE (Western Shoshone) Indians, located on the shores of the Great Salt Lake in present-day Utah. The Goshutes originally were thought to be related to the UTES, with whom they intermarried. Descendants hold the Goshute Reservation in Juab County, Utah, and White Pine County, Nevada, and the Skull Valley Reservation in Tooele County, Utah.

gouge A CHISEL with a grooved, scoop-shaped cutting edge, used for cutting channels in wood and stone or for removing bone marrow. Gouges typically were made from stone, bone, antler, or shell. A beaver tooth set in a wooden handle also served as a gouge.

gourd Native Americans used the shells of the gourd (family Cucurbitaceae) for a variety of tools, utensils, and containers, such as pottery smoothers, spoons, and water jugs, as well as for ceremonial objects, such as RATTLES and MASKS. (See also SQUASH.)

Gourd Dance (Gourd Clan Dance) A ceremony originating in 1838 among the KI-OWA Indians, where it was held by a warrior society after a victory. What became the Kiowa Gourd Dance Society (*T'anpeko*, for "skunkberry people") came to sponsor the tribe's annual SUN DANCE. Repressed along with the Sun Dance by federal officials in the late 19th and early 20th century, the Gourd Dance was revived in the 1950s. It is now sponsored annually by the Tian-paye (Tiah-pah) Society of Kiowas, held in early July, and includes the Brush Dance and other rituals.

government See FEDERAL INDIAN POL-ICY; SOVEREIGNTY; TRIBAL GOVERNMENT.

granary A storehouse or repository for grain. SOUTHWEST INDIANS typically stored

Southwest Indian granary

their grain in large baskets with thatched covers, raised on wooden platforms for protection from insects and animals.

grandfather Like GRANDMOTHER, the concept of grandfather is important to many Native American tribes since it refers to an ELDER of the tribe. The GREAT SPIRIT, i.e., the CREATOR, is sometimes referred to as grandfather, as in the SIOUAN (Nakota) phrase *Wakantanka Tunkasina*, translating as "god grandfather." The LENNI LENAPES (Delawares) were known as Grandfather among other ALGONQUIANS because their territory was the original homeland of the people in their legends.

Grand Medicine Society See MIDEWIWIN SOCIETY.

grandmother An expression of respect for a female ELDER among American Indians of many tribes. It also is applied to animals. Among the SHAWNEES, "Our Grandmother" (Lithikapo' shi, Papoothkwe, or Shikalapikshi) is considered the CREATOR. (See also GRANDFATHER; GRANDMOTHER SPIDER.)

Grandmother Spider (Spider Woman) A legendary being of SOUTHWEST INDIANS in particular the NAVAJOS and PUEBLO INDIANS. Grandmother Spider is considered a creative force who introduced WEAVING to the people.

grand sachem The CHIEF of a CONFEDERACY. (See also SACHEM; SAGAMORE.)

Grand Soleil See GREAT SUN.

Grass Dance (Omaha Dance, Omaha Society Dance) A ceremony of the PLAINS INDIANS as well as some NORTHEAST INDIANS, probably originating among the PAWNEES. The Grass Dance has elements in common with the IRUSKA DANCE; it has been called the Omaha Dance because the OMAHAS taught it to the SIOUX. The Sioux called it *Peji Mgnaka Wacipi*, meaning "they dance with grass tucked in their belts." While the braided grass BUSTLES symbolized scalps taken in battle, the Grass Dance was not a WAR DANCE, although whites sometimes called it that. Nor was it the true SCALP DANCE, which was performed only by women. It was, however, considered a victory celebration. The Grass Dance is thought to have led to the modern-day contest dancing known as the FANCY DANCE. Among the SHOSHONES, a ritual also known as the Grass Dance was performed in a circle by men and women to help the grass grow.

grass house (grass lodge) A house covered with grass, typical of the CADDOS and WICHITAS. Such a dwelling traditionally had

Wichita grass house

long poles erected in a circle, usually 40 to 50 feet in diameter, with the tops meeting in a domed or conical shape; the framework was tied together with CORDAGE, then covered with grass or THATCH. Sometimes four doors were built in the direction of the CARDINAL POINTS; or two doors were made, one facing east, to be used with the morning sun, and the other facing west, to be used with the afternoon sun.

grasswork The act, process, or resulting artifact of work made from any of the numerous grasses, i.e., plants of the family Gramineae, having narrow leaves and hollow, jointed stems; or work in any plants similar to true grasses. American Indians used grasses for covering houses; making bedding, rope, and brushes; weaving mats, baskets, and clothing; lining CACHES; igniting fires; plus numerous other applications. (See also GRASS HOUSE; SWEET GRASS; THATCH.)

grave A place of BURIAL, usually excavated. (See also GRAVEHOUSE.)

grave goods Objects found in a BURIAL along with the corpse, originally placed there as OFFERINGS.

gravehouse A house used for the deposit of ashes following CREMATION. The TLINGITS originally built log, then plank, gravehouses about eight feet square for family ashes. The front often was painted or carved with a family CREST. (See also HOUSE BURIAL.)

graver See BURIN.

Great Basin Culture Area A geographical and cultural region in the American West, corresponding to the central depression and surrounding highlands known as the Great Basin. To the east stand the Rocky Mountains; to the west, the Sierra Nevada; to the north, the Columbia Plateau; and to the south, the Colorado Plateau. This CULTURE AREA includes territory comprising almost all of present-day Nevada and Utah; parts of Idaho, Oregon, Wyoming, Colorado, and California; and small parts of Arizona and New Mexico; a total of about 210,000 square miles. The basin is a region of interior drainage, i.e., rivers and streams draining from the flanking higher ground and disappearing into sinks in the sandy soil. The mountains block the rain and snow blowing in from the ocean, resulting in low precipitation and high evaporation. In past ages, the Great Basin contained many large lakes, the largest body of water remaining being the Great Salt Lake in present-day Utah. The geological formation of the region led to the creation of alkaline flats, i.e., soil with mineral salts from evaporated bodies of water. Only occasional low and long rocky uplands break up the long stretches of barren desert. Because of the aridity, flora and fauna are scarce. The dominant plant life on the desert floor are low grasses and sagebrush. The hills have some trees that are adapted to dryness, such as juniper and PIÑON. The most common large mammal is the PRONGHORN, which grazes on grass and brush. Mountain goats subsist in the rocky highlands. Jackrabbits live in the desert, as do rodents, including field mice, kangaroo rats, muskrats, gophers, and ground squirrels. Certain birds and reptiles, particularly snakes and lizards, also are suited to desert life. As for insects, grasshoppers are in abundance. All these creatures provided food for the GREAT BASIN INDIANS, who also foraged and dug for edible wild plants. With a few exceptions, inhabitants practiced no agriculture in the extreme environment. Great Basin peoples traveled mostly in small bands of extended families and lived in WICKIUPS. In post-Contact times, some tribes began using TEPEES.

Great Basin Indians Four major tribal groups are considered part of the GREAT BASIN CULTURE AREA: PAIUTE, UTE, SHOSHONE, and BANNOCK. All four tribes, plus smaller tribal offshoots, speak dialects of the UTO-AZTECAN language families. The only exception is the WASHOE tribe in the western part of the culture area, who speak a HOKAN dialect. Great Basin peoples have been referred to collectively as DIGGER INDIANS.

Great House   A ceremonial house of the YUROK Indians. People belonged to the houses as if to a SECRET SOCIETY and together owned particular rituals.

Great Kiva   See KIVA.

Great Lakes Indians   Indian tribes living next to or near the Great Lakes, i.e., Lake Ontario, Lake Erie, Lake Huron, Lake Michigan, and Lake Superior. The phrase "upper (or western) Great Lakes Indians" refers to tribes of the geographical region including the drainage basins of Lake Huron, Lake Michigan, and Lake Superior. Except for the IROQUAOIAN speaking tribes in the east, and the SIOUAN-speaking WINNEBAGOS in the west, the Great Lakes Indians were ALGONQUIAN-speaking.

Great Plains Culture Area   The geographical and cultural region extending, east to west, from the Mississippi River Valley to the Rocky Mountains; and, north to south, from territory in present-day Manitoba, Saskatchewan, and Alberta in Canada as far as central Texas. The treeless grassland consists of two types: In the Mississippi Valley, a region sometimes called the Prairie Plains, or simply the "prairies," there is tall grass; to the west, in a region known as the high plains, or the Great Plains, there is short grass due to lesser rainfall. The plains are interrupted in places by some stands of trees, especially willows and cottonwoods along the numerous tributaries flowing eastward into the Missouri and Mississippi rivers. In some locations, highlands, dotted by pine trees, rise up from the plains: the Ozarks of Missouri and Arkansas; Black Hills of South Dakota and Wyoming; and Badlands of South Dakota. Deer, elk, pronghorns, bears, wolves, coyotes, and rabbits formerly were abundant on the grass-lands. The environment was especially suitable to the BUFFALO, which was central to the economy of the PLAINS INDIANS, providing meat for food as well as hides, bones, and horns for shelter, clothing, and tools. The typical way of life of this CULTURE AREA evolved after the arrival of whites. Ancient Indians once had lived in the region, but it is theorized that they left in the 13th century because of drought. With the arrival of the HORSE, first brought to North America by the Spanish in the 16th century, native peoples no longer had to depend on farming along the fertile river valleys to supply enough food for their people; they began ranging over a wide area in search of the buffalo herds, carrying their possessions with them. Portable TEPEES proved practical for life on the trail. Not all tribes on the plains abandoned farming and their permanent villages of EARTHLODGES or GRASS HOUSES. But, with horses, seminomadic PRAIRIE INDIANS—sometimes distinguished as separate from Plains Indians—tended to leave for longer periods of time on wide-ranging hunting expeditions.

Great Spirit (Great Mystery)   A translation of a variety of Indian names for the personification of the all-pervasive spirit; also called the CREATOR, supreme being, All-Power, or Master of Life. The Great Spirit is sometimes perceived as a figure. (See also GITCHEE MANITOU; GRANDFATHER; WAKAN-TANKA.)

Great Sun (Grand Soleil)   The hereditary title of a CHIEF of the NATCHEZ Indians, considered to be a descendant of the sun. Since the French were the first Europeans to write about the Natchez, their version of the title, *Grand Soleil*, is often found in English writings. "Suns," "Honored People," "Nobles," and "Stinkards" also were part of the Natchez CASTE SYSTEM.

"Great White Father"   A name used by certain tribes for the President of the United States. Originated either by whites or Indians.

Green Corn Ceremony (Green Corn Dance, busk) An annual renewal and thanksgiving festival performed by the CREEKS, SEMINOLES, and other SOUTH-EAST INDIANS, when the corn was in the roasting-ear stage, usually late July or August. The ceremony lasted four to eight days. Old fires were extinguished; a new SACRED FIRE was lit from which every household obtained fire. New tools and weapons were made; new clothing was donned. Wrongdoers were forgiven for most crimes except murder. There was ritual fasting, and the BLACK DRINK was taken for purification. Also called the busk, from the MUSKOGEAN word PUSKITA, meaning "fasting." The IROQUOIS and SHAWNEES have comparable Green Corn celebrations.

Grigra See TUNICAN.

grindstone (grinding stone) A stone for shaping and sharpening tools, a type of ABRADER. A WHETSTONE is a small hand-held variety. Indians commonly used sandstone as a grindstone.

Gros Ventre (Atsina) An ALGONQUIAN-speaking tribe of the GREAT PLAINS CULTURE AREA, located on the Milk River, a tributary of the Missouri in present-day northern Montana, ranging as far north as the Saskatchewan River in present-day Saskatchewan. The Gros Ventres may have lived formerly in the Red River region of present-day Minnesota and North Dakota, as one people with the ARAPAHOS; they are thought to have migrated westward to the headwaters of the Missouri River sometime in the 1700s and subdivided, the Gros Ventres heading north and the Arapahos south. For part of their history, the Gros Ventres were members of the Blackfoot Confederacy. Descendants share the Fort Belknap Reservation near Harlem, Montana, with the ASSINIBOINES. *Gros Ventre* is French for "big belly," because of their tribal name in the SIGN LANGUAGE of the PLAINS INDIANS, which was a sweeping pass over the abdomen to indicate that they were big eaters.

The alternate name *Atsina* probably is the BLACKFOOT term for "gut people." The French distinguished the *Gros Ventres des Plaines* ("of the plains"), i.e., the Atsinas, from the *Gros Ventres de la Rivière* ("of the river"), i.e., the HIDATSAS.

Guacata See MUSKOGEAN.

Guaicuruan See GUAYCURUAN.

Guale See MUSKOGEAN.

guanaco See LLAMA.

Guarani See TUPI-GUARANI.

guardian spirit (tutelar, tutelary) A legendary being or ANCESTOR spirit who takes special interest in an individual and protects him or her from dangers. In the VISION QUEST, a guardian spirit is sought. SPIRIT HELPER and spirit power are similar concepts. (See also OYARON.)

guava Any of various trees and shrubs of the genus *Psidium*, especially *P. guajava*, of tropical and semitropical America, with a berrylike fruit; also, the fruit itself. The word guava is of ARAWAKAN origin; the Spanish version is *guayaba*.

Guaycuruan (Guaicuruan) A language family and subdivision of the GE-PANO-CARIB phylum comprising dialects spoken by SOUTH AMERICAN INDIANS, including the Abipon, Matacoan, Mbaya, and Payagua tribes of present-day Paraguay; the Charrua tribe of present-day Uruguay; and others.

guessing game Guessing GAMES were widely distributed in many different forms and were often ritualized with accompanying songs. In the hand game (or simply hand), a player holds two bone or wooden cylinders, one plain and one marked, in the hands, while another player tries to guess which hand has the unmarked object. The game also is played by teams. Sometimes four cylinders are used. The hunt-the-button game is a similar hand game. In the hidden-ball game, a ball or stick is shuffled and hidden under one or four tubes or under moccasins (sometimes called the moccasin game). In the stick game, a player shuffles sticks, then divides them into bundles; another player has to guess which bundle has the marked stick. In the game of straw, players guess whether splints or reeds separated from a main bundle are odd or even-numbered. The Indian names and translations vary.

guide A person who shows the way to another person or group of people. Indian guides, such as the SHOSHONE woman Saca-jawea of the Lewis and Clark Expedition, helped European and Euroamerican explorers find their way through uncharted territory. Indians also served as guides and SCOUTS for military expeditions, often acting as INTERPRETERS, too.

guide flake See FLAKE.

gun See FIREARM.

gypsum See ALABASTER.

H

hacha An ax-shape stone sculpture, depicting a human face in profile; typical of the Totonacs of the Gulf Coast of present-day central Mexico. As with PALMAS and YUGOS, *hachas* are thought to be ceremonial. *Hacha* means "hatchet" in Spanish.

hacienda A large estate, especially one used for farming or ranching. Under the Spanish hacienda system of the 17th to 19th century, the *hacendado* (estate's owner) had a company store, where overpriced merchandise was supplied on credit to Indian laborers. Because in many cases the laborers never managed to eliminate their debt, the system amounted to a form of slavery. (See also ENCOMIENDA.)

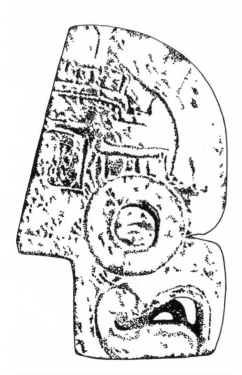

Mesoamerican *hacha*

haft The handle of a tool. A hafted tool has, or once had, a handle.

hageota An IROQUOIS term in IROQUOIAN for a traveling storyteller, typically a man, who journeys among his people, exchanging stories for lodging, food, and gifts.

Haida (Kaigani) A NADENE-speaking (Haida isolate) tribe of the NORTHWEST CULTURE AREA, located on the Queen Charlotte Islands in present-day British Columbia. In the early 1700s, one band settled on southern Prince Wales Island in present-day Alaska, where the people came to be known as Kaigani. The Masset band at Masset and Skidegate band at Queen Charlotte City maintain tribal identity in British Columbia. A community of Haidas also live at Hydaburg, Alaska. *Haida* means "people" in Nadene. The Haida language used to be classified as a distinct stock, Skittagetan.

hair pipe (shell hair pipe) A tubular bead, hollow, cylindrical, and more than an inch and a half in length; usually made of shell, but also of bone, copper, stone, and, in post-Contact times, glass and plastic. Hair pipes are suspended from clothing and used to make BREASTPLATES.

hairstyle (hairdo, hair form) Different hairstyles were typical of different tribes, although within most tribes individual expression was prevalent. Implements included grass brushes; wood, stone, and ivory combs; and pointed sticks. Both men and women used animal fat as a dressing, and plant products as perfumes and shampoos. (See also BRAIDWORK; HEADGEAR; ROACH; SCALPLOCK; SQUASH-BLOSSOM HAIRDO.)

hairwork The act, process, or resulting artifact of work in human and animal hair.

Hair from humans, horses, dogs, deer, and numerous other mammals was utilized in wigs, ornaments, and stuffing as well as for twisting rope and WEAVING. (See also FUR; ROACH.)

Haisla (Kitamat) A WAKASHAN-speaking tribe of the NORTHWEST COAST CULTURE AREA, located on the Douglas Channel in present-day British Columbia. The name Haisla is sometimes applied to a language dialect of the Kitamat and Kitlope bands; it is related to the HEILTSUK and KWAKIUTL dialects. A Haisla band known as Kitamaat has its tribal headquarters at Kitamaat Village, British Columbia.

Hako Ceremony (Pipe Dance) A springtime ceremony of the PAWNEE Indians, probably originally for the purpose of tribal fertility but now for ensuring good fortune and peace between bands or clans. In the five-day ceremony of about 100 different dances and other rituals—such as smoking a SACRED PIPE and exchanging gifts—one group, known as the Fathers, sponsors the ceremony and makes a ritual visit to a second group, the Children. *Hako* is a CADDOAN word for "pipe."

Halchidhoma See YUMAN.

"half-breed" A person of part-Indian and part-white ancestry, although not necessarily half and half. The term was widely used in the 19th century, often derogatorily; "MIXED-BLOOD," or "a person of mixed ancestry," are more common terms now. "Half-breed" was sometimes shortened to "breed." (See also METIS; MESTIZO.)

Halkomelem See COWICHAN.

hallucinogen See PSYCHOTROPIC SUBSTANCE.

Halyikwamai See YUMAN.

Hamatsa Dance (Cannibal Dance) A ceremony of the KWAKIUTL Indians for initiation into the Hamatsa Society, part of a series of dances in the Winter Ceremonial. An initiate had to fast for several days in the woods until he acted as if possessed by a cannibal spirit. Wearing hemlock boughs on his head and wrists, he would be lured into the Hamatsa lodge by a naked woman, then dance a frenzied dance while others sang. During the Hamatsa Dance, one member would impersonate Man Eater, a cannibilistic being. Other members represented Man Eater's army of creatures, most of them birdlike: the Crooked Beak of Heaven, who supposedly devours human flesh; the Raven, who devours human eyes; the Hoxhok, who has a taste for human brains; and the Grizzly Bear, who uses his massive paws to disembowel humans. A POTLATCH often followed the ritual.

hammer A tool, made of any hard material, especially stone, for striking, pounding, and chipping. Some were held directly in the hand; others had handles attached by thongs to a groove in the head. CLUBS sometimes doubled as hammers. Some large hammers—what might be called mauls and sledges—were designed for more than one person. (See also HAMMERSTONE.)

hammerstone A stone used as a HAMMER, typically rounded. Some were hafted, with grooves or pits for fastening handles.

hammock A swinging bed or couch suspended between two trees or other supports. A Native American invention—adopted worldwide—and the dominant sleeping place on European ships for centuries. Typical of SOUTH AMERICAN INDIANS, CIRCUM-CARIBBEAN INDIANS, and MESOAMERICAN INDIANS. The Spanish version *hamaca* derives from the ARAWAKAN word *amaca*.

Han An ATHAPASCAN-speaking tribe of the SUBARCTIC CULTURE AREA, located on the Yukon River in present-day east-central Alaska and the Yukon Territory. The Hans probably merged with other Athapascans.

hanblecheyapi (hanbleceya) The VISION QUEST of the SIOUX Indians. *Hanble* means "to fast and attain vision"; *cheyapi* means "to cry or weep" in Siouan; thus, the term means "crying for a vision." (See also LAMENTING.)

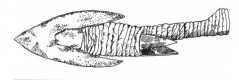

Makah harpoon point for whaling

handball Any BALL-GAME using hands as opposed to feet or rackets.

handgame See GUESSING GAME.

Handsome Lake Religion See LONGHOUSE RELIGION.

handstone See MANO.

hand-trembling A method of diagnosing or divining illness among the NAVAJOS. The hand-trembler obtains his or her powers though dreams and visions; various offerings of pollen, turquoise, and shells are made and songs or chants performed. The shaking during singing, i.e., the "motion-in-the-hand," gives the DIAGNOSTICIAN insight; he recommends particular HEALING ceremonies and a PRACTITIONER to perform them. (See also STARGAZING.)

"happy hunting ground" A non-Indian term to describe the Indian view of the AFTERWORLD; probably first used by whites in the 1800s.

Hare (Kawchottine, Kawchoddine) An ATHAPASCAN-speaking tribe of the SUBARCTIC CULTURE AREA, located to the west and northwest of Great Bear Lake in Canada's present-day Northwest Territories. Two current Hare bands, Fort Franklin and Fort Good Hope, hold reserves in their ancestral homeland. The alternate name *Kawchottine* means "people of the great hare" in Athapascan.

harpoon A spearlike weapon, typical of the INUITS and NORTHWEST COAST INDIANS, having a barbed and sometimes detachable head, used in fishing and hunting sea mammals. Lines between the heads and

foreshaft (also sometimes detachable from the main shaft) secure the catch. FLOATS often are attached, as in the case of a BLADDER DART. (See also LEISTER.)

harvest festival A ceremony or dance held by many agricultural tribes at harvesting time. Harvest ceremonies, such as the GREEN CORN CEREMONY, were used to give thanks and ensure continuing successful crops. Wild plant foods also were harvested and celebrated. (See also FIRST FOOD CEREMONY; THANKSGIVING.)

Hasinai Confederacy See CADDO.

hat See HEADDRESS; HEADGEAR; HELMET; NOOTKA HAT.

hatchet A small AX, designed for one hand. The term has been used by whites as interchangeable with TOMAHAWK. The expression "bury the hatchet" derives from the historical concept of making peace. European hatchets with iron heads (trade axes) became valuable trade items.

Hatteras An ALGONQUIAN-speaking tribe of the NORTHEAST CULTURE AREA, located on Cape Hatteras and Roanoke Island in present-day North Carolina. Some researchers have theorized that the CROATAN INDIANS, with whom the lost Roanoke colonists were thought to have taken refuge, were the Hatteras. The Hatteras merged with mainland Algonquians in the early 1700s and lost their tribal identity. (See also SECOTAN.)

Haudenosaunee See IROQUOIS.

hau kola   A SIOUX phrase of greetings and friendship in SIOUAN (Lakota). (See also HOW.)

Havasupai   A YUMAN-speaking tribe of the SOUTHWEST CULTURE AREA, located in Cataract Canyon (part of the Grand Canyon) on the Colorado River in present-day Arizona. Havasupais hold the Havasupai Reservation in Coconino County, Arizona, with headquarters at Supai. Their name is derived from the Yuman word *Kwaahahavasupaya*, meaning "blue water people."

hawk   Birds of prey of the order Falconiformes, known for their powerful hooked beaks and long claws, keen sight, and speed in flight. Like the EAGLE, the hawk has been revered by Native Americans, cited in legends and sought for AMULETS.

head deformation   (cranial deformation) An unintentional or intentional disfiguration of the human head. In the former, an infant's forehead was deformed because of prolonged contact with the head support of a CRADLEBOARD. In the latter, the forehead was purposely deformed, usually by means of a deerskin-covered block of wood or a bag of sand applied from the front to create a flattened shape, or by means of a series of bags around the head to create a more conical shape. As in other cultures around the world, certain Indian tribes, especially those of the SOUTHEAST CULTURE AREA and NORTHWEST COAST CULTURE AREA, practiced head deformation as a mark of beauty as well as status. "Lamboid flattening" refers to the flattening of the back skull.

headdress   A type of HEADGEAR, worn ceremonially or decoratively. Native Americans traditionally have worn a variety of headdresses, particular to each tribe. Many headdresses combine leather with feathers, quillwork, beadwork, and other materials. The number, direction, color, and type of feathers communicate tribal identity. The APACHES wear wooden-slat headdresses to impersonate the *GANS* in dances. The so-

Seneca headdress

called WARBONNET of PLAINS INDIANS is the most recognizable headdress. (See also FRONTLET; ROACH; TABLITA; *TUMA*.)

headgear   Any covering of the head, including hats, HEADDRESSES, HELMETS, and even MASKS. ARCTIC PEOPLES had hoods attached to their PARKAS; SUBARCTIC INDIANS and other northern peoples wore both hoods and fur caps for warmth; NORTHWEST COAST INDIANS carved wooden hats; SOUTHEAST INDIANS wore TURBANS made from sashes; CALIFORNIA INDIANS crafted basket hats and iris fiber hairnets, feather crowns, and feather headbands.

headman   A leader of a political and social organization, such as a tribe or village. The term is used in reference to INUIT leaders rather than the sometimes synonymous CHIEF. Among the IROQUOIS, a headman is the leader of a MOIETY, in charge of organizing various ceremonies. In modern usage, the head man or head woman at a POWWOW is the master of ceremonies. (See also CACIQUE; SACHEM.)

head pot Pottery in the shape of a human head, thought to represent a war trophy; typical of SOUTH AMERICAN INDIANS and Indians of the MISSISSIPPIAN CULTURE.

head-shrinking The ritual shrinking of human heads practiced by various SOUTH AMERICAN INDIANS, who believed that the keeping of such a trophy gave them supernatural power. "Head-shrinkers" would decapitate their slain enemy, remove the skin plus hair from the skull, boil it, then fill it with hot sand and pebbles. The Jivaros of present-day Ecuador were the first Indians associated with the custom; their shrunken heads are known as *tsantsas*.

healing (curing) Traditional Native American medical practices, including rituals, such as chanting for spiritual invocation, and herbal remedies. SHAMANS, or MEDICINE MEN, had special knowledge of healing. In some tribes, these healers were organized into MEDICINE SOCIETIES, such as the MIDEWIWIN SOCIETY. (See also BLOODLETTING; MEDICINE; SPIRIT HELPER; SUCKING DOCTOR.)

hearth See FIREPIT.

heartline A motif on POTTERY in which animal figures, especially deer, are painted with a line from the mouth to an arrowhead in the chest. Found on HOPI, KERES, and ZUNI pottery, beginning in the mid-1800s.

hecetu A SIOUX word for "so be it" or "it is so" in SIOUAN (Lakota), traditionally used in ceremonies.

Heiltsuk (Heiltsuq) A WAKASHAN-speaking tribe of the NORTHWEST COAST CULTURE AREA, located on the Pacific Coast of present-day British Columbia, from Rivers Inlet to Douglas Channel. The name Heiltsuk sometimes is applied to a language dialect of various bands, including BELLA BELLA, China Hat, Nohuntsitk, Somehulitk, and Wikeno; or to the Bella Bella subtribe in particular, since it is their native name.

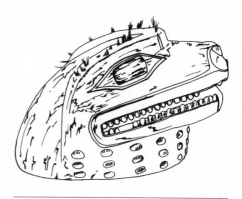

Tlingit wooden helmet

The Heiltsuk dialect is related to the HAISLA and KWAKIUTL dialects of Wakashan. The Heiltsuk and Oweekano bands maintain tribal identity in their ancestral homeland.

heishi See HESHI.

helmet A protective covering for the head. AZTEC warriors of rank wore wooden helmets carved to represent animals. TLINGIT Indians also crafted wooden helmets. Other tribes, such as the CHEROKEES, used strips of hide to protect their heads. (See also ARMOR.)

hematite An IRON ore valued in the making of tools; usually dark in color, especially grayish, brownish, or reddish. The red variety is called OCHER or red ocher.

hemisphere A prehistoric small stone object, typically polished, in the shape of a half-sphere, probably for ceremonial use.

herb The curing of disease with plant remedies was widespread throughout the Americas. Modern science has proven many to be effective, such as the bark of the cinchona tree of South America from which quinine is derived for the treatment of malaria; and the use of pine bark and needles, a source of vitamin C, for the treatment of scurvy. MEDICINE MEN and PRIESTS were trained in the use of plant remedies.

hereditary title   A position in a tribe, such as CHIEF, inherited through lineage. (See also RANK.)

heshi (heishi, heishe)   A type of BEAD-WORK, typical of PUEBLO INDIANS, in which pieces of shell, coral, bone, turquoise, or other semiprecious stone are drilled, strung, and rolled against an abrasive surface to make them uniform.

Hesi Ceremony   See KUKSU RELIGION.

heyoka   The sacred clown or contrary of the SIOUX (Lakota). Someone who has experienced visions of the *wakinyan*, or the THUNDER BEINGS, is obligated to speak and act out contradictively in the *Heyoka Kaga*, or Clownmaker Ceremony. The *heyokas* also performed the KETTLE DANCE.

Hidatsa (Minitaree, Minitari)   A SIOUAN-speaking tribe of the GREAT PLAINS CULTURE AREA, located on the Missouri River between the Heart and Little Missouri tributaries in present-day North Dakota and ranging into present-day eastern Montana. (The Hidatsas are believed to have formerly lived near Devil's Lake to the north but to have been pushed southwestward by the SIOUX.) There were three divisions: the Amahani (Mahaha), Awatixa (Amatiha), and Hidatsa, the name that came to be applied to all three. The Hidatsas' closest relatives linguistically were the CROWS (Absarokee), but their neighbors on the Missouri were the ARIKARAS and MANDANS, with whom they share the Fort Berthold Reservation near New Town, North Dakota. *Hidatsa* was originally the name of a village. The Mandan name for them was *Minitaree*, meaning "they crossed the water." The French called them *Gros Ventres de la Rivière* ("big bellies of the river") because their tribal name in the sign language of the PLAINS INDIANS was a sweeping pass in front of the abdomen to indicate the custom of tattooing parallel stripes across their chest. (See also GROS VENTRE.)

hidden-ball game   See GUESSING GAME.

hide   The SKIN of an animal, either raw or dressed. The term hide sometimes is used only for the skin of large animals, such as BUFFALO and DEER, with "skin" more likely to be used for smaller mammals, reptiles, birds, and fish. "Hidework" is the act, process, or resulting artifact of work in hide. (See also FUR; LEATHER; PELT; RAWHIDE; SKIN-DRESSING.)

hieroglyphics   See PICTOGRAPH.

hierohistory   Mythological history (literally "sacred history"), which gives meaning to a people's interpretation of their origin and reality.

hierophany   Revelation, believed to occur with the help of a SPIRITUAL BEING, as experienced in a VISION. "Hierophanic" is the adjective form.

high-steel   In 1886, MOHAWK Indians of the Caughnawaga (Kahnawake) Reserve in Quebec were trained in steel construction to work on a bridge across the St. Lawrence River, starting the high-steel tradition among the tribe and other IROQUOIS. Mohawk high-steel workers are contracted through their unions for work worldwide. They are known as "Skywalkers."

historic period   The age of written or recorded history, as opposed to PREHISTORY. (See also CONTACT.)

Hitchiti   A MUSKOGEAN-speaking tribe of the SOUTHEAST CULTURE AREA, located in present-day Chattahoochee County, Georgia. The Hitchitis spoke a dialect distinct from that of the CREEKS and other Muskogeans. Since they were part of the Creek Confederacy for much of their history and were relocated with the Creeks to the INDIAN TERRITORY, they are now considered a subtribe. Other Hitchitis migrated into Florida and were the ancestors of some of the SEMINOLES and MICCOSUKEES. *Hitchiti*

Hidatsa hoe

is thought to refer to a pile of ceremonial white ashes or to mean "to look upstream."

hocker A frontal depiction of the human figure, with arms and legs in a froglike position. Hocker sculptures are typical of MESOAMERICAN INDIANS.

hoe A tool with a flat blade attached at an angle to a long handle, used in cultivating soil and weeding. Blades of various shapes—either squared-off, rounded, or pointed—

were made from stone or bone for hoes. (See also SPADE.)

hogan A NAVAJO dwelling with a log and stick frame covered with mud or sod (or sometimes made from piled stone). Hogans usually have one room. They can be conical in shape (a "male" type with three poles extending from the tip) or domelike (a "female" type with stacked logs); the latter is typically six or eight-sided. The cone-shape hogans are used in ceremonies. Hogans face east, with the floor symbolizing Mother Earth and the roof, Father Sky. The original Navajo word for house or hut in ATHAPASCAN is *goghan*.

Hoh A subtribe of the QUILEUTE Indians, located on the Hoh River near the coast of present-day Washington. Descendants hold the Hoh Reservation, with tribal headquarters at Forks, Washington.

Hohokam Culture A cultural tradition of the American Southwest, lasting from about 100 B.C. to A.D. 1450. The core area of Hohokam Culture was along the Gila and Salt river valleys in present-day southern Arizona, desert country broken only by slow-flowing rivers and rugged volcanic hills. The Hohokam Indians had to use IRRIGATION techniques to cultivate the sandy

Navajo hogan

soil: They dug wide, shallow canals as long as 10 miles and made diversion dams with woven-mat valves to redirect the water from the rivers to their fields of corn, beans, squash, tobacco, and cotton. Because of their advanced farming techniques, the Hohokam Indians grew enough food to support a sizable population. The principal Hohokam village, known as Snaketown (near present-day Phoenix), had about 100 PIT-HOUSES. The Hohokam pithouses resembled those of the MOGOLLON CULTURE in construction but were larger and shallower. At Snaketown, the remains of two sunken BALL-COURTS and RUBBER balls have been found, indicating a connection between Hohokam Indians and MESOAMERICAN INDIANS. The Hohokams are considered the first people to practice ETCHING, starting in about A.D. 1000. They probably were the ancestors of the present-day PIMAS and PAPAGOS. *Hohokam* means "vanished ones" in the Pima dialect of UTO-AZTECAN. (See also PATAYAN CULTURE.)

hoka hey A SIOUX phrase for "hold fast, there is more" in SIOUAN (Lakota), spoken in times of duress.

Hokaltecan See HOKAN.

Hokan A phylum of language stocks, including the CHUMASHAN, PALAIHNIHAN, POMO, SALINAN, SHASTAN, TEQUISTLATECAN, TLAPANECAN, YANAN, and YUMAN families as well as the Chimariko, COAHUILTECAN, Esselen, KAROK, and WASHOE isolates. The Hokan phylum is sometimes grouped with the isolates Coalhuitecan, KARANKAWA, and TONKAWA under the name Hokaltecan.

holism A philosophy in which all aspects of reality and nature are viewed as a unified whole. Indians in general were a holistic people. (See also CIRCLE.)

Holy People The various deities in the NAVAJO pantheon, include Father Sun (Sun Father) and Mother Earth (Changing Woman); Begochiddy ("one who grabs breasts," the son of Sun); the Hero Twins, Born of Water and Monster Slayer (Elder Brother and Younger Brother); as well as Talking God (the maternal grandfather of all Navajos), First Man and First Woman, ANIMAL PEOPLE, Coyote, Great Snake, Old Grandmother Ant Person, Fire God, Water Monster, Rainbow, Corn, Thunders, Winds, and others. The Holy People are represented in SANDPAINTING and WEAVING. (See also MONSTER; WAYS; YEI.)

Holy Wind A concept of spiritual power of the NAVAJO Indians, existing within and around all living things, giving life and shaping behavior.

hominy A food made from CORN by pounding or cracking the dried kernals, then boiling; or hulling by soaking in water or steeping in lye or ashes, then boiling. Sometimes meat or fish is added for seasoning. The term hominy has come to refer to any boiled food made from dried corn that is coarser than cornmeal, as in hominy grits. "Hominy" is an ALGONQUIAN-derived word. SAMP, also an Algonquian word, is a coarse hominy or a porridge made from hominy. (See also ROCKAHOMINY.)

Honniasont See IROQUOIAN.

hook See FISHHOOK.

hook-stone A small stone artifact, typical of CALIFORNIA INDIANS, with a hooked head and a base, usually made from SOAPSTONE. The base, enabling it to stand upright, indicates a ceremonial function, although some scholars have classified hook-stones as tools.

hoop See HOOP-AND-POLE; HOOP DANCE; SACRED HOOP.

Hoopa (Hupa) An ATHAPASCAN-speaking tribe of the CALIFORNIA CULTURE AREA, located on the Trinity River, especially around Hoopa Valley, and on the New

River. Tribal members now hold the Hoopa
Valley Reservation in Humboldt County,
California. Their name is derived from
Hupo, the YUROK name of the valley.

hoop-and-pole A game or sport in which
a hoop or ring, sometimes webbed, is rolled
along the ground as a target for JAVELINS
or ARROWS.

Hoop Dance A dance performed with one
or more hoops, a sacred symbol. It probably
originated among Indians of the western
Great Lakes, in particular the CHIPPEWAS,
OTTAWAS, and POTAWATOMIS, who used
one hoop, and the MENOMINEES, who used
two. It was popularized in the 20th century
by the TIWA Indians of the Taos Pueblo,
and is now performed by various tribes at
POWWOWS with sometimes more than a
dozen hoops.

hootchenoo The word in CHINOOK JAR-
GON for homemade liquor, from which the
slang word "hooch" is derived.

Hopewell Culture A cultural tradition of
related archaeological sites, lasting from
about 100 B.C. to A.D. 700 in eastern North
America. Like the preceding ADENA CUL-
TURE, the Hopewell Culture was centered
along the Ohio Valley, although archaeologists have found Hopewell MOUNDS and
artifacts over a much wider area comprising
the Illinois River Valley, the Mississippi
River Valley, and other river valleys of the
Midwest and East. Hopewell Indians, also
called MOUNDBUILDERS, established a far-
flung trade network. At Hopewell sites, archaeologists have found artifacts made out
of raw materials from distant locations, such
as OBSIDIAN from the Rocky Mountains,
COPPER from the Great Lakes, shells from
the Atlantic Ocean, MICA from the Appalachian Mountains, and alligator skulls and
teeth from Florida. Hopewell burial mounds
generally were larger than Adena mounds;
many of them covered multiple burials and
stood 30 to 40 feet high. Other Hopewell
earthworks were effigy mounds, represent-

ing animals. Still others served as walls as
much as 50 feet high and 200 feet wide at
the base, often laid out in geometric shapes.
At a Hopewell site in Newark, Ohio comprising an area of four square miles are walls
or enclosures in different shapes, including
circles, parallel lines, a square, and an octa-
gon. The development of agriculture and
the growing of corn, beans, squash, and
other crops supported large, centralized
populations that might be called CITY-
STATES. Hopewell villagers lived in domed
structures, framed with poles and covered
with sheets of bark, woven mats, or animal
skins, much like the WIGWAMS of the later
ALGONQUIANS. Scholars theorize that the
Hopewell Indians were direct ancestors of
the later Indian tribes of eastern North
America. Drought and crop failures might
have brought about their cultural decline;
warfare and epidemics also might have depleted their numbers.

Hopi (Moqui, Moki) A UTO-AZTECAN-
speaking tribe of the SOUTHWEST CUL-
TURE AREA, located on Three Mesas in
present-day northeastern Arizona. The Hopis, who traditionally have lived in pueblos,
are classified as PUEBLO INDIANS. Tribal
members hold the Hopi Reservation in Coc-
ino and Navajo counties, Arizona, with
headquarters at Oraibi. "Hopi" is derived
from *Hopitu*, meaning "peaceful ones" in
Uto-Aztecan. The alternate name *Moqui*,
which means "dead," possibly first was used
by the NAVAJOS.

horizon In archaeology, a particular cultural period, as evidenced by a level or stratum. In geology, a deposit of a particular
time, usually identified by distinctive fossils.
A horizon style is a style of art or design
shared by the inhabitants of different regions during a particular period.

horn and antler work The act, process,
or resulting artifact of work in animal horns
and antlers. When heated, a horn can be
worked into different shapes; two pieces also
can be welded together. Horns were used

Pueblo Indian *horno*

for a variety of utensils, especially spoons, ladles, and dishes. The solid, harder antler, actually a bony outgrowth of the skull, was used for points, flakers, knives, awls, bows, and hoes. (See also BONEWORK; IVORY WORK.)

horno An outdoor oven, typical of PUEBLO INDIANS, made of stone and ADOBE and shaped like the upper half a beehive. Hornos have vents at the top and side doors; bread and other items to be baked are inserted with a flat wooden shovel.

horse The horse, *Equus caballus*, was domesticated by humans for riding and pull-ing. The horse native to the Americas became extinct at the end of the PLEISTO-CENE; Indian peoples did not have knowl-edge of the animal again until the arrival of the Spanish in the late 15th and early 16th centuries. As Spanish colonists spread out from the West Indies and Mexico, so did the horse, their dominant mode of land transportation. In North America, the PUEBLO INDIANS were the first peoples to become familiar with the animal, taking care of herds for colonists along the Rio Grande. By the mid-1700s, some APACHES, NAVAJOS, and southern PLAINS INDIANS had begun carrying out raids to acquire mounts. Dur-ing the Pueblo Rebellion of 1680, hundreds

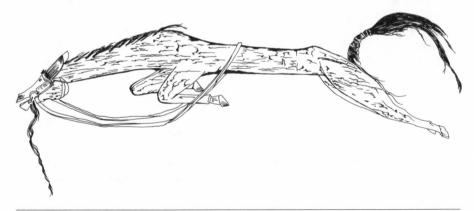

Sioux wooden horse effigy

of horses, fell into Indian hands. Trade in horses spread northward onto the Great Plains. In the 17th and 18th centuries, some EASTERN INDIANS, such as the IROQUOIS, acquired horses from the French, English, and Dutch and began breeding and trading them. Horses were widespread in the Americas by the end of the 18th century; Indians of many tribes had become highly skilled breeders, trainers, and riders. The horse became central to the way of life—traveling, trading, hunting, and warfare—of the GREAT PLAINS CULTURE AREA. A dominant symbol of wealth, prestige, and honor—especially the war pony for warfare and buffalo pony for hunting—the horse was celebrated in mythology and ritual. (See also APPALOOSA; CAYUSE PONY; RACING; SADDLE; *SUNKA WAKAN*; TRAVOIS.)

horticulture See FARMING.

Hotamitaneo See DOG SOLDIERS.

Houma (Huma) A MUSKOGEAN-speaking tribe of the SOUTHEAST CULTURE AREA, located on the east bank of the Mississippi River in present-day Mississippi. Close to the CHOCTAWS in language, the Houmas are thought to be an offshoot of the Chakchiumas. After 1706, they lived in the vicinity of present-day Houma, Louisiana; some descendants at Golden Meadows are known as the United Houma Nation. *Houma* means "red" in Muskogean; the name is an abbreviation of *saktci homma*, meaning "red crawfish."

Housatonic See STOCKBRIDGE INDIANS.

house A place of SHELTER, usually implying an erected structure as distinct from the all-inclusive DWELLING. Structures serving a public function are sometimes called buildings, especially when of stone, or LODGES or by their specific names, such as KIVAS, SWEATHOUSES, and TEMPLES. (See also CATEGORICAL APPENDIX, "HOUSES AND ARCHITECTURE.")

house burial A burial inside a structure, such as in a WIGWAM. (See also GRAVEHOUSE.)

house mound A visible rise in the land, indicating the site of a collapsed house.

housepost (house pillar) A post erected inside a house to support the roof. Those carved with images representing familial history and status, as typical of NORTHWEST INDIANS, are a kind of TOTEM POLE. (See also COSMIC TREE.)

"how" The white spelling of an expression of greeting among certain western tribes, such as the SIOUX. The original Native American term, more accurately spelled *hau* or *hao*, means "good" or "satisfactory" and was used as both a salutation and as a response in council. Non-Indians have mistakenly assumed it to be a shortening of "how are you?" or "howdy" and have stereotyped it, along with a raised-hand gesture, as typical Indian behavior. (See also *HAU KOLA*.)

hozhoni The NAVAJO concept of oneness or harmony with all that exists.

huaca A QUECHUA word, originally applied to the sacred forces of nature, or to a place or object believed to be the abode of spirits, i.e., a holy place. It also is applied to INCA ruins, especially a tomb, burial mound, or pottery from graves. As an adjective, *huaca* translates as "sacred."

Hualapai (Walapai) A YUMAN-speaking people of the SOUTHWEST CULTURE AREA, located on the middle course of the Colorado River in present-day northwestern Arizona. Hualapais now hold the Hualapai Reservation in Mojave, Cococino, and Yavapai counties, Arizona, with headquarters at Peach Springs. *Hualapai* is derived from the Yuman word *Hawalyapaya*, meaning "pine tree people."

Huchnom See YUKIAN.

Hudson's Bay blanket   A wool BLANKET used by the Hudson's Bay Company for trade with Indians. In the mid-1800s, the blankets came to replace beaver and otter pelts as the standard medium of exchange among NORTHWEST COAST INDIANS. They were often given away in the POTLATCH ceremony. (See also FUR TRADE.)

Huitzilopochtli   The AZTEC principal deity, god of war and hunting. His name translates as "left-handed hummingbird." One of the four children of TONACATECUHTLI, he eventually achieved the incarnation of Sun God.

human being   See PEOPLE.

human sacrifice   See AZTEC; SACRIFICE; SOUTHERN CULT.

humor (wit)   American Indians are known for their sense of humor. Many of their legends and stories have elements of humor. Some tribes have CLOWN societies. Practical jokes, teasing, puns, double-entendres, sarcasm, and satire play a large part in family and community interaction. *Ngagelicksi* is a LENNI LENAPE (Delaware) word for "I laugh" in ALGONQUIAN. (See also JOKING RELATIVE; TRICKSTER.)

Humptulips   See SALISHAN.

Hunab-Ku (Hunab)   The MAYA principal deity and creator of the world.

Hunkpapa   A subtribe of the TETON division of the SIOUX Indians, located on the upper Missouri River near the Cannonball River in present-day North Dakota and ranging throughout the Northern Plains, especially in present-day South Dakota, Montana, Wyoming, and Nebraska. *Hunkpapa* possibly means "at the entrance," "at the head end of the circle," "those who camp by themselves," or "wanderers" in SIOUAN.

Hunkpatina   A subtribe of the YANKTONAI division of the SIOUX Indians, located on the lower James River in present-day eastern South Dakota. *Hunkpatina* means "campers at the end of the circle" in SIOUAN.

hunting   Acquiring ANIMALS for food and other resources, especially hide, antler, and bone. Native Americans, for the most part the men of a tribe, traditionally hunted for survival, not for sport. Many different methods were used, including individual stalking and grabbing with bare hands; communal FIRE-DRIVES or SURROUNDS; pursuing with DOGS and HORSES; or capturing with TRAPS, SNARES, PITS, and POISONS. Hunting weapons included SPEARS, CLUBS, ATLATLS, BOWS and ARROWS, SLINGS, BOLAS. The term hunting sometimes includes FISHING. (See also CATEGORICAL APPENDIX, "ANIMALS"; CRUSTING; HUNTING-GATHERING; HUNTING GROUND; WHALING.)

hunting club   A CLUB used for striking game, as opposed to a WARCLUB.

hunting-gathering (hunting-and-gathering)   Subsistence in which food is obtained through hunting, fishing, and foraging for wild plant foods, without farming.

hunting ground   Territory for hunting. Tribes, clans, or families often had understandings with one another over the use and limits of such lands.

hunting party   A group, usually all men, leaving their village or camp to hunt. A party might range over a large area and be gone for days or weeks. (See also WAR PARTY.)

hunt-the-button   See GUESSING GAME.

Hupa   See HOOPA.

Huron (Wyandot, Wyandotte, Guyandot)   An IROQUOIAN-speaking tribe of the NORTHEAST CULTURE AREA, located on Lake Simcoe and south and east of Georgian Bay in present-day Ontario. (In the early

1500s, some bands lived along the St. Lawrence Valley as well.) Because of attacks by tribes of the IROQUOIS LEAGUE, the Hurons left their homeland. One band found safety among the French at Lorette near Quebec City. Many merged with the TOBACCO (Petun) Indians and, with them, began a series of migrations to territory around the Great Lakes in present day Michigan, Wisconsin, Illinois, Indiana, and Ohio. This group became known historically as the Wyandot tribe. By 1842, the Wyandots had been pressured into selling off their lands east of the Mississippi, and moved to present-day Wyandotte County, Kansas. In 1867, they were relocated to present-day northeastern Oklahoma. Descendants in Canada, centered at Huron Village, Huron, are known as the Hurons of Lorette; descendants in the United States, centered at Miami, Oklahoma, are known as the Wyandotte Tribe of Oklahoma. *Huron* is of French derivation, from the word *huré*, referring to an "unkempt," "rough," or "boorish" person. *Wyandot*, from *Wendat*, probably means "islanders" or "peninsula dwellers" in Iroquoian.

hurricane A tropical storm in the West Indies, characterized by a system of high-speed rotating winds along with driving rain, thunder, and lightning; known as a "cyclone" or a "typhoon" elsewhere. "Hurricane" is derived from an ARAWAKAN word, *huracan* or *hurrican*, that came to English via the Spanish *huracan*. To the ARAWAKS, Huracan was a furious god who visited them regularly.

huskanaw (huskany) A RITE OF PASSAGE among ALGONQUIAN-speaking Indians of Virginia, such as the POWHATANS, in which boys underwent solitary confinement and fasting in preparation for manhood.

husk See CORNHUSK.

Husk Face Society A MEDICINE SOCIETY of the IROQUOIS Indians, similar to the FALSE FACE Society; its members, both men and women, wear cornhusk masks, representing agricultural spirits.

husking pin (husking peg) A pin-shape tool attached to the hand with a strap, designed to aid in stripping the husk from corn.

husky (Siberian husky) A breed of DOG originally developed in the Siberian Arctic for pulling SLEDS. The term was first applied by white settlers in Labrador to INUITS, probably a corruption of one of their own band names, and was eventually applied to their wolflike sled dogs. (See also MALAMUTE.)

hutia Any large rodent of the genera *Capromys* and *Geocapromys*, found in the West Indies and hunted by the ARAWAKS for meat.

▲ I ▲

Ibitoupa See MUSKOGEAN.

Icafui See TIMUCUA.

Ice Age See PLEISTOCENE.

ice creeper Ivory or bone spikes, typical of the INUITS, attached to the bottom of footgear for traction on ice.

icon A picture or image, typically of a deity. MESOAMERICAN INDIANS and the INCAS represented their gods in images. Iconography is artistic representation in pictures and images; or the symbolism and meaning of the images. Iconology is the study of icons and iconography. (See also IDOL.)

ideograph See PICTOGRAPH.

idol An image or symbol of a deity, used as an object of worship. (See also ICON.)

igloo (iglu, snowhouse) A dome-shape dwelling of the INUITS, made from blocks of ice. Igloos were used only by the Central Eskimos in the winter. They were built mostly by men, with help in chinking and plastering with soft snow by women. An area of snow of the same consistency was chosen for the building material—ideally a layer of snow that fell in a storm then hardened into ice all at once. A circle nine to 15 feet in diameter was drawn as a floor plan. The builder used a SNOW KNIFE to cut large blocks of ice, each about 24 by 20 by four inches, for the first row along the circle's outline. The added rows of blocks spiraled upward and leaned inward slightly, so that each row was smaller than the previous one, until a final single block at the top completed the dome. A hole in the dome provided ventilation and a block of clear ice served as a window. The floor space of an igloo was near the entrance, where visitors stood. A platform of ice, an *ikliq*, about two feet above the floor, covered with furs, served as a bed. Igloos normally had a second smaller domed porch, a *hiqluaq*, for storage, with a covered, connecting passageway. A third dome was sometimes joined to the two so that a family could have a separate bedroom and living room. The igloos were warm, sometimes even too warm, when oil was burned in stone LAMPS for lighting and cooking. (See also QARMAQ; SOD HOUSE; TENT.)

ila An INUIT word (or root of a word) for "family" or "associates" in the ESKIMO-ALEUT language. It is combined with other words to define varying degrees of kinship.

Illinois (Illini) An ALGONQUIAN-speaking tribe of the NORTHEAST CULTURE AREA, located on the Illinois and Mississippi rivers in present-day Illinois as well as in present-day southern Wisconsin, northeastern Arkansas, and eastern Missouri. Subdivisions include the Cahokia, KASKASKIA, Michigamea, Moingwena, PEORIA, and Tamora bands; they were in effect an alliance of tribes, related linguistically and politically, and often referred to as a confederacy. By the 1760s, attacks by CHIPPEWAS, FOXES, KICKAPOOS, OTTAWAS, POTAWATOMIS, and SACS reduced Illinois territory. In 1832, Illinois survivors from the Kaskaskia and Peoria bands were relocated to present-day Paola, Kansas; in 1867–68, they were moved to present-day northeastern Oklahoma along with the PIANKASHAW and WEA bands of the MIAMI Indians. The Peoria Tribe of Oklahoma now has its headquarters at Miami, Oklahoma. *Illinois* means "people" in Algonquian.

impersonator One who assumes the identity of a god or legendary being in ceremonies by wearing a mask and costume and acting out a role; applied to PUEBLO INDIANS who impersonate KACHINAS. The term spirit impersonation also is used.

implement See TOOL.

Inca A QUECHUA-speaking people of the Andes Mountains of western South America. Some tribes may have been consolidated as early as A.D. 1000, in the pre-Inca period; they had evolved out of and had been influenced by earlier dominant cultures of the region, such as Tiahuanacan, Chavin, Chimu, Nazca, Moche (Mohica), and Paracas. The early Inca period is given as A.D. 1200 to 1440, during which time a centralized government was organized in the city of Cuzco. From 1440 to 1500, the Incas expanded their territory into the domain of the Aymara Indians of present-day Bolivia and the Araucanian Indians of present-day Chile. The Inca Empire of tributary tribes extended at the time of CONTACT along the Andes from what is now northern Ecuador to central Chile. An agricultural economy supported a highly organized civilization with classes of society. Everything was owned by the state, except houses, household goods, and some small parcels of land. The Incas built cities of highly refined stone architecture, such as Cuzco and Machu Picchu, and an extensive network of roads. They developed elaborate art forms, especially in metalwork and textiles, as well as writing, calendar, and counting systems (QUIPU). In 1533, the Spanish defeated the Incas and captured Cuzco. Descendants still speak the Quechua language. *Inca* is derived from *Ynca*, for the prince of the ruling family.

incense An aromatic substance burned ceremonially as an OFFERING. Favorite Native American incenses were *COPALLI* and other resins; the wood and needles of cedar, spruce, and pine; TOBACCO; SWEET GRASS; artemesia; and balsamroot.

incest taboo A TABOO i.e., prohibition, against mating with any person regarded as a genetic relative. Many tribes also had EXOGAMOUS rules against marriages within one's own CLAN.

incising See ENGRAVING.

Indian A native person of the Americas. Christopher Columbus applied the name to the ARAWAKS of the Greater Antilles in the Caribbean, believing he had reached the East Indies. The word first occurred in print in Columbus's letter of February 1493, mentioning a number of *indios* he had with him. The Spanish, Italian, and Portuguese version of "Indian" is *Indio;* the French, *Indien.* The slurred form "Injun" became a derogatory term among English non-Indians. Pre-Contact Indians had no names for themselves as a race; their native names often mean "people." (See also AMERICAN INDIAN; AMERIND; NATIVE AMERICAN.)

Indian affairs Isues, policies, and programs of the U.S. and Canadian governments involving native peoples. (See also BUREAU OF INDIAN AFFAIRS; DEPARTMENT OF INDIAN AFFAIRS AND NORTHERN DEPARTMENT.)

Indian agent The federal official representing the BUREAU OF INDIAN AFFAIRS on a reservation. After 1908, the position became known as INDIAN SUPERINTENDENT.

Indian bread Bread made by different tribes, including the FRY BREAD of the NAVAJOS and the *PIKI* of the HOPIS.

Indian college A college with Native American enrollment. Some modern-day colleges, such as Dartmouth (which began as Moor's Indian Charity School) and Hamilton College (which began as Hamilton Oneida Academy), were originally founded to educate Indian youth. "Indian college" is now used synonymously with "tribal college" to refer to any of the 26 such institutions run by Native Americans (both on and off reservations), such as the Navajo Community College, founded in Arizona in 1968 by the NAVAJO tribe, and the Oglala Lakota College, founded in South Dakota in 1971 by the SIOUX.

Indian corn   See CORN.

Indian Country   The concept of a separate "Indian Country" and a boundary line separating Indians from whites began with Great Britain's Royal Proclamation of 1763, which reserved territory and attempted to prevent white settlement west of the Appalachian watershed. With the Northwest Ordinance of 1787, the U.S. government reaffirmed this policy. In the 19th century, after the Louisiana Purchase of 1803, the United States viewed land west of the Mississippi as "Indian Country" and, in 1825, defined it as territory between the Red and Missouri rivers. In the Trade and Intercourse Act of 1834, the region was referred to as the INDIAN TERRITORY. When modern-day activists speak of "Indian Country," they are referring to all of the Americas.

"Indian file"   Single file, the way EASTERN INDIANS typically walked through woods.

"Indian giver"   Slang for someone who offers something as a gift, then wants it back, originally in reference to the custom of some tribes' expecting an equivalent gift or more after a display of generosity, as in the GIVEAWAY. The terms Indian gift or Indian giving are also used. Activists have applied the term to white officials who reneged on land rights to Indians. (See also BROKEN PROMISES.)

Indian market   A place where Native Americans sell foodstuffs and arts and crafts. An open market is held outside. A term used especially in the American Southwest. (See also FAIR.)

Indian police   Law enforcement officers on a reservation. Although Indian police generally are recruited from the reservation, the federal government provides funds for them, a policy established in 1878.

Indian rights   The political, cultural, religious, economic, and land rights of Indian tribes and individuals. The defense of Indian rights became formalized in the late 19th century with the founding of Friends of the Indian groups. In the 20th century, other Indian and non-Indian ORGANIZATIONS have continued to work for PAN-INDIAN goals. Indian ACTIVISM concerns Indian rights; in many instances, the struggle for Indian rights involves land tenure and land use as defined in historical TREATIES.

Indian school   Historically, a school operated by the BUREAU OF INDIAN AFFAIRS on a reservation; now used for schools operated by the tribes themselves. (See also BOARDING SCHOOL; INDIAN COLLEGE.)

Indian scout   See SCOUT.

Indian Shaker Religion   A religious revitalization movement of tribes of the Far West. In 1881, the SQUAXIN Indian John Slocum (Squ-sacht-un) founded *Tschadam*, known to whites as the Indian Shaker Religion. The name was derived from the shaking or twitching motion participants experienced while brushing off sins in a meditative state, a ritual introduced by Slocum's wife, Mary Thompson Slocum. The religion combined Chistian beliefs in God, heaven, and hell with traditional Indian teachings as in the WASHANI RELIGION. Slocum and his followers, especially among the Squaxin, SKOKOMISH, NISQUALLY, and CHEHALIS tribes, were imprisoned regularly by white officials for inciting resistance to ASSIMILATION programs.

Indian sugar   See MAPLE SUGAR.

Indian summer   A short period of mild weather occurring in mid-November, or any warm period in autumn in early winter. The term probably originated in New England, where there are four seasons.

Indian superintendent   The title of the federal official representing the BUREAU OF INDIAN AFFAIRS on a reservation after 1908 (formerly INDIAN AGENT). Indian superintendents are in charge of the transfer of federal funds to tribes. "Indian superintendent" also is a historical term: In 1754, the Albany Congress organized a centralized Indian program for England with a superintendent for a Northern Department and one for a Southern Department.

Indian Territory   A tract west of the Mississippi River in the central United States, set aside as a permanent homeland for Indians in 1834 (after originally being defined as the INDIAN COUNTRY), including much of present-day Nebraska, Kansas, and Oklahoma, then reduced over the following years. In 1854, with the Kansas-Nebraska Act, the northern part became Kansas and Nebraska territories. In 1862, the Homestead Act opened up many remaining Indian lands to white homesteaders. In 1890, Oklahoma Territory was carved out of much of it. In 1907, the so-called twin territories of the Indian Territory and Oklahoma Territory became the State of Oklahoma. (See also REMOVAL.)

Indian Two Step   A modern Indian social dance of couples, taken from non-Indian dances.

indigenismo   A political, economic, and social movement on behalf of SOUTH AMERICAN INDIANS, sometimes translated as an "Indiast" movement, striving to increase tribes' political power and raise their standard of living while preserving their culture. *Indigena* is the Spanish word for NATIVE.

indigenous   Originating in a particular place, as in the phrase indigenous peoples. (See also ABORIGINAL; NATIVE.)

informant   One who provides a historian or anthropologist with information about his or her history or culture. The term key informant describes that individual who

proves essential to a researcher's thesis. (See also FIELDWORK; LIFE HISTORY.)

Ingalik (Ingalit, Kaiyuhkhotana)   An ATHAPASCAN-speaking tribe of the SUBARCTIC CULTURE AREA, located on the lower Yukon River as well as on parts of the Anvik and Kuskokwim rivers in present-day Alaska. The Ingaliks were the westernmost of the Athapascans of Alaska and still hold a number of villages in Alaska. *Ingalik* is the INUIT name for the tribe in ESKIMO-ALEUT, meaning "having louse eggs"; the Russians used the name for all Athapascans.

inipi   The SWEATING ceremony of the SIOUX (Lakota).

initiation   A ceremony in which one is made a member of a SECRET SOCIETY. A RITE OF PASSAGE into adulthood is another form of initiation.

I'n-Lon-Schka   A ceremony of the OSAGE Indians. The four-day series of dances and rituals occurs in June, including as many as 200 songs, feasting, and GIVEAWAYS. Other rituals are Introduction to the Dance Ceremony and Feast for the Mourners as well as a Passing of the Drum Ceremony and Acceptance of the Drum Ceremony, if a new Drumkeeper of the Sacred Drum, always an eldest son, is being established. *I'n-Lon-Schka* translates from SIOUAN as "playground of the eldest son."

inscription   Writing carved in stone, wood, or some other material, as distinct from writing with paint or dyes. The verb form is "inscribe." Also used generally for any prominent or official writing.

in situ (in place)   Indicating the finding of an object in its original or natural position or place; Latin for "in place."

interpreter   Indians as well as non-Indians traveled with white explorers, settlers, and soldiers to communicate with fellow tribal members and members of other tribes. Interpreters often served as GUIDES and SCOUTS.

intoxicant See PSYCHOTROPIC SUBSTANCE.

inua The INUIT name of the shared power or SPIRIT inherent in animals, places, and objects. Translated as "person," it is not an individual soul, but rather that shared by and determining characteristics of phenomena, both animate and inanimate. *Inua* has been defined as the "generic spirit." The ALEUTS call it *yua*.

Inuit (Innuit, Innuin, Eskimo, Esquimaux) An ESKIMO-ALEUT-speaking people of the ARCTIC CULTURE AREA, located along the coasts of present-day Russia (coastal Siberia), Alaska, Yukon Territory, Northwest Territories, Quebec, Newfoundland, and Greenland. Some scholars organize the hundreds of Inuit bands into the following divisions: Siberian Eskimo, Saint Lawrence Island Eskimo, Alaskan Eskimo (North Alaskan, West Alaskan, and South Alaskan), Mackenzie Eskimo, Copper Eskimo, Caribou Eskimo, Netsilik Eskimo, Iglulik Eskimo, Baffinland Eskimo, Southampton Eskimo, Labrador Eskimo, Polar Eskimo, West Greenland Eskimo, and East Greenland Eskimo. Descendants live throughout their ancestral homeland. *Inuit* means "people" in the Eskimo-Aleut language. The alternate name *Eskimo*, more prevalent in historical writings, may be derived from the ALGONQUIAN term for "eaters of raw flesh" or, according to some scholars, "fish eaters."

inuk A "human being" in various INUIT dialects of the ESKIMO-ALEUT language.

invitation stick A long stick, typical of CALIFORNIA INDIANS, with an attached bundle of smaller sticks, having markings to indicate an invitation for a particular ceremony. The POMOS call it *hai di-ka-mu* in their HOKAN language.

Iowa (Ioway) A SIOUAN-speaking tribe of the GREAT PLAINS CULTURE AREA, located between the Mississippi and Missouri rivers in present-day Iowa; the Iowas' principal site for much of their history was on the Des Moines River. (According to tribal legend, the Iowas formerly were one people with the ancestors of the WINNEBAGOS living in present-day Wisconsin. A group supposedly traveled to the confluence of the Iowa and Mississippi rivers, then further divided: the band that continued westward became the Otos and Missouris; the band staying near the Mississippi became the Iowas.) Iowa bands ranged into northern Missouri and southwestern Minnesota. They were relocated to a reservation in present-day northeastern Kansas in 1836, which was later subdivided between the states of Kansas and Nebraska; other bands were moved to present-day Oklahoma in 1883. Tribal members hold the Iowa Reservation in Brown County, Kansas, and Richardson County, Nebraska. The Iowa Tribe of Oklahoma is centered in Shawnee. *Iowa* derives from the SIOUX name for them, *Ayuhwa*, meaning "sleepy ones" in Siouan. Their native name is *Pahodja*, meaning "dusty noses."

iron Iron tools, brought to the Americas by Europeans, revolutionized the technologies of native peoples, leading to extensive native IRONWORK. (See also HEMATITE; PYRITE.)

"iron horse" (steam horse) A 19th-century Indian term for a railroad locomotive.

ironwork The act, process, or resulting artifact of work in IRON. PREHISTORIC INDIANS flaked, pecked, hammered, or ground artifacts out of raw ores, such as HEMATITE, without smelting. In post-Contact times, Indians converted hoop iron (i.e., iron from barrel hoops) into POINTS, and files and other tools into KNIVES. The term ironwork can also refer to modern-day HIGH-STEEL work. (See also METALWORK.)

Iroquoian A language family and subdivision of the MACRO-SIOUAN phylum com-

Tlingit knife with ivory handle and iron blade

NEUTRAL, Neusiok (probably Iroquoian), Nottaway, SUSQUEHANNOCK, TOBACCO (Petun), and Wenro tribes; and of the SOUTHEAST CULTURE AREA, the CHEROKEE tribe.

Iroquois (Haudenosaunee, Haudenausaunee) A tribal name generally applied to tribes of the IROQUOIS LEAGUE, i.e., CAYUGA, ONEIDA, ONONDAGA, MOHAWK, SENECA, and TUSCARORA, as opposed to other IROQUOIAN-speaking tribes of the NORTHEAST CULTURE AREA with similar lifeways. "Iroquois" is derived from the ALGONQUIAN word *ireohkwa*, meaning "real snakes." The Iroquois native name is *Haudenosaunee*, for "people of the longhouse." (See also MINGO.)

Iroquois Confederacy See IROQUOIS LEAGUE.

Iroquois League (Iroquois Confederacy, Great League) A confederacy of tribes, made up of the MOHAWKS, ONEIDAS, ONONDAGAS, CAYUGAS, and SENECAS, founded in about 1570 by the Mohawk Indian Hiawatha and the HURON Indian Deganawida (the Peacemaker). The IROQUOIS alliance of tribes also is known as the League of Five Nations and, after the early 1700s — when the TUSCARORAS joined — as the League of Six Nations. (See also PINE TREE.)

irrigation The supplying of water to dry farmland by artificial means, such as ditches, canals, reservoirs, dams, and AQUEDUCTS, to make farming possible. Typical of SOUTHWEST INDIANS, especially the people of the HOHOKAM CULTURE, as well as MESOAMERICAN INDIANS and INCAS.

Iruska Dance (Irushka Dance) A healing ceremony of the PAWNEES, sponsored by the MEDICINE SOCIETY known as Iruska, whose members specialized in overcoming fire and healing burns. The Iruska Dance is named after a hair ROACH made from the tail of the deer. It may be an antecedent

prising dialects spoken by Indians of the NORTHEAST CULTURE AREA, among them the tribes of the IROQUOIS LEAGUE (CAYUGA, MOHAWK, ONEIDA, ONONDAGA, SENECA, and TUSCARORA) as well as the ERIE, Honniasont, HURON, MEHERRIN, of the widespread GRASS DANCE and has elements in common with the KETTLE DANCE of the SIOUX.

Isleta Pueblo   See TIWA.

isolate   See LANGUAGE ISOLATE.

italwa   The CREEK word for TOWN in MUSKOGEAN.

Itazipco   See SANS ARCS.

ivory work   The act, process, or resulting artifact of work in animal TUSKS. PREHISTORIC INDIANS used the ivory of MAMMOTHS and MASTODONS. INUITS are known for their elaborate carvings in ivory from walrus tusks as well as from sperm whale teeth. They have also used imported elephant ivory.

jacal In Mexico and the American Southwest, a type of architecture, or a type of house or hut, made of WATTLE-AND-DAUB, usually having upright poles. The word derives from the NAHUATL *xacalli* via Spanish.

jade Either of two distinct minerals, nephrite or jadeite, both pale green or yellow to white in color. Both stones take a high polish and are valued in the making of sculpture and jewelry. Because of their density, they also were used to make tools. Among MESOAMERICAN INDIANS, jade was highly valued because of its religious symbolism, associated with the AZTEC god TLALOC and the JAGUAR.

jaguar A large cat of tropical America (*Panthera onca*), with a heavier body, larger head, and shorter legs than a PUMA. The jaguar was worshipped as a principal deity among MESOAMERICAN INDIANS and the INCAS. The word derives from the TUPI-GUARANI *jaguara* via Spanish.

jar A container typically made of pottery or sometimes stone (or in modern-day usage, glass). Native Americans used jars for holding, serving, and storing food, water, herbs, seeds, or other materials in daily life or ceremonies. (See also SEED JAR; WEDDING JAR; WHISTLING JAR.)

jasper See CHALCEDONY.

javelin A small SPEAR for throwing. (See also LANCE.)

Jeaga See MUSKOGEAN.

Jemez Pueblo See TOWA.

jerky (charqui) Strips of meat smoked or dried in the sun, typically on wooden racks.

"Jerk" is a verb form, as in jerked meat. The original word *charqui* is of QUECHUA origin, referring to dried LLAMA meat, and is still used in South America. (See also PEMMICAN.)

jewelry In pre-Contact times, earrings and EARSPOOLS of shell, bone, and copper were worn by various tribes; sometimes the ear was pierced in more than one place for them. LABRETS were worn on the lips. GORGETS were worn on the neck and chest. Other PENDANTS, such as shell disks, were draped from the neck. BEAR-CLAW NECKLACES were highly valued. Nose-rings were favored by some tribes. Headbands, armlets, bracelets, collars, and ANKLETS also were crafted. The use of SILVER and GOLD in jewelry became widespread north of Mexico only in the 19th century. Glass BEADWORK also generally replaced SHELLWORK in post-Contact times. Some contemporary Native Americans have international reputations as jewelers, especially for their SILVERWORK.

Jicarilla A subtribe of the APACHE Indians, located in present-day northern New Mexico and southeastern Colorado and ranging into present-day Arizona, Texas, Oklahoma, and Kansas. Along with the KIOWA-APACHES and LIPANS, the Jicarillas are

Zuni silver and turquoise pin

classified as Eastern Apaches. The Jicarilla Reservation has its tribal headquarters in Dulce, New Mexico. *Jicarilla* means "little basket" in Spanish. Their native name, *Tinde*, means "the people."

jimsonweed (thorn apple) Plants of the nightshade family, especially *Datura stramonium* and *D. inoxia*, with large trumpet-shape flowers and prickly fruit. CALIFORNIA INDIANS, SOUTHWEST INDIANS, and MESOAMERICAN INDIANS made a tea from leaves, stems, and roots for ceremonial and medicinal purposes. The name, which was formerly Jamestown weed, derives from the Jamestown colony; in 1676, a troop of soldiers became sick after having cooked and eaten the poisonous leaves. (SOUTHEAST INDIANS of the region are not known to have used the plant.) The AZTECS knew jimsonweed as *toloache* in NAHUATL. (See also CHUNGICHNISH RELIGION.)

jingler See RATTLE; TINKLER.

Jivaroan A language family and subdivision of the ANDEAN-EQUATORIAL phylum comprising dialects spoken by SOUTH AMERICAN INDIANS, including the Jivaro tribe of present-day Peru and the Palta tribe of present-day Ecuador.

joined frame See POST-AND-BEAM.

joking relative A relative, often a cousin, who has the assigned task of ridiculing a child or adolescent as part of shaping character and preparation for adulthood; typical of PLAINS INDIANS.

Juaneno A UTO-AZTECAN-speaking tribe of the CALIFORNIA CULTURE AREA, located south of present-day Los Angeles, California, from the coast to Sierra Santa Ana. Like the Gabrielinos to their north and the LUISENOS to their south, the Juanenos were missionized by the Spanish, becoming known as MISSION INDIANS. A group in Santa Ana, California, still uses the tribal name, taken from the San Juan Capistrano mission.

juggling Keeping two or more objects in the air at the same time by repetitive tossing and catching. In juggling competitions, the object is to keep juggling the longest without a mistake. Among Native Americans, women, not men, traditionally juggled, using clay balls.

Jumano See UTO-AZTECAN.

Jump Dance (Jumping Dance, Redheaded Woodpecker Dance) A unity dance of the HOOPA, KAROK, and YUROK Indians, held during the World Renewal Ceremonial Cycle. The name derives from the leaping of the dancers, who wear headdresses made from the scalps of the redheaded woodpecker and carry wands woven out of plant materials.

juniper Any of various evergreen shrubs or trees of the genus *Juniperus*, especially *J. communis*, having small bluish-gray berrylike cones; considered a CEDAR. Native Americans chewed the berries to ward off diseases and relieve coughing and cramps. Juniper wood was burned in a number of ceremonies.

▲ K ▲

kachina (katchina, katcina, katsina, katzina, kacina, cachina) A spiritual being in the religion of the HOPIS and other PUEBLO INDIANS. Equivalent beings of other tribes—the KERES *shiwana;* the TEWA *okhua;* and the ZUNI, *koko*—also are referred to by the Hopi name. There are many different kachina beings—250, according to the Hopis—with distinct identities, representing different forces; some of them are ancestral. They are believed to live in mountains, lakes, and springs and represent animals, plants, and other natural phenomena, in particular rain. They stay in the other world for half the year and move invisibly among human beings the other half. In kachina dances, members of kachina societies wear kachina masks to call forth the invisible presences. Kachina dolls are carved icons of the deities, given to children to instruct them; they have been referred to as ancestral breath bodies. A scare-kachina is a representation in mask or doll used to discipline a child. "Kachina Cult" is sometimes used for the SECRET SOCIETY within a particular pueblo, the male members of whom participate in kachina ceremonies; in some instances, women also belong. In the UTO-AZTECAN language of the Hopis, *k'a-ci'nna* (i.e., *kachina*) means "spirit-father" or "those from over the horizon." (See also IMPERSONATOR.)

Kadohadacho Confederacy See CADDO.

Kahnawake See MOHAWK.

Kainah See BLOOD.

Kalapooian See KALAPUYAN.

Kalapuya (Kalapooya, Calapooya) A KALAPUYAN-speaking tribe of the NORTHWEST COAST CULTURE AREA, located at the headwaters of the Willamette River in present-day Oregon. In the mid-1800s, the Kalapuyas were settled on the Grande Ronde Reservation (now the Grande Ronde Indian Community) in Grande Ronde, Oregon, along with other tribes of the same language family.

Kalapuyan (Kalapooian) A language family and subdivision of the PENUTIAN phylum comprising dialects spoken by the Ahantchuyuk, Atfalati, Chelamela, Chepenafa, KALAPUYA, Luckiamute, Santiam, Yamel, and Yoncalla tribes of the NORTHWEST COAST CULTURE AREA.

Kalispel (Pend d'Oreille) A SALISHAN-speaking tribe of the PLATEAU CULTURE AREA, located on the Pend Oreille River,

Hopi kachina

Pend Oreille Lake, Priest Lake, and lower Clark's Fork in present-day Idaho and eastern Washington. Tribal members now hold the Kalispel Reservation near Usk, Washington; other Kalispels share the Colville Reservation near Nespelem, Washington, and the Flathead Reservation near Dixon, Montana, with other tribes. *Kalispel* derives from the native word for CAMAS; the alternate name, *Pend d'Oreille*, is French for "earrings," in reference to large shells tribal members wore dangling from their ears.

Kalopaling (pl., Kalopalit; Mitiling) A legendary being in INUIT tradition, a merman who wears a PARKA of eider-duck skins and has feet the size of sealskin floats. Kalopalits (plural form) were thought to delight in capsizing KAYAKS and putting drowned people in PARKA hoods. The alternate name, *Mitiling*, means "with eider ducks."

Kamia See DIEGUEÑO; YUMAN.

Kansa See KAW.

Karankawa A Karankawa-speaking (or Karankawan, a language isolate with undetermined phylum affiliation) tribe of the SOUTHWEST CULTURE AREA. The name originally was applied to one band living near Matagorda Bay in present-day Texas but came to include linguistically related coastal bands between Galveston Bay and Padre Island. Attacks by whites caused the Karankawas to become extinct in the mid-1800s.

karmak A type of earth-covered PITHOUSE of the INUITS, about five to six feet underground and two to three feet above, with a frame of wood or whalebone. The entrance is an underground passageway.

Karok (Karuk) A HOKAN-speaking tribe (Karok isolate) of the CALIFORNIA CULTURE AREA, located on the middle course of the Klamath River and some of its tributaries in present-day northwestern California. Members make up the Karok Indian

Community near Happy Camp, California. *Karok* means "upstream" in Hokan. The Karok language was formerly classified as a distinct stock, Quoretean.

kashim (kazgi, kazigi, karigi, qashe, qasqig, qaggi, qalegi, qaggi) A CEREMONIAL HOUSE and clubhouse of the INUITS. In Alaska, these structures typically were rectangular; in eastern regions, circular *kashims* generally were found. They were constructed with POST-AND-BEAM framework and sod covering, as well as of ice blocks, like IGLOOS. Many were semisubterranean (PITHOUSES) with secret passageways that only the *angagok* (SHAMANS) knew about. Ropes inside the *kashims* enabled the shamans to entertain and create illusions with acrobatics. Like the KIVA of PUEBLO INDIANS, the *kashim* evolved into a social institution for men. *Kashim* is the Russian version, probably taken from a Kodiak Island dialect. Other Inuit dialects have differing pronunciations, with a variety of spellings used by whites. These structures also have been referred to by non-Inuits as men's houses, dance houses, and feast houses.

Kaska See NAHANE.

Kaskaskia A subtribe of the ILLINOIS Indians, located on the upper Illinois River in present-day Illinois and later near present-day Kaskaskia. The Kaskaskias first were relocated to Kansas with the PEORIAS and then to the INDIAN TERRITORY.

Kaskinampo See MUSKOGEAN.

Kaw (Kansa) A SIOUAN-speaking tribe of the GREAT PLAINS CULTURE AREA, located on the Kansas River in present-day Kansas and ranging into present-day southeastern Nebraska. (The ancestors of the Kaws may have been among those of the OMAHA, OSAGE, PONCA, and QUAPAW tribes living along the Ohio River, then migrating onto the plains west of the Mississippi River and dividing.) In 1873, the Kaws were relocated to the northeastern part of the INDIAN TER-

RITORY. The Kaw tribe holds trust lands in Osage County, Oklahoma. *Kaw*, a shortened form of *Kansa*, means "people of the south wind" in Siouan.

Kawaiisu See UTO-AZTECAN.

Kawchottine See HARE.

Kawia See CAHUILLA.

kayak (kaiak) A boat, typical of the INU-ITS, with an enclosed cockpit, made by stretching hide, usually from a walrus or seal (in post-Contact times, canvas has also been used), over a wooden or whale-rib frame. Most kayaks are for a single passenger (some hold two), who uses a double paddle to propel the boat. (See also BAI-DARKA; UMIAK.)

keeper A tribal member who stores and protects a PALLADIUM, such as a MEDICINE BUNDLE, and carries out prescribed rituals. The terms caretaker, custodian, and guardian also are used.

Keres (Keresan, Queres) A Keresan-speaking (Keres or Keresan isolate) tribe of the SOUTHWEST CULTURE AREA, located on the upper Rio Grande in present-day New Mexico. Keres peoples lived in politically distinct PUEBLOS and are classified as PUEBLO INDIANS. Descendants hold the Acoma and Laguna pueblos west of Albuquerque, New Mexico, and the Cochiti, San Felipe, Santa Ana, Santo Domingo, and Zia pueblos north of Albuquerque.

Keresan See KERES.

kero A large wooden goblet, typical of the INCAS, narrow at the bottom and wide at the top, inlaid with colored resins depicting scenes of humans, animals, plants, along with abstract designs. The term is also applied to POTTERY of a similar shape.

Kettle Dance A dance of the SIOUX (Lakota) Indians, performed by the HEYOKAS

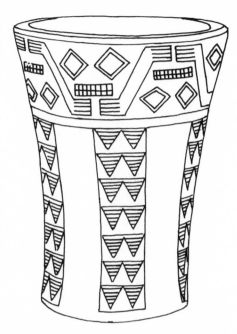

Inca kero

around a boiling kettle of dog meat to honor the THUNDER BEINGS during the Heyoka Kaga (Clownmaker Ceremony) and the YU-WIPI. Dancers would thrust their hands into the hot water to retrieve the meat, while insisting the water was cold. In SIOUAN, the dance is called *cehohomni wacipi*, meaning "dance around the kettle."

Keyauwee See SIOUAN.

ki A PITHOUSE of the PIMAS and PA-PAGOS, constructed over a shallow pit with an inner square POST-AND-BEAM framework and an attached circular BENT-FRAME, forming a domed shape. Brush and plant stalks are woven to it, then sealed with mud. Sometimes an ADOBE roof is added. *Kis* are usually less than 10 feet in diameter, but sometimes larger for a chief house or community house.

kiaha A BASKET for carrying food or possessions, made by the PIMAS and PAPAGOS, who traditionally supported it with a TUMPLINE.

Kichai See CADDOAN; WICHITA.

Kickapoo An ALGONQUIAN-speaking tribe of the NORTHEAST CULTURE AREA, located between the Wisconsin and Fox rivers in present-day Wisconsin. The Kickapoos are related linguistically to the FOXES and SACS. In the early 1700s, some among them lived on the Milwaukee River. After 1765, most Kickapoo bands lived on territory formerly held by the ILLINOIS Indians on the Illinois River in present-day Illinois. The tribe eventually divided: Some members headed farther south to the Sangamon River, becoming known as the Prairie band; others headed east to the Vermilion branch of the Wabash River, now part of the border of Illinois and Indiana, becoming known as the Vermilion band. By the 1830s, the Kickapoos had been relocated to present-day Missouri. The tribe soon was forced to move to Kansas. Some managed to stay there; others were relocated to INDIAN TERRITORY. A band of Kickapoos headed for Texas in 1852, finally settling in Mexico, becoming known as the Mexican Kickapoos. In the 1870s, many joined fellow tribal members in Oklahoma. Kickapoos hold the Kickapoo Reservation in Brown County, Kansas, as well as trust lands in Oklahoma, Lincoln, and Pottawatomi counties, Oklahoma. Other Kickapoos still live in the Santa Rosa Mountains of Mexico. *Kickapoo* derives from *Kiwegapaw* meaning "he moves about, standing now here, now there."

kickball (football) INUIT kickball is played with a soft leather ball stuffed with caribou hair; a player and his or her team try to control the ball longer than the other side. Men, women, and children can play. In the kick-stick or kicked stick race of the ZUNIS and other PUEBLO INDIANS, players use two small painted sticks. (See also FOOTBALL.)

kick-stick See KICKBALL.

kihus A rectangular surface ceremonial room, typical of PUEBLO INDIANS, similar in design and function to a KIVA.

killed pottery A type of POTTERY buried with a deceased person, often the pot's maker; supposedly holding the SOUL and having a kill hole, a perforation in the bottom, which supposedly allows a soul to escape to the afterworld.

kill site A place where remains of many animals have been found along with human artifacts. Sometimes POINTS are found in or among the bones, indicating the act of hunting.

kiln An oven in which the FIRING of POTTERY takes place. Modern kilns use electricity. PIT OVENS are used for traditional pottery.

kilt See APRON.

kinnikinnick (kinnikkinnik, kinnikinik, kinnikinic, kinikinik, kinic-kinic, kinnikkinnuk, k'nickk'neck, killikinnick) A mixture for SMOKING, made from TOBACCO and other plant matter, such as the inner bark of willow and dogwood or sumac leaves. Buffalo bone marrow sometimes was added. An ALGONQUIAN word, meaning "what is mixed."

kinship Shared DESCENT or other culturally recognized links, i.e., a common group relationship (a kin group) as in a FAMILY or CLAN. (See also SIB.)

Kiowa A KIOWA-TANOAN-speaking tribe of the GREAT PLAINS CULTURE AREA, located south of the Arkansas River in present-day southern Kansas and northern Oklahoma; the principal site was on the Cimarron River. (The first known homeland of the Kiowas was in present-day Montana, then eastern Wyoming and western South Dakota, and, by the early 1800s, Nebraska, before they settled to the south.) In 1868, the Kiowas were placed on a reservation in the INDIAN TERRITORY, along with

COMANCHES. Tribal members hold trust lands near Anadarko, Oklahoma. *Kiowa* derives from *Kaigwu*, meaning "principal people."

Kiowa-Apache A subtribe of the APACHE Indians, related linguistically to the JICARILLAS and LIPANS, other Eastern Apaches, but living among the KIOWA Indians as part of their CAMP CIRCLE. The Kiowa-Apaches continue to live near the Kiowas, with tribal headquarters also in Anadarko, Oklahoma. Their native name, *Naishandina*, means "our people."

Kiowa calendar The sacred WINTER COUNT of the KIOWA Indians. Years are depicted in PICTOGRAPHS, painted spirally on animal hide, each named after a remarkable event.

Kiowa-Tanoan A language family and subdivision of the Aztec-Tanoan phylum comprising dialects spoken by the KIOWA tribe of the GREAT PLAINS CULTURE AREA and the Pecos, Piro, TEWA, TIWA, and TOWA Indians of the SOUTHWEST CULTURE AREA.

kisi A small structure made of evergreen trees or cottonwood and used to house snakes for the SNAKE DANCE of the HOPIS.

Kitamat See HAISLA.

Kitanemuk See UTO-AZTECAN.

kitchen midden See MIDDEN.

Kitchigami See ALGONQUIAN.

Kite See CROW.

Kitksan See GITKSAN.

Kitunahan See KOOTENAY.

kiva An underground CEREMONIAL HOUSE of the PUEBLO INDIANS, a kind of PITHOUSE, serving as a sacred chamber and clubhouse. Kivas are either circular or rectangular in shape; the flat roof is sometimes built partly above ground with stone or ADOBE. The entrance symbolizes where the first people emerged to inhabit the earth's surface; a ladder leads inside, where are found a FIREPIT, ALTAR, SIPAPU, and some-

Anasazi kiva

times a *BANCO*. When a ceremony is in process, a *nachi* (a feathered stick or sticks) is raised on the top. Villages usually have more than one kiva, representing individual clans. Women generally are not permitted to enter kivas. *Kiva* is a HOPI word. "Great kiva" applies to large circular structures of the ANASAZI CULTURE, used for councils and ceremonies. (See also DEFLECTOR; PROTOKIVA.)

Klallam   See CLALLAM.

Klamath   A PENUTIAN-speaking (Klamath-Modoc or Lutuamian isolate) tribe of the PLATEAU CULTURE AREA, located on Upper Klamath Lake, the Klamath River, and the Sprague and William rivers in present-day southern Oregon. Tribal members are centered in Chiloquin, Oregon. Their native name is *Maklaks*, meaning "people" or "community."

Klickitat (Klikitat)   A SAHAPTIN-speaking tribe of the PLATEAU CULTURE AREA, located at the headwaters of the Klickitat, Cowlitz, Lewis, and White Salmon rivers in present-day Washington. The Klickitats also lived for a time north of the Columbia River. They settled among the YAKIMAS on the Yakima Reservation near present-day Toppenish, Washington. Their name means "beyond" in CHINOOKAN, referring to their homeland being west of the Cascade Range.

Knaiakhotana   See TANAINA.

knapping   See FLAKING.

knife   Native Americans made knives out of any material that would take an edge, including stone (especially FLINT), wood, reed, bone, antler, teeth, shell, and, in post-Contact times, iron. Knives had numerous purposes, in crafts, food preparation, surgery, warfare, and ceremonies. "Dagger" refers to a knife or small sword used for stabbing. (See also SACRIFICIAL KNIFE; SNOW KNIFE; ULU.)

Koasati   See COUSHATTA.

Kohuana   See YUMAN.

Kokopelli   A legendary being of the ANASAZI CULTURE, depicted in artwork as humpbacked, wearing a feathered headdress, and playing a FLAGEOLET. He is thought to bring rain and fertility.

Koluschan   See TLINGIT.

Konkau   A subtribe of the MAIDU Indians, located on the lower course of the North Fork of the Feather River in present-day Butte County, California. Konkaus hold the Round Valley Reservation in Mendocino County, California.

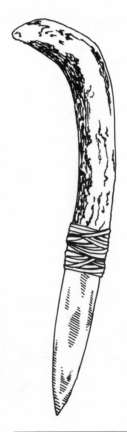

Iroquois antler and bone knife

Konomihu See SHASTAN.

Kootenay (Kootenai, Kutenai) A Kutenai-speaking (language isolate with undetermined phylum affiliation) tribe of the PLATEAU CULTURE AREA, located on Kootenay River, Kootenay Lake, Arrow Lake, and the upper Columbia River in present-day southeastern British Columbia, northwestern Montana, northeastern Washington, and northern Idaho. The tribe is classified into two general divisions: the Upper Kootenay to the east on the upper Kootenay River and the Lower Kootenay to the west. Tribal members hold the Kootenai Reservation near Bonners Ferry, Idaho; others share the Flathead Reservation near Dixon, Montana, with FLATHEAD Indians. In British Columbia, the Columbia Lake, Lower Kootenay, and Tobacco Plains bands maintain tribal identity. The Kootenay language was formerly classified as a distinct stock, Kitunahan.

Koroa See TUNICAN.

Koshare (Koshari) A SECRET SOCIETY of the KERES Indians, the members of which wear black-and-white horizontal stripes and horns to impersonate the spirits also known as Koshare and perform comedies between ceremonial dances. They are associated with fertility and control of the weather. The name Koshare has been translated as CLOWNS or "delight-makers." Equivalent societies among other PUEBLO INDIANS are the Kossa (Kosa) of the TEWAS; the Tabosh of the TOWAS; the Paiakyamu of the HOPIS; and the Nekwekwe of the ZUNIS. KWERANA is another Keres clown society.

Kotikilli A SECRET SOCIETY of the ZUNI Indians. There were traditionally six divisions of the Kotikilli, each with its own particular KIVA, corresponding to the six world-realms. Members included every male of the tribe and some females. They were below the PRIESTHOOD OF THE BOW and RAIN PRIESTHOOD in rank, but shared some of the same functions, such as RAINMAKING.

Koyemshi (Koyenci) A SECRET SOCIETY of the ZUNIS, members of which are ritual CLOWNS. The Koyemshis are called MUDHEADS because of their earth-colored masks; they also wear packets of corn around their necks. They begin the SHALAKO FESTIVAL, visiting all the houses in the pueblo.

Koyukon An ATHAPASCAN-speaking tribe of the SUBARCTIC CULTURE AREA, located on the Koyukuk, Innoko, and Yukon rivers in present-day north-central Alaska. Descendants live in their ancestral homeland; the Koyukuk Village Council is centered in Koyukuk. *Koyukon* is the shortened form of *Koyukukhotana*, meaning "people of Koyukuk River" in Athapascan. (The long form is considered a subdivision of the tribe, along with the Kaiyuhkhotana and Yukonikhotana bands.)

Kuitsh (Lower Umpqua) A YAKONAN-speaking tribe of the NORTHWEST COAST CULTURE AREA, located on the lower Umpqua River in present-day Oregon. The Kuitsh Indians, also known as Lower Umpquas, were related linguistically to the SIUSLAWS, with whom they merged; their neighbors on the river, UMPQUAS, or Upper Umpquas, were ATHAPASCAN-speaking. The Confederated Tribes of Coos, Lower Umpqua and Siuslaw Indians are centered in Coos Bay, Oregon. (See also COOS.)

Kuksu Religion (Kuksu Cult) A religion of central CALIFORNIA INDIANS, among them the CAHTOS, COSTANOANS, Esselens, MAIDUS, PATWINS, POMOS, SALINAS, Wappos, WINTUNS, and YUKIS. Members of the Kuksu Society impersonate spiritual beings in order to acquire their power. Participants wear "big-head" feather or grass headdresses as disguises representing different deities. Moki represents the most powerful god-figure to the Patwins; other beings in the Patwin pantheon are Tuya the Big-Headed and Chelitu the Unmasked. The Kuksu Society holds its ceremonies in the cold months to bring an abundant harvest and successful hunt the following spring and summer. The Patwins, Maidus, and Wintuns call the first ceremony *Hesi;* it is a four-day dance, with one Kuksu acting out Moki and pairs of others representing different versions of Tuya and Chelitu as well as other beings. While villagers look on, drummers provide a beat for the dancers, usually by stomping on a FOOT DRUM, and singers chant sacred Kuksu songs.

Kukulkan The MAYA god of wind, also symbolizing life, light, water, and motion; the principal deity during the Maya-Toltec period, the Maya version of QUETZALCOATL, who supposedly helped the Mayas conquer their enemies.

Kulanapan See POMO.

Kusan (Coos) A language family and subdivision of the PENUTIAN phylum comprising dialects spoken by bands of the COOS tribe of the NORTHWEST COAST CULTURE Area.

Kutchin An ATHAPASCAN-speaking tribe of the SUBARCTIC CULTURE AREA, located in present-day eastern Alaska, northern Yukon Territory, and northwestern Northwest Territories. The Alaskan Kutchins consist of the following subtribes: Dihai-Kutchin, Kutcha-Kutchin, Natsit-Kutchin, Tennuth-Kutchin, Tranjik-Kutchin, and Vunta-Kut-chin. The Canadian Kutchins include the following: Nakotcho-Kutchin, Takkuth-Kutchin, and Tatlit-Kutchin. The name Loucheux has been applied to the Kutchin tribes, especially in Canada. Descendants of these various groups live in their ancestral homelands in both Alaska and Canada. *Kutchin* means "people" in Athapascan.

Kutenai See KOOTENAY.

Kwaiailk See CHEHALIS.

Kwakiutl (Kwaguilth, Kwa-Gulth) A WAKASHAN-speaking tribe of the NORTHWEST COAST CULTURE AREA, located on both shores of Queen Charlotte Sound and northern Vancouver Island in present-day British Columbia. Many Kwakiutl bands live in their ancestral homeland. *Kwakiutl* means "smoke of the world" or "beach at the north side of the river" in Wakashan.

Kwalhioqua See ATHAPASCAN.

Kwerana (Kwirana, Kwiraina, Kwirena, Kurena, Quirana) A SECRET SOCIETY of the KERES Indians, involving sacred CLOWNS and fertility. The Kwerana SODALITY shares ceremonial functions with the KOSHARE. Members' faces are painted with orange and black stripes for ceremonies; bodies are orange on the right side and white on the left.

labret An ornamental plug, often cylindrical in shape, usually wood, cane, shell, ivory, or stone, worn in the lip. Labrets were usually inserted in the lower lip, or just below it, by both men and women. Typical of the INUITS, YUMAN Indians, and SOUTHEAST INDIANS of present-day Florida.

lacrosse A game or sport invented and played by EASTERN INDIANS, using rackets (originally a wooden stick with a curved head, then long wooden handles and netting); a small ball (originally a spherical block of wood, such as a burl, then deerskin stuffed with hair or moss); and two goals, or "gates" (two poles about 10 feet high), under which the ball is tossed. Among NORTHEAST INDIANS, such as the IROQUOIS, each player used a single racket; among SOUTHEAST INDIANS, players generally used two. The games lasted for days and were sometimes violent, a kind of SHAM BATTLE that served as training for real warfare. The CHOCTAW Indians called the game *toli* in Muskogean, sometimes translated as "stickball"; the term stickball also is used by CREEKS and SEMINOLES. Southeast Indians referred to the game as "little brother of war." A modern version, introduced in colleges in 1877, now is played widely. The Iroquois have intertribal competition. The word lacrosse derives from the French *la crosse*, meaning "the crosier."

ladle See SPOON.

Laguna Pueblo See KERES.

Lake (Senijextee) A SALISHAN-speaking tribe of the PLATEAU CULTURE AREA, located on the Columbia River, from Kettle Falls to the Canadian boundary in present-day Washington and around Arrow Lakes in present-day British Columbia. Descendants share the Colville Reservation near Nespelem, Washington, with other tribes. The name Lake Indians also applies to GREAT LAKES INDIANS.

Choctaw lacrosse stick and ball

Lakota   See SIOUX; TETON.

lamenting   A synonym of "mourning," applied in Indian studies to the ritual practice among the PLAINS INDIANS of the VISION QUEST, i.e., seeking a vision in solitude.

lamp   The INUITS provided lighting with a stone device, known as a *kudlek* or *qulliq*, typically shaped like a saucer and designed to hold burning animal or fish oil, especially from sea mammals, along with moss wicks. SOAPSTONE was a favored material for carving these stone lamps or oil lamps. Other American Indians in present-day California and Virginia had similar stone artifacts believed to be lamps. Most tribes used campfires or TORCHES for lighting. (See also FIRE.)

lance   A weapon designed for thrusting with a long wooden handle and a sharp stone or metal head. The term lance sometimes is used interchangeably with SPEAR, but the long handles make them more suited to thrusting and not throwing. A JAVELIN is designed primarily for throwing. PLAINS INDIANS used long spears, or lances, from horseback. They often were decorated with featherwork or other insignia and had special sheaths. MILITARY SOCIETIES often had ceremonial lances. Medicine lances were carried to bring good fortune in war and the hunt.

land   Defining "land" as the solid ground of the earth or a region inhabited by a particular people only partly communicates the traditional concept of land among Native Americans. For many Indian peoples, land was alive, pervaded by a spirit or spirits; many tribes speak of land as "mother," something akin to the concept of "mother earth." "Ancestral homeland" imparts more of the Indian view of land, referring to a "home" and to the long-standing ties to that home through CULTURE HEROES. (See also LAND CESSION; LAND CLAIM; LAND TENURE.)

land bridge   See BERINGIA.

land cession   Land given up by Indians in a TREATY. Most land cessions were forced upon tribes against their will following defeat in war. In many cases, white officials negotiated with a particular element of a tribe that was not representative of all the bands, using bribes and alcohol as negotiating tools.

land claim   A tribe's assertion of rights to a particular tract of land based on ancestral use. The term has been used in the 20th century in reference to legal claims to land, most based on historical TREATIES. In 1946, the U.S. Congress created the Indian Claims Commission to settle tribal land claims against the United States (which formerly had been handled by the Court of Claims) and to provide financial compensation; it lasted until 1978. Since then claims have been handled by the judicial system. In 1974, Canada established the Office of Native Claims to resolve its native peoples' land and treaty claims. Relevant to contemporary land claims are WATER RIGHTS, mineral rights, and grazing rights. The colonial powers in the Americas made "claims" to land, based on the fact that they had arrived before other powers, with little regard for the rights of indigenous peoples. (See also BROKEN PROMISES; LAND TENURE.)

land tenure   The holding of LAND and the rights to that land. For American Indians, occupancy determined land tenure, i.e., occupancy at the tribal level. Tribes claimed and protected their homelands and made territorial claims to HUNTING GROUNDS against other tribes. But tribes and individuals did not generally "own" land as in the non-Indian notion of "real estate"; land was considered a natural resource for all to use. In many cases, when a tribe signed a land agreement, it did not realize it could no longer use the land and continued to do so. Whites went to war with tribes over such violations of their property deeds. Concerning land use, tribes had customs and rules governing individual rights to placement of lodges and the use of certain plots for farming. (See also LAND CLAIM.)

language   In Indian linguistic studies, the term language usually applies to that which is distinct in vocabulary, grammar, and phonetics. A DIALECT is a variation of a language; and a LANGUAGE FAMILY or a LANGUAGE PHYLUM is a grouping of two or more languages. The classification of Indian languages into these various groups is theoretical because so many of them are extinct. It is estimated that 1,800 to 2,200 different languages were spoken by native peoples in the Americas at the time of early contacts with Europeans (and many more dialects), as many as 300 north of Mexico, 300 to 350 in Mexico and Central America, and the rest in South America and the West Indies. About 200 native languages still are spoken in the United States and Canada, but many are on the verge of extinction. (See also CATEGORICAL APPENDIX, "TRIBES, BANDS, PEOPLES, LANGUAGES, AND CULTURES;" LANGUAGE ISOLATE; LINGUISTICS; PROTO-LANGUAGE; SIGN LANGUAGE; TRADE LANGUAGE.)

language family (language stock)   A LINGUISTICS term to describe two or more languages, distinct but with elements in common and related historically in that they are descended (or assumed to be descended) from a common language. (See also CATEGORICAL APPENDIX, "TRIBES, BANDS, PEOPLES, LANGUAGES, AND CULTURES.")

language isolate   A unique language with no recognizable elements in common with other languages.

language phylum (language superstock) A grouping of LANGUAGE FAMILIES, based on elements in common, including vocabulary, grammar, and phonetics. (See also CATEGORICAL APPENDIX, "TRIBES, BANDS, PEOPLES, LANGUAGES, AND CULTURES.")

language stock   See LANGUAGE FAMILY.

lapstone   See METATE.

lariat   See ROPE.

Lassik   See ATHAPASCAN.

Latgawa (Upper Takelma)   A PENUTIAN-speaking (Takelma or Takilman isolate) tribe of the NORTHWEST COAST CULTURE AREA, located on the upper Rogue River in present-day Oregon. The Latgawas sometimes are grouped as a subtribe of the TAKELMAS. Along with other Rogue River Indians, the Latgawas were placed on the Siletz Reservation near Siletz, Oregon, in the mid-1800s. *Latgawa* means "those living in the uplands" in Penutian.

leaf bread   A bread of the IROQUOIS, made by boiling corn paste wrapped in cornhusks. Other ingredients, such as nuts and berries, sometimes were added.

lean-to   A temporary open brush shelter, generally consisting of a single-pitched sloping roof. Some western SUBARCTIC INDIANS constructed double lean-tos with two roofs meeting in a peak.

leather   The dressed or tanned HIDE of an animal, usually with the hair removed. "Leatherwork" is the act, process, or resulting artifact of work in leather. (See also SKIN-DRESSING.)

ledger art (ledger drawing)   A drawing representing an incident in the life of an individual, often in pencil or crayon, typically on the page of a ledger book obtained from a white trader or soldier. Many imprisoned PLAINS INDIANS, especially CHEYENNES, COMANCHES, and KIOWAS at Fort Marion near St. Augustine, Florida, filled ledger books with drawings.

legend   A story from the past. Legends often are associated with the history of a people and have an element of truth, but are not verifiable. (See also MYTH.)

legendary being   A being with human attributes and associated with LEGENDS. Variations include SPIRITUAL BEING, spirit being, supernatural being, man-being, mythological figure, deity, and demigod. (See also CATEGORICAL APPENDIX, "SPIRITS AND LEGENDARY BEINGS;" CULTURE HERO; MYTHICAL ANCESTOR; SPIRIT.)

legging   A covering for the leg. Indians used both animal skin and woven cloth to make leggings, decorating them with fringe, quillwork, and beadwork. Men's leggings typically extended from the ankles to the hips and were attached by thongs to a belt, which also held a BREECHCLOTH. Women's leggings extended from the ankles to the knee; depending on the tribe, they were attached to moccasins, wrapped around the calf, or fastened with buttons.

leister   A barbed HARPOON, typical of the INUITS, having three or more prongs.

Lenni Lenape   (Leni-lenape, Delaware) An ALGONQUIAN-speaking tribe of the NORTHEAST CULTURE AREA, located in present-day New Jersey; New York (west of the Hudson River and the western end of Long Island); eastern Pennsylvania; northern Delaware; and northeastern Maryland. In the course of their post-Contact history, Lenni Lenape bands also lived in present-day Ohio, Illinois, Indiana, Arkansas, Texas, Missouri, Kansas, Wisconsin, Oklahoma, and Ontario. The three major divisions are MUNSEE, UNALACHTIGO, and UNAMI, each having numerous bands. Since the various bands were politically independent with their own territories and leaders, they are sometimes referred to as being united in the Delaware Confederacy. The Delaware Indian Tribe now holds trust lands near Anadarko, Oklahoma. Munsee descendants share the Stockbridge-Munsee Reservation near Bowler, Wisconsin; others live in Ontario, part of the Moravian of the Thames and Muncey of the Thames bands. In New Jersey, the Native Delaware Indians, the Nanticoke-Lenni Lenape Tribe (with the

NANTICOKES), and the Ramapough Mountain Indians maintain tribal identity. A group known as the Delaware-Muncie Tribe is centered in Pomono, Kansas. The Delawares of Idaho operate out of Boise. Lenni Lenape descendants also live in the Allentown, Pennsylvania region. *Lenni Lenape* means "true men" in Algonquian. The non-Indian name, Delaware, was taken from the Delaware River, named after Lord De La Warr, the second governor of Virginia. (See also BROTHERTON INDIANS; MORAVIAN INDIANS.)

lichen   Any of the thallophytic plants of the group *Lichenes*, consisting of a fungus in symbiotic union with an algae and growing crustlike on rocks and trees in the Arctic. Reindeer moss, a primary food of the CARIBOU, is one variety.

life history   An individual's account of his or her experiences as gathered by a researcher in interviews. (See also INFORMANT.)

lifeways   See   CULTURAL   TRAIT; CULTURE.

lightning   For many American Indians, lightning is associated with the ARROW. In NAVAJO mythology, children in the sky fire shafts of lightning toward earth, and the legendary beings known as the Hero Twins use thunderbolts to slay monsters. *Itsiniklizh* is the Navajo word for "lightning" in their ATHAPASCAN language, depicted as a zigzag symbol. (See also AVANYU; THUNDER BEINGS.)

Lillooet   A SALISHAN-speaking tribe of the PLATEAU CULTURE AREA, located on the Lillooet, Bridge, and Fraser rivers and Harrison Lake in present-day British Columbia. A number of Lillooet bands live in their ancestral homeland.

lineage   See DESCENT.

linguistic family   See LANGUAGE FAMILY.

linguistics The science and study of LAN-GUAGE, including structure (descriptive linguistics) and origin (historical linguistics). A linguist studies human speech as it is spoken and written. (See also COGNATE; MORPHEME; PHONEME; PHONOLOGY; POLYSYNTHESISM.)

linguistic stock See LANGUAGE FAMILY.

lintel A horizontal member spanning a window or door to support the weight of the structure above it.

Lipan A subtribe of the APACHE Indians, ranging from the lower Rio Grande in present-day New Mexico and Mexico eastward to the Gulf Coast of present-day Texas. With the JICARILLAS and KIOWA-APACHES, the Lipans are defined as Eastern Apaches. Surviving tribal members at the end of the 19th century settled with the MESCALEROS; others, with the Kiowa-Apaches. *Lipan* is derived from *Ipa-n'de*, *Ipa* probably being a personal name and *n'de* meaning "people." Their native name is *Naizhan*, meaning "our kind."

literature The term ORAL TRADITION is encountered more often in Indian studies than "literature," since many Native American texts are derived from traditional STORYTELLING, i.e., spoken tales and LEGENDS, and ORATORY. Yet many contemporary Native Americans work in written prose—the novel and short-story forms—and in POETRY.

Lithic period See PALEOLITHIC PERIOD.

Little Bighorn A famous battle in the Sioux Wars. On June 25, 1876, SIOUX, Northern CHEYENNES, and Northern ARAPAHOS, under Sitting Bull, Crazy Horse, and Gall, defeated Lieutenant Colonel George Armstrong Custer's Seventh Cavalry on the Little Bighorn in present-day southern Montana. The Battle of the Little Bighorn is considered the greatest victory for the PLAINS INDIANS, but it set the stage for the ultimate defeat of the Northern Plains tribes. In 1991, what had been known as the Custer Battlefield National Monument became the Little Bighorn Battlefield National Monument.

Little People Spiritual beings small in size, existing in the legends of many native peoples and generally believed to be mischievous. They are also referred to as little folks and pygmies by the IROQUOIS, who have a Little People Society to appease them and draw power from them. In CATAWBA tradition, small creatures known as *Yehasuri*, for "not human ones," dwell in the forest and attack and kidnap the unwary.

llama Any of several wild or domesticated South American ruminants, related to camels, but smaller and without a hump. The alpaca (*Lama pacos*) is domesticated in Peru, with long woolly hair. The guanaco (*L. guanicoe*) is perhaps the ancestor of domesticated llamas. The vicuña (*L. vigugna*), another wild species, also is related to the guanaco, but smaller. The INCAS domesticated llamas as a pack animal and as a source of wool, meat, and milk.

Inca silver llama

lodge   A term for a dwelling, referring to TEPEES, WICKIUPS, WIGWAMS, and other types of North American Indian structures. (See also EARTHLODGE; GRASS HOUSE; SWEATHOUSE.)

log cabin   A small dwelling made of un-hewn timber. American Indians used logs in traditional construction, but typically for framing and not in the stacked fashion of the log cabins associated with non-Indian pioneers. In post-Contact times, however, various tribes copied the design of pioneer log cabins, among them CHEROKEES and IR-OQUOIS.

longhorn buffalo   See BUFFALO.

longhouse   A dwelling, about 60 feet long by 18 feet wide, with a pointed or rounded roof about 18 feet high and doors at both ends, made with a POST-AND-BEAM or bent sapling frame, and usually covered with slabs of ELM BARK about four feet wide by six to eight feet long. The IROQUOIS and HURONS

lived in longhouses, which had central fires and were divided into compartments with raised platforms for sleeping for different families. Plants were dried from the inner cross poles. The longhouse also served as a political or social grouping within the tribe. Some ALGONQUIAN Indians, such as the LENNI LENAPES (Delawares), MAHICANS, and WAPPINGERS, built longhouses along with their domed WIGWAMS, often as coun-cil houses. (See also LONGHOUSE RE-LIGION.)

Long House People   See IROQUOIS.

Longhouse Religion   A religious revital-ization movement of the IROQUOIS Indians. In 1799, the SENECA Indian Handsome Lake (Ganiodaiyo), alcoholic and sick, expe-rienced a series of visions in which he claimed he was taken on a spiritual journey by four messengers. Afterward, he stopped drinking and regained his health. He began preaching to his people, his teachings be-coming known as *Gaiwiio,* or "Good Word."

Southeast Indian log cabin

Iroquois longhouse

Handsome Lake rejected many white customs, especially the use of alcohol, advocating self-purification through traditional beliefs. He also encouraged the values of family, community, and sharing. He denounced any form of witchcraft. Agriculture, he believed, was central to tribal self-sufficiency. As it came to be defined in the *Code of Handsome Lake* (published in 1850, with the help of Blacksnake, Handsome Lake's nephew and disciple) and as practiced today, the Longhouse Religion combines elements of Quakerism, in particular good deeds and silent prayer, with traditional Iroquois beliefs. Those traditional beliefs, predating Handsome Lake's teachings and involving a series of Iroquois seasonal ceremonies, such as the MIDWINTER CERE-MONY and four sacred rituals—the FEATHER DANCE, Thanksgiving Dance, Personal Chant, and Bowl Game—are sometimes also referred to as the Longhouse Religion. A distinction is thus sometimes made between the traditional practices in ceremonial longhouses and Handsome Lake's revamped version, which is also referred to as the Handsome Lake Religion or the Code of Handsome Lake. (See also FAITHKEEPER; WASHANI RELIGION.)

Long Walk A historical event of the Navajo War in 1864, when NAVAJOS were forced by white troops to leave their ancestral homeland in present-day northern Arizona and New Mexico and southern Utah and Colorado and relocate to Bosque Redondo in eastern New Mexico. Hundreds died during and after the march. Survivors were allowed to return to their Chuska Mountain homeland in 1868. Like the TRAIL OF TEARS, the Long Walk has come to symbolize all forced relocations of Indian peoples.

loom A device used to interweave thread or yarn to make cloth. Basic means of supporting materials while WEAVING, such as trees, poles, and frames, were widespread in the Americas. North of Mexico, only the SOUTHWEST INDIANS used true looms—two-bar, fixed-WARP frames with heddles, i.e., sticks, cords, or wire to which some of the warp strands are attached in order to separate and guide them.

lost wax See CIRE PERDUE.

Loucheux See KUTCHIN.

Luckiamute See KALAPUYAN.

Luiseno   A UTO-AZTECAN-speaking tribe of the CALIFORNIA CULTURE AREA, located in the area of the San Luis Rey River in present-day California. With their neighbors, the DIEGUENOS and the Gabrielinos, the Luisenos were missionized by the Spanish, becoming known as MISSION INDIANS. Contemporary Luisenos hold the following reservations: La Jolla, Los Coyotes, Pala, Pauma and Yuima, and Rincon in San Diego County, California; Pechanga and Soboba in Riverside County; and Twenty-Nine Palms in San Bernardino County. Their name derives from the San Luis Rey de Francia mission.

Lumbee   A tribe of combined ancestry, possibly ALGONQUIAN, IROQUOIAN, or SI-OUAN, located in North Carolina and South Carolina. Previously referred to as Croatan Indians, Robeson County Indians, and then Cherokee Indians of Robeson County, they formally adopted the name Lumbee in 1953 after the Lumber River. The Lumbee Tribe is centered in Pembroke, North Carolina.

Lumni   A SALISHAN-speaking tribe of the NORTHWEST COAST CULTURE AREA, located on Bellingham Bay and the mouth of the Nooksack River in present-day Washington. Tribal members hold the Lumni Reservation in Whatcom County, Washington.

Lutuamian   See KLAMATH; MODOC.

▲ M ▲

Macaw See MAKAH.

Machapunga See ALGONQUIAN.

Macro-Algonquian A phylum of language stocks, including the ALGONQUIAN and MUSKOGEAN families as well as the ATAKAPA, CHITIMACHA, TONKAWA, TUNICAN, WIYOT, and YUROK isolates.

Macro-Chibchan A phylum of language stocks, including the CHIBCHAN and PAEZAN families.

Macro-Siouan A phylum of language stocks, including the CADDOAN, IROQUOIAN, and SIOUAN families as well as the YUCHI isolate and, according to some scholars, the CATAWBA isolate.

magic A force of or pertaining to the supernatural; also, the use of ritual to control or change the natural laws, as in WITCHCRAFT; and sleight-of-hand or other tricks to create a supernatural effect. In Indian studies, the term magic is also applied to the mysterious force behind nature, i.e., a synonym of MEDICINE, SPIRIT, or "power."

magpie Any of two birds of the family Corvidae (*Pica pica* or *P. nuttalli*) having long tails and blue-black and white plumage and a chatterlike call. Magpies, related to CROWS, are noisy and mischievous and are considered TRICKSTER figures by a number of tribes, such as the NAVAJOS. According to legend, Magpie has been known to trick Coyote by flattering him. (See also COYOTE.)

maguey See AGAVE.

mahala (mahaly) A term for SQUAW in the American and Canadian West, from the YOKUTS word *muk'ela,* meaning "woman" in PENUTIAN. A mahala mat is a type of shrub (*Ceanothus prostratus*) found on the Pacific Coast and used by Indian women to make MATS.

Mahican An ALGONQUIAN-speaking tribe of the NORTHEAST CULTURE AREA, located on the upper Hudson River in present-day New York as well as in present-day western Massachusetts, northwestern Connecticut, and southwestern Vermont. The various Mahican bands sometimes are referred to as members of the Mahican Confederacy. Some of the Mahicans became known historically as STOCKBRIDGE INDIANS and BROTHERTON INDIANS. Mahican descendants share the Stockbridge-Munsee Reservation in Shawano County, Wisconsin, with LENNI LENAPE (Delaware) descendants. *Mahican* means "wolf" in Algonquian. (See also MOHICAN.)

Maidu A PENUTIAN-speaking tribe of the CALIFORNIA CULTURE AREA, located in the Sacramento Valley and the adjacent Sierra. Nevada, especially the drainage areas of the American and Feather rivers, in present-day California. Tribal members hold the Berry Creek and Enterprise rancherias near Oroville, California and share the Susanville Indian Rancheria near Susanville with ACHOMAWIS and PAIUTES. A band known as Maidu Historical Tribal and Cultural Elders Organization operates out of Dobbins, California; and the Northern Maidu tribe is centered in Greenville. Some scholars group the various dialects spoken by the Maidu bands in a distinct language family called Maidu, a subdivision of the Penutian phylum; it was formerly known as Pujunan. *Maidu* means "person" in Penutian. (See also KONKAU.)

maize See CORN.

maka A SIOUX name for the "earth" in SIOUAN (Lakota). Earth is considered the Womb-Mother nourishing all of life.

Makah (Macaw) A WAKASHAN-speaking tribe of the NORTHWEST COAST CULTURE AREA, located on Cape Flattery and Neah Bay as well as on Ozette River and Ozette Lake in present-day Washington. (The southern branch of the tribe is usually referred to as Ozette.) The Makahs are related linguistically to the NOOTKAS. Tribal members hold the Makah and Ozette reservations in Clallam County, Washington. *Makah* means "cape people" in Wakashan.

malamute (Alaskan malamute, malemute) A breed of DOG, originally developed as a sled dog by the Malemiuts (Mahlemuts), an INUIT people of Alaska. Like the HUSKY, the malamute is descended from the WOLF.

Malecite (Maliseet, Maliset, Etchemin) An ALGONQUIAN-speaking tribe of the NORTHEAST CULTURE AREA, located on the St. John River in present-day New Brunswick and in present-day northeastern Maine, to the north of the ABENAKIS. For much of their history, the Malecites were part of the Abenaki Confederacy. The Edmundston, Kingsclear, Oromocto, St. Mary's, Tobique, and Woodstock bands in New Brunswick maintain tribal identity; Malecites also live in Quebec. The Maliseet Band holds the Houlton Reservation near Houlton, Maine. *Malecite* possibly means "broken talkers" in the MICMAC dialect of Algonquian.

mammoth A large, extinct grazing mammal of the genus *Mammuthus*, similar to the elephant, once common in the Northern Hemisphere and hunted by PALEO-INDIANS. The woolly mammoth (*M. primigenius*) was one variety. (See also BIG-GAME HUNTING; MASTODON.)

Manahoac See SIOUAN.

Manakin See MONACAN.

man-being See LEGENDARY BEING.

Mandan A SIOUAN-speaking tribe of the GREAT PLAINS CULTURE AREA, located on the Missouri River, between the Heart and Little Missouri rivers in present-day North Dakota and ranging into present-day eastern Montana. (After separating from other Siouans, the Mandans lived on the Missouri at the mouth of the White River in present-day South Dakota before continuing northward.) The ARIKARAS and HIDATSAS were their neighbors. The Three Affiliated Tribes now share the Fort Berthold Reservation near New Town, North Dakota.

Manebozho (Manabozho, Nanabozho, Nenabozho, Nehnehbush, Nanabojo, Winabojo, Old Man) A legendary being in the traditions of various ALGONQUIAN tribes, such as the CHIPPEWAS. Manebozho is considered the Giver of Life and provider of MEDICINE for the MIDEWIWIN SOCIETY; he also is characterized as a TRICKSTER figure. Among the POTAWATOMIS, Manebozho is known as Chipiyapos and is the twin of Wiske. Among other Algonquians, Chipiyapos is considered the younger brother of Manebozho. (See also GLUSKAP.)

Manguean (Chorotegan) A language family and subdivision of the OTO-MANGUEAN phylum comprising dialects spoken by Indians of the MESOAMERICAN CULTURE AREA, including the Chiapanec (Chiapaneco) tribe of what is now southern Mexico and the Mangue tribe of what is now Nicaragua.

manioc See CASSAVA.

manitou (manito, manitu, manido, manitoa, manitto, manetto, mana) In ALGONQUIAN tradition, the force of nature and life, the mysterious SPIRIT or supernatural power inherent in all living and nonliving things (often capitalized when referring to a personified SPIRITUAL BEING). *Manitou* is known by other names in other religions and language families. (See also GITCHEE MANITOU; ORENDA; WAKANDA.)

mano (handstone, muller)   A stone, held in the hand, usually cylindrical in shape, for grinding CORN and other grains; used with a METATE. *Metlapilli*, or "son of metate," is the NAHUATL word for a mano. *Mano* is Spanish for "hand." (See also MORTAR AND PESTLE.)

mano and metate   See MANO; METATE; MORTAR AND PESTLE.

mantle   See CLOAK; ROBE.

manuscript   See CODEX.

maple sugar (Indian sugar)   NORTHEAST INDIANS taught the technique of boiling sap down to sugar to English and French settlers. Less boiling and evaporation is required to make maple syrup. Indians used the sap itself, either fresh or fermented, as a drink.

Maricopa (Marikapa)   A YUMAN-speaking tribe of the SOUTHWEST CULTURE AREA, located on the Gila River in present-day Arizona near the PIMAS. The two tribes make up the Gila River Indian Community, with tribal headquarters at Sacaton, Arizona. *Maricopa* is UTO-AZTECAN, given to them by the Pimas; the Maricopa native name is *Pipatsje*, meaning "people."

Mariposa   See YOKUTS.

marriage   The union of a man and woman, usually with an accompanying CEREMONY and the sharing of a household. Rules governing marital relationships and postmarital residence vary from tribe to tribe. (See also AFFINAL; AGAMOUS; ENDOGAMOUS; EXOGAMOUS; MATRILOCAL; NEOLOCAL; PATRILOCAL; RITE OF PASSAGE.)

Mascouten   See PEORIA. POTAWATOMI.

mask   Indian masks representing animal spirits or legendary beings are used in cere-

Inuit fur and leather mask

monies to give the wearer power. Complex rituals are involved in the making, storing, and wearing of masks. Some are made from animal heads; others are crafted from wood, basketry, pottery, hide, or ivory, and painted and decorated with a variety of materials. Some masks have two or more faces. (See also ARTICULATE MASK; BOOGER MASK; CHAPAYEKA; FALSE FACE; HUSK FACE SOCIETY; KACHINA; MOURNING MASK; MUDHEAD; PASCOLA; YEIBICHAI MASK.)

Maskegon   See CREE.

masonry   See STONEWORK.

masquette   A miniature mask, made of wood or cornhusks, serving as an AMULET. Masquettes were sometimes attached to full-size masks. Typical of the IROQUOIS.

Massachuset (Massachusett)   An ALGONQUIAN-speaking tribe of the NORTHEAST CULTURE AREA, located around Massachusetts Bay, between Plymouth and Salem in present-day eastern Massachusetts. In the 1600s, Christian converts from the tribe were gathered into Natick and 16 other villages. The Massachusets are now extinct as a tribal entity. Their name means "at the range of hills" in Algonquian, referring to the hills of Milton.

"massacre" Indiscriminate, wholesale, and cruel killing of human beings (or animals); in historical texts, used mostly in an ETHNOCENTRIC sense, referring to the defeat of whites by Indians in battle. What might be called a massacre by whites of Indians has been referred to more often as a battle or incident. During the four centuries of on-and-off warfare between American Indians and Euroamericans, both sides committed atrocities. (In some cases, one colonial power encouraged Indian allies to carry out atrocities against an opposing colonial power.) (See also WAR.)

Massaum Ceremony A ceremony of the CHEYENNE Indians, lasting five days and depicting the creation of the universe. The name Massaum derives from the Cheyenne word *massa'ne*, meaning "crazy" in ALGONQUIAN, and refers to the comical behavior of dancers disguised as animals. (See also CLOWN.)

mastodon (mastodont) Any large extinct mammal of the genus *Mammut* (or *Mastodon*). The variety found in the Americas is known as *M. americanum* (or *M. giganteum*). Mastodons resembled elephants. They lived in forested as well as grassland regions and ate grasses as well as leaves and twigs from trees. They differ from the also-extinct MAMMOTHS and existing elephants chiefly in the molar teeth.

mat A piece of coarse fabric, made by WEAVING rushes, husks, straw, or similar plant materials (and sometimes animal hair). Mats were used by Native Americans in many different applications, among them coverings of dwellings and bedding. "Matting" is used as a synonym of "mats."

matchcoat A type of CLOAK, worn especially by ALGONQUIAN-speaking Indians. The Indians originally crafted cloaks out of fur and later out of a coarse woolen European-made textile, known as matchcloth. The term derives from the CHIPPEWA name for the cloak in Algonquian, *matshigode*.

material culture The artifacts a given people possess and utilize in their daily life, involving the way they dress, make their homes, and prepare their food.

matrilineal (matrilineal descent) A term describing a type of social organization, such as in a matriclan, in which descent and property are passed through the female line; a type of unilineal DESCENT. (See also PATRILINEAL.)

matrilocal (matrilocal residence, uxorilocal) Residence after marriage in which the husband lives with or near his wife's family, as opposed to PATRILOCAL, another type of unilocal residence. A matrilocal extended family might describe an extended FAMILY consisting of a woman, her husband, their unmarried children as well as their married daughters and their husbands and children. (See also NEOLOCAL.)

Mattabesec See ALGONQUIAN.

Mattaponi (Mattapony) A subtribe of the POWHATAN Indians, located on the Mattaponi River in present-day Virginia. The Mattaponi Indian Tribe holds the Mattaponi Reservation in King William County, Virginia; the Upper Mattaponi Indian Tribal Association is centered at St. Stephens Church.

mattock A digging tool with a bone or stone blade set at right angles to the handle. It is shaped like a pickax, but with at least one of the two blades broad and flat instead of pointed.

Mattole See ATHAPASCAN.

maul See HAMMER.

Maya A MAYAN-speaking people of the MESOAMERICAN CULTURE AREA, located in what is now Guatemala and the Yucatan Peninsula of Mexico. The stage of Maya development and consolidation in the centuries before A.D. 300, during the time of the OLMEC civilization, is referred to as the Preclassic period. The period of Maya dominance and highest expression of culture is called the CLASSIC PERIOD, from about A.D. 300 to 900. CITY-STATES such as Tikal and Palenque in what is now Guatemala prospered during the Classic period; their inhabitants are sometimes called Lowland Mayas. The phase of Maya culture from about A.D. 900 to 1500 is known as the Postclassic period, during which Maya culture thrived in the Guatemalan mountains to the south. The Mayas of such sites as Chama, Utatlan, and Kaminaljuya are called Highland Mayas. These peoples learned METALWORK, probably through trade with the Indians living to their south in Peru and Ecuador, and crafted objects out of gold, silver, tin, and zinc. After about A.D. 1000, also during the Postclassic period, still another strain of Maya culture flourished on the Yucatan Peninsula in what is now eastern Mexico; an invasion of TOLTECS from the west spurred this new flowering of culture. The Toltecs interbred with the Mayas and adopted many of their cultural traits. Inhabitants of Chichen Itza, Mayapan, and Tulum reached their peak with many of the same traits as the Classic Lowland Mayas, such as stone architecture and carving. Mayan CITY-STATES consisted of numerous stone constructions, including PYRAMIDS with TEMPLES on top; shrines; platforms that served as astronomical observatories; monasteries; palaces; baths; vaulted tombs; BALL-COURTS; paved roads; bridges; plazas; terraces; causeways; reservoirs; and AQUE-DUCTS. Each of these ceremonial and economic centers had distinct social classes. In the countryside surrounding the central complex of buildings, farmers lived in one-room houses, built with pole frames and covered with THATCH. They practiced slash-and-burn agriculture as well as IRRIGA-TION techniques. Descendants of the Mayas still speaking the Mayan language live in Mexico, Guatemala, and other Central American countries, most of them peasant farmers.

Mayan A language family and subdivision of the PENUTIAN phylum comprising dialects spoken by Indians of the MESOAMERI-CAN CULTURE AREA, including the MAYAS of the Yucatan Peninsula in present-day Mexico and Guatemala; the Huastecs of what is now east-central Mexico; and other peoples of present-day Mexico, Guatemala, Belize, El Salvador, and Honduras.

Mdewakanton (Mdawakanton, Mdewkanton) A subtribe of the SANTEE (Dakota) division of the SIOUX Indians, located on Mille Lacs in present-day central Minnesota and later on the lower Minnesota River. *Mdewakanton* means "mystery lake village" in SIOUAN.

meal (Indian meal) Coarsely ground seeds, or nuts, or other food; used in reference to cereal grains.

mealing bin A rectangular box of stone or wood, containing stones used to grind grain and other foodstuffs in the making of MEAL.

medal A piece of metal with a figure, design, or inscription commemorating an event or person. Spanish, French, English, and American officials bestowed medals on Indians, often with a representation of a king or president, as emblems of authority and symbols of peace; they also were called peace medals. Medals often were engraved on both sides and had a means of attachment, such as a loop for a cord hung over the neck or a ribbon and pin. "Medallion" can refer to a large medal or to an ornament that resembles a medal, such as oval beadwork.

medicine (power)　In general, the mysterious power inherent in the universe; more specifically, power that cures the sick, or the object or substance itself that effects change or HEALING. A MEDICINE MAN uses his special abilities to channel medicine, or "power," to influence events as well as to heal the sick. There is "good medicine" and "bad medicine." "Medicine" in many cases is interchangeable with "sacred," as in medicine pipe. "Medicine power" can be said to mean "spiritual power." The use of the term medicine with regard to Indian lifeways might derive from MIDEWIWIN SOCIETY, translated as "Grand Medicine Society." (See also MIDE; SHAMAN; SPIRIT.)

Medicine Arrows (Sacred Arrows, Maahotse, Mahuts)　A set of four arrows, each one differing in color, considered sacred by the CHEYENNE Indians; a gift from Maheo, the CREATOR, to SWEET MEDICINE, a CULTURE HERO. The tribe traditionally has used them in a purification ceremony, when a Cheyenne had been killed by a fellow tribal member. The Renewal of Medicine Arrows is a ceremony for renewing the power of the Sacred Arrows and unifying the tribe. (See also SACRED BUFFALO HAT.)

medicine bag (medicine pouch)　A pouch with one or more objects believed to have spiritual power. Medicine bags traditionally are worn around the neck or waist. (See also MEDICINE BUNDLE.)

medicine bundle (fetish bundle, sacred bundle)　A package, such as a hide or cloth wrapping, pouch, or box, containing one or more objects or materials considered to be sacred and have spiritual power. In addition to pipes, medicine bundles contain objects seen in a DREAM or VISION such as a stone or arrow or part of an animal. Individuals have kept their own personal medicine bundles for good fortune, but tribal chiefs or SHAMANS keep bundles for the entire tribe.

The TALISMANS inside have special meanings with regard to tribal legends. An individual, clan, or tribe might have a particular medicine bundle. The NAVAJO word in ATHAPASCAN for a sacred bundle is *jish*. The POTAWATOMI word in ALGONQUIAN is *bidjgosan*. (See also KEEPER; MEDICINE BAG.)

medicine lodge　Any structure used for HEALING ceremonies, such as the dwelling of a SHAMAN.

medicine man　A spiritual mediator and healer; either a SHAMAN, who conducts a variety of ceremonies, or, more specifically, an Indian doctor, who treats the sick with herbal remedies, the use of charms, and psychiatry. The term medicine woman also is used. Tribes have varying names for these individuals in their own languages. (See also BEAR DOCTOR; CACIQUE; DIAGNOSTICIAN; HAND-TREMBLING; PRACTITIONER; PRIEST; PROPHET; STARGAZING; SUCKING DOCTOR.)

medicine pipe　See CALUMET; SACRED PIPE.

medicine pouch　See MEDICINE BAG; MEDICINE BUNDLE.

medicine society (curing society)　A SECRET SOCIETY of SHAMANS, the rituals of which are used in HEALING. (See also MIDEWIWIN SOCIETY.)

medicine wheel　A circular arrangement of boulders from pre-Contact times found especially on the Northern Plains in present-day Alberta, Saskatchewan, Montana, and Wyoming. Medicine wheels are thought to have an astronomical as well as ceremonial purpose. A site known as Sacred Medicine Wheel in the Big Horn Mountains of Wyoming is a circle 80 feet in diameter, constructed of mountain rock and boulders, with 28 rock spokes and a central cairn hub. The ARAPAHOS and other Indian peoples consider it a SACRED SITE and use it for religious ceremonies. Like many other

Indian sacred places, Sacred Medicine Wheel is in danger of desecration and destruction; the U.S. Forest Service plans to make it a tourist attraction.

medium of exchange (measure of value) A TRADE item that comes to represent a fixed value among different tribes or between Indians and whites. WAMPUM, DENTALIUM, FURS, and HUDSON'S BAY BLANKETS were some among many different standardized goods.

Meherrin An IROQUOIAN-speaking tribe of the NORTHEAST CULTURE AREA, located on the Meherrin River on both sides of the present-day Virginia-North Carolina border. Descendants are centered in Winton, North Carolina.

Menominee (Menomini, Rice) An ALGONQUIAN-speaking tribe of the NORTHEAST CULTURE AREA, located on the northwestern shore of Lake Michigan in present-day Wisconsin and Michigan, especially in the region of the Menominee and Fox rivers. Menominees hold the Menominee Reservation near Keshena, Wisconsin. Their name means "wild rice people" in Algonquian, from the CHIPPEWA term for WILD RICE, *manomin*, which translates literally as "good berry" or "spirit delicacy."

mescal An alcoholic beverage, typical of SOUTHWEST INDIANS and MESOAMERICAN INDIANS, distilled from a variety of AGAVE species, especially *Agave atrovirens*. The PEYOTE plant also is sometimes referred to as mescal.

Mescalero A subtribe of the APACHE Indians, located between the Rio Grande and the Pecos River in present-day Mexico and ranging into the Staked Plains of present-day Texas and into Coahuila, Mexico. The Mescaleros are grouped with the CHIRICAHUAS, a division referred to as Chiricahua-Mescalero. Tribal members hold the Mescalero Reservation in Otero County, New

Mexico. Their name is Spanish for "mescal people."

Mesoamerica (Meso-America) The region comprising northern Mexico south of the Sinaloa, Lerma, and Panuco rivers; central Mexico, southern Mexico, and the Yucatan Peninsula; Guatemala; and parts of Belize, Honduras, El Salvador, Nicaragua, and Costa Rica. "Mesoamerican" is the adjective form. (See also MESOAMERICAN CULTURE AREA; MIDDLE AMERICA.)

Mesoamerican Culture Area The geographical and cultural region of MESOAMERICA, comprising territory within the boundaries of the following countries: Mexico, except the northern part, which is included in the SOUTHWEST CULTURE AREA; all of Guatemala, Belize, and El Salvador; and parts of Honduras, Nicaragua, and Costa Rica. This CULTURE AREA was a densely populated region with a wide range of lifeways, from organized and centralized agricultural societies to nomadic hunter-gatherers. MESOAMERICAN INDIANS, such as the OLMECS, MAYAS, TOLTECS, and AZTECS, created cities with elaborate stone architecture. Among the cultural traits these people had in common were FARMING; CITY-STATES of stone architecture, including PYRAMIDS; CASTE SYSTEMS; regimented armies; extensive trade networks; refined artwork, using many different raw materials; and writing systems, in particular PICTOGRAPHS, as well as CALENDAR and COUNTING systems.

Mesoamerican Indians ("Mesoamericans") Peoples of the MESOAMERICAN CULTURE AREA. The Indians of this region spoke dialects from the following language families: CHINANTECAN, MANGUEAN, MAYAN, MIXE-ZOQUEAN, MIXTECAN, OTOMIAN, POPOLOCAN, TEQUISTLATECAN, TLAPANECAN, TOTONACAN, UTO-AZTECAN, and ZAPOTECAN, and the language isolate Tarascan. (See also AZTEC; CLASSIC PERIOD; MAYA; OLMEC; TOLTEC.)

Mesquakie See FOX.

mesquite (mesquit, algarroba, honey locust) A spiny, deep-rooted tree or shrub of the genus *Prosopis*, especially *P. juliflora* and *P. glandulosa*, found in the American Southwest and Mexico. *P. pubescens* is known as the screw bean. The mesquite tree bears a pod full of seeds. The beans are rich in sugar and are eaten green, or dried and ground. The fruit, leaves, and stalk also are edible, and the juice can be drunk. An alcoholic beverage was made from the mesquite plant by SOUTHWEST INDIANS, especially the PIMAS and PAPAGOS. Nowadays, mesquite is used as a feed for livestock. Also known as algarroba and honey locust.

Messenger Feast (Inviting In Ceremony) A ceremony of the INUITS, centered around trading and socializing. It lasts about four days to two weeks at the end of December or in January. Beforehand, messengers are sent out to neighboring villages carrying carved sticks, which serve as a record or mnemonic device for what the festival hosts hope to receive in trade.

messiah Many different Native American REVITALIZATION MOVEMENTS, established during post-Contact times—especially in the 19th century—drew on Christian themes. Some of them predicted the arrival of a messiah, a divinely sent savior, who would liberate Indians from their oppressors. (See also PROPHET.)

mestizo A Spanish-derived term for a person of part-European and part-Indian ancestry, i.e., a MIXED-BLOOD. In the Americas, the term originally was applied to the offspring of a Spaniard and Indian, with other names for varying percentages of American Indian blood. "Mestee" or "mustee," formerly in use in the American Southeast, are corruptions of "mestizo."

metalwork (metallurgy) The act, process, or resulting artifact of work in any metal. The synonym "metallurgy" also refers to the art and science of extracting metals from their ores. Metalwork includes any of the following: smelting, casting; hammering, embossing, ENGRAVING, ANNEALING, sheathing, welding, and soldering. SOUTH AMERICAN INDIANS, especially in present-day Colombia and Peru, as well as MESOAMERICAN INDIANS, were advanced in many of these techniques. (See also CIRE PERDUE; COLD-HAMMERING; COPPER; GOLDWORK; HIGH-STEEL; IRONWORK; MISE EN COULEUR; REPOUSSÉ; SILVERWORK.)

metate (lapstone, milling stone) A flat or hollowed-out and curved stone, used with a MANO, on which grain is ground. The surfaces of metates are of different textures for different refinement of grain. *Metate*, a Spanish word, derives from the NAHUATL word *metlatl*. (See also MORTAR AND PESTLE.)

Methow A SALISHAN-speaking tribe of the PLATEAU CULTURE AREA, located on the Methow and Okanogan rivers and Chelan Lake in present-day Washington. Descendants share the Colville Reservation near Nespelem, Washington, with other tribes.

Metis (Métis, Bois Brulés) Literally, French for "mixed," referring to people of mixed Indian and white ancestry. *Métisse* is the feminine form. Many Canadian fur traders of French Canadian ancestry, as well as Scottish and Irish ancestry, lived among and intermarried with the Indians, especially the ALGONQUIAN-speaking CREES. Their offspring constituted a special class of people, like an Indian tribe, but with a combined Indian-white culture. The word is capitalized when it identifies this special group, descendants of which now live in both Canada and Montana; an accent is sometimes used. (See also HALF-BLOOD; MESTIZO; MIXED-BLOOD; VOYAGEUR.)

Me-Wuk See MIWOK.

Mexica See AZTEC.

Mexican-American An American with cultural and language ties to Mexico. Some Mexican-Americans migrated to the United States from Mexico; others lived in the American Southwest when it was still part of Mexico. The term is used in historical discussions of the Southwest as distinguished from ANGLO-AMERICANS.

Miami (Twightwee) An ALGONQUIAN-speaking tribe of the NORTHEAST CULTURE AREA, located south of Lake Michigan in present-day northern Indiana, especially on the St. Joseph and Eel rivers, and in present-day western and northern Ohio, on the Miami, Little Miami, and Maumee rivers. (Earlier, in the 1600s, Miamis had lived in present-day Wisconsin, Michigan, and Illinois.) Subdivisions include the Atchatchakangouen, Kilatika, Mengakonkia, Pepicokia, PIANKASHAW, and WEA bands. The latter two bands were relocated to Kansas in 1832 with ILLINOIS bands; other Miamis joined them. In 1867–68, they were moved to the INDIAN TERRITORY. The Miami Tribe of Oklahoma holds trust lands near Miami, Oklahoma. The Indiana Miami Organizational Council is centered at Huntington. *Miami* may derive from the Algonquian word for "people on the peninsula" or the word for "pigeon."

mica Any of a group of crystalline mineral silicates, commonly found in igneous rocks and metamorphic rocks. Mica separates readily into thin, translucent layers and was used by native peoples in ornaments and MIRRORS.

Miccosukee (Mikasuki) A subtribe of the SEMINOLE Indians, located in present-day Jefferson and Madison counties in northern Florida and later near present-day Gainesville in Alachua County. The Miccosukees probably branched off from the HITCHITIS or the CHIAHAS or both, and possibly from other MUSKOGEAN-speaking tribes as well. Starting in the 1830s, some were relocated to the INDIAN TERRITORY; others avoided relocation by hiding out in the Everglades.

The Miccosukees now constitute a tribal entity in southern Florida, holding the Miccosukee Reservation in Dade County. Their dialect of Muskogean is usually spelled Mikasuki.

Michabo A legendary being in the tradition of various ALGONQUIAN tribes. Michabo, or the Great Hare, is associated both with GITCHEE MANITOU and MANEBOZHO.

Micmac An ALGONQUIAN-speaking tribe of the NORTHEAST CULTURE AREA, located in present-day Nova Scotia, Prince Edward Island, Cape Breton Island (Quebec), eastern New Brunswick, and, later, southern Newfoundland. For much of their history, the Micmacs were part of the Abenaki Confederacy with the ABENAKIS and other tribes. Contemporary Micmac bands hold reserve tracts throughout their ancestral homeland. Their name derives from *Migmac*, meaning "allies" in Algonquian.

Mictlantecuhtli The AZTEC god of death and lord of Mictlan, land of the dead. He is depicted holding a skull or wearing a skull mask.

midden A refuse heap marking the site of human habitation. "Kitchen midden" refers to a pile containing remains of food, such as shells and bones. (See also SHELL-HEAP.)

Middle America The part of the Americas comprising Mexico and Central America; usually described as the area south from the Rio Grande to the Panama Canal, and including the West Indies. "Middle America" can be used synonymously with MESOAMERICA, although the latter when defining the MESOAMERICAN CULTURE AREA does not include all of Mexico.

mide (mida) A CHIPPEWA term in ALGONQUIAN, meaning MEDICINE, SPIRIT, or "mystically powerful"; used as both a noun and adjective. The POTAWATOMIS spell it *mida*.

Midewiwin Society (Grand Medicine Society, Mide Cult) A MEDICINE SOCIETY, originating in about 1700 among the CHIPPEWAS and spreading to other GREAT LAKES INDIANS and eastern SIOUX. The SODALITY was organized around four degrees, or "lodges," into which members were inducted. The initiates sponsored feasts and in return were instructed in the secrets of myths and sacred animals, and in the rituals of HEALING and the medicinal properties of plants. *Midewiwin* has been translated from ALGONQUIAN as "mystical doings" or "spirit doings"; as "good-hearted"; and as "to summon the spirit of well-being." The POTAWATOMI spelling is *Midawin*.

Midwinter Ceremony (New Year's Ceremony) A nine-day ceremony, beginning in January or February, of the IROQUOIS Indians, the first in the seasonal cycle. Rituals vary from LONGHOUSE to longhouse, but generally include the Four Sacred Rituals of the LONGHOUSE RELIGION: the FEATHER DANCE, Thanksgiving Dance, Personal Chant, and Bowl Game. The Life Supporting Dances celebrating the THREE SISTERS, corn, beans, and squash, are sometimes performed. The FALSE FACE Society and other sodalities participate.

migration The act or process of moving from one place—continent, country, or region—to another. (See also DEMOGRAPHY; RELOCATION; REMOVAL.)

Mikasuki See MICCOSUKEE.

military society (soldier society, war society) A SODALITY, typical of PLAINS INDIANS, organized around the rituals of war. Each society had its particular songs, dances, ceremonial costumes, insignia, obligations, and taboos. Members often assumed leadership in war and fought side by side. A military society is one type of SECRET SOCIETY. (See also DOG SOLDIERS; PRIESTHOOD OF THE BOW; SOLDIERS' LODGE.)

milling stone See METATE.

milpa (swidden) A cultivated field or, more specifically, a small field of corn; also applies to an agricultural technique in which forests are cut down annually and burned in place for planting. The word came to English via Spanish, originally from the NAHUATL *milpan*, meaning "in the fields."

Mimbreno (Mimbrena, Mimbres, Coppermine Apache) A subtribe of the GILENOS division of APACHE Indians, centered in the Mimbres Mountains in present-day southwestern New Mexico and ranging into present-day eastern Arizona and northern Chiahuahua, Mexico. *Mimbreno* derives from the Spanish name for the mountain range and means "people of the willows."

Mimbres Culture See MOGOLLON CULTURE.

Minataree See HIDATSA.

Mingo A subtribe of the IROQUOIS Indians, which branched off sometime before 1750 and settled on the upper Ohio River in present-day Pennsylvania near the SHAWNEES and LENNI LENAPES (Delawares). By the 1770s, Mingos had moved down the Ohio to the area of present-day Steubenville, Ohio. They eventually moved westward to the headwaters of the Sciota and Sandusky rivers, where they became known as the SENECAS of Sandusky, even though their descendants were mostly from other tribes of the IROQUOIS LEAGUE as well as SUSQUEHANNOCK Indians. In about 1800, a group of Cayugas from New York settled among them. In 1831, both bands moved to a tract of land on the Neosho River in Kansas, then, in 1867, to the INDIAN TERRITORY. Their descendants now are known as the Seneca-Cayuga Tribe of Oklahoma, centered in Ottawa County. *Mingo* or *Mingwe*, an ALGONQUIAN word meaning "stealthy," originally was used by the Lenni Lenapes in reference to all Iroquois.

miniature canteen See TOBACCO FLASK.

Miniconjou (Minneconjo) A subtribe of the TETON division of the SIOUX Indians, located on the upper Missouri River north of the mouth of the Cheyenne River in present-day South Dakota and ranging throughout the Northern Plains, especially in present-day North Dakota, Montana, Wyoming, and Nebraska. *Miniconjou* means "those who plant beside the stream" in SIOUAN.

mining The process of extracting metals, salt, or other minerals form the earth. "Mining" usually refers to extracting metals, whereas QUARRYING refers to stones. In pre-Contact times, MESOAMERICAN INDIANS and SOUTH AMERICAN INDIANS obtained their GOLD by the washing of gravel from streambeds. SILVER was obtained from pits and possibly the smelting of ores. COPPER, also mined by North American Indians, was obtained in nugget form. A mine is the excavation itself, usually a tunnel; whereas a quarry is an open excavation or pit. There were no true mines with tunnels and caverns north of Mexico until the arrival of whites. Spanish colonists mandated forced labor from the Indian populations for their mining operations. (See also GOLD RUSH.)

minototak The NASKAPI term for "morality" or "ethical conduct" in ALGONQUIAN.

mirror Water served as a mirror for Native Americans, as did inlaid shiny stones. Indians of the HOHOKAM CULTURE, among others, made mirrors by inlaying small pieces of MICA and other shiny minerals in stone disks. The MAYAS and AZTECS used PYRITE inlays. In post-Contact times, European-made mirrors of glass with a metallic backing were utilized to flash SIGNALS.

mise en couleur A method of GOLDWORK in which an object is cast in *TUMBAGA*, an alloy of gold and copper, then treated with the acidic sap of a plant to dissolve the copper, leaving gilding on the surface. In pre-Contact Central and South America, in particular the region now comprising Colombia, goldworkers used the process. The term translates from the French as "setting in color."

Mishikhwutmetunne See ATHAPASCAN.

mission Persons sent to do religious work in a foreign land; also, a religious center established there. Missions in Indian lands consisted of churches and schools and were centers of operation for MISSIONARIES. (See also MISSION INDIANS.)

missionary An advocate sent to a region to convert people of other religions to a particular faith and, in some cases, carry on educational and medical work. Jesuits, Franciscans, Congregationalists, Presbyterians, Episcopalians, Methodists, Quakers, and representatives of other denominations established MISSIONS among Indian peoples.

Mission Indians Indians who gave up their tribal way of life to live at MISSIONS. The term especially refers to CALIFORNIA INDIANS missionized by the Spanish. New England Indians are more often referred to as PRAYING INDIANS or Christian Indians. The MORAVIAN INDIANS were another missionized group. (See also CAHUILLA; CHUMASH; COSTANOAN; DIEGUENO; JUANENO; LUISENO; SALINAS; SERRANO.)

Missisauga (Mississauga, Mississagi) A subtribe of the CHIPPEWA Indians, located at the mouth of the Mississagi River on the the north shore of Lake Huron and on nearby Manitoulin Island in present-day Ontario, and later on the north shore of Lake Erie and west shore of Lake Ontario. Bands known as Mississauga and Mississaugas Credit have tribal headquarters at Blind River and Hagersville in Ontario. Their name means "large outlet" in ALGONQUIAN, referring to the mouth of the Missassagi.

Mississippian Culture A cultural tradition of related archaeological sites that evolved in eastern North America starting about A.D. 700, following the decline of the

HOPEWELL CULTURE. Mississippian Culture was located along the Mississippi River; the center of development is referred to as the Middle Mississippi Culture, with related Mississippian sites extending from present-day Florida and the Carolinas as far west as Oklahoma and as far north as Wisconsin. Mississippian Indians built flat-topped MOUNDS to hold TEMPLES, and can be referred to as Temple Mound Builders or MOUNDBUILDERS. (The Mississippian Indians may have been influenced by MESOAMERICAN INDIANS, who placed temples on top of stone pyramids.) Log steps ran up one side to the WATTLE-AND-DAUB and THATCH structure. Some of the mounds had terraced sides on which smaller structures were built, the homes of priests and nobles. Other villagers—merchants, craftsmen, soldiers, hunters, farmers, and laborers—lived in thatch huts surrounding the mounds. Some Mississippian dwellings were PITHOUSES, having vertical logs extending from rectangular pits. Villagers conducted their business in the village's central open plaza. Cahokia in present-day Illinois was the largest Mississippian population center. The city, covering about 4,000 acres near the Mississippi River where the Illinois River flows into it, had more than 100 mounds, both temple mounds and burial mounds. Mississippian farmers grew crops in the rich alluvial soil of riverbeds. For some reason, perhaps warfare, overpopulation, drought, or famine, the great Mississippian villages were abandoned. Or coastal Indians might have unknowingly spread European diseases inland through trade, starting deadly epidemics. Sometime after 1500, the custom of mound-building was no longer practiced. Many EASTERN INDIANS, especially the tribes of the SOUTHEAST CULTURE AREA, continued to use the ancient mounds. Some of them, such as the CREEKS, possibly were direct descendants of Mississippian Indians. The NATCHEZ shared many cultural traits with their forerunners. (See also SOUTHERN CULT.)

Missouri (Missouria) A SIOUAN-speaking tribe of the GREAT PLAINS CULTURE AREA, located on the Missouri River near the mouth of the Grand River; in the early 1800s, Missouris settled south of the Platte River in present-day Nebraska. (According to tribal legend, the Missouris formerly were one people with the ancestors of the IOWA, OTO, and WINNEBAGO tribes in present-day Wisconsin. A group supposedly separated from the Winnebagos and migrated to the confluence of the Iowa and Mississippi rivers. This group further divided: The band staying near the Mississippi became the Iowas; the band that continued westward to the Missouri River divided again, becoming the Missouris and Otos.) The Missouris merged with the Otos in 1829. The two tribes were relocated to the INDIAN TERRITORY in 1882. The Otoe-Missouria Tribe holds trust lands in Noble County, Oklahoma. *Missouri* possibly means "people with dugout (or wooden) canoes" in Siouan.

Mistassini (Mistassin) A subtribe of the CREE Indians, located on Lake Mistassini in present-day Quebec. The Mistassini band still lives in its ancestral homeland. The name means "great stone" in ALGONQUIAN, referring to a boulder jutting out of Lake Mistassini.

mitakuye oyasin (mitakuyase oyate) A SIOUAN phrase for "all my relations," "all my relatives," or "we are all related," repeated during various rituals, indicating the connectedness of all that exists, animate and inanimate. "*Mitakuye oyasin*" is the TETON (Lakota) version; "*mitakuyase oyate*," the YANKTON and YANKTONAI (Nakota) version. The first word refers to all things around a person, both past and present; the second means "nation," indicating groups of beings.

mitten Mittens traditionally have been worn by ARCTIC INDIANS and SUBARCTIC INDIANS as well as by some PLATEAU and northern PLAINS INDIANS. Some INUITS had PARKAS with mittens attached. Native American mittens sometimes were insulated with down or moss.

Miwok (Me-Wuk) A MIWOK-COSTA-NOAN-speaking tribe of the CALIFORNIA CULTURE AREA, located in present-day central California. The Miwoks are classified into three groups: the Valley Miwoks, living on the western slope of the Sierra Nevada along the San Joaquin and Sacramento rivers and their tributaries; the Lake Miwoks, living near Clear Lake; and the Coast Miwoks, living on the Pacific Coast north of San Francisco Bay. Miwoks have been referred to historically along with the YOKUTS as Chowchilla Indians. The Me-Wuk Tribe holds a number of rancherias: Jackson in Amador County, California; Sheep Ranch in Calaveras County; and Tuolumne in Tuolumne. *Miwok* means "people" in Miwok-Costanoan. (See also POMO.)

Miwok-Costanoan A language family and subdivision of the PENUTIAN phylum comprising dialects spoken by the MIWOK and COSTANOAN tribes of the CALIFORNIA CULTURE AREA. The Miwok language formerly was referred to as Moquelumnan.

mixed-blood A person of mixed ancestry, such as Indian-white or Indian-black. (See also HALF-BREED; MESTIZO; METIS.)

Mixe-Zoquean A language family and subdivision of the PENUTIAN phylum comprising dialects spoken by Indians of the MESOAMERICAN CULTURE AREA, including the Mixe, Zoque, Sierra Popoluca (Chocho), Oluta, Sayula, and Texixtepec tribes of what is now central Mexico. The Mixe languages also have been called Mizocuavean.

Mixtecan A language family and subdivision of the OTO-MANGUEAN phylum comprising dialects spoken by Indians of the MESOAMERICAN CULTURE AREA, including the Amuzgo (Amishgo), Cuicatec, Mixtec, and Trique tribes of what is now central Mexico.

Mobile A MUSKOGEAN-speaking tribe of the SOUTHEAST CULTURE AREA, located on the west side of the Mobile River just south of the junction of the Alabama and Tombig-bee rivers in present-day Alabama and later on Mobile Bay. The Mobiles probably merged with the CHOCTAWS. *Mobile* may derive from the Choctaw word for "to paddle" in Muskogean.

Mobilian trade language (Chickasaw trade language) An intertribal TRADE LANGUAGE, combining MUSKOGEAN and other dialects of SOUTHEAST INDIANS; utilized on the lower Mississippi River as well as in present-day coastal Louisiana, Alabama, and Florida.

moccasin Originally an ALGONQUIAN word, with variations depending on the dialect (*mocussin* in NARRAGANSET; *makisin* in CHIPPEWA; *m'cusun* in MICMAC; among others), but now referring to footwear of many Indian peoples of differing designs. There are two basic types of moccasin: one made from a single piece of leather with a seam at the instep and heel, more common in the East; and the other, with a rawhide sole attached to a leather upper, typical in the West. Boot moccasins or legging moccasins, worn by women, have an attached leather piece, designed to wrap around the calf. Moccasins typically were made of leather and often decorated with fur, quills, shells, beads, and eventually buttons and cloth; the IROQUOIS were known to make moccasins from CORNHUSKS and basswood fiber.

moccasin game See GUESSING GAME.

Mococo See TIMUCUA.

Sioux moccasins

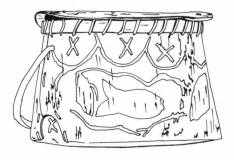

Chippewa *mocuck*

mocuck (macaque, makak, mocock, mow-kowk, mukuk) A BIRCHBARK container for holding sugar and other food, sometimes with a rawhide handle and carved design. Typical of the CHIPPEWAS, from whose AL-GONQUIAN dialect the word derives.

Modoc A PENUTIAN-speaking (Klamath-Modoc or Lutuamian isolate) tribe of the CALIFORNIA CULTURE AREA, located on Modoc Lake, Little Klamath Lake, Tule Lake, Clear Lake, Lost River Valley, and Goose Lake in present-day southern Oregon and northern California. In 1873, after war with the whites, some Modocs were relocated to the INDIAN TERRITORY among the QUAPAWS. Modocs now live among the KLAMATHS in Oregon and the Quapaws in Oklahoma. *Modoc* derives from *Moatokni*, meaning "southerners" in Penutian.

Mogollon A subtribe of the GILENOS division of the APACHE Indians, centered in the Mogollon Mountains of present-day western New Mexico and ranging into eastern Arizona. Mogollon descendants live on the San Carlos and Fort Apache reservations, although they no longer maintain a tribal identity distinct from other Apaches. *Mogollon* derives from the mountains, named after a Spanish official.

Mogollon Culture A cultural tradition in the American Southwest, lasting from about 300 B.C. to A.D. 1400. The Mogollon Moun-tains along the southern Arizona-New Mexico border were this group's core area. Mogollon Indians, probably direct descendants of the earlier COCHISE CULTURE, are considered the first Southwest people to adopt farming, house-building, and pottery. They cultivated the high valleys in the rugged mountains, planting corn, beans, squash, tobacco, and cotton. They also gathered edible wild plants and hunted small game, adopting the BOW and ARROW in about A.D. 500. For their villages, they chose sites near mountain streams or along ridges that were easy to defend. They lived in PITHOUSES with log frames covered with reeds, saplings, and mud; large structures served as KIVAS. The earliest Mogollon pottery was brown in color. Later Mogollon Indians painted their pottery with intricate designs. A subgroup of the Mogollon Culture, known as Mimbres, is famous for black-on-white pottery made from about A.D. 900 to A.D. 1300. Mogollon Indians wove plant matter into baskets and used both cultivated cotton and animal fur to make yarn for weaving clothing and blankets. Mogollon Indians probably were ancestors of the present-day ZUNI Indians. *Mogollon* derives from the Spanish name of the mountain range.

Mohave See MOJAVE.

Mohawk (Ganeagaono, Kaniengehaga, Kanienkahegeh) An IROQUOIAN-speaking tribe of the NORTHEAST CULTURE AREA, located on the Mohawk River in present-day New York. The Mohawks are part of the IROQUOIS LEAGUE. The Gibson Mohawks and Mohawks of the Bay of Quinte bands hold reserve lands in Ontario; and the Kahnawake (Caughnawaga) and Oka bands, in Quebec. The Akwesasne band (Iroquois of St. Regis) has lands in both Ontario and New York. Mohawk descendants also are part of the Six Nations of the Grand River band in Ontario. Some Mohawks make their home in Brooklyn, New York. *Mohawk* derives from the NARRAGANSET word for "man-eaters" in ALGONQUIAN.

Their native name, *Kaniengehaga,* means "people of the place of flint."

Mohegan An ALGONQUIAN-speaking tribe of the NORTHEAST CULTURE AREA, located on the Thames River in present-day Connecticut. The Mohegans branched off from the PEQUOTS in the early 1600s. The Mohegan Tribe, centered in Uncasville, Connecticut, maintains tribal identity. *Mohegan* means "wolf" in Algonquian. (See also MOHICAN.)

Mohican Algonquian for "wolf"; an alternate spelling for both the MAHICAN and MOHEGAN tribal names.

moiety One of the dual divisions within a tribe. The word means "half." Some tribes with CLANS (or SIBS) organized them into moieties as well. Moieties traditionally were responsible for different chores and played each other in games. The IROQUOIS divided their LONGHOUSES into moieties.

Mojave (Mohave) A YUMAN-speaking tribe of the SOUTHWEST CULTURE AREA, located on the Colorado River near present-day Fort Mohave, Arizona, and Needles, California. Tribal members hold the Fort Mojave Reservation in Arizona, California, and Nevada, with tribal headquarters at Needles. Mojaves share the Colorado River Reservation in Arizona and California with the CHEMEHUEVIS, with headquarters at Parker, Arizona; and the Fort McDowell Reservation in Arizona with APACHES and YAVAPAIS, with headquarters at Scottsdale, Arizona. *Mojave* derives from *Hamakhava,* meaning "three mountains," referring to the Needles. The original Mojave native name was *Tzi-na-ma-a,* probably meaning "people."

Molala See PENUTIAN.

Monacan (Manakin) A SIOUAN-speaking tribe of the SOUTHEAST CULTURE AREA, located on the upper James River in present-day Virginia. The Monacans actually were a confederacy of subtribes, allies of the Manahoacs to the north and enemies of the POWHATANS to the east. They probably merged with the SAPONIS and Tutelos. *Monacan,* if ALGONQUIAN-derived, means "digging stick," but it is more likely from their own Siouan dialect.

Monache See MONO.

Moneton See SIOUAN.

money See MEDIUM OF EXCHANGE.

monitor pipe See PIPE.

Mono (Monache, Monachi) A UTO-AZTECAN-speaking tribe of the GREAT BASIN CULTURE AREA, located near Mono Lake in present-day eastern California and near Walker Lake in present-day western Nevada. Some scholars group the Monos with the Northern PAIUTES. Their descendants hold the Big Sandy and Cold Spring rancherias in Fresno County, California; some live with other tribes on the Round Valley Reservation in Mendocino County; the Dunlap Band of Mono Indians operates out of Dunlap, California.

monogamy Marriage to a single person, i.e., the practice of having only one wife or husband at a time. (See also POLYGAMY.)

monolith A single block or slab of stone, usually large, erected as a unit in architecture or sculpture. Typical of MESOAMERICAN INDIANS and SOUTH AMERICAN INDIANS. (See also OBELISK; STELA.)

monophony Music with a single melodic line. "Monophonic" is the adjective form. Most traditional Native American music is monophonic, not polyphonic. A melody might be accompanied by a drone, a note held on a single pitch. Several voices or instruments might perform the single melody in unison; octave harmonies sometimes are used. (See also SONG.)

monotheism The belief in a single, all-powerful god. An all-pervasive Master of Life or CREATOR, translated by whites as GREAT SPIRIT, is part of many Native American religions. In Indian traditions this one spirit manifests itself as many different spirits found in all aspects of nature. (See also ANIMISM; PANTHEISM; POLYTHEISM.)

Monster Monsters or demons exist in many Indian mythologies. Some of them were believed to be cannibalistic, such as WINDIGO of the CREES and other SUBARCTIC INDIANS. Among the NAVAJOS, supernatural beings were Big Monster (or Big Lonely Monster); Burrowing Monster (or Horned Monster); Cliff Monster (or Throwing Monster); Kicking Monster; and Water Monster. Monster Slayer, one of the HOLY PEOPLE, subdues them in different legends. Similarly, the APACHES have a CULTURE HERO known as Slayer of Monster. The ZUNIS speak of POSHAYANKI, a Beast God. The OTKON of IROQUOIS tradition have monstrous characteristics.

Montagnais An ALGONQUIAN-speaking tribe of the SUBARCTIC CULTURE AREA, located in present-day central Quebec, from James Bay to the Gulf of St. Lawrence. The Montagnais are related linguistically to the NASKAPI Indians. (Some scholars discuss the two tribes as subdivisions of one, the Montagnais-Naskapi.) The Bersimis, Escoumains, Lac St. Jean, Mingan, Montagnais of Schefferville, Natashquam, Romaine, St. Augustin, and Sept-Iles bands hold reserve lands in Quebec. *Montagnais* means "mountaineers" in French.

Montauk An ALGONQUIAN-speaking tribe of the NORTHEAST CULTURE AREA, located on present-day eastern and central Long Island, New York. The Montauk proper, after whom the Montauk Confederacy is named, held territory in present-day Southampton Township. The alliance also included the Corchaug, Manhasset, Massapequa, Matinecock, Merric, Nesaquake, POOSPATUCK, Rockaway, Secatogue, Setauket, and SHINNECOCK Indians. The Montauk Indian tribe is centered in Sag Harbor, New York. The Poospatucks and Shinnecocks hold reservation lands in their ancestral homeland. *Montauk* possibly derives from the ALGONQUIAN word *Meuntauket*, meaning "at the fort."

moon Native peoples traditionally considered the moon a powerful spirit. To the Alaskan INUITS, the Moon Spirit was a male force having control of animals as well as the fertility of women. Many North American Indians refer to months as "moons." Their tribal calendars have descriptive names for the moons, usually based on natural events or the availability of food, such as the Moon When the Leaves Break Forth of the TEWAS (April); Moon When the Acorns Begin to Ripen of the MAIDUS (August); Caribou Are Abundant in the Woods Moon of the DOGRIBS (September); Moon When the Ducks Fly of the KUTCHINS (September); Moon When the Cold Makes the Trees Crack of the LENNI LENAPES (December); and Hard Time to Build a Fire Moon of the NEZ PERCES (February).

moose A large hoofed mammal of the deer family (*Alces alces* or *A. americana*), sometimes more than seven feet tall and more than 1,000 pounds in weight. Found in the northern forests of North America, moose were a valuable resource of meat, fur, and antlers for NORTHEAST INDIANS and SUBARCTIC INDIANS. The word moose is of ALGONQUIAN origin for "he strips off," referring to the animal's eating of bark and twigs from trees.

Moquelumnan See MIWOK-COSTANOAN.

Moratok See ALGONQUIAN.

Moravian Indians Some Indians of the LENNI LENAPE (Delaware) tribe, especially MUNSEES, and including some MAHICAN and WAPPINGER Indians, were converted by Moravian missionaries, beginning in the mid-1700s. The first mission was in New York among the Mahicans and Wappingers, but it was moved to various sites in Pennsylvania, where Lenni Lenapes were missionized, and then to Ohio. The Moravian Indians finally settled in Ontario in 1791. The Moravian of the Thames band holds reserve lands near Bothwell.

Morning Star Ceremony   The Skidi band of PAWNEES believed that the Sun and Mother Earth conceived the Morning Star, the God of Vegetation. As late as the early 19th century, once a year, the Skidis would raid another tribe for a young girl, about 13, and keep her among them for months as an honored guest. At the summer SOLSTICE, early in the morning, the priests would paint half the girl's body in red, for day, and half in black, for night. Then they would tie her to a rectangular frame in a field outside the village. As the morning star rose, three priests would sacrifice her with a torch, arrow, and knife. Then every male old enough to handle a bow would shoot arrows into her body. In 1816 or 1817, Petalesharo, the son of a chief, rallied support against the priests in protest of the ritual, which was soon abandoned. Petalesharo went on to become principal chief himself.

morpheme   A unit of relatively consistent meaning that cannot be broken into a smaller unit. The morpheme can be a word, or a word part, i.e., a prefix or suffix. Morphemes help linguists define relations between different languages and dialects.

mortar and pestle   A two-part milling tool, with a bowl-shaped lower part, the mortar, plus a club-shape, hand-held upper part, the pestle, used for pulverizing plant or animal matter. A MANO and METATE refers to a stone pestle and mortar; other mortar and pestles might also be of wood or bone. In original usage, a mano or muller referred to an object with a flat undersurface and shaped to be held under the hand; a pestle referred to an object with a rounded or flat undersurface shaped to be held in the hand in an upright position; and a metate was not a true bowl, as a mortar might be.

mortuary customs   See   BURIAL; MOURNING.

mosaic   A picture or design, made by placing small colorful pieces of stone, shell, feathers, or other material in a cement mixture. The art of mosaics was highly developed among the MAYAS, AZTECS, and INCAS. It was practiced little north of Mexico, except by the Indians of the ANASAZI CULTURE and HOHOKAM CULTURE. In post-Contact times, SOUTHWEST INDIANS began inlaying TURQUOISE in black PIÑON gum.

Mosan   See SALISHAN; WAKASHAN.

Moses   See COLUMBIA.

Mosquito   See TIMUCUA.

Mosquito Dance   A dance of CHEROKEE women, who use thorns, sticks, or pins to jab men who fall asleep during ceremonies and neglect their duties. The NATCHEZ supposedly taught the dance to the Cherokees.

moss   Any of the Musci class of plants, part of the division Bryophyta, which includes true mosses, peat moss (or sphagnum), and liverworts. Mosses are green or brown and grow in clusters on the ground, rocks, and trees. Native Americans used moss for insulation and bedding.

moss-bag   A carrier for babies, typical of ATHAPASCAN Indians and the western Crees, made from leather and lined with moss. (See also CRADLEBOARD.)

Mouache (Moache)   A SUBTRIBE of the UTE Indians, located in southern Colorado and northern New Mexico. Mouache Indians hold the Southern Ute Reservation near Ignacio, Colorado, with the CAPOTE band.

mound An EARTHWORK used for BURIALS; as EFFIGY figures; to hold TEMPLES or houses; for enclosures; and for fortifications. Some mounds have more rock than earth in them; the term is also sometimes applied to SHELL-HEAPS and other MIDDENS. A burial mound (tumulus, pl. tumuli) is an earthwork containing a GRAVE and GRAVE GOODS, or more than one grave. An effigy mound is an earthwork representing an animal or legendary being, such as a bird or serpent. A temple mound is a flat-topped earthwork designed to hold a *temple;* the term is sometimes applied to earthen substructures for other buildings as well, such as a chief's or priest's home. Those peoples who constructed these earthworks are known as MOUNDBUILDERS. Most Indian mounds are located east of the Mississippi River. (See also HOUSE MOUND.)

moundbuilders PREHISTORIC INDIANS who constructed MOUNDS. The three mound-building cultures, ADENA CULTURE, HOPEWELL CULTURE, and MISSISSIPPIAN CULTURE, were active during the FORMATIVE PERIOD.

mound ware POTTERY found at mound sites.

Mountain Indians See TUTCHONE.

mountain lion See PUMA.

mountain man A fur trapper and trader working the Rocky Mountains and surrounding regions in the 1820s and 1830s. The mountain men adopted many Indian customs, living off the land and typically wearing deerskin and fur. Some married Indian women and lived among the tribes. They were the first non-Indians to explore much of the American West. Following the drop-off in the international demand for furs, many mountain men worked as GUIDES for white settlers emigrating westward. (See also FUR TRADE.)

Mountain Spirit Dance (Crown Dance) A dance of the APACHE Indians in which performers impersonate the GANS, or Mountain Spirits. They wear hooded deerskin or cloth masks, tall wooden headdresses, and kilts; they decorate themselves with body paint; and they carry painted wooden wands.

mourning The expression of grief for the dead, either in behavior or through symbolism. Typical mourning behavior and symbolism includes wailing, cutting hair, and black body paint. Some participants went as far as SCARIFICATION. The HOPIS, ZUNIS, and MOJAVES have professional mourners who lead in mourning ceremonies and observances. (See also MOURNING MASK.)

mourning mask A mask, typical of CALIFORNIA INDIANS, made of ashes from the funeral pyre. The ashes, mixed with water, were smeared over the face of the mourner until they wore off, thus determining the length of the mourning period.

Muckleshoot A SALISHAN-speaking tribe of the NORTHWEST COAST CULTURE AREA, located on the White and Green rivers in present-day Washington. Descendants hold the Muckleshoot Reservation in King County, Washington; others live on Puyallup Reservation with the PUYALLUPS and other Salishans.

mudhead The popular name of members of the ZUNI society KOYEMSHI and of the HOPI society TACHUKTU.

Muklasa See CREEK; MUSKOGEAN.

mukluk A soft and supple INUIT boot, usually made from sealskin or caribou skin, sometimes with as many as four layers. Mukluks often were insulated with down or moss.

muller See MANO; MORTAR AND PESTLE.

Multomah   See CHINOOKAN.

mummy   The body of a human being or animal embalmed or treated for BURIAL by removing internal organs and applying various preservatives, as in ancient Egypt. In Indian studies, the term has come to be used for any remains resembling Egyptian mummies because of special preparations, such as removing organs and wrapping in mats, or because of arid burial conditions. The Mixtecs, INCAS, and ALEUTS, among other native peoples, practiced techniques of mummification.

Munsee (Muncie, Muncey)   A subtribe of the LENNI LENAPE (Delaware) Indians, located west of the Hudson River in present-day New Jersey and adjacent parts of New York. Munsee bands include Catskill, Mamekoting, Minisink, Ramapough, Waranawonkong, and Wawarsink. *Munsee* derives from the ALGONQUIAN word *Min-asin-ink*, meaning "at the place where stones are gathered together."

mushroom   Native Americans ritually ingested certain mushrooms for their hallucinogenic properties. The *Teonanacatl* reportedly used by the AZTECS was possibly *Panaeolus, Psilocybe, Conocybe,* or *Stropharia;* the chemical psilocybine can be isolated from all of them. Mazatec SHAMANS of Mexico still use mushrooms to induce visions and for healing rituals. The terms sacred mushroom and magic mushroom are used in discussions of ceremonial mushroom use.

music   The art of combining and regulating sounds of different pitch, as produced by voice or a MUSICAL INSTRUMENT. (See also CHANT; DANCE; MONOPHONY; PENTATONIC SCALE; SONG.)

musical bow   A hunting BOW, typical of GREAT BASIN INDIANS, CALIFORNIA INDIANS, and SOUTHWEST INDIANS, used as a rhythm instrument. One end is held in the teeth, while the string is struck with a stick; the moving of the mouth creates different pitch. (See also APACHE FIDDLE.)

musical instrument   Native Americans have used many different devices for making MUSIC, both melodic and rhythmic, such as the APACHE FIDDLE, BELL, BULLROARER, CLAPPER, DRUM, FLAGEOLET, MUSICAL BOW, NOTCHED STICK, OCARINA, PANPIPE, RATTLE, and WHISTLE.

musical rasp   See NOTCHED STICK.

muskeg   A swamp or bog, formed by the accumulation of sphagnum and decaying plant matter, usually with clumps of grass or sedge and sometimes black spruce and tamarack trees; common to the Subarctic. The word is of ALGONQUIAN origin, *maskeek* in the CREE dialect and *mashkig* in the CHIPPEWA dialect.

Muskogean (Muskhogean, Muskogian)   A language family and subdivision of the MACRO-ALGONQUIAN phylum comprising dialects spoken by Indians of the SOUTHEAST CULTURE AREA, among them the Acolapissa, Ais, ALABAMA, APALACHEE, Apalachicola, Avoyel, Bayogoula, CALUSA, Chakchiuma, Chatot, CHIAHA, CHICKASAW, CHOCTAW, COUSHATTA, CREEK, CUSABO, Guale, HITCHITI, HOUMA, Kaskinampo, Koasati, MOBILE, Muklasa, OCONEE, Okelousa, Okmulgee, Pawokti, Pensacola, Quinipissa, Sawokli, SEMINOLE, Taensa, Tamathli, Tangipahoa, Taposa, Tawasa, Tohome, Tuskegee, and YAMASEE tribes. The following tribes also are believed to be Muskogean-speaking: Amacano, Choula, Guacata, Ibitoupa, Jeaga, Osochi, Pascagoula, and Tekesta.

Muskogee   See CREEK.

myth   A traditional story, typically of the distant past with supernatural elements, such as SPIRITUAL BEINGS or LEGENDARY BEINGS; often describing the origins of a people or a natural phenomenon. In Indian studies, "myth" and LEGEND often are used interchangeably. A myth more likely involves deities, whereas a legend concerns human beings or legendary beings with humanlike traits. Many Native Americans prefer the term STORY because the term myth implies the supernatural.

mythical ancestor (mythological ancestor) A LEGENDARY BEING considered an ANCESTOR of a particular lineage. (See also CULTURE HERO.)

mythology   The body of MYTHS of a people or the study of myths. (See also LEGEND; RELIGION.)

▲N▲

Nabesna (Upper Tanana) An ATHAPAS-CAN-speaking tribe of the SUBARCTIC CULTURE AREA, located in the drainage area of the Nabesna and Chisana rivers in present-day Alaska. The Nabesnas are related linguistically to the TANANAS living to the north. Descendants of both tribes are among Alaska's Athapascans.

Nadene (Na-Dene) A phylum of language stocks, including the ATHAPASCAN family and TLINGIT and HAIDA isolates.

nagual A GUARDIAN SPIRIT among various Mexican tribes or, more generally, MEDICINE or "power." A Spanish word, derived from the NAHUATL word *nahualli*, meaning "sorcerer."

Nahane (Nahani) An ATHAPASCAN-speaking tribe of the SUBARCTIC CULTURE AREA, located in present-day northern British Columbia and southern Yukon Territory. Nahane subtribes include Esbataottine, Etagottine, Kaska, Pelly River, TAGISH, Takutine, and Titshotina. (Some scholars also consider the TAHLTANS a subdivision.) Descendants constitute some of the contemporary Athapascan bands of western Canada. *Nahane* means "people of the west" in Athapascan.

Nahuatl (Nahuatlan) The language of the AZTECS, the TOLTECS, and other related peoples of the MESOAMERICAN CULTURE AREA. More than 1 million people still use the Nahuatl language, mostly the rural population living outside Mexico City. The Nahuatl (or Nahuatlan) language is part of the UTO-AZTECAN language family. *Nahuatl* is sometimes used as a tribal name for the Aztecs; it means "mouth," "opening," or "ring." A *Nahua* is an individual of the various Nahuatl-speaking tribes.

Nahyssan See SIOUAN.

naja A crescent-shape pendant, typically of silver, placed centrally in NAVAJO and ZUNI necklaces. An ATHAPASCAN word.

Nakota See SIOUX; YANKTON; YANKTONAI.

Nambe Pueblo See TEWA.

naming ceremony Tribes had varying practices of naming an individual. Some names were bestowed, often taken from a respected predecessor; others were earned though deeds. An individual might have numerous names in a lifetime. (See also CHILDHOOD NAME; DREAM NAME.)

Nanabozho See MANEBOZHO.

Nanaimo (Nanaimuk) A SALISHAN-speaking tribe of the NORTHWEST COAST CULTURE AREA, located at Nanaimo Harbor and Nanoose Bay on the east coast of Vancouver Island in present-day British Columbia. The Nanaimo dialect is similar to that of their neighbors, the COWICHANS. Two contemporary bands, Nanaimo and Nanoose, maintain tribal identity.

Nanticoke An ALGONQUIAN-speaking tribe of the NORTHEAST CULTURE AREA, located on the Eastern Shore of present-day Maryland and southern Delaware. The Nanticokes are related linguistically to the LENNI LENAPES (Delawares) and CONOYS. After 1722, some Nanticokes migrated northward up the Susquehanna River, living in Pennsylvania then, in 1753, joining the IROQUOIS in western New York; others merged with the Lenni Lenapes in Ohio and Indiana in the 1780s. The Nanticoke Tribe operates out of Millsboro, Delaware.

Nanticoke derives from *Nentego* (as does UN-ALACHTIGO), meaning "tidewater people" in Algonquian.

nanuk (nanook, nanuq)   An INUIT term for "bear" in the ESKIMO-ALEUT language. When capitalized, it refers to the cluster of stars known as the Pleiades.

narcotic   See PSYCHOTROPIC SUBSTANCE.

Narraganset (Narragansett)   An ALGON-QUIAN-speaking tribe of the NORTHEAST CULTURE AREA, located west of Narragansett Bay, between the Providence and Pawcatuck rivers in present-day Rhode Island. Tribal members hold the Narragansett Indian Reservation near Kenyon, Rhode Island. *Narraganset* means "people of the small point" in Algonquian.

narrative   See ORAL TRADITION; RITUAL DRAMA; STORYTELLING.

Naskapi (Nascapee)   An ALGONQUIAN-speaking tribe of the SUBARCTIC' CULTURE AREA, located on the Labrador Peninsula in present-day Quebec. The Naskapis are related linguistically to the MONTAGNAIS Indians. (Some scholars discuss the two tribes as subdivisions of one.) The Naskapis of Schefferville hold reserve tracts in their ancestral homeland. *Naskapi* is a term of reproach among the Montagnais in Algonquian.

Natchesan   See NATCHEZ.

Natchez   A MACRO-ALGONQUIAN-speaking (Natchez or Natchesan isolate) tribe of the SOUTHEAST CULTURE AREA, located east of present-day Natchez, Mississippi, ranging across the Mississippi River into present-day Louisiana. The neighboring Taensas of Louisiana spoke a similar dialect. After 1731, one band of Natchez settled among the CREEKS near the Coosa River in present-day Alabama and migrated with them to the INDIAN TERRITORY (present-day Oklahoma); another band settled among the CHEROKEES in present-day North Carolina and Tennessee, migrating westward with them. The Natchez now are extinct as a tribal entity.

Natchitoches Confederacy   See CADDO.

nation   Originally applied by the French to tribes in Quebec, distinguishing "*Les grandes Nations*" from "*Les petites Nations.*" "Nation" was later applied by English-speaking peoples to large Indian confederacies, especially in the SOUTHEAST CULTURE AREA. It became the official name for the CHEROKEE, CHICKASAW, CHOC-TAW, CREEK, and SEMINOLE tribal entities in the INDIAN TERRITORY after their relocation in the 1830s. "Nation" often is used synonymously with TRIBE and is favored by many Native Americans because it implies the concept of SOVEREIGNTY.

native   Originating in a particular place; not introduced from outside. In the United States, the term is applied more often in the adjective form, as in NATIVE AMERICAN or NATIVE PEOPLES, than in noun form. In Canada, "Native" is used interchangeably with INDIAN and INUIT. (See also AB-ORIGINAL.)

Native American   An aboriginal inhabitant of the Americas; a term considered less ETHNOCENTRIC than INDIAN, which was a misnomer by Europeans and which became the shortened form of AMERICAN INDIAN. Before contact with whites, Native Americans had no general name for themselves; many still prefer being identified by their tribal name as opposed to either "Native American" or "Indian." "Native North American" sometimes specifies indigenous peoples of the United States and Canada. Aboriginal Hawaiians are also referred to as Native Americans. (See also PEOPLE.)

Native American Church   A religious revitalization movement, founded in 1918 by followers of the PEYOTE RELIGION. This organized religion incorporates certain Christian beliefs, such as nonviolence, with the sacramental use of peyote. In 1944, the original church organization became the Native American Church of the United States; it has since become incorporated in about one-third of the states. In 1954, a Native American Church of Canada was chartered. The Native American Church, in resisting legal attempts to suppress the use of PEYOTE, has played a central role in the native struggle for freedom of religion. (See also ROADMAN.)

Native American Day A holiday for the celebration of Native American heritage. There is no such national legal holiday in the United States, but there have been attempts to set aside a day to honor the "First Americans." It has been argued that Columbus Day should equally be theirs, since it was the beginning of cultural exchange for American Indians and Europeans alike. Thanksgiving also is relevant to Indian descendants, since Massasoit, Squanto, and other WAMPANOAGS provided the agricultural knowledge that enabled the Pilgrims to survive. In the early 1900s, during the time of the Indian struggle for citizenship, a movement gained momentum to establish such a holiday. In 1915, the Congress of the American Indian Association issued a proclamation declaring the second Saturday of each May as American Indian Day. The next year, New York State complied with official state observance. In 1919, Illinois recognized the fourth Friday in September as American Indian Day. In 1935, Massachusetts enacted a law stating that the governor name the date for such a celebration for any given year; other states have sponsored Native American Awareness Weeks and Indian Rights Days. Yet even in those states, few non-Indians seem to take notice. Activists call for a national legal holiday, a national POWWOW, when work shuts down and celebrations surrounding Native American traditions and contributions take place.

(See also COLUMBIAN EXCHANGE; THANKSGIVING.)

native peoples The earliest-known inhabitants of a particular region; ABORIGINAL or INDIGENOUS peoples; used synonymously with NATIVE AMERICANS.

nativism A policy or philosophy of encouragement of NATIVE cultural traits, as in "nativistic movement," as opposed to ACCULTURATION. (See also INDIGENISMO; REVITALIZATION MOVEMENT; SELF-DETERMINATION.)

Nauset See ALGONQUIAN; WAMPANOAG.

Navajo (Navaho, Dineh, Dine) An ATHAPASCAN-speaking tribe of the SOUTHWEST CULTURE AREA, located in present-day northern Arizona and New Mexico and southern Utah and Colorado. The Navajos are related linguistically to the APACHE Indians. Tribal members now hold the Navajo Reservation in Arizona, New Mexico, and Utah, with tribal headquarters in Window Rock, Arizona. ("Navajoland," the largest reservation in the United States, is structured as a number of smaller reservations.) In New Mexico, Navajos also hold the Alamo Reservation, with tribal headquarters at Alamo; Canoncito Reservation, with headquarters at Canoncito; and Ramah Reservation, with headquarters at Ramah. *Navajo* derives from *Tewa Navahu*, a region of cultivated land and a former TEWA pueblo; the Spanish originally referred to the Navajos as *Apaches de Navajo*. The Navajo native name is *Dineh* or *Dine*, meaning "people."

Navajo blanket Woolen BLANKETS with bright-colored geometric designs, typical of the NAVAJOS. The geometric designs are cosmic symbols. In post-Contact times, Navajo women learned to spin the wool from sheep (introduced to the American Southwest by the Spanish), dye the threads (with traditional vegetal dyes or modern aniline dyes), then weave them on a LOOM.

Navajo blanket

Navajo blankets also are used as rugs and wall-hangings. (See also CHIEF'S BLANKET; EYE DAZZLER.)

Navajo Ways See WAY.

necklace See BEAR-CLAW NECKLACE; JEWELRY; NAJA; PENDANT.

necropolis (cemetery) A "city of dead" or place of BURIAL, especially belonging to an ancient city, as in the MESOAMERICAN CULTURE AREA.

needle Indians of the Americas used bone, ivory, thorn, and copper needles for sewing in pre-Contact times. The term bodkin is used for large blunt needles. Some needles, such as used by California Indians, had eyes. For tough materials, AWLS were used. European steel needles made hidework and beadwork easier.

negative painting (resist-negative, resist painting, resist dye) A process in POTTERY-making in which the surface is partly covered in wax or gum before the SLIP or PAINT is applied. FIRING creates color, except on the waxed or gummed portions; i.e., the design is in the fired color of the clay. Negative painting, the opposite of POSITIVE PAINTING, in which the colored design is

applied directly, is used on other surfaces. (See also RESERVE DECORATION.)

neolocal (neolocal residence) Residence after marriage in which the husband and wife live in a new home or locality without their parents present, as opposed to a MATRILOCAL or PATRILOCAL residence.

nephrite See JADE.

Nespelem See SANPOIL.

net A device made from NETTING, used in FISHING and HUNTING. The term refers to all netting or network. (See also SEINE; SNARE.)

netting (network) A material or fabric with woven, knotted, or twisted threads forming openwork meshes, made from animal tissues (hair, wool, hide, sinew, intestines) and vegetable fibers (roots, stems, bark, leaves). Netting is used to make NETS for fishing and hunting; for clothing; for BASKETRY; for lacing on SNOWSHOES, LACROSSE STICKS, TRAVOIS, and other objects; and also as a foundation for FEATHERWORK.

Neusiok See IROQUOIAN.

Neutral (Neutre Nation, Attiwandaronk) An IROQUOIAN-speaking tribe of the NORTHEAST CULTURE AREA, located between Lake Ontario, Lake Erie, and Lake Huron in present-day southern Ontario, western New York, and southeastern Michigan. In the mid-1600s, the tribes of the IROQUOIS LEAGUE, especially the neighboring SENECAS, defeated and absorbed the Neutrals. Their name was given to them by the French (*Neutre Nation*) because the tribe remained neutral in the wars between the IROQUOIS and the HURONS. The Hurons called them *Attiwandaronk*, meaning "their language is awry" in Iroquoian.

Nevome See PIMA.

"New World" In historical texts, the Western Hemisphere, i.e., the Americas, are sometimes referred to as the New World, with the Eastern Hemisphere, i.e., Europe, Africa, and Asia, referred to as the Old World. Such terms are ETHNOCENTRIC, ignoring the Indian WORLDVIEW.

Nez Perce (Nez Percé, Chopunnish, Sahaptin) A SAHAPTIN-speaking tribe of the PLATEAU CULTURE AREA, located in present-day central Idaho, southeastern Washington, and northeastern Oregon, and ranging into southwestern Montana. In 1878–85, a band of Nez Perces also lived in the INDIAN TERRITORY. Tribal members now hold the Nez Perce Reservation near Lapwai, Idaho; other Nez Perces share the Colville Reservation near Nespelem, Washington, with other tribes. The Nez Perce native name is *Tsutpeli* (also recorded as *Choo-pin-it-pa-loo*), meaning "people of the mountain," which the French confused with *Chopunnish*, meaning "pierced noses," leading to the French translation *Nez Percé*.

Niantic An ALGONQUIAN-speaking tribe of the NORTHEAST CULTURE AREA; the Eastern Niantics lived on the western coast of present-day Rhode Island and nearby Connecticut; the Western Niantics lived on the coast of present-day Connecticut between Niantic Bay and the Connecticut River. The two groups were separated by PEQUOT lands. The eastern group merged with the NARRAGANSETS in the 1600s; and the western group, with the MOHEGANS. Some joined the BROTHERTON INDIANS. *Niantic* probably means "at a point of land on an estuary" in Algonquian.

nickel silver See GERMAN SILVER.

Nicoleno See MISSION INDIANS; UTO-AZTECAN.

Nipissing (Nipissingue) A subtribe of the CHIPPEWA Indians, located on Lake Nipissing in present-day Ontario. In the mid-1600s, because of attacks by IROQUOIS, the Nipissings moved westward to Lake Nipigon. Their name means "little-water people" in ALGONQUIAN, referring to Lake Nipissing. The Nipissing band has its headquarters at Sturgeon Falls, Ontario.

Nipmuc (Nipmuck) An ALGONQUIAN-speaking tribe of the NORTHEAST CULTURE AREA, located in present-day central Massachusetts, especially in southern Worcester County, and extending into present-day northern Connecticut and Rhode Island. The Nipmuc Tribal Council of Massachusetts holds the Hassanamisco Reservation near Grafton. *Nipmuc* derives from the Algonquian *Nipmaug*, meaning "freshwater fishing place."

Nisga'a (Niska, Nishga, Nass River Indians) A PENUTIAN-speaking (TSIMSHIAN isolate) tribe of the NORTHWEST COAST CULTURE AREA, located on the Nass River in present-day northwestern British Columbia. The Nisga'as are related linguistically to the Tsimshians. Two bands, the Gitlakdamix at New Aiyansh and the Lakalzap at Greenville, maintain tribal identity.

Nisqually (Nisqualli, Qualliamish, Skalliahmish, Skwale) A SALISHAN-speaking tribe of the NORTHWEST COAST CULTURE AREA, located on the Nisqually River and the upper Puyallup River in present-day Washington. The Nisqually Indian Community is centered at Yelm in Thurston County, Washington; other tribal members share the Puyallup and Squaxin Island reservations with PUYALLUPS, SQUAXINS, and other Salishans.

nistsistanowan A CHEYENNE word for "our shared life (or existence)" in ALGONQUIAN.

nith-song A SONG FIGHT of the Greenland INUITS, in which a dispute between individuals is resolved through a debate consisting of song, dance, and humor. The audience chooses the victor depending on the wit, wisdom, and creativity of each contestant. Once a decision has been made, the point of contention can no longer be discussed. *Nith* is a Norwegian word, meaning "contention."

nomadic A migratory way of life in which people move from one location to another in search of food. Seminomadic people have permanent villages, but leave them seasonally to hunt, fish, or gather wild plant foods. PLAINS INDIANS were nomadic; some among them, also known as PRAIRIE INDIANS, were seminomadic. "Free wandering" is an unrestricted movement based on the availability of food resources; "restricted wandering" refers to movement within a defined territory. Nomadic is the opposite of SEDENTARY.

Nomelacki (Nomlaki, Nom-laka, Noamlaki, Nom-kewel) A subtribe of the WINTUN Indians, located on Thomas, Long, and Elder creeks in present-day Colusa and Tehama counties, California. Descendants maintain their identity on the Round Valley Reservation in Mendocino County, California, which they share with other tribes.

Nongatl See ATHAPASCAN.

Nooksack (Nooksak) A SALISHAN-speaking tribe of the NORTHWEST COAST CULTURE AREA, located on the Nooksack River in present-day Whatcom County, Washington. Nooksacks hold the Nooksack Reservation, with tribal headquarters at Deming, Washington; other tribal members are on the LUMNI Reservation near Bellingham; the Marietta Band of Nooksack Indians is centered at Marietta. *Nooksack* means "men of the mountains" in Salishan.

Nootka (Aht) A WAKASHAN-speaking tribe of the NORTHWEST COAST CULTURE AREA, located on the west coast of Vancouver Island in present-day British Columbia. The Nootkas are related linguistically to the MAKAH Indians. Nootka bands hold reserve tracts in their ancestral homeland. (See also CLAYOQUOT.)

Nootka hat A hat of woven fiber made by the NOOTKA Indians.

Noquet See ALGONQUIAN.

North American Indian See AMERICAN INDIAN.

Northeast Culture Area The geographical and cultural region extending, east to west, from the Atlantic Ocean to the Mississippi River; and north to south, from the Great Lakes to the Ohio Valley, including the Chesapeake Bay and Tidewater region. All of the following present-day states are included in this huge expanse of land: Maine, Vermont, New Hampshire, Massachusetts, Rhode Island, Connecticut, New York, New Jersey, Pennsylvania, Delaware, Ohio, Indiana, Illinois, and Michigan. Most of Maryland, West Virginia, Kentucky, and Wisconsin also are part of this CULTURE AREA, as are smaller parts of Virginia, North Carolina, Missouri, Iowa, and Minnesota. The following present-day provinces of Canada are included as well: Nova Scotia, New Brunswick, and Prince Edward Island, plus parts of Quebec and Ontario, in addition to a small part of Manitoba. Most of the region is woodland. (The region sometimes is called the Northeast Woodland Culture Area.) The physiography of the culture area also includes seacoast, hills, mountains, lakes, and river valleys. The Appalachian Mountains run in a general north-south direction. The five Great Lakes are located in the north-central region. The largest of the rivers are the St. Lawrence, Ottawa, Connecticut, Hudson, Delaware, Susquehanna, Allegheny, Ohio, Wabash, and Illinois. The forests provided natural resources for NORTHEAST INDIANS: wood for houses, boats, tools, and fuel; plus abundant game. Of the mammals, DEER were the most important resource. The oceans, lakes, and rivers were a source of plentiful fish and shellfish. In addition to hunting-gathering, Northeast Indians practiced farming. Many of their villages of LONG-

HOUSES or WIGWAMS had cultivated fields nearby.

Northeast Indians   The Indians of the NORTHEAST CULTURE AREA spoke dialects of two language families: ALGONQUIAN and IROQUOIAN. The only exception were the WINNEBAGOS, who spoke a dialect of SIOUAN. (See also CATEGORICAL APPENDIX, "TRIBES, BANDS, PEOPLES, LANGUAGES, AND CULTURES.")

Northwest Coast Culture Area   A geographical and cultural region extending, in the north, from present-day southern Alaska as far as, in the south, present-day northern California, and, in between, including the western parts of present-day British Columbia, Washington, and Oregon as well as numerous islands, including Vancouver Island, the Queen Charlotte Islands, and the Alexander Archipelago. This CULTURE AREA is elongated in shape, from north to south about 2,000 miles long, but from east to west about 150 miles at the widest. The many islands are actually the tips of submerged mountains, part of the Coast Range; the rugged mountains form a spine running north-south along the culture area, in some places extending to the ocean, forming rocky cliffs. There are numerous inlets and sounds along the shoreline as well as many straits between the islands. Farther inland, in Washington and Oregon, another mountain range, the Cascade Range, also lies on a north-south axis. The climate of the region is warm for northern latitudes; an ocean current known as the Japanese Current warms the water as well as winds blowing inland. The westerly winds also carry abundant moisture; the mountains block the moisture, which turns to rainfall—as much as 100 inches or more a year—more than in any other part of North America. Abundant springs and streams run from the mountains to the ocean. Except on mountain tops and rock faces too steep to have soil, these climatic conditions have produced vast forests, with some of the tallest evergreen trees in the world; the branches of tall trees form a dense canopy, blocking out sunlight and making the forest floor dark and wet with little undergrowth other than ferns and mosses. NORTHWEST COAST INDIANS usually placed their PLANK HOUSES at the ocean's edge on typically narrow sand and gravel beaches. With travel over the rugged land so difficult, Indians moved up and down the coast by sea. They hunted SEA MAMMALS, including WHALES, seals, and sea lions; they also caught SALMON, halibut, herring, cod, and flounder. When salmon left the ocean waters to lay their eggs, Northwest Coast Indians also fished the rivers. Their land game included deer, elk, bear, and mountain goat. The region had plenty of food to support large populations in seaside villages without farming.

Northwest Coast Indians   The tribes of the NORTHWEST COAST CULTURE AREA. The many languages spoken in the region include those of the NADENE and PENUTIAN language phyla as well as the CHIMAKUM, SALISHAN, and WAKASHAN language families. (See also CATEGORICAL APPENDIX, "TRIBES, BANDS, PEOPLES, LANGUAGES, AND CULTURES.")

nose-ring   See JEWELRY.

notched plate   A stone plate, either round or rectangular, with notches or scallops along the edge. (The rectangular plates had notches on the ends only.) Often the surfaces bear representational and abstract engravings or grooves. The purpose of notched plates is unknown, but, based on their coarse stone, they might have been used as a type of METATE to grind PIGMENTS. Typical of MOUNDBUILDERS.

notched stick (notched resonator, musical rasp)   A musical instrument that creates a rhythmic sound by rasping one stick with grooves against another, or against a gourd, bone, or basket. The Spanish word is *morache*.

Nottaway   See IROQUOIAN.

Ntlakyapamuk (Thompson)   A SALISHAN-speaking tribe of the PLATEAU CULTURE AREA, located on the Fraser and Thompson rivers in present-day British Columbia and ranging into present-day northern Washington. Subdivisions include the Lower Thompson and Upper Thompson (the latter is further subdivided into the Lytton, Upper Fraser, Spences Bridge, and Nicola bands). A number of Ntlakyapamuk bands hold reserve tracts in their ancestral homeland.

Nuclear America   Those regions in the Americas where FARMING, POTTERY, and other cultural traits were invented and developed and from where they spread, specifically the central Andes in South America (the home of the INCAS) as well as parts of Mexico and Central America (the home of the OLMECS, MAYAS, TOLTECS, and AZTECS).

nuclear family   See FAMILY.

nugluktag   An indoor game of the INUITS, in which players try to poke sticks through a twirling spool that dangles from above.

numeral system   See COUNTING.

nutstone   See CUPSTONE.

nyaweh gowah (niawenkowa)   A MOHAWK phrase for "great thanks" in IROQUOIAN.

obelisk A four-sided pillar of stone, typical of the INCAS and MESOAMERICAN INDIANS, usually tapering to a point. Many obelisks are MONOLITHS.

obsidian A natural glass formed by volcanic action; typically lustrous and black, brown, reddish, or greenish. Like FLINT, obsidian can be worked to a sharp point or edge for tools and weapons. It also was used to make ceremonial objects. MESOAMERICAN INDIANS used obsidian for spear points and mirrors; it was associated with the world of the dead.

Ocale See TIMUCUA.

ocarina A musical instrument with four tones, made of POTTERY, usually with a mouthpiece at almost a right angle from the body. Typical of SOUTH AMERICAN INDIANS.

Occaneechi See SIOUAN.

ocher Any of a variety of natural earths, consisting of mineral oxides of iron, clay, or sand. Red ocher (HEMATITE) and yellow ocher (limonite) are used as PIGMENTS.

Oconee (Ocon, Oconi) A MUSKOGEAN-speaking tribe of the SOUTHEAST CULTURE AREA, located on the Oconee River in present-day Georgia. The Oconees also lived on the Chattahoochee River for a time, after which, in the mid-1700s, they settled in present-day Alachua County, Florida. Along with other Muskogeans, they became known historically as SEMINOLES.

offering A gift to a spiritual being to bring about good fortune. Animals once were common offerings, as were plants, especially TOBACCO. The burning of tobacco and other plants as INCENSE likewise was considered a gift to the SPIRIT WORLD. Tools and other valued possessions were given as well. PRAYER STICKS and PRAYER FEATHERS are symbolic offerings. Offerings are made at ALTARS, SHRINES, and SACRED SITES, or to SACRED OBJECTS. A GIVEAWAY can be called an offering to people. Offerings Lodge is a ceremony of the ARAPAHOS, in which participants offer devotion through prayer, fasting, and personal SACRIFICE in return for spiritual aid in survival. (See also SACRIFICE.)

Ofo See SIOUAN.

Oglala A subtribe of the TETON division of the SIOUX Indians, located on the upper Missouri River between the Cheyenne and Bad rivers in present-day South Dakota and ranging throughout the Northern Plains, especially in present-day North Dakota, Montana, Wyoming, and Nebraska. *Oglala* means "to scatter one's own" in SIOUAN.

ohwachira The MOHAWK term for "family" in IROQUOIAN.

Ojibway See CHIPPEWA.

Oka See MOHAWK.

Okanagan (Okanogan, Okinagan, Okanagon) A SALISHAN-speaking tribe of the PLATEAU CULTURE AREA, located on the Okanogan River in present-day Washington and on Okanagan Lake in present-day British Columbia. The Sinkaietk Indians are sometimes classified as a subtribe. The Lower Similkameen, Okanagan, Osoyoos, Penticton, Upper Similkameen, and Westbank bands are active in British Columbia; Okanagan descendants in Washington live among other Salishans, in particular on the

Colville Reservation in Ferry and Okanogan counties.

Okelousa   See MUSKOGEAN.

okey   The CHOCTAW word for "yes" in MUSKOGEAN, used in COUNCILS to indicate agreement. Probably the derivation of the expression "okay" or "O.K."

Okipa   (O-kee-pa)   A ceremony of the MANDAN Indians, held in late spring or summer and usually lasting four days; centered around a sacred cedar post erected on the village plaza inside a small enclosure. The various rituals, among them a Bull Dance and a Feast of the Buffalo, celebrated the creation of the Mandans and attempted to ensure food supplies and bring about visions for youths passing into adulthood. The Okipa ceremony had elements in common with the SUN DANCE and VISION QUEST of other PLAINS INDIANS. To prove their manhood, Mandan youths fasted; had their chests, backs, and legs slashed; and were raised toward the roof of a ceremonial lodge on rawhide thongs and ropes. The last Okipa Ceremony was held in about 1890. *Okipa* possibly means "to look alike" in SIOUAN, referring to the Bull Dancers resembling one another.

Okmulgee   See CREEK; MUSKOGEAN.

Okwanuchu   See SHASTAN.

Old Copper Culture   A cultural tradition of ARCHAIC INDIANS in the western Great Lakes region of present-day Michigan and Wisconsin, lasting from about 4000 to 1500 B.C. The name of the culture is based on the COPPER artifacts discovered among remains, indicating the earliest use of metal known among Indians north of Mexico. Old Copper Indians used natural copper deposits, both sheets in rock fissures or nuggets in the soil, to make tools and ornaments. They shaped it by heating, then hammering it. Their copper artifacts have been found be-

yond their homeland, proving widespread trade relationships.

Old Cordilleran Culture   (Cascade)   A cultural tradition of ARCHAIC INDIANS in the Pacific Northwest along the Columbia River, beginning about 9000 B.C. until 5000 B.C. or afterward. Old Cordilleran or Cascade POINTS have the shape of willow leaves (without FLUTING) and were probably used to hunt small game.

oleohneh   An ABENAKI expression of "thank you" in ALGONQUIAN.

olla   An earthenware jar or jug, typical of SOUTHWEST INDIANS, with a globular body, flared neck, wide mouth, and, in some cases, looped handles, generally used to hold water or grain or for cooking. Animal skin is used to cover the mouth. The word is of Spanish origin.

Olmec   (Olmeca)   A people of the MESOAMERICAN CULTURE AREA, located on the Gulf Coast east of present-day Mexico City, Mexico. Olmec culture dominated the region from about 1500 B.C. to A.D. 300. Olmec peoples probably established the "mother civilization" of MESOAMERICA, which influenced later inhabitants of the region, including the MAYAS, TOLTECS, and AZTECS. The Olmecs developed extensive trade contacts. Unlike the societies of most Indian tribes, Olmec society had a class of powerful PRIESTS, as well as bureaucrats, merchants, and craftsmen. The Olmec upper classes lived in structures (some of which were pyramids with temples on top) of highly finished stone architecture. The buildings were situated along paved streets. AQUEDUCTS carried water to them. The Olmec population centers are not thought of as true cities, but rather as ceremonial and economic centers. Farmers lived in the nearby countryside, supporting the upper classes through SLASH-AND-BURN farming, with corn as the main crop. Another Olmec cultural development passed to later Indians was a BALL-GAME played with a ball made from RUBBER on a paved BALL-COURT. The Olmecs were also the first known Indians to have number and CALENDAR systems as well as PICTOGRAPHS. The most important Olmec population centers were San Lorenzo, dominant from 1200 to 900 B.C.; La Venta, dominant from 800 to 400 B.C.; and Tres Zapotes, dominant from about 100 B.C. to A.D. 300. La Venta was the location of the largest Olmec pyramid. Invading tribes, drought, failing crops, or disease all could have played a part in the decline of Olmec culture. Descendants of the Olmecs, who might have been the ancestors of later Mesoamerican peoples, are sometimes referred to as epi-Olmecs.

ololiuqui A morning glory plant (*Rivea corymbosa* or *Ipomoea violacea*), the seeds of which act as a narcotic. The AZTECS used it ritually for divination and as a kind of truth serum.

Omaha A SIOUAN-speaking tribe of the GREAT PLAINS CULTURE AREA, located on the Missouri River in present-day northeastern Nebraska. (The ancestors of the Omahas probably were one people with those of the KAW, OSAGE, PONCA, and QUAPAW tribes, formerly living along the Ohio River, then migrating onto the prairies and plains west of the Mississippi River where they divided. The Omahas and their closest relatives, the Poncas, probably lived in present-day Minnesota and Iowa before separating in South Dakota.) Tribal members hold the Omaha Reservation in Thurston County, Nebraska. *Omaha* means "those going against the wind (or current)" in Siouan.

Oneida An IROQUOIAN-speaking tribe of the NORTHEAST CULTURE AREA, located in present-day Oneida County, New York and surrounding areas. The Oneidas are part of the IROQUOIS LEAGUE. In 1838, many among them relocated to present-day Wisconsin, purchasing land from the MENOMINEES. Tribal members hold the Oneida Reservation near Oneida, New York as well as the Oneida Reservation near Oneida,

Wisconsin. Oneidas living in Ontario include the Oneida of the Thames band and members of the Six Nations of the Grand River band. Their name, derived from *Onayatakono*, means "people of the boulder" or "people of the standing stone" in Iroquoian, referring to a large rock within their territory.

Onondaga An IROQUOIAN-speaking tribe of the NORTHEAST CULTURE AREA, located in present-day Onondaga County, New York and surrounding areas. Onondagas are part of the IROQUOIS LEAGUE. Tribal members hold the Onondaga Reservation near Nedrow, New York; other Onondagas are part of the Six Nations of the Thames band in present-day Ontario. Their name, derived from *Onondagaono*, means "people of the hills" in Iroquoian.

Oohenonpa (Oohenonpah, Two Kettles) A subtribe of the TETON division of the SIOUX Indians, located near the Cheyenne River in present-day South Dakota and ranging throughout the Northern Plains, especially in present-day North Dakota, Montana, Wyoming, and Nebraska. *Oohenonpa* means "two boilings" in Siouan.

Opelousa See ATAKAPA.

oral tradition (oral literature) The preservation of tribal knowledge and LEGENDS through the spoken or sung word. The phrase oral tradition usually refers to memorized tribal history and mythology, as found in narration, SONGS, and CHANTS, but it can apply to any nonwritten shared beliefs or information. (See also DRAMA; ORATORY; POETRY; SPEAKER; STORYTELLING.)

oratory Public speaking, the art of oration, has played an important part in the governing of tribes and bands, with leaders arguing their cases in COUNCILS. Oratory also has been important in tribal negotiations with representatives of other tribes and of governments. Some tribes had official SPEAKERS, talkers, or spokesmen, known for their eloquence and having varying powers; some spoke as a chief, others for a chief. Many of them traveled widely to make their cases before foreign governments and their representatives. In some cases their speeches, recorded by non-Indian officials, are considered literature, helping to bring alive Indian history and the Indian viewpoint. Those repeated in specific ceremonies are referred to as "ritual speeches" or "ritual addresses." Indian oratory is known for its passion, drama, poetry, and references to nature. Contemporary Indian activists continue the Native American tradition of compelling oratory. (See also STORY-TELLING.)

ordeal A trial of courage, strength, and endurance, either to determine guilt or innocence or to prove readiness for adulthood in a RITE OF PASSAGE. (See also *HUSKANAW*; RUNNING THE GAUNTLET; SUN DANCE; VISION QUEST.)

orenda IROQUOIAN for the magic power, force of energy, or SPIRIT inherent in every being or object; sometimes capitalized. (See also *MANITOU*; *WAKANDA*.)

organization A group of people united for a common purpose. In Indian studies, the term is used for political, social, and economic groups working to protect INDIAN RIGHTS and develop Indian resources. Some of those playing an important role in Indian history are the All-Pueblo Council, founded in 1922; the Indian Defense League, 1925; the National Congress of American Indians (NCAI), 1944; the National Indian Youth Council, 1961; the Survival of American Indians Associations, 1964; the Alaska Federation of Natives (AFN), 1966; the American Indian Movement (AIM), 1968; the Native American Rights Fund (NARF), 1971; the International Indian Treaty Council, 1974; the Council of Energy Resource Tribes (CERT), 1975; National Indian Urban Council, 1977; and the Women of All Red Nations (WARN), 1978. Many other political, educational, historical, religious, and social organizations are working to improve the lives of native peoples. (See also ACTIVISM; REFORMER.)

ornament An adornment, decoration, or embellishment. The term is usually applied to objects worn on the person or hand held; but it can also refer to "design." A ceremonial ornament has symbolic meaning. (See also CATEGORICAL APPENDIX, "ARTS AND CRAFTS"; APPLIQUÉ; GORGET; JEWELRY.)

Osage A SIOUAN-speaking tribe of the GREAT PLAINS CULTURE AREA, located on the Osage River (the Great Osages) and on the Missouri River (Little Osages) in present-day Missouri. (The ancestors of the Osages probably were one people with those of the KAW, OMAHA, PONCA, and QUAPAW tribes, formerly living along the Ohio River, then migrating onto the prairies and plains west of the Mississippi River and dividing.) The Osages also claimed territory in present-day northern Arkansas and Oklahoma and in southeastern Kansas. A band dividing from the Great Osages in the early 1800s became known as the Arkansas Osages. The Osage Tribe holds trust lands in Osage County, Oklahoma. *Osage* is the French version of *Wazhazhe*, the native name of the Great Osages. The native name of the Osages as a whole is *Ni-U-kon'-Skah*, for "people of the middle waters."

Osochi See CREEK; MUSKOGEAN.

ossuary A place or container where the bones of the dead are deposited. (See also BURIAL.)

Otkon Evil beings in IROQUOIS tradition. The name can be translated as "demon" or "monster"; the opposite of OYARON. Also used as an adjective, meaning "monstrous" or "mysterious," and often applied to FETISHES.

Oto (Otoe) A SIOUAN-speaking tribe of the GREAT PLAINS CULTURE AREA, located on the lower Platte and Missouri rivers in present-day Nebraska. (According to tribal legend, the Otos formerly were one people with the ancestors of the IOWA, MISSOURI, and WINNEBAGO tribes, living in present-day Wisconsin. A group supposedly separated from the Winnebagos and traveled to the confluence of the Iowa and Mississippi rivers. This group further divided: The band staying near the Mississippi became the Iowas; the band that continued westward to the Missouri River divided again, becoming the Otos and Missouris, with the Otos continuing farther up the Missouri.) The Missouris and Otos joined up in present-day Nebraska in 1829 and were relocated to the INDIAN TERRITORY in 1882. The Otoe-Missouria Tribe holds trust lands in Noble County, Oklahoma. *Oto* derives from *Wat'ota*, meaning "lechers" in Siouan, referring to a chief's son who seduced another chief's daughter, causing the original split between the Otos and Missouris. The Oto native name is *Che-wae-rae*, probably meaning "people."

Oto-Manguean A phylum of language stocks, including the CHINANTECAN, MANGUEAN, MIXTECAN, OTOMIAN, POPOLOCAN, and ZAPOTECAN families.

Otomian (Otomi-Pame) A language family and subdivision of the OTO-MANGUEAN phylum comprising dialects spoken by Indians of the SOUTHWEST CULTURE AREA, including the Jonaz and Pame tribes of north-central Mexico and tribes of the MESOAMERICAN CULTURE AREA, among them the Matlatzinca (Pirinda), Mazahua, Ocuiltec (Ocuilteca), and Otomi tribes of central Mexico.

Ottawa (Outauois) An ALGONQUIAN-speaking tribe of the NORTHEAST CULTURE AREA, located on Manitoulin Island and the north shore of Georgian Bay, part of Lake Huron, in present-day Ontario. The closest linguistic relatives of the Ottawas are the CHIPPEWAS and POTAWATOMIS. In the course of their history, Ottawa bands lived on Lake Michigan in present-day Michigan and Wisconsin as well as in present-day Minnesota, Illinois, Indiana, Ohio, Kansas, and Oklahoma. Tribal members hold trust lands near Miami, Oklahoma. Others make their homes in Kansas, Michigan, and Ontario. *Ottawa* means "to trade," probably in an Algonquian dialect, referring to the acting of middlemen among other tribes.

Otter Society A MEDICINE SOCIETY of IROQUOIS women who draw their power from water animals. Members ritually obtain water from a spring, which they then sprinkle on the sick from buckets with cornhusks.

Outagamie See FOX.

oven A closed compartment for baking; used in cooking food and in POTTERY-making. (See also HORNO; KILN; PIT OVEN.)

owl Owls, of the order Strigiformes, are generally nocturnal birds of prey, having large heads, round frontal eyes, short hooked beaks, and feathered and hooked talons. Because of their nocturnal and predatory habits, they traditionally have been regarded as symbols of death, either as an

Flathead owl effigy bowl

ominous messenger or as the vehicle of human souls. But Owl also is regarded as a teacher. Owl feathers and talons are valued highly for ceremonial use. The HOPI word for "owl" in UTO-AZTECAN is *mongwau*.

Oyaron An Iroquois name of a GUARDIAN SPIRIT. A person's Oyaron supposedly protects him or her from the OTKON.

Ozette See MAKAH.

Pacarina (Conopa, Chanca, Chuarchar) The collective name of the INCA guardian spirits, symbolizing natural forces and representing clans; known as *Conopa* on the coast and *Chanca* and *Chuarchar* in the mountains in other QUECHUA dialects.

paddle A wooden implement, wide at one end. The term refers to CANOE and other boat paddles, sometimes carved and painted with intricate designs; to paddles used in mixing and stirring, such as corn or acorn mush paddles; and to paddles used in adding designs in pottery, as in PADDLE-AND-ANVIL designs.

paddle-and-anvil A technique of finishing POTTERY in which the walls of the pot, made by COILING, are smoothed by striking the exterior with a paddle, while holding a round or mushroom-shape implement known as an anvil on the interior to counter the force of the blow. (See also PADDLING.)

paddling A technique of decorating POTTERY by pressing a flat or curved wooden PADDLE against the wet clay before FIRING; the paddle or paddle stamp has a design carved in it or cords wrapped around it. The term also refers to the "paddling" of boats. (See also PADDLE-AND-ANVIL.)

Paezan A language family and subdivision of the MACRO-CHIBCHAN phylum comprising dialects spoken by SOUTH AMERICAN INDIANS, including the Atacameno tribe of present-day northern Chile; the Canari and Puruha tribes of present-day Ecuador; the Jirajara tribe of present-day Venezuela; the Mura tribe on the Amazon River in present-day Brazil; and others.

Paha Sapa The SIOUAN name for the Black Hills, a mountainous region of southwestern South Dakota and northeastern Wyoming. A GOLD RUSH to the Black Hills beginning in 1874 resulted in the eventual loss of SIOUX rights to what they considered sacred lands. The carving of Mt. Rushmore and the establishment of Custer State Park added symbolic insult to the loss of ancestral territory.

Pahko A FIESTA in YAQUI tradition. Pahkos are sponsored jointly by individual households as well as tribal church organizations. The household of those persons hosting the Pahko, such as for a rite of passage, is transformed into a church. Both church officials and traditional PASCOLA dancers carry out their assigned rituals.

paho The HOPI word for a PRAYER STICK in UTO-AZTECAN. The typical *paho* is six to 12 inches long, with a cottonwood handle that is decorated with paint, feathers, and cornhusks.

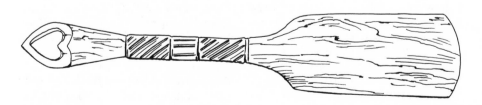

Seneca corn paddle

paint American Indians derived paint from minerals, such as iron oxides (mineral paint); from vegetable matter, such as berries, flowers, and bark (vegetal paint); and from animal sources, such as blood or a yellowish substance in the gall bladder of the BUFFALO. (See also PAINTING; PIGMENT.)

painting Native American methods of painting include applying PAINT with fingers; with pieces of chalk, charcoal, or clay; with wood, bark, or reeds softened at the end; or with bones, especially the spongy knee joint of the buffalo; and sometimes spraying it on with the mouth. Shells and pottery were used as paint cups. Horses, dwellings, totem poles, masks, pottery, bags, and other objects were painted ceremonially. ROCK ART included rock painting as well as PETROGLYPHS. Body-painting and face-painting preceded various ceremonies and also served as protection from wind and sun. ("War paint," a misused term, is but one type of body paint, i.e., the paint worn into battle.) It is possible Indians were first called "red men" or "redskins" by whites because they often used red body paint, a symbol of strength and success for many tribes. In all types of painting, colors had differing meaning and symbolism for different people. The APACHES speak of any object with ceremonial designs as "painted on"; such objects have to be created, handled, and disposed of with the proper ritual. Many contemporary Indians have achieved international reputations as painters in the FINE ARTS, blending traditional themes with modern. (See also FRONTIER PAINTER; NEGATIVE PAINTING; POSITIVE PAINTING; SANDPAINTING.)

Paiute (Piute, Pahute) A UTO-AZTECAN-speaking tribe of the GREAT BASIN CULTURE AREA, located in present-day western Nevada, southeastern Oregon, eastern California, and southwestern Idaho (Northern Paiutes, or Paviotso) as well as in present-day southeastern Nevada, western Utah, northwestern Arizona, and southeastern California (Southern Paiutes). The Paiutes, both the Northern and Southern branches,

are discussed more properly as a number of seminomadic bands with related dialects. In Arizona, Paiutes hold the Kaibab Reservation near Pipe Springs. In California, Paiutes hold the Benton Paiute Reservation near Benton; Big Pine Reservation (with SHOSHONES) near Big Pine; Bishop Indian Reservation (with Shoshones) near Bishop; Bridgeport Indian Colony near Bridgeport; Cedarville Rancheria near Cedarville; Fort Bidwell Reservation near Fort Bidwell; Fort Independence Reservation near Independence; Lone Pine Reservation (with Shoshones) near Lone Pine; Susanville Indian Rancheria (with ACHOMAWIS and MAIDUS) near Susanville; and the X L Ranch Reservation (with Achomawis) near Alturas. In Idaho and (Nevada), Paiutes hold the Duck Valley Reservation (with Shoshones) near Elko (Nevada), and the Summit Lake Reservation near Fort Hall (Idaho). In Nevada, Paiutes hold the Fallon Reservation and Colony (with Shoshones) near Fallon; Las Vegas Indian Colony near Las Vegas; Lovelock Indian Colony near Lovelock; Moapa River Indian Reservation near Las Vegas; Pyramid Lake Reservation near Nixon; Reno-Sparks Indian Colony (with WASHOES) near Reno; Walker River Reservation near Schurz; Winnemucca Indian Colony near Winnemucca; and Yerrington Indian Colony and Campbell Ranch near Yerrington. In Nevada and Oregon, Paiutes hold the Fort McDermitt Reservation (with Shoshones) near McDermitt. In Oregon, Paiutes hold the Burns Paiute Indian Colony near Burns and the Warm Springs Reservation (with other tribes) near Warm Springs. In Utah, Paiutes hold the Paiute Indians of Utah Reservation near Cedar City. A band known as San Juan Northern Paiute operates out of Tuba City, Arizona. *Paiute* possibly means "water UTE" or "true Ute" in Uto-Aztecan. (See also DIGGER INDIANS; SNAKE INDIANS.)

Palaihnihan A language family and subdivision of the HOKAN phylum comprising dialects spoken by the ACHOMAWI and Atsugewei tribes of the CALIFORNIA CULTURE AREA. The name Palaihnihan is taken from the KLAMATH word *p'laikni*, meaning "mountaineers" in PENUTIAN.

"paleface" Indian term for whites, more common in fiction than in real life. (See also WHITE.)

Paleo-Indians (Lithic Indians) PREHISTORIC INDIANS of the PALEOLITHIC PERIOD, the period before the invention of metal tools, also known as the Old STONE AGE. The Paleo-Indians or Lithic Indians had only wood, stone, and bone tools and no metal. They lived mostly in caves, under overhangs, and in brushwood lean-tos. They wore hide and fur clothing. They used fire to keep warm, to cook, to protect themselves from animals while sleeping, and to hunt. By lighting fires on the grasslands, the hunters could drive herds of animals over cliffs and into swamps and bogs. Early Indians had different methods for lighting fires: striking a spark with certain stones, such as FLINT, into kindling; or by rubbing wood together. FIRE DRILLS enabled the rapid spinning of wood against wood. The first Indians are thought of primarily as big-game hunters, but they also were gatherers of wild plant foods, including greens, seeds, berries, roots, and bulbs. In addition to longhorn BUFFALO, woolly MAMMOTHS, MASTODONS, and SABER-TOOTHED TIGERS, Paleo-Indians hunted other extinct mammals: American lions, camels, short-faced bears, dire wolves, native horses, plus smaller game. The first Paleo-Indians did not have stone POINTS but probably used fire to harden the tips of wooden spears. Early Paleo-Indians did have roughly shaped stone and bone tools for scraping and chopping. Later Paleo-Indians developed methods of FLAKING. They also invented the ATLATL. Scholars use the different types of points found at campsites, kill sites, and quarry sites to determine different technological phases, or cultures, among the Paleo-Indians, such as CLOVIS CULTURE, FOLSOM CULTURE, PLANO CULTURE, and SANDIA CULTURE. (See also BERINGIA; BIG-GAME HUNTING.)

Paleolithic period (Paleo-Indian period, Lithic period, Old Stone Age) The cultural period beginning with the FLAKING of stone tools; first defined in Europe, then applied to other continents (although the terms mesolithic and neolithic are generally not applied to the Americas). Paleolithic cultures occurred in the latter part of the PLEISTOCENE. PALEO-INDIANS are known to have been widespread in the Americas by at least 11,000 years B.P. (before the present), i.e., 13000 B.C. Recent archaeological evidence at Meadowcroft Rock-shelter in southwestern Pennsylvania indicates human presence as far back as 14225 B.C. The Monte Verde site in Chile indicates early human presence as well. Paleo-Indians possibly may have are reached the Americas more than 50,000 years ago. Most scholars date 8000 B.C. as the end of the Paleolithic period and the start of the ARCHAIC PERIOD. Some apply various terms to a transitional period between the periods, such as Paleo-transitional period and protoarchaic period, when cultural traits defined under one category resemble in part those in the other without clear distinctions. Other transitional terms, such as Pluvial period, postglacial period, and WATERSHED AGE, refer to climatic changes at the end of the Pleistocene.

paleontology The study of FOSSIL remains and ancient life forms. A paleontologist specializes in this science. Paleozoology, the study of ancient vertebrates and invertebrates, and paleobotany, the study of ancient plants, are subdivisions of paleontology. Paleontological studies are relevant to ARCHAEOLOGY.

Paleo-Siberians Peoples of the PALEOLITHIC PERIOD living in Siberia, some of whom eventually migrated to North America via BERINGIA.

palisade (stockade) A fence of upright logs, placed around a village for purposes of fortification. Some palisades supported an inner raised walkway. EASTERN INDIANS were known for their palisaded villages.

palladium   An object considered sacred to a people and that helps safeguard them. Customs and laws also are sometimes referred to as palladiums. The BUFFALO CALF PIPE of the SIOUX, the MEDICINE ARROWS of the CHEYENNES, the FLAT PIPE of the GROS VENTRES, the TAIMÉ of the KIOWAS, and the SACRED POLE of the OMAHAS are considered palladiums. A Latin word derived from the Greek *Palladion*, a statue of the goddess Pallas Athena that watched over Troy. (See also PRESTIGE ITEM.)

palma   A type of stone sculpture found on the Gulf Coast of what is now Mexico; about 20 inches long, narrow and thick at the bottom, wide and thin at the top, typically of BASALT with carvings in BAS-RELIEF. As with *HACHAS* and *YUGOS*, the purpose

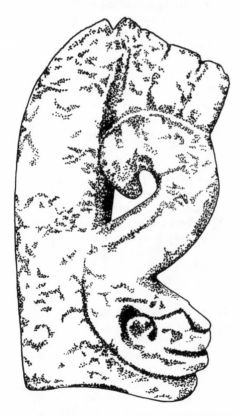

Mesoamerican *palma*, showing serpent

of *palmas* is unknown, although it probably was ceremonial. *Palma* is Spanish for "palm tree"; the sculptures are so named because of their shape.

palmetto   Any of several small trees in the palm family, in particular *Sabal palmetto* (cabbage palmetto) native to the SOUTHEAST CULTURE AREA. The SEMINOLE Indians traditionally have used palmetto trunks in framing CHICKEES and the leaves for THATCH, BASKETRY, bedding, and rope. They also eat the buds raw or baked.

Palouse   (Palus)   A SAHAPTIN-speaking tribe of the PLATEAU CULTURE AREA located on the Palouse and Snake rivers in present-day southeastern Washington and northern Idaho. Descendants share the Colville Reservation near Nespelem, Washington, with other tribes.

palynology   The study of spores and POLLENS, often in their fossil form. A palynologist specializes in this discipline. Ancient pollen grains can help date artifacts.

Pamlico   See ALGONQUIAN.

Pamunkey   A subtribe of the POWHATAN Indians, located in present-day King William County, Virginia. Descendants hold the Pamunkey Reservation, with tribal headquarters at King William, Virginia. *Pamunkey* means "sloping hill" or "rising upland" in ALGONQUIAN.

Panamint   See UTO-AZTECAN.

pan-Indian   Pertaining to Indians of more than one tribe; refers to ORGANIZATIONS, activities, goals, and culture (ritual and art) relevant to all Indian peoples. A pan-Indian culture refers to shared cultural traits, as among the PLAINS INDIANS. The pan-Indian movement refers to Indians of more than one tribe united for political ACTIVISM. (See also COMPOSITE TRIBE.)

Panoan   A language family and subdivision of the GE-PANO-CARIB phylum comprising

dialects spoken by SOUTH AMERICAN INDI-
ANS, including the Conibo and Shipibo
tribes in present-day Peru, and others.

panpipe (pan flute, mouth organ) A musical instrument consisting of a series of pipes
or reeds of different lengths bound together,
with the open tops for blowing even and
the stopped-up bottoms graduated, thus creating varying tones in a scale. Typical of
SOUTH AMERICAN INDIANS.

pantheism A doctrine of belief in which
god is viewed as identical to or an expression
of the physical forces of nature. (See also
ANIMISM.)

pantheon All the gods of a particular people, as in the "pantheon of AZTEC deities."

panther See PUMA.

Papago (Tohono O'odham) A UTO-
AZTECAN-speaking tribe of the SOUTH-
WEST CULTURE AREA, located south and
southeast of the Gila River and on the Santa
Cruz River in southwestern Arizona and in
present-day northern Mexico. Papagos are
related linguistically to the PIMAS. Descendants hold the Ak Chin Reservation in Pinal
County, Arizona and the Papago Reservation in Maricopa, Pima, and Pinal counties.
Their name derives from the Uto-Aztecan
name *Papah-ootam*, meaning "bean people."
Their native and official tribal name since
1984 is *Tohono O'odham*, meaning "desert
people."

paper bread See PIKI.

papoose (pappoose, pappouse) An infant
child of North American Indian parents.
The word probably derives from *papu*, an
infant's way of addressing his father in the
NARRAGANSET dialect of the ALGONQUIAN
language, to which the Narragansets added
an "s" sound referring to the child. White
traders and settlers carried it throughout
North America, and it has come to be applied to any Indian baby. A papoose board
is a CRADLEBOARD.

parallel flaking See FLAKING.

parfleche RAWHIDE with the hair removed. The rawhide is soaked in lye to
remove the hair, then lashed together while
wet and dried until stiff. The term also
refers to a BOX or saddlebag made from
this material by the PLAINS INDIANS. These
parfleches were crafted in a variety of shapes
and sizes, often rectangular and about two
by three feet, and usually were painted.
Clothing, ceremonial objects, and food, especially meat, were carried in parfleches,
which also are called meat cases. The word
parfleche is of French origin, probably from

Plains Indian parfleche

parer, "to parry," and *flèche,* "arrow," referring to a hide SHIELD; or possibly from
pour, "for," and *flèche,* "arrow," referring to
a QUIVER.

parka A hooded outer garment made by
the INUITS and ALEUTS from the skin of
mammals or birds. The length varies from
people to people, from the hips to below
the knees. Women's parkas are cut larger
for carrying infants; they also are longer in
back for insulation when sitting. Sometimes
MITTENS are attached. Elongated jackets
with hoods, made of wool and other wind-
resistant materials, now also are referred to
as parkas. The word is of Samoyed origin
(a Siberian native people), passed to the
Aleuts by the Russians. One of the Inuit
words for a parka in the ESKIMO-ALEUT
language is *attige.*

parrot Any of various tropical and semitropical birds of the order Psittaciformes,
having hooked bills and bright plumage.
Parrot feathers were a valued trade item in
much of the Americas, reaching as far north
as the American Southwest, such as among
Indians of the HOHOKAM CULTURE, where
the long-tailed macaws were valued. In the
CORN DANCE of the KERES, TEWAS, and
other PUEBLO INDIANS, the dancers traditionally have worn clusters of parrot feathers
on the head.

Pascagoula   See MUSKOGEAN.

Pascola   A YAQUI Indian dancer. Although
the Pascolas predate Catholicism among the
Yaquis, they now are featured performers in
the tribe's elaborate Easter celebration and
other ceremonial events derived from the
Christian calendar as well as in traditional
rites of passage. The Pascolas bring comic
elements to their performances. The word
translates from the Yaqui dialect of UTO-
AZTECAN as "old man of the fiesta." (See
also PAHKO.)

Passamaquoddy   An   ALGONQUIAN-
speaking tribe of the NORTHEAST CULTURE

AREA, located on Passamaquoddy Bay, St.
Croix River, and the Schoodic Lakes in
present-day Maine. The Passamaquoddies
were part of the Abenaki Confederacy and
have been referred to as ABENAKIS. Tribal
members hold the Indian Township Passamaquoddy and Pleasant Point Passamaquoddy reservations in Washington County,
Maine. *Passamaquoddy* means "those who
pursue the pollock" or "at the place where
pollock are plenty" in Algonquian.

Patayan Culture (Hakataya Culture) A
cultural tradition of the American Southwest, starting about A.D. 500. Patayan peoples were centered along the Colorado River
south of the Grand Canyon in present-day
western Arizona. They sometimes are
grouped with the Indians of the early HO-
HOKAM CULTURE. Unlike the Hohokams,
the Patayans did not develop extensive IRRI-
GATION techniques, but planted their crops
in river flood lands; nor did they live in
PITHOUSES, but in brush huts. They made
a brownish pottery, sometimes painted in
red, and baskets; they also carved seashells
from the Gulf of California for trade. Patayan peoples probably are ancestral to YU-
MAN-speaking Indians.

Patchogue   See POOSPATUCK.

patojo (patoho)   A POTTERY vessel in the
shape of a shoe; typical of MESOAMERICAN
INDIANS, SOUTH AMERICAN INDIANS, and
SOUTHWEST INDIANS. A Spanish word,
which also means "waddling like a duck."

patolli   A GAME of DICE, typical of MES-
OAMERICAN INDIANS and PUEBLO INDIANS,
in which beans are tossed onto a painted
mat. *Patolli* is a NAHUATL word; the Spanish
version is *patol.*

patrilineal (patrilineal descent)   A term describing social organization, such as in a
patriclan, in which descent and property are
passed through the male line; a type of
unilineal DESCENT. (See also MATRI-
LINEAL.)

patrilocal (patrilocal residence, virilocal) Residence after marriage in which the wife lives with or near her husband's family, as opposed to MATRILOCAL; both are types of unilocal residence. (See also NEOLOCAL.)

Patwin A PENUTIAN-speaking tribe of the CALIFORNIA CULTURE AREA, located on the western side of Sacramento Valley and on San Francisco Bay in present-day California. The Patwins are classified as having two major subdivisions, Hill Patwin and River Patwin. They merged with the WINTUN Indians. *Patwin* means "person" in Penutian. Some scholars group the various dialects spoken by the Patwin and Wintun bands in a distinct language family, Wintun, a subdivision of the Penutian phylum; it was formerly known as Copehan.

Paugussett (Paugusset) A subtribe of the WAPPINGER Indians, located on the Housatonic River, near the mouth of the Naugatuk River, in present-day Connecticut. Some among the Paugussetts merged with the SCHAGHTICOKES. The Golden Hill Paugussett Tribe has its headquarters at Colchester, Connecticut. *Paugussett* means "where the narrows open out" in ALGONQUIAN.

Paviotso See PAIUTE.

Pawnee A CADDOAN-speaking tribe of the GREAT PLAINS CULTURE AREA, located in present-day Kansas and Nebraska. In pre-Contact times, the Pawnees separated from other Caddoans, migrating northward from present-day Texas, to the Red River region of present-day southern Oklahoma, and then to the Arkansas River region of present-day northern Oklahoma and southern Kansas. By the early 1700s, the Pawnees had divided into four major bands: the Grand, Republican, Tapage (or Noisy), and Skidi. The Grand, Republican, and Tapage bands stayed along the Arkansas River for much of their history and came to be known collectively as the Southern Pawnees (or Black Pawnees). The Skidis migrated farther north to the Platte River, Loup River, and the Republican Fork of the Kansas River in present-day southern Nebraska and northern Kansas, becoming known as the Northern Pawnees. Many Pawnees were relocated to the INDIAN TERRITORY in 1876. Tribal members hold trust lands in Pawnee County, Oklahoma; others still live in and near Fullerton, Nebraska. Their name possibly derives from the Caddoan word *pariki*, meaning "horn," referring to their hornlike hairstyle. The Pawnee native name is *Chahiksichahiks*, meaning "men of men."

Pawokti See CREEK; MUSKOGEAN.

peace pipe See CALUMET.

pearl A dense, lustrous concretion, mostly calcium carbonate, formed around a grain of sand in some mollusks. EASTERN INDIANS used pearls for decoration and in BURIAL ceremonies. The great number of pearls found among Gulf Coast tribes as well as Virginia Indians helped spur on Spanish and English colonization and exploitation.

pecan (Illinois nut) A tree, *Carya illinoensis*, and its edible nuts. Pecan trees grew in the river bottoms of present-day southern Illinois, and Indiana, Iowa, Louisiana, Texas, and other southern states, and the nuts were a staple of various tribes, such as the ILLINOIS. An ALGONQUIAN-derived word, with variations in many different tribal dialects.

peccary Either of two types of wild boar, *Tayassu pecari* or *T. tajacu*. Peccaries are nocturnal and travel in numbers. Once ranging from present-day Texas to Paraguay, they were hunted by Indians of the tropical forest. "Peccary" is from the CARIBAN word *pakira* via the Spanish *pecari*.

pecking To strike with a hard and often pointed implement. Stones that are difficult to shape by FLAKING, such as sandstone, were worked with a pecking implement, such as a HAMMER, and then further shaped with an ABRADER.

Pecos   See KIOWA-TANOAN.

Pee Dee (Pedee) A SIOUAN-speaking tribe of the SOUTHEAST CULTURE AREA, located on the middle course of the Pee Dee River in present-day South Carolina. Most Pee Dee bands merged with the CATAWBAS in the mid-1700s. Pee Dee descendants have organized the Pee Dee Indian Association in Clio, South Carolina. Their name, if from the Catawba dialect of Siouan, means "something good" or "smart."

pellet-bow (stonebow) A BOW that shoots clay pellets or stones instead of ARROWS. Two strings are used instead of one with a cradle between them and a small wooden fork to keep them separated. SOUTH AMERICAN INDIANS may have first learned of the technology from Portuguese sailors, who had brought it from India.

pelt The undressed SKIN of an animal with the hair still attached. (See also FUR; SKIN-DRESSING.)

pemmican (pemican) A food made from strips of lean meat, usually deer or buffalo, sun-dried or smoked, pounded into a paste, mixed with melted fat and berries, and packed in hide bags to be stored. The mixture lasted as long as five years. SUBARCTIC INDIANS depended on pemmican, but there were varieties among other peoples. NORTHWEST COAST INDIANS made a similar food product using fish, sometimes called fish pemmican. White explorers used dried beef, suet, raisins, and sugars, which also came to be called pemmican; traders and trappers made a soup from pemmican, known as robbiboe. *Pemmican* is ALGONQUIAN, probably of CREE origin, from *pemmi*, meaning "meat, and *kon*, meaning "fat." (See also JERKY.)

pendant An artifact, usually with a perforation, designed to hang around the neck.

(See also BAR-GORGET; GORGET; JEWELRY; PERFORATED STONE; RUNTEE.)

Pend d'Oreille   See KALISPEL.

Pennacook An ALGONQUIAN-speaking tribe of the NORTHEAST CULTURE AREA, located in what is now central and southern New Hampshire, northeastern Massachusetts, and southern Maine. The Pennacooks were part of the Abenaki Confederacy, many of them eventually merging with the ABENAKI proper. A band known as the Pennacook New Hampshire Indian Tribe operates out of Manchester, New Hampshire. *Pennacook* means "at the bottom of the hill" or "down hill" in Algonquian.

Penobscot An ALGONQUIAN-speaking tribe of the NORTHEAST CULTURE AREA, located on Penobscot Bay and the Penobscot River in present-day Maine. The Penobscots were part of the Abenaki Confederacy and have been referred to as ABENAKIS. Tribal members hold the Penobscot Reservation in Penobscot County, Maine. *Penobscot* means "rocky place" or "descending ledge place" in Algonquian, referring to falls on the Penobscot River.

Pensacola   See MUSKOGEAN.

pentatonic scale Any musical scale of five tones, the octave being reached at the sixth tone (rather than at the eighth tone as in a diatonic scale). Traditional Native American music varies considerably among tribes, but the most widespread pattern is a pentatonic tune with chains of major or minor thirds.

Penutian A phylum of language stocks, including the CHINOOKAN, CHIPAYU-URU, KALAPUYAN, KUSAN, MAIDU, MAYAN, MIWOK-COSTANOAN, MIXE-ZOQUEAN, SAHAPTIN, TOTONACAN, WINTUN, YAKONAN, and YOKUTS families as well as the CAYUSE, Molala, TAKELMA, TSIMSHIAN, ZUNI, and Huave isolates.

people Many native tribal names translate as "people" or "the people," such as the

NAVAJO *Dineh* and APACHE *Tineh*. Moreover, a particular tribe's names for another tribe often translates as "people" of a particular place or "people" of a particular custom.

Peoria (Mascouten) A subtribe of the ILLINOIS Indians, located originally in present-day northeastern Iowa and later on the Illinois River near present-day Peoria, Illinois. The Peorias eventually lived on the Blackwater River in present-day Missouri; then on the Osage River, Kansas, with the KASKASKIAS; and then in the INDIAN TERRITORY. Descendants are centered at Miami, Oklahoma. *Peoria* means "carriers" in ALGONQUIAN.

pepper See CHILI.

Pequot (Pequod) An ALGONQUIAN-speaking tribe of the NORTHEAST CULTURE AREA, located in present-day Connecticut, especially on the Atlantic Coast, from the Niantic River to the border of present-day Rhode Island. Pequots hold the Eastern Pequot Reservation near North Stonington, Connecticut; the Golden Hill Reservation near Trumbull; the Mashantucket Pequot Reservation near Ledyard; and the Schaghticoke Indian Reservation near Kent. A band known as the Paucatuck Pequot Tribe is centered in Ledyard, Connecticut. The New England Coastal Schagticoke Indian Association operates out of Avon, Massachusetts. *Pequot* means "destroyers," a name applied to them by other Algonquians. (See also MOHEGAN; SCHAGHTICOKE.)

percussion flaking See FLAKING.

perforated stone Stone artifacts with holes, with an unknown purpose; found especially in southern California. RINGSTONES are types of perforated stones. (See also BAR-GORGET; PENDANT; PIERCED TABLET; SINKER; SPADE-STONE.)

permafrost Permanently frozen subsoil, typical of the TUNDRA of the ARCTIC CULTURE AREA.

persimmon (dateplum, possum-wood) Any of the trees of the genus *Diospyros*, especially *D. virginiana*, having hard wood and small orange-red plumlike fruit, edible when ripe. (The fruit of the tree is also known as persimmon.) A staple of the POWHATAN Indians as well as other EASTERN INDIANS, it was eaten in a variety of ways: dried, cooked, or made into a kind of bread and into a wine. The seeds were used as DICE. "Persimmon" is an ALGONQUIAN-derived word.

pestle See MORTAR AND PESTLE.

petroglyph (pectrograph) A PICTOGRAPH, pecked or incised on rock surfaces; a type of ROCK ART, found on boulders as well as on cliff and cave walls. Petroglyphs often are oriented directionally. Many Indian peoples believed in spiritual beings who presided over the creation of petroglyphs. The ABENAKIS called the beings *Oonagamessok*. (See also GLYPH.)

Petun See TOBACCO (Petun).

peyote A type of cactus (*Lophophora williamsii*), native to northern Mexico and the American Southwest. American Indians have chewed and eaten peyote buttons, the plant's dried buttonlike blossoms, for HEALING purposes as well as for spiritual purposes, their hallucinogenic effect including a heightening of the senses, feelings of well-being, and visions. Use of peyote is considered a sacrament and channel for prayer in the PEYOTE RELIGION, which has been formalized as the NATIVE AMERICAN CHURCH. "Peyotism" refers to the use and advocacy of peyote for religious purposes, as by a "peyotist." "Peyote" comes to English via Spanish, originally from the NAHUATL *peyotl* for "caterpillar," referring to the appearance of the button's downy tuft. The plant is sometimes also called MESCAL, because of confusion with AGAVE. The COMANCHE word for peyote is *wokowi* in their UTO-AZTECAN language; the KIOWA word is *seni* in KIOWA-TANOAN.

peyote fan A fan, usually made from a bundle of feathers, used in rites of the PEYOTE RELIGION to shield a participant's eyes from the fire and force purifying CEDAR smoke in the direction of other participants.

Peyote Religion (Peyote Cult, Peyote Road, Peyote Way, Mescal Cult) A religious movement involving the sacramental use of PEYOTE. The ingesting of peyote buttons for medicinal, hallucinogenic, and ceremonial purposes has been widespread in what is now the American Southwest and Mexico for perhaps as long as 10,000 years. The Spanish attempted to suppress peyote use from early colonial times. PLAINS INDIANS, in particular the COMANCHES, probably brought back knowledge of the plant after raids in Mexico. Quanah Parker discovered what is sometimes called the "Peyote Road" after 1890 and the collapse of the GHOST DANCE RELIGION. His work, and that of other peyotists such as Big Moon of the KIOWAS, led to peyote spreading among other tribes. Oklahoma Territory tried to ban peyote in 1899, as did some states in later years. In 1918, the NATIVE AMERICAN CHURCH was chartered, drawing on elements of the Peyote Religion.

phase Archaeological evidence of an ancient culture and its period of existence. The term can refer to a group of archaeological sites with similar determinants or to an interval of culture.

philosophy See COSMOLOGY; RELIGION; WORLDVIEW.

phoneme In LINGUISTICS, a speech sound, i.e., the basic unit of sound differentiating meanings in a language. Phonemics, a branch of PHONOLOGY, is the study of phonemes.

phonology The study of speech sounds, a branch of LINGUISTICS. Phonology includes phonemics, the study of PHONEMES, as well as phonetics, the study of how speech sounds are represented in written symbols.

phratry A term for two or more CLANS or SIBS within a TRIBE. A phratry generally is considered an EXOGAMOUS social grouping. (See also MOIETY.)

phylum See LANGUAGE PHYLUM.

Piankashaw (Piankeshaw) A subtribe of the MIAMI Indians, located on the Wabash River, with a village at the junction of the Vermillion, in present-day Indiana. The Piankashaws later lived at the site of present-day Vincennes, Indiana, then in Kansas, and eventually in the INDIAN TERRITORY. Today, Piankashaws live in Oklahoma, with tribal headquarters at Miami. Their name possibly means "those who separate" in ALGONQUIAN.

pick A tool with a pointed blade, used for breaking hard surfaces. Indians used the points of antlers or walrus tusks as blades as well as bone and stone. Wooden handles often were added.

pictograph (pictogram, hieroglyph) A picture or sign representing a word or idea (as opposed to a sound, as in alphabet-writing or in SYLLABARIES). Indians etched pictographs in wood, bark, shell, and stone; painted them on hide; and tattooed them on the human body. When present, the colors in pictographs also had symbolic meaning. The term pictography is synonymous with "picture writing." The terms hieroglyphics and glyph writing sometimes are used interchangeably with "pictography." "Hieroglyphics" and "hieroglyph" were originally applied to the picture writing of ancient Egyptians before that of MESOAMERICAN INDIANS. GLYPH originally referred to carved pictographs, either incised or in relief, as found in stone. Pictograph and ideograph (or ideogram) are used synonymously; the latter sometimes refers to a series of concepts as opposed to a representation of one event. A PETROGLYPH is a pictograph on rock. (See also CALENDAR; WINTER COUNT.)

picture writing See PICTOGRAPH.

Picuris Pueblo See TIWA.

pièce esquille A small stone WEDGE used to work bone and antler. A French term, translating as "splinter piece."

Piegan A subtribe of the BLACKFOOT Indians, located in present-day southern Alberta and northern Montana. The Piegan band now is centered at Brocket, Alberta. The Blackfeet Reservation in Glacier and Pondera counties, Montana, has predominantly Piegan descendants. *Piegan* derives from the Algonquian word *pikuni*, meaning "people wearing badly dressed robes."

pierced tablet A prehistoric artifact of stone, bone, shell, or copper, having a flat and oblong shape, from two to 14 inches long, with usually two or more holes. The holes suggest use as a PENDANT. Pierced tablets, types of PERFORATED STONES, sometimes are close in shape to BANNERSTONES or BOATSTONES.

pigment Any substance used as a coloring. (See also DYE; PAINT.)

piki (bunjabe, paper bread, wafer bread) A type of bread made by the HOPIS and other PUEBLO INDIANS. Cornmeal is the basic ingredient, with wood ashes added; the mixture is spread over a BAKING STONE. After baking, the thin bread is rolled up. Color depends on whether the corn is white, yellow, blue, or red. The Hopi name for *piki*-making day in UTO-AZTECAN is *piktotokya*.

pila'mayan A SIOUX expression of "thank you" in SIOUAN (Lakota).

pilaster A roof-supporting column or pier, typical of the INCAS and MESOAMERICAN INDIANS, which projects out beyond the roof, sometimes with an ornamental motif. Certain KIVAS of the ANASAZI CULTURE also had pilasters.

pillma A volleyballlike sport played by the Araucanians and other SOUTH AMERICAN INDIANS in present-day Chile. Players stood in a circle and kept a ball in the air by tapping it with the hands.

Pima (Pima Alto, Akimel O-odham) A UTO-AZTECAN-speaking tribe of the SOUTHWEST CULTURE AREA, located on the Gila and Salt rivers in present-day southern Arizona and extending into present-day northern Mexico. There are two major subdivisions: a northern group, the Pima Alto, or Upper Pima; and a southern group in Mexico, the Pima Bajo, or Lower Pima. The latter group in Mexico now are known as the Nevome Indians. The Pimas are related linguistically to the PAPAGOS. Descendants of the Pima Alto branch share the Gila River Indian Community in Maricopa and Pinal counties, Arizona and the Salt River Reservation in Maricopa County with the MARICOPAS. *Pima* means "no" in the Nevome dialect of Uto-Aztecan. The Pima native name is *Akimel O-odham*, for "river people." (Another spelling of "people" is *O-o-dam*.) The Pima language formerly was classified as a distinct stock, Piman.

Pinal (Pinaleno) A subtribe of the APACHE Indians, part of the SAN CARLOS grouping. The Pinals once lived between the Salt and Gila rivers in present-day Pinal and Gila counties, Arizona. Descendants live on the San Carlos and Fort Apache reservations in Arizona with other Apache groups. *Pinal* means "pine people" in Spanish.

Pine Tree (Pine Tree Sachem) A title of the IROQUOIS Indians, earned through deeds rather than through heredity. The Pine Trees often spoke at the Great Council of the IROQUOIS LEAGUE as representatives of the Six Nations. Deganawida, one of the founders of the confederacy, was the first to hold the title.

pinole Parched or roasted, then ground, corn (or some other grain or nut) mixed

Cheyenne buffalo effigy pipe

with water to make flour or gruel. A Spanish word from the NAHUATL *pinolli*. (See also ROCKAHOMINY.)

piñon (pinyon, nut pine) Any of various low-growing pine trees, especially *Pinus cembroides edulis*, which produce large, edible seeds; found in the American West and Mexico, especially the southern Rocky Mountain region.

pipe A device for SMOKING, consisting of a tube or stem with a mouthpiece and an opening or bowl. American Indians made pipes from stone, clay, bone, wood, reed, and, in post-Contact times, metal, or a combination of various materials. Carvings or feathers and beads decorated them and added symbolic meaning. In a platform pipe, the bowl is upright in the middle of the stem. In an elbow pipe, the stem and bowl form a right angle. A self pipe is a one-piece pipe in which the stone or clay forms the stem as well as the bowl. An effigy pipe is a pipe with a bowl, either stone or pottery, carved in the shape of a human, animal; bird, or legendary being. A monitor pipe, a kind of effigy pipe typical of MOUNDBUILDERS, has a flat, sometimes arched stem, with an upright bowl. (See also CALUMET; PIPESTONE; PIPE-TOMAHAWK; SACRED PIPE.)

pipe bag A POUCH to hold a PIPE, made of leather with QUILLWORK or BEADWORK.

pipestone (catlinite) A compacted clay, pale grayish red to dark red, sometimes mottled, soft enough to carve intricate PIPE bowls. The alternate term catlinite derives from the name of frontier painter George Catlin, who wrote about the PIPESTONE QUARRY in Minnesota in the 1830s.

Pipestone Quarry An outcropping in southwestern Minnesota where Indians obtained red PIPESTONE (catlinite) for their carvings, i.e., a QUARRY SITE. Since the quarry was considered a sacred place, different tribes could use it without fear of attack. The stone for the SACRED PIPE of the SIOUX was mined there. Since the 1850s, tribes have had to struggle with whites to retain access to the quarry. In 1937, Congress created the Pipestone National Monument; access is granted to pipe makers through permit.

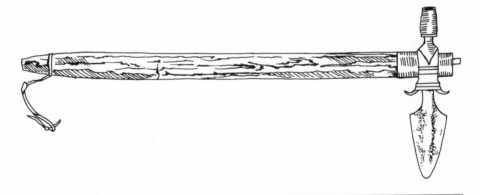

French-made pipe-tomahawk

pipe-tomahawk (tomahawk pipe, hatchet pipe) A combination PIPE and TOMA-HAWK. The smoking mixture is placed in a bowl in the metal head and smoke drawn through the wooden handle. Europeans made pipe-tomahawks, or tomahawk pipes, for trade with Indians, who used them more often ceremonially than as a HATCHET or WARCLUB.

Piro See KIOWA-TANOAN.

pirogue See DUGOUT.

Piscataway See CONOY.

pisé A kind of ADOBE work, typical of SOUTHWEST INDIANS in PUEBLO architecture, in which the clay mixture is poured and stuffed into a mold constructed of pole frames interwoven with reeds. *Pisé* is a French-derived word.

pit Indians dug open holes or pits for a variety of purposes: for cooking and storing food; for building houses; for SWEATING; for CACHES; for TRAPS; and for BURIALS. (See also CAIRN BURIAL; CIST; FIREPIT; PIT-FALL; PITHOUSE; PIT OVEN.)

pitch Any of a number of viscous materials, such as asphalt or tree RESIN, used as sealants in the making of birchbark CANOES, GLUE, and in other applications. *Bigiu* is the CHIPPEWA word for "pitch" in ALGON-QUIAN. Bitumen, also called mineral pitch or asphalt, is any of various mixtures of hydrocarbons and other substances occurring naturally; it is used for waterproofing and as a PIGMENT.

pitfall An excavated hole concealed at the opening, used as a trap to catch animals. GREAT BASIN INDIANS trapped grasshoppers and locusts by digging a large shallow pit in a field, then setting fire to surrounding grasses. (See also DEADFALL.)

pithouse (semisubterranean house) A dwelling over an excavated hole. To construct a pithouse, a superstructure, usually made with a POST-AND-BEAM frame with walls and roof of saplings, reeds, earth, mats, or skins, is placed over a typically shallow pit. PLATEAU INDIANS built pithouses, as did Indians of the HOHOKAM CULTURE and MOGOLLON CULTURE. (See also KARMAK; KASHIM; KI; KIVA.)

pit oven An OVEN consisting of a hole in the ground, sometimes lined with stones, which is heated with fire, filled with food to be cooked or POTTERY to be fired, then covered with earth, clay, or stone. Some pit ovens have draft holes.

Pit River Indians See ACHOMAWI.

place name Many names of geographical locations throughout the Americas derive from Indian words, including names of more than half of the states in the United States and four out of 10 Canadian provinces, plus the name Canada itself, which is thought to be from the IROQUOIAN word *kanata* or *kanada*, meaning "cabin" or "lodge."

Plains Indians Inhabitants of the GREAT PLAINS CULTURE AREA, including tribes of the following language groupings: ALGON-QUIAN, ATHAPASCAN, CADDOAN, KIOWA-TANOAN, SIOUAN, TONKAWA, and UTO-AZTECAN. Plains tribes consisted of bands of related families, who lived apart most of the year but gathered in the summer for communal buffalo hunts and ceremonies. (See also CATEGORICAL APPENDIX, "TRIBES, BANDS PEOPLES, LANGUAGES, AND CULTURES.")

Plainview Culture See PLANO CULTURE.

plaiting A technique used in weaving baskets and cloth in which two different elements cross each other. The four basic types of plaiting in BASKETRY are CHECKER-BOARD, TWILLING, WICKER, and hexagonal.

plank boat A boat made with boards, typical of CHUMASH Indians, the only Indians to use that technology for boat-making in pre-Contact times. Cedar was split with antler wedges into planks, then smoothed with shell or stone rubbing tools. The planks were lashed together with sinew or plant bindings and caulked with asphalt to form 25-foot double-bowed hulls. A crew of four could paddle these boats in ocean waters. Not one such plank boat remains intact; design and technique are recreated from fragments.

plank house   A rectangular dwelling, typical of NORTHWEST COAST INDIANS, from about 20 by 30 feet, to 50 by 60 feet (sometimes even 60 by 100 feet), made of hand-split planks lashed either vertically or horizontally to a POST-AND-BEAM frame, CEDAR being the wood of choice. The roofs, also plank-covered, are either gabled or shed.

Tlingit Bear House plank screen

Planks also are used for flooring, sometimes on two different levels. There is usually a central FIREPIT. Platforms run along the walls for sleeping and storage. Mats are hung on the inside for additional insulation. The fronts of the houses are carved and painted, in some cases having added facades, or screens. TOTEM POLES are sometimes used as HOUSEPOSTS. Plank houses provided shelter for several families. (See also SMOKE HOUSE.)

Plano Culture (Plainview culture)   A cultural tradition lasting from about 8000 B.C. to 6000 B.C.; also called Plainview after the Plainview site in Texas. Plano Culture is associated with the Great Plains and long-horn BUFFALO, based on findings of leaf-shape points. Plano Indians demonstrated a more varied culture than the Indians before them and are considered a transitional culture between PALEO-INDIANS and ARCHAIC INDIANS. They built CORRALS to trap animals and developed a method of preserving meat by mixing it with animal fat and berries and packing it in hide or gut containers.

plant   See   CATEGORICAL   APPENDIX, "PLANTS."

plate   See DISCOID; DISH; FLINT DISK.

Plateau Culture Area   The geographical and cultural region situated between the Cascades to the west and the Rockies to the east, and the Fraser River to the north and the Great Basin to the south. The CULTURE AREA includes territory of present-day southeastern British Columbia, eastern Washington, northeast and central Oregon, northern Idaho, western Montana, and a small part of northern California. The name derives from the Columbia Plateau, a region of highlands through which the Columbia River flows. The Columbia starts in the southeastern part of British Columbia, then flows to the Pacific Ocean, forming much of the border between Washington and Oregon; tributaries include the Snake, Thompson, Okanagan, Deschutes, Umatilla, Willamette, and Kootenai rivers. Water comes from three mountain ranges: the Rocky Mountains, Cascade Mountains, and Coast Range. Another large river, the Fraser River, also starting in the Rocky Mountains in British Columbia, is not part of the Columbia watershed. The mountains and river valleys have enough precipitation to support some of the tallest trees in the world, mostly evergreen forests of needle-bearing conifers. The Columbia Plateau lying between the mountain ranges has little rainfall since the Cascades block the rain clouds blowing in from the ocean. Grasses and sagebrush are the dominant vegetation on the plateau's flatlands and rolling hills. The sparse ground vegetation on both mountain and plateau meant little game for the PLATEAU INDIANS. Elk, deer, and bear could be found at the edge of the forest. PRONGHORNS and jackrabbits lived out on the dry plains of the plateau. Yet the many rivers and streams offered plentiful food, especially SALMON. The river valleys also provide abundant berries. On the grasslands of the plateau, the Indians found other wild plant foods, such as roots and bulbs, especially from the CAMAS plant, bitterroot, wild carrots, and wild onions. Plateau Indians subsisted through fishing and gathering first, then hunting; they did not farm. In cold weather, most inhabitants lived along rivers in villages of semisubterranean earth-covered PITHOUSES which provided natural ground insulation. In warm weather, most lived in temporary lodges with basswood frames and bulrush-mat coverings, either along the rivers at salmon-spawning time or in open country at camas-digging time. Plateau Indians used the rivers as avenues of trade, with many contacts among different tribes.

Plateau Indians The inhabitants of the PLATEAU CULTURE AREA. Plateau Indians spoke predominantly dialects of the PENUTIAN language phylum and the SALISHAN language family. The KOOTENAY Indians are an exception, speaking a unique language, probably related to ALGONQUIAN. (See also CATEGORICAL APPENDIX, "TRIBES, BANDS, PEOPLES, LANGUAGES, and CULTURES.")

platform house See CHICKEE.

plaza A public central area or square in a community, village, town, or city, used for religious, political, and social gatherings.

Pleistocene (Ice Age) The geological era from about one and a half million years ago until about 8000 B.C., or 10,000 B.P. (before present); the first of two geological epochs of the Quartenary period (part of the Cenozoic era, i.e., the Age of Mammals), the second being the present Holocene, or Recent, epoch. The Pleistocene age, sometimes called the Ice Age, is actually a series of four ice ages during which much of the world was covered with GLACIERS. Interstadials (interglacial periods of warmer weather and melting ice) separated the ice ages. During the last of the ice ages, PALEO-INDIANS first arrived in the Americas. (See also BERINGIA; WATERSHED AGE.)

Pleistocene Overkill The killing of more animals than necessary by PALEO-INDIANS during the PLEISTOCENE is sometimes referred to as the Pleistocene Overkill. The changing climate of the WATERSHED AGE probably contributed to the extinction of big-game animals, i.e., MAMMOTHS, MASTODONS, and longhorn BUFFALO, although Paleo-Indians also might have played a part. Their techniques of hunting became so proficient, as in the communal drives of huge herds, that hunters killed more game than they needed, as indicated by the number of bones with stone POINTS among them as found at KILL SITES.

Plumed Serpent See QUETZALCOATL.

plummet A conical artifact of stone, bone, shell, or copper that resembles a plumb bob (a device for determining if building materials are exactly vertical) or top (a spinning toy). Plummets of varying shapes typically have a groove, indicating their use as PENDANTS, perhaps worn ceremonially since they are associated with burials. Others might have been SINKERS for fishing.

Pocomtuc   See ALGONQUIAN.

pod corn   A type of corn (*Zea mays tunicata*), having each kernel enclosed in a husk.

poetry   Indian SONGS and CHANTS, presented in written verse, are now studied as poetry. Past and contemporary Native Americans have explored the written form of poetry as well. (See also LITERATURE; ORAL TRADITION.)

pogamoggan (pagamagan, pakamagan)   A type of WARCLUB. An ALGONQUIAN term meaning "used for striking"; probably from the CHIPPEWA or CREE dialect, referring to both CLUBS and HAMMERS. The name spread to other GREAT LAKES INDIANS and PLAINS INDIANS, among whom it was applied to warclubs.

pogonip (ice fog)   A type of dense fog with suspended ice particles, as common in the deep valleys of the Sierra Nevada. Originally a UTO-AZTECAN term in both PAIUTE and SHOSHONE dialects.

Pohoy   See TIMUCUA.

point   A SPEAR point or ARROWHEAD; also referred to as PROJECTILE POINT. Points were made out of stone, bone, antler, and, in post-Contact times, metal. A birdpoint is a small point from the late pre-Contact period with a stemmed or notched base; a gempoint is a small point made of colorful or translucent flint, found especially in the Pacific Northwest; and a warpoint is a small point from the late pre-Contact period, triangular in shape without a stem or notches. (See also CLOVIS CULTURE; FLAKING; FLUTED POINT; FOLSOM CULTURE; PLANO CULTURE; SANDIA CULTURE.)

poison   Indians used poisons taken from plants and animals in fishing, hunting, and war. Certain barks and roots were placed in ponds and pools to stun fish. Poisons also were added to ARROWS to make them more deadly. Other poisons were used as stimulants. (See also CURARE.)

Pojoaque Pueblo   See TEWA.

polishing implement   Any stone, wood, bone, shell, clay, hide, or textile tool used to smooth and shine artifacts by friction. A polishing stone is small, hard, smooth stone used to polish SLIPS in POTTERY.

pollen   The fertilizing element of flowering plants; their mass of microspores. Many native peoples have used pollen ritually as an offering and to sanctify events and sites. (See also PALYNOLOGY.)

polychrome ware (polychrome pottery)   POTTERY of more than two colors. The term sometimes is applied to two-color pottery as well.

polygamy   A plural marriage, or the practice of having more than one wife or husband at the same time. Polyandry is a type of polygamy in which a wife has more than one husband; polygyny is polygamy in which a man has more than one wife. Among various Indian peoples, the latter took the form of a man marrying sisters. (See also MONOGAMY.)

polysynthesism   The grammatical characteristic of composite words, i.e., various words (or word elements) combined into a single word that is the equivalent of a sentence in another language. Native American languages were for the most part polysynthetic. A famous example is *wiitoku-chumpunkuruganiyugwivantumu*, a PAIUTE word in their UTO-AZTECAN language for "they-who-are-going-to-sit-and-cut-up-with-a-knife-a-black-female-(or male)-buffalo."

polytheism Belief in and worship of more than a single god, as in the religions of the OLMECS, MAYAS, TOLTECS, AZTECS, and INCAS. (See also MONOTHEISM.)

Pomo A HOKAN-speaking tribe of the CALIFORNIA CULTURE AREA, located on the Pacific Coast in present-day northern California and inland as far as Clear Lake. ("Clear Lake" is a collective name applied to the Pomos as well as to some MIWOK Indians living near Clear Lake.) The Pomos are organized into the following subdivisions: Northern; Northeastern (or Salt); Eastern; Central; Southeastern; Southern (or Gallinomero); and Southwestern (or Gualala). Pomos hold a number of reservations in their ancestral homeland, including Dry Creek Rancheria; Hopland Rancheria; Laytonville Rancheria (with the CAHTOS); Manchester Rancheria; Middletown Rancheria; Round Valley Reservation (with other tribes); Sherwood Valley Rancheria; Stewarts Point Rancheria; Sulphur Bank Rancheria; and Yokayo Pomo Rancheria. The Mendo Lake Pomo Council band operates out of Ukiah, California. *Pomo* derives from a native word-ending in Hokan, placed after the names of villages. Some scholars group the various dialects spoken by the Pomo bands in a distinct language, Pomo, a subdivision of the Hokan phylum; it was formerly known as Kulanapan.

Ponca A SIOUAN-speaking tribe of the GREAT PLAINS CULTURE AREA, located at the confluence of the Niobrara and Missouri rivers on both sides of the present-day boundary between Nebraska and South Dakota. (The ancestors of the Omahas probably were one people with those of the KAW, OMAHA, OSAGE, and QUAPAW tribes, formerly living along the Ohio River, then migrating onto the prairies and plains west of the Mississippi River and dividing. The Poncas, along with their closest relatives, the Omahas, perhaps lived in present-day Minnesota and Iowa before separating in South Dakota.) Many Poncas were relocated to INDIAN TERRITORY in 1877. Tribal members hold trust lands in Kay and Noble counties, Oklahoma; others still live in Nebraska.

poncho A blanketlike cloak with a slit in the middle for the head. "Poncho" is from the ARAUCANIAN-CHON word *pantho*. (See also SERAPE.)

pony See HORSE.

pony beads (trade beads) Small glass BEADS, introduced by European traders in the early 1800s. Originally only black and white, later they were produced in a variety of colors.

Poospatuck (Poospetuck, Poosepatuck, Patchogue, Patchoag, Unkechaug, Uncachogue) A subtribe of the MONTAUK Indians, located on southern Long Island, from present-day Patchogue, New York, to Westhampton. Descendants hold the Poospatuck Reservation near Mastic, New York. *Poospatuck* means "where a creek flows out" in ALGONQUIAN.

popcorn A type of CORN (*Zea mays everta*) cultivated by Native Americans, having small hard kernels with contained moisture that, on exposure to dry heat, burst to form white irregularly shaped puffs.

Popolocan A language family and subdivision of the OTO-MANGUEAN phylum comprising dialects spoken by Indians of the MESOAMERICAN CULTURE AREA, including the Chocho, Ixcatec (Ixcateco), Mazatec (Mazateco), and Popoloc (Popoloca) tribes of what is now central Mexico.

population Scholars disagree on the number of American Indians at the time of Contact. It has been estimated that there were 30 million SOUTH AMERICAN INDIANS (i.e., from the Isthmus of Panama to Tierra del Fuego); 7 million to 30 million Indians in MIDDLE AMERICA (i.e., all of present-day Mexico, Central America, and the West Indies); and 1 million to 12 million Native

Americans in the present-day United States and Canada. There were no accurate counts by early explorers, and European DISEASES, passed by intertribal contact, may have decimated tribes before whites even visited them. Native Americans currently make up less than 1 percent of the U.S. population and about 2 percent of the Canadian population. The term population density applies to comparative measurements of populations. For example, the coastal regions of North America had much greater population density than inland regions. (See also DEMOGRAPHY.)

porcupine A mammal of the rodent family (in North America, the genus *Erethizon*) with sharp spines or quills that detach on contact. The quills are valued by Native Americans for decoration of clothing, containers, and other articles. (See also QUILLWORK.)

portage The act of carrying, especially transporting a boat or CANOE and supplies overland from one navigable waterway to another. The term also applies to the route taken between bodies of water.

posah-tai-vo The COMANCHE word for "crazy white man" in UTO-AZTECAN; used by the tribe's CODE TALKERS in World War II to refer to Adolf Hitler.

Poshayanki A spiritual being in ZUNI tradition, the leader of the Beast Gods, many of whom have features of predatory animals and who live in a realm known as Shipapolina. The Beast Gods supposedly determine health and long life. Poshayanki passed knowledge of healing to the MEDICINE SOCIETIES.

positive painting A type of PAINTING in which the design is applied directly with PIGMENTS; refers especially to POTTERY design. The opposite process is NEGATIVE PAINTING (resist painting).

post-and-beam (joined frame) A type of construction with straight poles or timbers,

tied together with CORDAGE (or otherwise fastened), as in a LONGHOUSE or PLANK HOUSE. The posts are vertical members; the beams, horizontal. Often sloping roof members, or rafters, are added. Other basic types of Native American construction are BENT-FRAME and COMPRESSION SHELL.

Postclassic period See CLASSIC PERIOD.

post-Contact See CONTACT.

post mold An area of discolored ground remains, indicating where wooden posts were placed for housing.

pot See POTTERY.

Potano See TIMUCUA.

potato A plant, *Solanum tuberosum*, with an edible starchy tuber; native to South America. Like CORN, the TOMATO, the SWEET POTATO, and many other plants, the potato was first cultivated by American Indians and passed to the rest of the world, becoming a staple in many different cultures, especially in northern Europe, within two centuries.

Potawatomi (Potawatami, Pottawatami, Pottawatomie) An ALGONQUIAN-speaking tribe of the NORTHEAST CULTURE AREA, located on the lower peninsula of present-day Michigan. The Potawatomis are related linguistically to the CHIPPEWAS and OTTAWAS. By 1670, Potawatomis were living west of Lake Michigan near Green Bay in present-day Wisconsin. Over the next years, bands migrated to Illinois and Indiana. In the 1800s, some among them migrated from the Great Lakes country to present-day Missouri, then to Iowa, and eventually to Kansas. Others were relocated directly from the Great Lakes to Kansas. Many Potawatomis were then relocated from Kansas to the INDIAN TERRITORY (present-day Oklahoma). Still other Potawatomis settled in present-day Ontario. In Michigan, Potawatomis hold the Hannahville Indian Community in Menominee County; the Huron

Potawatomi Band is centered in Fulton; the Potawatomi Indian Tribe of Indiana and Michigan is centered in Dowgiac. In Wisconsin, Potawatomis make up the Forest County Potawatomi Indian Community. In Kansas, tribal members hold the Prairie Potawatomi Reservation in Jackson County. In Oklahoma, the Citizen Band of Potawatomis holds trust lands in Pottawatomi and Cleveland counties. In Ontario, the Caldwell band operates out of Kingsville. *Potawatomi* means "people of the place of fire." Their native name is *Neshnabe*, meaning "people."

potlatch A ceremony in which possessions are given away or destroyed to demonstrate wealth and rank and validate social claims, involving feasting, speechmaking, singing, and the GIVEAWAY; traditionally held in wintertime among NORTHWEST COAST INDIANS to celebrate a wedding, dedicate a new house, raise a TOTEM POLE, or a similar event. Some individuals saved for years in preparation for a potlatch. BLANKETS were a common gift. Some sponsors were known to give away all their possessions as a form of competition with someone who had previously held a potlatch. The resulting prestige usually led to a return in goods from others, or increased rank within the tribe, serving as a form of investment. "Potlatch" can be used as a verb. From the NOOTKA word *patshatl* for "sharing," passed into the CHINOOK JARGON.

potsherd (potshard, shard, sherd) A fragment of broken POTTERY. Potsherds, the most durable of archaeological evidence, are valuable in dating sites. Indian potters sometimes ground sherds to be used as a TEMPER in clay mixture for new pots.

pottery Objects of fired clay, or the making of objects such as CONTAINERS, utensils, PIPES, EFFIGY figures, and TOYS. Pottery-making was developed among the INCAS and MESOAMERICAN INDIANS about the same time as agriculture. The skill spread to ancient peoples of the Southwest and the Southeast, then to much of the Americas.

Keres pottery bowl

Pottery was found in the SOUTHWEST CULTURE AREA, SOUTHEAST CULTURE AREA, and to a lesser extent in the GREAT PLAINS CULTURE AREA and NORTHEAST CULTURE AREA. Pots originally were molded without a wheel, often by means of COILING. Among Indian peoples, pottery-making has been for the most part a woman's activity. Traditional pottery is pottery that is handmade using ancient techniques, materials, and tools to create long-established shapes and designs. Prehistoric pottery is by definition traditional; both historic pottery, made in post-Contact times until the early 1900s, and modern pottery (or contemporary pottery), made since 1930, can be traditional. (See also CATEGORICAL APPENDIX, "ARTS AND CRAFTS"; CERAMIC.)

pouch A small container, made from a flexible material, such as leather, cloth, or gut, used to carry objects and supplies. (See also BAG; MEDICINE BAG.)

power See MEDICINE.

Powhatan (Powhattan) An ALGONQUIAN-speaking tribe of the NORTHEAST CULTURE AREA, located in the tidewater region of present-day Virginia and extending into present-day Maryland. The Powhatan proper, after whom the Powhatan Confederacy of at least 30 tribes was named, had villages in present-day Henrico County, Virginia. A number of Powhatan subtribes live in their ancestral homeland, using the CHICKAHOMINY, MATTAPONI, PAMUNKEY, and RAPPAHANNOCK names. The Powhattan Renape Nation is located in Rancocas, New Jersey. *Powhatan* means "falls in a current of water" in Algonquian.

powwow (powow, pauwau)   A social gathering and celebration, including feasting, dancing, and singing, prior to a COUNCIL, hunt, or war expedition; or the council itself. Powwows often were intertribal with socializing and trade. Today, a "powwow" has elements of both a FAIR and a FESTIVAL, with arts and crafts on display and open to non-Indians; a contest powwow offers prize money for dancing. "Powwow" also can be used as a verb. It is a MASSACHUSET and NARRAGANSET word in ALGONQUIAN, originally meaning "he dreams" or "he uses divination," referring to a SHAMAN. First used in New England, the term was spread by whites to other parts of North America.

practitioner   A person engaged in religious practices, typically for HEALING; used synonymously with MEDICINE MAN or SHAMAN. In NAVAJO tradition the functions of a DIAGNOSTICIAN who diagnoses a condition and a practitioner who treats it are different.

Prairie Indians   Inhabitants of the prairies of the central United States. The word prairie or (the phrase Prairie Plains) applies to the grasslands flanking the Mississippi and Missouri rivers. The Prairie Plains' grasses grow taller than the Great Plains' grasses to the west because of greater rainfall. To the east, the prairies give way to woodlands. The present-day states of Illinois and Iowa are mostly prairie country; North Dakota, South Dakota, Nebraska, Kansas, Oklahoma, Arkansas, and Texas all have prairies in their eastern parts; Missouri, in its northern and western parts; Minnesota, in its southern and western parts; Indiana, in its northern part; Ohio, in its western part; and Michigan and Wisconsin, to a certain extent in the south. Some of these states, especially Illinois and Iowa, are referred to as Prairie States. The Native Americans sometimes cited as Prairie Indians shared cultural traits with both the NORTHEAST INDIANS and the

PLAINS INDIANS. Many of them inhabited semipermanent villages along wooded river valleys, for the most part in sizable EARTHLODGES or in dome-shape GRASS HOUSES, and had extensive cultivated fields where they grew corn, beans, squash, tobacco, and other crops. Most Prairie Indians left their homes to hunt BUFFALO part of the year. While on the trail, they lived in temporary LEAN-TOS or TEPEES. In post-Contact times, Prairie Indians acquired use of the HORSE for hunting and raiding. The Prairie tribes peoples east of the Mississippi generally are classified in the NORTHEAST CULTURE AREA: FOX, KICKAPOO, MENOMINEE, POTAWATOMI, SAC, WINNEBAGO, as well as tribes to their south, ILLINOIS, MIAMI, and SHAWNEE. (Some of these tribes also have been classified as western GREAT LAKES INDIANS.) The Prairie tribes west of the Mississippi, mostly occupying the stretch of land from the Mississippi River to the Missouri, generally are classified as part of the GREAT PLAINS CULTURE AREA: ARIKARA, HIDATSA, IOWA, KAW, MANDAN, MISSOURI, OMAHA, OSAGE, OTO, PAWNEE, PONCA, QUAPAW, and WICHITA.

prayer   An act of communion with, or a petition to, a deity or supernatural being. The term prayer is sometimes used interchangeably with CHANT or SONG, or combined into "prayer-song." Prayers, invocations, or incantations often accompanied a SACRIFICE or other rituals. In post-Contact times, some Indians began practicing Christian prayers. (See also OFFERING; PRAYER FEATHER; PRAYER STICK.)

prayer feather (breath feather)   A ceremonial FEATHER, used in devotional OFFERINGS.

prayer stick (prayer board)   A ceremonial stick or board, used in ritual as a devotional OFFERING; carved and painted, with objects added to them, especially feathers. SOUTHWEST INDIANS planted them in the ground to mark sacred sites and summon spiritual beings. (See also PAHO.)

Praying Indians (Christian Indians) American Indians of various tribes who accepted the teachings of Christian MISSIONARIES. Applied especially to New England Indians, in particular to some MASSACHUSETS, who were converted by the Protestant missionary John Eliot, starting in 1646. Natick and other settlements became known as praying villages. Also applied to the MOHAWKS of Kahnawake (Caughnawaga) who adopted Catholicism. "MISSION INDIANS" more often refers to California peoples.

preacher The individual who ritually recites the Code of Handsome Lake in the LONGHOUSE RELIGION of the IROQUOIS. (See also FAITHKEEPER.)

pre-ceramic The period before the invention of POTTERY; or, within a particular culture, before the manufacture of pottery.

Preclassic period See CLASSIC PERIOD.

pre-Columbian The period of history in the Americas before Christopher Columbus's voyage in 1492. (See also COLUMBIAN EXCHANGE; CONTACT; PREHISTORY.)

pre-Contact See CONTACT; PREHISTORY.

Prehistoric Indians The peoples of PREHISTORY in the Americas, i.e., before there were written records. "Pre-Contact," sometimes used synonymously with "prehistory," refers to the period before Indian-white contacts. "PRE-COLUMBIAN" refers to the period before the arrival of Christopher Columbus and other explorers in the Americas. "Ancient Indians" also is used. ARCHAEOLOGY provides information about Prehistoric Indians. Much of it is largely hypothetical. Most human remains, other than scattered bones, have perished; most ancient artifacts, other than stone ones, have decayed. Moreover, scientific techniques for dating ancient matter, such as RADIOCARBON DATING, are inexact and must allow for a margin of error. (See also CATEGORICAL APPENDIX, "TRIBES, BANDS, PEOPLES, LANGUAGES, AND CULTURES"; ARCHAIC INDIANS; CONTACT; FORMATIVE INDIANS; PALEO-INDIANS.)

prehistoric pottery See POTTERY.

prehistory The cultural stage of a given people before written records; in Native American studies, applied to the pre-Contact or PRE-COLUMBIAN time frame, although various types of writing were in use, such as PICTOGRAPHS. (See also CONTACT.)

presidio A fort built by the Spanish near MISSIONS to native peoples.

pressure flaking See FLAKING.

prestige item An object of great craftsmanship, rare materials, or symbolic value. The possession of such prestige items was often hereditary. (See also FETISH; PALLADIUM; TROPHY.)

priest A person who performs public religious acts; most often applied to religions with a strict hierarchy, as in the case of the INCAS, AZTECS, MAYAS, OLMECS, TOLTECS, and MOUNDBUILDERS. The religious leaders of these societies often wielded political power. The concept of PRIESTHOOD, i.e., more than one priest having a common purpose, also is implied in the term, as opposed to the more individualistic SHAMAN or MEDICINE MAN. (See also CACIQUE.)

priesthood A class of "priests" in a society, such as among the AZTECS and other MESOAMERICAN INDIANS. With regard to PUEBLO INDIANS, the term is used in reference to members of certain SECRET SOCIETIES, such as PRIESTHOOD OF THE BOW and RAIN PRIESTHOOD. (See also THEOCRACY.)

Priesthood of the Bow (Bow Priesthood) A MILITARY SOCIETY of the ZUNI Indians, made up of PRIESTS overseeing the rituals of war. The two head Bow Priests, along with priests of the RAIN PRIESTHOOD, traditionally have held high civil and judicial rank within the tribe. (See also KOTIKILLI.)

primogeniture   The system of succession or inheritance in which the firstborn child, typically the firstborn son, has primary rights.

projectile   See ARROW; ATLATL; BOLA; DART; JAVELIN; PROJECTILE POINT; RABBIT STICK; SLING; SPEAR.

projectile point   A POINT for any weapon designed to be hurled, i.e., an arrow, dart, or spear point.

promyshlenniki   The Russian term for the fur traders who extended their domain out of Siberia to Alaska and south along the Pacific Coast in the late 18th century and early 19th century. The traders exploited the ALEUTS for their labor; the TLINGITS offered stubborn resistance to Russian encroachment on their lands. (See also FUR TRADE.)

pronghorn   (pronghorn antelope)   A small ruminant, deerlike mammal (*Antilocapra americana*) with short forked horns. Native to the western plains of North America, pronghorns resemble the antelopes of Africa and Asia.

property   Scholars distinguish corporeal property, such as land and chattels (a "chattel" is a movable article); and incorporeal property, i.e., nonmaterial possessions such as a SONG, DANCE, CREST, HEREDITARY TITLE, or HEALING ritual. Both types of property can be given or passed through inheritance. Most Indian peoples considered the use of land an inalienable right. (See also LAND TENURE; POTLATCH.)

prophet   A person who, having experienced religious inspiration, predicts the future and becomes a proponent of change and often the leader of a REVITALIZATION MOVEMENT. In Indian history, a number of men — often influenced by the Christian concept of revelation — called for a return to traditional beliefs and lifeways. Some among them became known to whites as prophets rather than as SHAMANS or MEDICINE MEN. Delaware Prophet, Kickapoo Prophet, Shawnee Prophet, and Winnebago Prophet are all historical figures. Some Indian prophets founded new religions. (See also DREAMER RELIGION; GHOST DANCE RELIGION; INDIAN SHAKER RELIGION; WASHANI RELIGION.)

protohistory   The cultural stage of a given people at the end of their PREHISTORY and immediately preceding their earliest recorded history. "Protohistoric" is the adjective form.

protokiva   A subterranean chamber of the ANASAZI CULTURE, which evolved into the KIVAS of the PUEBLO INDIANS.

protolanguage   The parent LANGUAGE, linguistically reconstructed, from which a set of known languages evolved.

provenance   The place of origin or source; used in reference to the archaeological site of an artifact as well as its cultural context. (See also PROVENIENCE.)

provenience   An artifact's archaeological location as based on depth from the surface, stratification, and mapping. Although "provenience" can be used in a general sense — as a synonym of PROVENANCE — the more specific meaning is usually applied.

Pshwanwapam   See SAHAPTIN; YAKIMA.

psychotropic substance   Any substance that affects mental activity. Hallucinogens, intoxicants, narcotics, and stimulants are all psychotropic, or "psychoactive." Native Americans have made use of the mind-altering and hallucinogenic qualities of certain substances to facilitate the quest for VISIONS and contact with the spiritual world. Practical applications of psychotropic plants are medicinal, as cures and pain-killers; stimulative, for energy and bravery; and social, to create bonds of friendship. The practical applications also have been ritualized. (See also AKUHUA; ALCOHOLIC BEVERAGE; BLACK DRINK; COCA; JIMSONWEED; MESCAL; MUSHROOM; OLOLIUQUI; PEYOTE; TOBACCO; YOPO.)

puberty rite (puberty ceremony, puberty custom) A ritual to mark the passage of an individual's entrance to physiological maturity and adulthood. (See also RITE OF PASSAGE.)

puccoon (puccon, poccon, pocon) Any of several plants yielding a red or yellow DYE or PIGMENT; applied especially to bloodroot (*Sanguinaria canadensis*) and goldenseal (*Hydrastis canadensis*). "Hoary puccoon" refers to *Lithospermum canescens*. *Puccoon*, an ALGONQUIAN word, derives from Virginia Indians.

pueblo Originally, the Spanish word for an Indian village; also used for a particular type of apartmentlike structure of the PUEBLO INDIANS made from ADOBE and wooden beams, up to five stories high, with the levels interconnected by ladders. The entrances are through hatchways in the roofs and down ladders that can be drawn up. In addition to communal houses, pueblos have KIVAS and plazas.

Hopi pueblo architecture

Pueblo Indians A grouping of Native Americans of the SOUTHWEST CULTURE AREA, the name taken from their PUEBLO dwellings. Pueblo Indians include the HOPI and ZUNI tribes as well as Indians of the Rio Grande pueblos—the KERES, Pecos, Piro, TEWA, TIWA, and TOWA (Jemez) tribes.

Pujunan See MAIDU.

pulque A milky alcoholic beverage made by MESOAMERICAN INDIANS from AGAVE. The TOLTECS probably developed it, passing it to the AZTECS among other peoples.

puma (catamount, cougar, mountain lion, panther) A large wildcat (*Felis concolor*) found throughout the Americas and known by many names. The fur is yellow brown, red brown, or gray. The skin was valued by North American Indians to make QUIVERS. Some tribes, such as the SEMINOLES, ate the meat of the puma ceremonially. "Puma" derives from the QUECHUA language via Spanish; the alternative word "cougar" is from the TUPI-GUARANI word *suasarana*, meaning "false deer" because of the color. (See also JAGUAR.)

pump drill See DRILL.

pumpkin See SQUASH.

punctation (punctate decoration) A design formed by punching holes. Punctation is created in the wet clay of POTTERY before FIRING.

Puntlatch (Puntlatsh, Pentlatch) A SALISHAN-speaking tribe of the NORTHWEST COAST CULTURE AREA, located on the east coast of Vancouver Island in present-day British Columbia. The Qualicum band at Qualicum Beach, British Columbia, maintains tribal identity.

puppet A figure of a human or animal, the head, limbs, and torso of which can be moved with strings, wires, or sticks. KWAKIUTLS and TSIMSHIANS among other

NORTHWEST COAST INDIANS used wooden puppets representing legendary beings in ceremonies.

purification (cleansing) Rites of cleansing the body and spirit are a part of many Native American ceremonies, such as the GREEN CORN CEREMONY. "Going to the water," i.e., bathing, and SWEATING are means of purification.

puskita (pushkita, boskita, boos-ke-tau). The MUSKOGEAN word for fasting, corrupted to "busk" by white traders. The GREEN CORN CEREMONY also is known by this name.

Puyallup A SALISHAN-speaking tribe of the NORTHWEST COAST CULTURE AREA, located at the mouth of the Puyallup River and the neighboring coastal areas in present-day Washington. Tribal members hold the Puyallup Reservation in Pierce County, Washington, with their headquarters at Puyallup. (See also STEILACOOM.)

pyramid A massive stone monument, having a rectangular base and four sides extending upward to a point; found in the MESOAMERICAN CULTURE AREA as well as in ancient Peru. Native American pyramids, as tall as 140 feet, were a series of superimposed platforms used to hold TEMPLES. (See also TEMPLE MOUND.)

pyrite (iron pyrites) A pale yellow to brown, glistening mineral sulfide. Indians throughout the Americas used pyrite as an IRON ore to make ORNAMENTS and AMULETS and in FIRE-MAKING. The MAYAS and AZTECS used pyrite inlays to make MIRRORS and as eyes for statues. Pyrite is sometimes called "fool's gold" because it can be mistaken for GOLD.

▲ Q ▲

qarmaq (qaqmaq) A circular dwelling of the INUITS, with walls of ice (or sometimes stone) and a roof of skin; used interseasonally in autumn or spring, when it is too cold for TENTS and too warm for warm IGLOOS. (See also SOD HOUSE.)

Quaitso See SALISHAN.

Quapaw (Arkansa) A SIOUAN-speaking tribe of the GREAT PLAINS CULTURE AREA, located near the confluence of the Arkansas and Mississippi rivers in present-day Arkansas and Mississippi. (The ancestors of the Quapaws probably were one people with those of the KAWS, OMAHAS, OSAGES, and PONCAS, formerly living along the Ohio River, then migrating onto the prairies and plains west of the Mississippi River and dividing.) In 1823–33, some Quapaws lived among the CADDOS in present-day northwestern Louisiana and northeastern Texas. In 1833, the Quapaws were relocated to the INDIAN TERRITORY, their new lands in present-day northeastern Oklahoma and southeastern Kansas. Quapaws hold trust lands in Ottawa County, Oklahoma. *Quapaw* means "downstream people" or "those going with the current." The alternate name *Arkansa* derives from *Kansa*, Siouan for "people of the south wind," and *arc*, French for "bow," referring to the Osage orange, a type of mulberry tree in their territory prized in the making of BOWS.

quarrying The procuring of stone from the earth; the open excavation or pit is a quarry. In archaeology, the term QUARRY SITE is used. (See also MINING.)

quarry site A location that has an abundance of workable stone, such as FLINT or PIPESTONE. American Indians visited quarry sites to make stone tools. Archaeologists identify such sites by the number of CHIPS or spalls, i.e., stone waste matter from FLAKING.

quartz A hard, glassy mineral, a form of silica, found as a component of sandstone or as pure crystals in CHALCEDONY, CHERT, FLINT, opal, and rock crystal. Quartz is used for tools because of its hardness and workability, and for ORNAMENTS and AMULETS because of its appearance. Quartzite is a compact, granular rock metamorphosed from the recrystallization of the quartz content of sandstone, also valued in FLAKING.

Quechan See YUMA.

Quechua (Quetchua, Quichua, Kechua, Quechuan) A South American people and the language they speak. The language is sometimes grouped with the related language of the Aymaras as part of the QUECHUAMARAN language family. Quechua became the official language of the INCA Empire, which united diverse peoples. There are Quechua peoples in present-day Peru, Argentina, Brazil, Chile, Colombia, and Ecuador. More than 7 million people speak Quechua today; at least 28 Quechua or "Quechuan" dialects are still in use.

Quechuamaran A language family and subdivision of the ANDEAN-EQUATORIAL phylum comprising dialects spoken by SOUTH AMERICAN INDIANS, including the Aymara and QUECHUA tribes in the Andes Mountains of present-day Bolivia and Peru.

quetzal A large Central American bird of the trogon family *Pharomachrus mocinna*. Its long green tail feathers were highly valued by MESOAMERICAN INDIANS. The bird was associated with the worship of QUETZALCOATL.

Quetzalcoatl (Quetzalcohuatl, Feathered Serpent, Plumed Serpent) A god of the

OLMECS; the god of nature and a water deity among the inhabitants of the city of Teotihuacan; and the god of the heavens, earth, the wind, and fertility for the TOL-TECS and AZTECS. He is also considered the creator of mankind, organizer of religious rites, inventor of agriculture, and patron of learning. His name was taken by particular leaders. The MAYAS knew him as KUKUL-KUN. *Quetzalcoatl* translates as "feathered serpent" or "bird-serpent" from the NAHU-ATL; the deity combines traits of the QUET-ZAL and rattlesnake.

quid   Any vegetable chewed for its juice and nutrients, then spat out. CORNHUSKS, TULE, and YUCCA are among the many quids utilized by Native Americans.

Quileute (Quilayute, Quilayutte)   A CHI-MAKUAN-speaking tribe of the NORTH-WEST COAST CULTURE AREA, located on the Quilayute River and the neighboring coastal areas of present-day Washington. Tribal members hold the Quileute Reservation in Clallam County, Washington, with headquarters at La Push; other Quileutes live among the MAKAHS on the Makah Reservation, also in Clallam County. (See also HOH.)

quill   See QUILLWORK.

Quiller's Society   See QUILLWORKER SOCIETY.

quillwork   The act, process, or resulting artifact of work in PORCUPINE spines, such as WEAVING and EMBROIDERY. Quillwork is found on clothing, bags, pipes, and other items. The shafts of feathers also are used. Quills were softened in water or the mouth; flattened by drawing them through the teeth or with a special rock or bone tool called a quill flattener; colored with DYES; and then applied as a form of APPLIQUÉ on various materials, especially animal skins. The northern ALGONQUIAN-speaking tribes, such as the CHIPPEWAS, CREES, and OTTA-WAS, are known for their traditional quill-work on both leather and BIRCHBARK.

Quillworker Society (Quiller's Society)   A SECRET SOCIETY of CHEYENNE women who practiced the ritual art of QUILLWORK on various artifacts, including clothing, containers, and ceremonial objects, for members of other sodalities.

Quinault (Quinaielt)   A SALISHAN-speaking tribe of the NORTHWEST COAST CUL-TURE AREA, located at the mouth of the Quinault River in present-day Washington and the neighboring coastal areas. Tribal members hold the Quinault Reservation in Grays and Jefferson counties, Washington; other Quinaults share the Shoalwater Reservation in Pacific County with CHEHALIS and CHINOOK Indians.

Quinipissa   See MUSKOGEAN.

quinoa (Andean rice)   A type of pigweed (*Chenopodium quinoa*) growing in the high Andes Mountains of South America and cultivated as a cereal by native peoples. The word is of QUECHUA derivation, via Spanish to English.

quipu   A device, typical of the INCAS, consisting of a main cord with smaller cords of different colors knotted at varying distances, for the purpose of counting, record keeping, and registering events. A QUECHUA word, meaning "knot."

quirt   A riding whip, typical of Spanish Americans as well as PLAINS INDIANS, with a wood, bone, or horn handle and a braided leather lash; or simply a short wooden staff. Quirts sometimes doubled as ceremonial staffs or COUP STICKS.

quiver   A case or sheath for carrying ARROWS, usually made from skins or wood and decorated with a variety of materials, including feathers, quills, or beads.

quoits   A game common to many tribes in which rings or disks are thrown at a peg or pin to encircle it.

▲ R ▲

rabbit Rabbits, long-eared and short-tailed mammals of the family Leporidae, were widely hunted, sometimes communally, in rabbit drives. In the SOUTHWEST CULTURE AREA, they were the main source of meat. The fur also was used, typically sewn together in patchwork or joined at the ends, then twisted or braided into strips and woven.

Rabbit Dance A contemporary dance common to many North American Indians in which men and women dance arm in arm; adapted from non-Indian dances, in particular the waltz and fox trot.

rabbit stick (throwing stick) A flat, curved CLUB, typical of CALIFORNIA INDIANS and SOUTHWEST INDIANS, designed to be thrown at small game. Although a rabbit stick resembles an Australian boomerang with a similar aerodynamic design, it does not return to the thrower. The chosen wood is Gambell's oak, painted black, red, and green; sometimes a rabbit figure is drawn. The HOPIS call the weapon *putshkohu*.

racing Native Americans have traditionally engaged in foot races and, in post-Contact times, horse races. Races often were intertribal and sometimes included GAMBLING. Ritual races or runs were held to affect the weather and hasten the growth of crops. KICKBALL and kick-stick are kinds of races.

radiocarbon dating (carbon-14 dating) A technique for dating ancient materials with organic content, i.e., plant or animal material, by measuring the amount of C-14 (the radioactive isotope of carbon) present and deducing its degree of decay at a known rate since the organism's death. A type of ABSOLUTE DATING.

raft Logs or some other material, such as bulrushes, tied together to bear weight and float on water. (See also BALSA.)

rain god A type of POTTERY figurine made by TEWA Indians of the Tesuque Pueblo, beginning in the late 19th century, for sale to tourists at the encouragement of white traders.

rainmaking (rain dance) A ceremony for bringing rain and ensuring plentiful crops. Many agricultural tribes, especially in the SOUTHWEST CULTURE AREA, conducted rainmaking ceremonies or rain dances, such as the KACHINA dance. Other peoples, such as CALIFORNIA INDIANS of the KUKSU RELIGION, participated in rainmaking rituals for continuing fertility of wild plant foods. One sees the term Rain Powers for the spirits controlling rain.

Rain Priesthood (Ashiwanni) A SECRET SOCIETY of the ZUNI Indians that, through prayers and fasting, strives to bring about plentiful rain. Along with members of the PRIESTHOOD OF THE BOW, the Rain Priests, organized into more than one SODALITY, traditionally have held great authority within the tribe—civil and judicial as well as religious. (See also KOTIKILLI.)

rake A tool with a handle and head of long teeth, used to clear brush and leaves. The ARIKARAS, HIDATSAS, and MANDANS used rakes with an antler head for clearing and smoothing land. The HOPIS used a wooden version.

ramada An ARBOR or sun shade, made with branches of trees or shrubs, used by SOUTHWEST INDIANS for outdoor cooking and craftwork. A ramada sometimes was attached to a house as a porch. Special rama-

Hidatsa rake

das were constructed for ceremonial purposes, such as the *watto* of the PAPAGOS, built as part of a *VAHKI*. "Ramada" is a Spanish-derived word.

Ramapough   See LENNI LENAPE.

rancheria   The Spanish term for a small rural village, often dependent on a larger village; also, a group of huts. The Spanish used the term in California to refer to native villages, usually of Indians not converted to Christianity. Today, in California in particular, it refers to a small RESERVATION.

rank   Relative position within a social organization. Rank was hereditary among some peoples; the NATCHEZ, for example, had a CASTE SYSTEM. Other peoples earned rank through deeds; PLAINS INDIAN war chiefs proved themselves in battle. Rank or "status" also was accomplished by certain rituals, such as the POTLATCH. (See also HEREDITARY TITLE.)

Rappahannock   A subtribe of the POWHATAN Indians, located on the Rappahannock River in present-day Virginia. The United Rappahannock Tribe, Inc. is centered at Indian Neck, Virginia. In ALGONQUIAN, the name means "alternating stream."

rattle   A musical instrument that makes short percussive sounds in rapid succession when shaken. Some rattles had small objects, such as pebbles and seeds, in a larger hollow piece (shaker); rawhide, wood, gourds, turtle shells, hooves, and horns were commonly used as receptacles, often with a handle attached. Other rattles were crafted out of two objects of about equal size that make a rhythmic noise when coming in

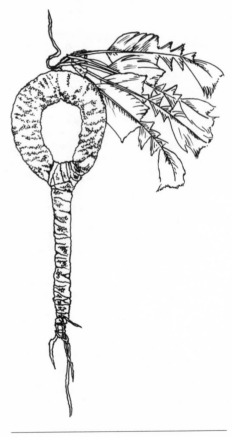

Sioux hoop rattle

contact; pods, shells, bird beaks, and other materials were used in this design. Still others had a number of small objects, such as hooves, claws, or teeth, strung together; this last variety was often attached to the body or clothing as jinglers. Among the PUEBLO INDIANS and INUITS, rattles were utilized as toys. For most tribes, however, rattles were sacred objects, sometimes called medicine rattles or spirit rattles, to be used only by a SHAMAN. In the SIGN LANGUAGE of the PLAINS INDIANS, the sign for "rattle" was used to mean "sacred." (See also CLAPPER.)

raven A bird, *Corvus corax*, related to the CROW but larger, with glossy black plumage and a croaking cry, and known for its intelligence and mischievousness. "Raven" capitalized is a TRICKSTER figure in many NORTHWEST COAST INDIAN legends.

rawhide The untanned SKIN or HIDE of animals. In preparing rawhide, fresh hide is stretched, fleshed, and usually dehaired, but not tanned as in the making of LEATHER. Rawhide was valued among native peoples and used for numerous artifacts, large and small. The fact that the hide would shrink considerably when drying was incorporated in the design of certain objects, such as securing handles to tools and attaching drumheads. Because of its hardness, rawhide has been referred to as Indian iron. (See also BABICHE; PARFLECHE; *SHAGANAPPI*.)

rebozo A long woven scarf, worn over the head and shoulders. Of Spanish origin, rebozos also are worn by native women in Mexico and other parts of Latin America.

Redheaded Woodpecker Dance See JUMP DANCE.

Red Paint Culture A cultural tradition of ARCHAIC INDIANS in present-day New England and eastern Canada, lasting from about 3000 B.C. to 500 B.C. The Red Paint people were so named because of their use of ground-up red iron ore to line graves.

"redskin" (red man) A term applied historically to Native Americans by non-Indians. It was probably first used by early English and French explorers to refer to the BEOTHUKS of Newfoundland, who colored their bodies, cloths, and tools with red OCHER. The French version is *peau-rouge* or, plural, *peaux-rouges*.

Red Stick A term applied by whites to the militant faction of the CREEK Indians in the early 19th century, after the tall red poles erected as declarations of war. Tribal members who allied themselves with whites were called WHITE STICKS.

redware A type of POTTERY made from red clay, fired so that it keeps its red color. Typical of PUEBLO INDIANS, especially of the Santa Clara and San Ildefonso pueblos. (See also BLACKWARE.)

Ree See ARIKARA.

reformer A term applied to non-Indians who worked on behalf of INDIAN RIGHTS in the late 19th and early 20th century. Reformers known as Friends of the Indian were non-Indian individuals and the organizations they formed to lobby the federal government. Among them were the Indian Protection Committee, Indian Rights Association, Women's National Indian Association, and National Indian Defense Association. Most of the early non-Indian activists supported the policies of ASSIMILATION, with Indian citizenship a major goal. In the Lake Mohonk Conferences from 1883 to 1916, reformers met at New Paltz, New York, to formulate Indian policy.

reindeer See CARIBOU.

relative dating The dating of ancient materials relative to one another, as opposed to the fixed time scales of ABSOLUTE DATING. CROSS DATING and STRATIGRAPHY are types of relative dating.

religion A system of belief and worship. In Native American studies, a distinction generally is not made between religion and philosophy, since the Indian WORLDVIEW is traditionally one of HOLISM, ANIMISM, and reverence for nature. Most Indian languages do not have a separate word for religion since it is considered central to existence. (See also CATEGORICAL APPENDIX, "RELIGION and RITUAL.")

relocation The forced or encouraged REMOVAL of a tribe from one location to another. A common governmental practice in the 19th century, when EASTERN INDIANS were relocated to INDIAN TERRITORY. From the early 1950s into the 1960s, the federal government adopted a modern relocation policy, pressuring Indians to move from reservations to urban areas. (See also TERMINATION; TRAIL OF TEARS.)

removal A federal policy formalized with the Indian Removal Act of 1830; the U.S. government forced EASTERN INDIANS to leave their ancestral homelands and move west of the Mississippi River to INDIAN TERRITORY. Those Indians who stayed in the East were subject to state laws. (See also RELOCATION; TRAIL OF TEARS.)

repartimiento Spanish term for "distribution" or "apportionment"; used historically for a grant of lands in a conquered territory and the right to exploit some among the Indian population with an annual levy for labor and produce. The *repartimiento* system replaced the ENCOMIENDA system in 1542 and lasted through the Spanish colonial period.

repatriation The act of restoring to one's country or place of origin; used to refer to the reacquisition by a tribe of human remains or SACRED OBJECTS from the government, museums, or private owners. In 1990, the Native American Graves Protection and Repatriation Act required federal agencies and any museums receiving federal grants to return human remains and sacred objects to requesting tribes.

repoussé In METALWORK, a design hammered in relief; or the technique itself. In one method of creating such a design, the reverse side is hammered out, then additional hammering and filing work is done on the front. Another method is hammering over a carved model.

requerimiento A Spanish word for "request," "requisition," or "summons"; used historically to refer to the royal decree read by conquistadors to tribal representatives, informing Indians of their duty to king and pope, including their right to freedom if they submitted and the threat of war and enslavement if they did not. To obtain freedom, the Indians had to prove themselves "civilized" in terms of language, religion, shelter, and dress.

reservation A tract of land set aside by the federal or state governments for occupation by and use of Indians, based on treaty negotiations. Reservations originally served as a kind of prison for Indians, who were restricted to them. Today, reservations are tribally held lands, protected by the government, where Indians are free to come and go as they choose. (See also RANCHERIA; RESERVE.)

reservation state A state in which there is at least one Indian tribe having FEDERAL RECOGNITION and receiving funds for special Indian programs.

reserve The Canadian equivalent of a RESERVATION. Different Canadian BANDS usually have more than one reserve tract of land.

reserve decoration A process in POTTERY-making in which paint is applied to the background, allowing the natural color of the clay to form a design. (See also NEGATIVE PAINTING.)

resin Any of numerous viscous substances of plant origin. Indians used the resins or gum of evergreen trees for medicinal purposes; to make torches; as glue; and for waterproofing boats and baskets. One resin, known as chicle (from the NAHUATL word *chictli*), taken from the sapodilla tree, was utilized by MESOAMERICAN INDIANS in a number of applications; now it is used in the making of chewing gum, as in Chiclets. (See also PITCH.)

resistance ACTIVISM and defensive WARFARE, i.e., the Indian fight throughout history for tribal homelands and rights. Certain Indian-white conflicts have come down through history with specific names, such as the Second Seminole War. The terms rebellion, revolt, and uprising are also used, as in Pontiac's Rebellion and the Natchez Revolt. But other periods of warfare—especially prolonged ones with many different periods of engagement—are now called resistance, such as the Apache Resistance or Geronimo's Resistance. "Resistance" was originally applied to underground fighters battling Nazi occupation of their countries in World War II.

resist painting See NEGATIVE PAINTING.

restoration Cultural renewal, or a return to traditional ways and values; often appears as "tribal restoration," indicating the establishment of autonomous tribal governments, the rediscovery of tribal identity, and the development of tribal resources. Tribal restoration became widespread as of 1930, when the federal government's Indian Reorganization Act (IRA, or Wheeler-Collier Act) launched a "New Deal" for Native Americans and ended the policies of ALLOTMENT and ASSIMILATION. Indian language, customs, and religions were no longer suppressed; an Indian Arts and Crafts board was established; and loan and scholarship funds were organized.

revitalization movement A religious or cultural movement in which Indian lifeways are reintroduced and SELF-DETERMINATION is encouraged; usually following defeat in war, displacement from lands, and CULTURAL DISPOSSESSION. Some such movements have drawn on elements of Christianity. The DREAMER RELIGION, GHOST DANCE RELIGION, INDIAN SHAKER RELIGION, LONGHOUSE RELIGION, and NATIVE AMERICAN CHURCH are considered revitalization movements. (See also MESSIAH; PROPHET.)

rhombus See BULLROARER.

ribbonwork Patchwork or APPLIQUÉ, typical of the SEMINOLES, in which silk ribbons are sewn in strips on a dress. Also called ribbon appliqué, silk appliqué, and rickrack.

Ricaree See ARIKARA.

Rice See MENOMINEE.

rickrack See RIBBONWORK.

ring-and-pin A game or toy involving two objects, connected by a string, for swinging and catching one on the other (or a series of objects onto another). In a common variety among Native Americans, a pin-shape object is held and swung in such a way as to catch a ring (or series of rings). In cup-and-ball (the Mexican *balero*, or European *bilboquet*), a ball is caught in a cup. In the SIOUX version, called the deer-toe game, bones strung together are caught on a needle.

ringstone (doughnut-stone) A round stone with a hole through its middle, perhaps for ceremonial use. (See also PERFORATED STONE.)

rite A formal religious act or series of acts. "Rite" can be used interchangeably with RITUAL or CEREMONY; but also more specifically in the sense that a people's general body of ritualistic behavior is made up of particular rites. (See also RITE OF PASSAGE.)

rite of passage A ceremony associated with the change of status of an individual, such as CHILDBIRTH, PUBERTY RITE, INITIATION, MARRIAGE, or death. (See also VISION QUEST.)

ritual Prescribed and symbolic behavior surrounding a religion or religious event; used in reference to the body of ceremonies of a particular religion as well as specifically as that part of a CEREMONY that is spoken or sung. Both "ritual" and "ritualistic" are adjective forms.

ritual drama See DRAMA.

ritual speech See ORATORY; SPEAKER.

roach A clump of hair, usually deer, horse, or porcupine hair, attached to the top of the head to create the effect of a SCALPLOCK. (The term roach can be used synonymously with "scalplock.") A roach spreader is a piece of bone, antler, or metal plate inserted in the roach above its base, to keep the hair, and sometimes an added eagle feather, upright.

roadman (Road Chief) One who runs the prayer meeting in the NATIVE AMERICAN CHURCH.

robe The SKIN of an animal, dressed with the fur on, and used as a wrap. In North America, BUFFALO furs were commonly used to make robes. The terms CLOAK and mantle sometimes are synonymous with "robe," but usually only if made from some other material than fur, such as a "feather mantle." Among the SIOUX, an animal's "laying down of his robe" refers to its dying. (See also BLANKET; BUFFALO ROBE.)

rockahominy A food preparation, consisting of parched CORN pounded into a fine powder, used especially by hunting and war parties away from home. Other ingredients sometimes are added to the corn flour, such as MAPLE SUGAR, cane sugar, CHOCOLATE, or powdered MESQUITE beans. "Rockahom-

iny" is an ALGONQUIAN-derived word, but the food is used by many other Indian peoples and known by different names in their languages. *PINOLE* is the Spanish name. (See also HOMINY.)

rock art PICTOGRAPHS drawn on rocks, i.e., on boulders, in caves, in rock shelters, on overhangs, etc. They are carved, pecked, or abraded, forming PETROGLYPHS; or painted, forming rock paintings. Most rock art is in the West. The CHUMASH Indians of California are known for their rock art.

rocker stamping A decorative technique in which a sharp, curved edge, often a shell, is rocked back and forth on wet POTTERY before FIRING, resulting in connecting zigzag lines. *Sello* is Spanish for "rocker stamp."

rock shelter See CAVE.

Rogue River Indians See CHASTACOSTA; LATGAWA; TAKELMA; TUTUTNI.

root craft The act, process, or resulting artifact of work with roots; or the general use of roots as a resource. Native Americans have used roots, the normally underground portion of a plant (bulbs, tubers, and rootstocks often are categorized with true roots), to make BASKETS, TEXTILES, MEDICINES, POISONS, and DYES, and for FOOD.

rope A thick cord, usually consisting of twisted or braided strands. Native Americans made lariats (throw ropes or lassos) and tie ropes (stake ropes) from hair, rawhide, and plant fibers. (See also CORDAGE; NETTING.)

rubber An elastic material obtained by means of the coagulation and drying of the milky sap of various tropical plants, especially the rubber tree (*Hevea brasiliensis*). SOUTH AMERICAN INDIANS, MESOAMERICAN INDIANS, and CIRCUM-CARIBBEAN INDIANS used rubber for balls, bags, footwear, drums and drumsticks, and torches. The rubber boom in the 19th century led to a virtual invasion by colonial rubber traders and the displacement of many tribes, especially in the Amazon.

running the gauntlet   An IROQUOIS ritual in which captives were forced to run between two lines of people who attacked them with clubs. Those who survived the ORDEAL generally were spared.

runtee   A type of SHELLWORK, consisting of a shell disk with one or more perforations drilled edgewise through the middle; probably worn as a PENDANT. Common among Virginia ALGONQUIANS and other coastal Indians. Europeans also began manufacturing runtee for trade. The word is thought to be a corruption of the French *arrondi* for "rounded," from *écaille arrondie*, "shell made round." (See also GORGERIN.)

▲ S ▲

saber-toothed tiger (saber-toothed cat, sabertooth)   Extinct mammals of the cat family, especially of the genera *Machairodus* and *Smilodon*, equaling the tiger in size but with long, curved upper canine teeth. PALEO-INDIANS hunted them and other big game.

Sac (Sauk)   An ALGONQUIAN-speaking tribe of the NORTHEAST CULTURE AREA, located on upper Green Bay and the lower Fox River in present-day Wisconsin. (In pre-Contact times, the Sacs lived on Saginaw Bay in present-day Michigan, named after them.) The Sacs are related linguistically to the FOXES and the KICKAPOOS. Beginning in the early 1700s, they occupied lands in present-day Illinois near their allies, the Foxes. In 1832, the two tribes were pressured by whites to cede territory east of the Mississippi in exchange for land in present-day Iowa. In 1842, some bands were relocated to present-day Kansas and then, in 1867, to Oklahoma; others stayed in or returned to Iowa. The Sac and Fox Tribe holds trust lands near Shawnee, Oklahoma; other Sacs and Foxes hold the Sac and Fox Reservation near Tama, Iowa. *Sac* or *Sauk*, derives from the Algonquian term *Osa'ki-wug*, meaning "yellow earth people" or "people of the outlet."

sachem   The CHIEF of a TRIBE. Among the ALGONQUIANS of New England, the position was hereditary. The title sometimes refers to IROQUOIS chiefs and to leaders of other tribes as well. The term sachem can apply to a leader of a CONFEDERACY of tribes, with SAGAMORE indicating the leader of a particular tribe. But GRAND SACHEM now more often applies to the head of an alliance, with "sachem" designating the tribe's leader and "sagamore" a leader of subordinate rank within the sachem's own tribe. "Sachemship" refers to the sachem's political entity; "sachemdom" refers to the sachem's domain; "sachemic" means "sachemlike." *Sacimau* (or *Sakimau*) is the NARRAGANSET and ABENAKI form.

Sacred Arrows   See MEDICINE ARROWS.

Sacred Buffalo Hat (Esevone)   A holy object, or PALLADIUM, of the CHEYENNE Indians, representing a gift from the SPIRIT WORLD. The Cheyenne name in ALGON-QUIAN, *Esevone*, refers to a herd of female buffalo. (See also MEDICINE ARROWS.)

sacred bundle   See MEDICINE BUNDLE.

Sacred Hoop   A SIOUX symbol, representing togetherness among the tribe's various bands. (See CIRCLE; HOOP DANCE.)

sacred object (ceremonial object)   Any object believed to possess spiritual power, being a gift from the SPIRIT WORLD. Sacred objects are used in ceremonies. *Godiyo* is an APACHE term in ATHAPASCAN for a category of objects considered holy. (See also AMU-LET; FETISH; KEEPER; MEDICINE BUNDLE; PALLADIUM; PRESTIGE ITEM; TALISMAN.)

sacred pipe   A pipe with special religious and political significance to a tribe. The care and smoking of the Sacred Pipe is part of SIOUX religion and that of other PLAINS INDIANS, the pipe being the symbolic channel to the SPIRIT WORLD. Sometimes the Sacred Pipe and its rituals are discussed as a religion unto itself. (See also BUFFALO CALF PIPE; CALUMET; FLAT PIPE.)

Sacred Pole (Venerable Man)   A holy object, or PALLADIUM, of the OMAHAS. The Sacred Pole consists of a cottonwood pole, resting on a wooden "leg," with a scalp on its "head." It is the personification of a human being, symbolizing both man as protector and provider of the home and woman as mother. It is stored in a Sacred Tent, watched over by a hereditary KEEPER. A two-part ceremony celebrating both the male and female roles, known as Anointing the Sacred Pole, is held annually. Other tribes, such as the CHICKASAWS, have sacred poles in their mythology, representing the COSMIC TREE.

Sacred Shield See SHIELD.

sacred site A location with special mythological or historical meaning to a tribe. Sacred natural places include mountains, lakes, rivers, caves, and rock quarries; sacred man-made places include burial grounds, mounds, rock piles, and rock art. Many tribes have had long-term struggles to preserve and use their sacred sites. (See PAHA SAPA.)

sacrifice A gift to a spiritual power. A sacrifice is a kind of OFFERING, but the former implies giving up something highly valued. The terms animal sacrifice and human sacrifice also are used, the latter practice institutionalized by INCAS, TOLTECS, and AZTECS. *Sacrifice* is a Latin word, meaning "to make sacred." (See also SACRIFICIAL KNIFE.)

sacrificial knife A KNIFE, typical of the AZTECS, used in human or animal SACRIFICE. Sacrificial knives were elaborately carved, often in wood and stone.

saddle Many Indians rode bareback, especially when hunting buffalo and in warfare. Some Indians used BLANKETS as saddles. Some used pad saddles, hide stuffed with animal hair and attached with a rawhide cinch or girth, and having short stirrups. Others used frame saddles, modeled after Moorish saddles (brought to North America by the Spanish), often made from cottonwood covered with rawhide and with horn pommels in front and back. Leather and beadwork ornaments sometimes were

attached to bridles or draped over the horse's shoulders. Saddlebags were used to carry food and possessions. PARFLECHES also were hung from saddles. Thongs looped around the horse's lower jaw usually served as a bridle.

saddlebag See BAG; PARFLECHE; SADDLE.

sagamite A kind of cornmeal mush. Typical of the CREES; derived from the word *kisagamitew*, meaning "hot liquid" in their ALGONQUIAN language.

sagamore A subordinate CHIEF or lieutenant chief of the ALGONQUIAN Indians, below a SACHEM in rank. "Sagamore" is a corruption of the ABENAKI *sakimau*, their word for chief (not "lesser chief," as it evolved among whites).

saguaro A giant cactus, *Carnegiea gigantea*, growing in the American Southwest and northern Mexico, having upturned branches, white flowers, and red fruit; also, the fruit itself. SOUTHWEST INDIANS, especially the PAPAGOS and PIMAS, gathered and ate the sweet and fleshy fruit, fresh or dried. The Papagos used a long pole, called a *kuibit*, made from the ribs of the plant, to knock down the fruit. Recipes included boiling the fresh fruit into a jam or syrup; or grinding the dried fruit into powder and mixing it with water for a drink. The syrup also was made into a wine. The Indians of the HOHOKAM CULTURE used the acid of the plant in their ETCHING procedure.

Sahaptin (Shahaptin, Shahaptian) A language family and subdivision of the PENUTIAN phylum comprising dialects spoken by peoples of the PLATEAU CULTURE AREA, among them the KLICKITAT, NEZ PERCE, PALOUSE, Pshwanwapam, Skin (Tapanash), Taidnapam, TENINO, Tyigh, UMATILLA, WALLAWALLA, Wanapam, Wauyukma, and YAKIMA tribes. This language family also is referred to as Sahaptin-Nez Perce.

Sahehwamish See SALISHAN.

Salado Culture A cultural tradition of the American Southwest, lasting from about A.D. 1300 to 1400, and centered in the Gila River region of present-day Arizona. The Salado Indians, or the Saladoans, are considered an offshoot of the combined SINAGUA CULTURE and ANASAZI CULTURE; they passed ADOBE building techniques to the Indians of the HOHOKAM CULTURE.

Salinan A language family and subdivision of the HOKAN phylum comprising dialects spoken by the bands of the SALINAS tribe of the CALIFORNIA CULTURE AREA.

Salinas A SALINAN-speaking tribe of the CALIFORNIA CULTURE AREA, located on the Salinas River in present-day San Luis Obispo, Monterey, and probably San Benito counties, California. The now-extinct Salinas were missionized by the Spanish along with YOKUTS Indians at the San Antonio and San Miguel missions, becoming known as MISSION INDIANS. *Salinas*, the Spanish name of the river, means "salt-pit."

Salish See FLATHEAD.

Salish, Coast See SALISHAN.

Salish, Inland See SALISHAN.

Salishan A language family of undetermined phylum affiliation comprising dialects spoken by Indians of the NORTHWEST COAST CULTURE AREA (Coast Salish), among them the BELLA COOLA, CHEHALIS, CLALLAM, COMOX, Copalis, COWICHAN, COWLITZ, DUWAMISH, Humptulips, LUMNI, MUCKLESHOOT, NANAIMO, NISQUALLY, NOOKSACK, PUNTLATCH, PUYALLUP, Quaitso, QUINAULT, Sahehwamish, Satsop, SEECHELT, SEMIAHMOO, SILETZ, SKAGIT, SNOHOMISH, SNOQUALMIE, SONGISH, SQUAMISH, SQUAXIN, SUQUAMISH, Swallah, SWINOMISH, Tillamook, TWANA, and Wynoochee tribes; and Indians of the PLATEAU CULTURE AREA (Inland or Interior Salish), among them the Chelan, COEUR D'ALENE, COLUMBIA, COLVILLE, FLATHEAD, KALISPEL, LAKE, LILLOOET, METHOW, NTLAKYAPAMUK, OKANAGAN, SANPOIL, SHUSWAP, Sinkaietk, Sinkakaius, and Wenatchee tribes. The Salishan and WAKASHAN language families have been classified as part of a combined "Mosan" language family. *Salish* possibly comes from the Okanagan word *salst*, meaning "the people."

salmon Any fish of the genera *Salmo* and *Oncorhynchus*, having pinkish flesh. There are at least five salmon species in the Pacific Northwest. When salmon ran upriver from the ocean to spawn, NORTHWEST COAST INDIANS and PLATEAU INDIANS used nets, weirs, spears, and gaffs (hooks) to catch them. The men passed the caught fish to the women, who split them open and hung them in the sun to dry.

salt A colorless or white crystalline solid, composed mainly of sodium chloride; used as a condiment or, less frequently, a food preservative. Indians in northern climates who subsisted predominantly on meat, which contains salts, needed less salt as an additive. Those peoples living in hot climates sweated more, losing body salt, and thus had a greater need. Indians obtained salt both from the surface of the land around dry lake beds and by evaporating saltwater. Salt became an important trade item among SOUTHEAST INDIANS, SOUTHWEST INDIANS, CALIFORNIA INDIANS, and MESOAMERICAN INDIANS. Among many peoples, salt was collected ritually and used in ceremonies. Some tribes in Mesoamerica and the Southwest had salt deities.

Samish A SALISHAN-speaking tribe of the NORTHWEST COAST CULTURE AREA, located on Samish Bay and Samish Island as well as Guemes Island and Fidalgo Island in present-day Washington. Samish Indians were placed on the Lumni Reservation in Whatcom County, Washington, and the Tulalip Reservation in Snohomish County with other Salishans. Another group, the Samish Indian Tribe, operates out of Anacortes, Washington.

samp A CORN porridge made from HOMINY. Corruption of an ALGONQUIAN word.

San Carlos A subtribe of the APACHE Indians. The name is used for the San Carlos division, a large grouping of Western Apaches, including the CIBECUE, TONTO, WHITE MOUNTAIN, and San Carlos subdivisions. The last consists of the APACHE PEAKS, ARAVAIPA, and PINAL bands, as well as the San Carlos band proper. The San Carlos band lived near the San Carlos River between the Gila and Salt rivers. San Carlos is also a reservation in Gila and Graham counties, Arizona.

sandal Native Americans living in warm climates traditionally have worn sandals, especially SOUTHWEST INDIANS and MESOAMERICAN INDIANS. In the Southwest, the most common materials in early sandal-making were the leaves and stems of the YUCCA plant. Some PUEBLO INDIANS added sandals to BURIALS to help guide the deceased to the SIPAPU.

Sand Creek An incident in Indian history that, like the TRAIL OF TEARS, the LONG WALK, and WOUNDED KNEE, has come to symbolize the suffering of Indian peoples. On November 19, 1864, Colorado volunteers under Colonel John Chivington attacked Black Kettle's peaceful encampment of Southern CHEYENNES and Southern ARAPAHOS at Sand Creek near Fort Lyon in Colorado, killing about 200 men, women, and children.

Sandia Culture A cultural tradition of the PALEOLITHIC PERIOD, existing about 10000 B.C., and possibly much earlier. The culture, localized in the Southwest, is named for a cave site in the Sandia Mountains of New Mexico. Sandia POINTS are about two

Sandia point

to four inches long with rounded bases and a bulge on one side where they were attached to wooden shafts.

Sandia Pueblo See TIWA.

sandpainting (dry-painting) A ceremonial art involving the trickling of sand colored with minerals onto neutral sand; and the work of art itself. A custom of the NAVAJOS and PUEBLO INDIANS, but also found to a lesser extent among the APACHES, CHEYENNES, ARAPAHOS, BLACKFEET, and some CALIFORNIA INDIANS. In Navajo tradition, sandpainters, under the guidance of SHAMANS, create the mosaic on the floor of a LODGE at dawn; using five sacred colors—white, black, blue, red, and yellow—they depict the HOLY PEOPLE, their legendary beings, as well as natural phenomena; at the end of the ceremony, often a HEALING ceremony, they destroy the work. No painting is kept after sunset. Sandpaintings also are referred to as dry-paintings, sand pictures, and sand altars.

San Felipe Pueblo   See KERES.

San Ildefonso Pueblo   See TEWA.

San Juan Pueblo   See TEWA.

sannup (sanop)   A married Indian man, a correlative of SQUAW, used in some historical writings to designate an ordinary warrior, as distinguished from a SACHEM or SAGAMORE.   An   ALGONQUIAN-derived word.

Sanpoil   A SALISHAN-speaking tribe of the PLATEAU CULTURE AREA, located on the Sanpoil River and on the Columbia River below Big Bend in present-day Washington. The Nespelem Indians, located on Nespelem Creek, generally are considered a subtribe. Descendants of both groups live on the Colville Reservation near Nespelem, Washington, with other Salishans.

Sans Arcs (Itazipco, Itazipcho)   A subtribe of the TETON division of the SIOUX Indians, located near the Grand River in present-day South Dakota and ranging throughout the Northern Plains, especially in present-day North Dakota, Montana, Wyoming, and Nebraska. *Sans Arcs* is French for "without bows," the translation from the SIOUAN of *Itazipco*.

Santa Ana Pueblo   See KERES.

Santa Clara Pueblo   See TEWA.

Santee (Dakota)   A subtribe of the SIOUX Indians, located on the Minnesota River in present-day Minnesota. The Santee division includes the MDEWAKANTON, SISSETON, WAHPEKUTE, and WAHPETON, bands. The Santee Sioux sometimes are referred to as Eastern Sioux to distinguish them from the TETONS, YANKTONS, and YANKTONAIS. *Santee* possibly derives from the SIOUAN word *isanyati*, meaning "to pitch tents at Knife Lake," referring to Mille Lacs. The Santees call themselves *Dakota*, meaning "allies."

Santee (Issati, Isanyati)   A SIOUAN-speaking tribe of the SOUTHEAST CULTURE AREA, located on the Santee River in present-day South Carolina. In the early 1700s, many Santees were sold into slavery in the West Indies; others probably merged with the CATAWBAS. Santees of the White Oak Indian Community at Holly Hill, South Carolina, maintain tribal identity. *Santee* possibly means "river" in eastern dialects of Siouan.

Santiam   See KALAPUYAN.

Santo Domingo Pueblo   See KERES.

Saponi   A SIOUAN-speaking tribe of the SOUTHEAST CULTURE AREA, located in present-day Albemarle County, Virginia. Saponi bands later lived in Rowan, Bertie, Brunswick, and Granville counties in present-day North Carolina. In about 1740, they migrated northward into Pennsylvania, along with the linguistically related Tutelos, living for a time at Shamokin. In 1743, they were adopted by the CAYUGAS and settled among them in New York; others, who had stayed behind in North Carolina, eventually also went to New York with the TUSCARORAS. The Halliwa-Saponi tribe is centered in Maxton, North Carolina. *Saponi* derives from the Siouan term for "shallow water."

Sarcee (Sarsi)   An ATHAPASCAN-speaking tribe of the GREAT PLAINS CULTURE AREA, located on the upper Saskatchewan and Athabasca rivers near the Rocky Mountains in present-day Alberta. For part of their history, the Sarcees were members of the Blackfoot Confederacy. The Sarcee band has its headquarters at Calgary, Alberta. Their name means "not good" in the BLACKFOOT dialect of ALGONQUIAN.

sash   A band or strip worn around the waist or over the shoulder. Indians have worn sashes for decoration and for ceremonial purposes, often adding quillwork or beadwork designs. Sashes woven in bright geometric colors are typical of EASTERN INDIANS, and were sometimes wrapped around the head as TURBANS. Sashes also were used to decorate weapons. (See also BELT.)

Satsop See SALISHAN.

Saturiwa See TIMUCUA.

Sauk See SAC.

Sauk-Suiattle A subtribe of the SKAGIT Indians, comprising the Sauk band on the Sauk River and the Suiattle band on the Suiattle River in present-day Washington. Tribal members hold the Sauk-Suiattle Indian Reservation, with tribal headquarters at Darien, Washington.

Saulteaux See CHIPPEWA.

"savage" The term savage, or *sauvage* in French, has been used ETHNOCENTRICALLY in many historical writings to refer to Native Americans, despite the fact that in any warfare fighters on both sides demonstrate "savage" behavior. *Siwash*, meaning "Indian" in the CHINOOK JARGON, derives from the French word.

saw Indians chipped notches into stone to make saws for cutting wood, bone, and other materials. They also placed sand between the material to be cut and a second material, making the cut through abrasion. Water sometimes was added as a lubricant while sawing.

Sawokli See CREEK; MUSKOGEAN.

scaffold burial A BURIAL on a wooden platform, with roofing sometimes added. Typical of PLAINS INDIANS, PRAIRIE INDIANS, NORTHWEST COAST INDIANS, and SUBARCTIC INDIANS. (See also TREE BURIAL.)

Scalp Dance (Victory Dance) A dance performed by women after the men had returned from a successful war party. (See also WAR DANCE.)

scalping The cutting of a small, circular portion of the skin and hair from the top of the human head. Scalping mistakenly has come to be associated with all North American Indians. Scholars disagree on just how widespread the practice was before the coming of whites, or whether it was practiced at all. In any case, the custom spread after various wars of the 17th and 18th century, during which white officials placed a bounty on Indian scalps, because they were easier to transport than heads. Certain tribes developed customs and TABOOS concerning the taking of scalps. In some instances, the scalp was given back to the enemy to shame him. (Scalping is not necessarily fatal.) A second person—not always the victim's opponent in battle—sometimes took the scalp, since for some tribes scalp-taking was one way to count COUP. Although not all scalps were kept as TROPHIES, some were prepared for that purpose or for OFFERINGS by stretching them on a small hoop and drying them; the hair was braided and decorated with ornaments; the skin side was painted red or red and black. (See also SCALP DANCE.)

scalplock A lock of hair on an otherwise shaved head. (See also ROACH.)

scarification The cutting of human skin for the purpose of producing a scar. Certain tribes practiced scarification for cosmetic purposes, a kind of TATTOO; others created scars as a RITE OF PASSAGE to prepare individuals for future suffering. (See also BLOODLETTING.)

Schaghticoke (Schagticoke, Scaticook) A subtribe of the PEQUOT Indians, located on the Housatonic River in present-day Connecticut. Tribal members hold the Schaghticoke Indian Reservation in Litchfield, Connecticut. The New England Coastal

Schagticoke Indian Association operates out of Avon, Massachusetts. *Schagticoke* means "at the river fork" in ALGONQUIAN.

"schmoehawk" A derogatory term used by Native Americans for a non-Indian who poses as an Indian for profit.

scout A person sent out to gather information; scouts also served as GUIDES, trackers, and INTERPRETERS. "Indian scout" in historical writings refers to Native Americans scouting for the army. In 1866, the federal government's War Department created the U.S. Indian Scouts, a force not to exceed 1,000, to serve as scouts and hunters. Many PAWNEES and CROWS (Absarokees) were recruited. Many MOUNTAIN MEN ended up scouting for the army and for migrants westward. (See also TRACKING.)

scraper A tool for scraping wood, bone, hide, and other materials. Various sharp pieces of stone, bone, or shell having wide edges could be used, but some were specially shaped and had elaborate handles. KNIVES, ADZES, and GOUGES were sometimes used for scraping as well. (See also FLESHER.)

scrimshaw A process of decorating shell, bone, or ivory by means of ENGRAVING, then rubbing ink or pigments into the incised lines; or the work itself. The term, originally applied to ivory carved by whalers, is now commonly used for carvings by INUITS in ivory and bone.

sculpture Traditional Native American figurines and other ceremonial objects are often referred to as "sculpture" because they display a strong esthetic. Other Indian STONEWORK, WOODWORK, BONEWORK, SHELLWORK, etc., even when utilitarian, can be categorized as such because of its creativity and expressiveness. Contemporary Indian sculptors work in the sculptural arts with both traditional and modern materials.

sealing dart A weapon for hunting seals with a barbed head on a four- or five-foot shaft; typical of the INUITS. (See also BLADDER DART.)

seal killer A round stone tied to a leather thong, or encased in rawhide netting, for the purpose of killing seals after harpooning; typical of the INUITS.

seal scratcher A device with prongs, sometimes with actual seal claws attached to the tips, used for scratching ice in order to imitate the sound of a seal at a breathing hole and lure seals or other game; typical of the INUITS.

sea mammal (marine mammal) Any of various mammals living in the ocean, such as species of WHALES, dolphins, walruses, seals, and sea lions; a staple of ARCTIC PEOPLES and NORTHWEST COAST INDIANS. The INUITS call sea mammals *puiji*, meaning "those who show their noses," because mammals surface to breathe, unlike fish.

Secotan An ALGONQUIAN-speaking tribe of the NORTHEAST CULTURE AREA, located on the peninsula between Albemarle Sound and the Pamlico River and on nearby islands in present-day North Carolina. The Secotans, who were known to whites only in the late 1500s, probably were ancestors of the HATTERAS, Machapunga, and Pamlico Indians, who came to inhabit the same region. *Secotan* possibly means "burned place."

secret society A SODALITY, with exclusive membership, a common purpose, and particular ritual. Some tribes have many different societies; the majority are made up of men only, but some are exclusively for women and others for both sexes. The term usually refers to clubs of a predominantly religious nature, often surrounding HEALING rituals, i.e., a MEDICINE SOCIETY as opposed to a MILITARY SOCIETY, the latter being organized around war rituals. "Dance society" ("dancing society") also is used, since secret societies have special dances. "Ceremonial society" and "religious society" are other variations found in writings about

Native American religion. "Shamans' society" applies specifically to NORTHWEST COAST INDIANS. Functions of secret societies include passing knowledge of tribal mythology, protecting sacred objects, and preserving tribal records. Membership is usually for life, following an elaborate INITIATION ritual.

sedentary A way of life in which people live in permanent villages. Most sedentary tribes practiced agriculture. "Sedentism" is a noun form referring to the practice of living most of the time in settled communities. "Sedentary" is the opposite of NOMADIC.

Seechelt (Sechelt, Sishiatl, Siciatl) A SALISHAN-speaking tribe of the NORTHWEST COAST CULTURE AREA, located on Jervis and Seechelt inlets and on Nelson and Texada islands in present-day British Columbia. A band known as Sechelt operates out of Sechelt, British Columbia.

seed jar (seed bowl) A POTTERY vessel with a round base, high shoulder, flat top, and small opening in the center, designed for holding seeds; found at archaeological sites of the ANASAZI CULTURE.

seine A long net for fishing that hangs vertically in the water, with FLOATS on top and SINKERS on the bottom.

Sekani An ATHAPASCAN-speaking tribe of the SUBARCTIC CULTURE AREA, located on the upper Peace and Liard rivers and the nearby western slopes of the Rocky Mountains in present-day British Columbia. The Fort Ware, Ingenika, and McLeod Lake bands maintain tribal identity in their ancestral homeland. *Sekani* means "dwellers on the rocks."

self-determination A tribal and governmental policy calling for Indian self-government, self-sufficiency, and cultural renewal. In 1975, the U.S. federal government's Indian Self-Determination and Education Assistance Act called for maximum tribal participation in federal programs, refuting the policies of TERMINATION. (See also RESTORATION; SOVEREIGNTY.)

self-torture See SCARIFICATION; TORTURE.

Semiahmoo A SALISHAN-speaking tribe of the NORTHWEST COAST CULTURE AREA, located along Semiahmoo Bay in present-day northwestern Washington and southwestern British Columbia. The Semiahmoo band operates out of Surrey, British Columbia.

Seminole A MUSKOGEAN-speaking tribe of the SOUTHEAST CULTURE AREA, located in present-day Florida. The original Seminoles migrated southward from present-day Georgia and Alabama in the 1700s, breaking off mostly from CREEK Indians, especially the EUFAULA band, as well as from the ALABAMA, CHIAHA, HITCHITI, OCONEE, YAMASEE, and YUCHI tribes. Other local tribes are thought to have merged with these groups. The Seminoles settled on the Apalachicola River in northern Florida and in central Florida in present-day Alachua County, with scattered groups along both coasts. Starting in the 1830s, while some Seminoles were forced to relocate to the INDIAN TERRITORY, others hid out to the south in Everglades country, permanently making their home in that region. In Florida, tribal members hold the Big Cypress Reservation in Hendry County; Brighton Reservation in Glades County; Seminole Reservation in Broward County; and Miccosukee Reservation in Dade County. In Oklahoma, Seminoles hold trust lands in Seminole County. *Seminole* means "one who has camped away from the regular towns" or "runaway in Muskogean." (See also MICCOSUKEE.)

Seminole doll A doll made by the SEMINOLE Indians out of PALMETTO, having a brightly colored patchwork and RIBBONWORK dress.

Seneca An IROQUOIAN-speaking tribe of the NORTHEAST CULTURE AREA, located between Lake Seneca and Genesee River in present-day western New York. The Senecas are part of the IROQUOIS LEAGUE. Tribal members hold the Allegheny Reservation (with the CAYUGAS) near Salamanca, New York; the Cattaraugus Reservation near Irving; and the Oil Spring Reservation near Cuba Lake. Another group, the Tonawanda Band of Seneca Indians holds the Tonawanda Reservation near Basom, New York. *Seneca* is a Latinized version of the Iroquoian word *Osininka*, meaning "people of the stone." The Seneca native name is *Nundawaono*, meaning "people of the great hill."

Senijextee See LAKE.

sept See CLAN.

serape A blanket or shawl, usually of brightly colored wool, worn as a wrap by Spanish Americans and adopted by the NAVAJO Indians. (See also PONCHO.)

serpent See SNAKE.

Serrano A UTO-AZTECAN-speaking tribe of the CALIFORNIA CULTURE AREA, located in the San Bernardino and San Gabriel mountains and southward along part of the Mojave River and into the Mojave Desert of present-day California. The San Manuel Band of Mission Indians, holding the San Manuel Reservation in San Bernardino County, has Serrano ancestry. *Serrano* is Spanish for "mountaineers." (See also MISSION INDIANS.)

setline (trawl line, trotline) A long fishing line supporting a series of shorter lines with baited hooks (set hooks).

sewan Dutch for shell-beads or WAMPUM, derived from the ALGONQUIAN term *siwan*, meaning "loose or scattered."

Sewee See SIOUAN.

shaganappi (shaganappy, shaggunappy, shaggineppi) Thong, cord, or thread of RAWHIDE; derived from the CREE dialect of ALGONQUIAN. A corresponding word to BABICHE. The METIS made harnesses with *shaganappi* for their Red River carts used to haul fur.

Shahaptian See SAHAPTIN.

Shaker Religion See INDIAN SHAKER RELIGION.

shaking tent (conjuring lodge) A small BENT-FRAME structure of saplings covered with bark, hide, mats, or textiles, used for a divinity rite. RATTLES were tied to the frame. After a SHAMAN had entered, the coverings were put in place. The shaking and swaying motion created by the shaman as he made contact with the SPIRIT WORLD gave the structure its name. Tribal members questioned the shaman while he was inside. One sees the terms "Shaking Tent Ceremony" and "Shaking Tent Shaman." Typical of the CHIPPEWAS, CREES, and other ALGONQUIANS.

Shakori See SIOUAN.

Shalako Festival (House Blessing Ceremony) A ceremony of the ZUNI Indians, held annually in late December or early November. Various SECRET SOCIETIES participate, including the KOYEMSHI, also known as MUDHEADS. The series of rituals include the impersonation of *kokos* (KACHINAS); the blessing of homes; races; music; and dances, such as the all-night Shalako Dance.

shaman A mediator between the world of SPIRITS and that of humans and animals; a tribal member who interprets and attempts to control the supernatural, using his powers to bring success in food gathering and warfare and to cure the sick. Shamans also are the keepers and interpreters of tribal lore and sometimes act as CHIEFS, their religious functions and political power varying from tribe to tribe. Shamans use herbal remedies as well as "suggestion cures," such as sleight-of-hand, to make a patient believe that a foreign substance was extracted from his or her body. "Shaman," although basically a synonym of MEDICINE MAN or medicine woman, is now preferred by many scholars because of the latter's limiting concept of HEALING implied by MEDICINE. A shaman who uses his skills to practice "bad medicine (or magic)" as opposed to "good medicine (or magic)" might be referred to as a SOR-CERER, WITCH, wizard, or necromancer. *Shaman* is thought to be a Tungusic word, referring to religious leaders and healers. (The Tungus were a Mongoloid people of eastern Siberia.) "Shamanic" is the adjective form. (See also BEAR DOCTOR; CACIQUE; DIAGNOSTICIAN; HAND-TREMBLING; PRAC-TITIONER; PRIEST; PROPHET; SHAMANISM; STARGAZING; SUCKING DOCTOR.)

shamanism The religion of peoples of northern Europe, Asia, and Oceania as well as North America in which the unseen world of deities, LEGENDARY BEINGS, and ancestor SPIRITS is considered responsive to SHAMANS. Shamanism has elements of ANIMISM. "Shamanistic" is the adjective form.

shamans' society See SECRET SOCIETY.

sham battle (sham warfare) A battle held for training and entertainment. Among the AZTECS, sham battles were part of religious festivals. Among the MANDANS and other PLAINS INDIANS, experienced warriors would lead youths in competitions. The CREEKS conducted sham battles against ef-figies of their enemies.

shape shifter A human or legendary being believed to possess the ability to transform its physical appearance, taking on the iden-tity of different animals. The legendary be-ings known as TRICKSTERS are thought to practice shape-shifting. (See also SKIN-WALKER; WITCH.)

shard See POTSHERD.

Shasta A SHASTAN-speaking tribe of the CALIFORNIA CULTURE AREA, located on the Klamath, Scott, and Shasta rivers in present-day northern California and on the Stewart River and Little Butte Creek in present-day southern Oregon. Some Shasta descendants settled on the Grande Ronde Reservation (now the Grande Ronde Indian Commu-nity); others merged with the ACHOMAWIS. A group known as the Shasta Tribe is cen-tered in Yreka, California.

Shastan (Sastean) A language family and subdivision of the HOKAN phylum compris-ing dialects spoken by the Konomihu, Ok-wanuchu, and SHASTA tribes of the CALIFORNIA CULTURE AREA.

Shawl See REBOZO.

Shawnee (Shawanese, Savannah, Chaoua-non) An ALGONQUIAN-speaking tribe of the NORTHEAST CULTURE AREA, located on the Cumberland, Ohio, and Tennessee riv-ers in present-day Tennessee, Ohio, West Virginia, and Kentucky. Comprising a num-ber of bands that migrated often, the Shaw-nees also had temporary villages in present-day southern Indiana and Illinois; present-day western Maryland, Virginia, Pennsylva-nia, and New York; and present-day north-ern South Carolina, Georgia, and Alabama. In the 1800s, they were relocated to present-day Kansas and Missouri, then to the IN-DIAN TERRITORY. Some Shawnees also mi-grated to Texas. Tribal members hold trust lands in Pottawatomi, Cleveland, and Ot-tawa counties, Oklahoma. Others hold the Eastern Shawnee Reservation near Seneca, Missouri. The Shawnee Nation United Remnant Band is centered in Dayton, Ohio. *Shawnee* means "southerners" in Algon-quian.

sheep Any of various ruminant mammals of the genus *Ovis* especially the domesti-cated *O. aries.* The Spanish introduced sheep-raising to the Indians. The NAVAJOS and other SOUTHWEST INDIANS have become known for their herds, which they breed for wool.

Sheepeater A band of BANNOCKS and SHOSHONES, living in the Salmon River Mountains of present-day central Idaho in the middle to late 1800s.

shell See SHELLFISH; SHELLWORK.

shellfish Any aquatic animal having a shell, including both mollusks and crustaceans such as clams, oysters, crabs, lobsters, mussels, and crayfish. Shellfish have been important to Indian peoples living near water for food and for their shells. (See also SHELL-HEAP; SHELLWORK.)

shell hair pipe See HAIR PIPE.

shell-heap (shell midden) A refuse pile, or MIDDEN, resulting from the consumption of SHELLFISH as food. Such concentrations of deposited shells, especially clams and oysters, have been located on seashores, tidewater bays, and inlets; there are also deposits along rivers, consisting especially of mussels. These shell MOUNDS have been known to cover 20 acres. Fish bones and artifacts sometimes are found within the mounds, as are the remains of FIREPITS. Indians often used the shell material in the construction of burial mounds and temple mounds and for fortifications.

shell trumpet A spiral conch shell from a marine gastropod that makes a trumpetlike sound when blown. MESOAMERICAN INDIANS, CIRCUM-CARIBBEAN INDIANS, and SOUTHEAST INDIANS used shell trumpets as signals in warfare. AZTEC priests used them in rituals.

shellwork The act, process, or resulting artifact of work in shell, the hard outer casing of certain animals, especially SHELLFISH. Native Americans made tools, ornaments, and ceremonial objects out of shells. Some seashells, chosen for their beauty,

were crafted—cut up, trimmed, ground, drilled, and polished—and used as jewelry or as a form of APPLIQUÉ. Shells also were engraved with designs. The bony shells of TURTLES were used to make RATTLES and other objects. (See also BEADWORK; DENTALIUM; RUNTEE; WAMPUM.)

shelter The most general term for a place of abode; sometimes used interchangeably with DWELLING and HOUSE, but it also can refer to a refuge from the natural elements, such as a CAVE or rock overhang, i.e., rock shelter.

sherd See POTSHERD.

shield A defensive weapon, worn on the arm to ward off blows or projectiles. PLAINS INDIANS and SOUTHWEST INDIANS made shields of RAWHIDE stretched over a wooden frame. Some PUEBLO INDIAN crafted shields out of BASKETRY. The typical Plains Indian shield, for use on horseback, was round and about 12 to 20 inches in diameter, with two leather covers, both painted. The inside cover was exposed only in warfare. Ornaments, especially feathers, were added. A shield was considered a sacred possession (Sacred Shield), its design determined in dreams: The paintings on

Arapaho shield

shields served as a link between the natural and spiritual worlds, pointing to mystical places and were intended to offer magical protection to the bearer. Some shields were crafted for ceremonial purposes. Few EASTERN INDIANS used shields, although some tribes, such as the IROQUOIS, were known to fashion them from bark or woven willow. NORTHWEST COAST INDIANS, although they wore ARMOR, rarely used them. The AZTECS had shields covered with feather mosaics.

Shield and Spear Dance A modern derivative of traditional dancing, performed at intertribal POWWOWS by two male dancers, each holding a shield and spear.

Shinnecock A subtribe of the MONTAUK Indians, located on southern Long Island in present-day New York, from Shinnecock Bay to Montauk Point. Shinnecocks hold the Shinnecock Reservation near Southampton, New York. Their name derives from the ALGONQUIAN word *Shinne-auk-ut*, meaning "at the level land."

shinny A hockeylike game, played with a curved stick and ball usually by women of many North American tribes. The CHEYENNE name in ALGONQUIAN is *ohonistuts*. (See also DOUBLE-BALL.)

shirt The shirt, clothing for the upper body, is most common to Native Americans in northern climates. A widespread PLAINS INDIAN design consisted of two deerskins sewn together at the shoulders and tied at the sides, with flaps for sleeves. PLATEAU INDIANS and EASTERN INDIANS had shirts sewn together at the shoulders, sides, and under the arms. SOUTHWEST INDIANS wore a COTTON shirt, made from a rectangular piece of cloth with a hole for the head and tied together at the sides, in some cases with additional rectangular pieces attached for sleeves. Plains Indian war shirts had symbols on the front for victory and on the back for protection. Often they were fringed, some-

times with hair offered by women and occasionally with TROPHIES from a slain enemy. (See also GHOST SHIRT.)

Shoshone (Shoshoni) A UTO-AZTECAN-speaking tribe of the GREAT BASIN CULTURE AREA. The tribe is subdivided into the Northern Shoshones (Wind River, Snakes) in present-day western Wyoming, eastern Idaho, and northeastern Utah, and the Western Shoshones in present-day central and northeastern Nevada, central and western Idaho, northwestern Utah, and eastern California. The Snake River in present-day Idaho is considered the heart of Shoshone territory. In California, tribal members share the Big Pine Reservation near Big Pine, Bishop Indian Reservation near Bishop, Fort Independence near Independence, and Lone Pine Reservation near Lone Pine with PAIUTES. In Idaho, Shoshones share the Fort Hall Reservation near Fort Hall with BANNOCKS and BLACKFEET. In Idaho and Nevada, Shoshones share the Duck Valley Reservation near Owyhee with Paiutes. In Nevada, tribal members hold the Duckwater Reservation near Duckwater; Ely Indian Colony near Ely; Fallon Reservation and Colony (with Paiutes) near Fallon; Ruby Valley (Te-Moak) Reservation near Elko; South Fork Indian Colony near Lee; and Yomba Reservation near Austin. In Nevada and Oregon, Shoshones share the Fort McDermitt Reservation with Paiutes. In Utah, Shoshones hold the Washakie Reservation. In Wyoming, Shoshones share the Wind River Reservation near Fort Washakie with ARAPAHOS. The Northwestern Band of Shoshone Nation operates out of Rock Springs, Wyoming; and the Northeastern Band of Shoshone Indians is centered in Brigham City, Utah. (See also GOSHUTE; SHEEPEATER.)

Shoshonean A language family comprising dialects spoken by the COMANCHE; HOPI, PAIUTE, SHOSHONE, and UTE tribes. Most scholars now place Shoshonean in a larger linguistic family known as UTO-AZTECAN.

shovel See SPADE.

shrine A holy place, where legendary events once occurred and where ceremonies are held repeatedly. The term shrine generally is used for a permanent place of worship, whereas ALTAR is more often used for a structure or object that can be moved. (See also SACRED SITE; TEMPLE.)

shrunken head See HEAD-SHRINKING.

Shuswap A SALISHAN-speaking tribe of the PLATEAU CULTURE AREA, located on the middle Fraser and upper Columbia rivers in present-day British Columbia. The Shuswaps were the largest Salishan tribe in Canada. Several bands continue to live in their ancestral homeland.

sib A relative by blood; also, a group consisting of persons descended from a common ancestor, among whose members marriage is forbidden. Sibs are therefore EXOGAMOUS. CLAN has been used as a synonym of "sib"; in discussion of KINSHIP, anthropologists have to make distinctions between such terms. (See also CONSANGUINITY; MOIETY; PHRATRY.)

Sicangu See BRULE.

sierra A mountain range, typically with a jagged, irregular profile. The Spanish word originally meant a "saw."

sign Evidence of human or animal presence on a trail. In TRACKING, the tracker "reads sign." A "sign" is also a gesture in SIGN LANGUAGE.

signal A means of communication from a distance. Indians used a variety of signals, such as starting fires, making puffs of smoke, shooting fire-arrows, waving blankets, throwing dust in the air, flashing mirrors, walking or riding in certain patterns, and drawing figures in the ground, on trees, or on rocks. (See also SMOKE SIGNAL.)

sign language A communication system of hand and arm gestures used by tribes of differing languages. Gestures, or combinations of gestures, stood for objects and ideas. Each tribe had a representative SIGN. Typical of PLAINS INDIANS.

Sihasapa (Blackfoot Sioux, Blackfeet Sioux) A subtribe of the TETON division of the SIOUX Indians, located near the Grand River in present-day South Dakota and ranging throughout the Northern Plains, especially in present-day North Dakota, Montana, Wyoming, and Nebraska. *Sihasapa* means "black feet" in SIOUAN, referring to black moccasins.

Siksika See BLACKFOOT.

sila The Air Spirit of INUIT tradition, associated with the weather. To some Inuit peoples, *sila* is a personified deity, the Creator of Life; to others it is an all-pervasive spirit, manifesting itself in many forms.

Siletz a SALISHAN-speaking tribe of the NORTHWEST COAST CULTURE AREA, located on the Siletz River in present-day Oregon. The Siletz were the southernmost of the Salishans. Tribal members now share the Siletz Reservation near Siletz, Oregon, with other Salishans.

silver Malleable, ductile, and capable of a high polish, silver is one of the most highly valued metals. Coin silver is obtained by melting down coins. (See also GERMAN SILVER; MINING; SILVERWORK.)

silverwork The act, process, or resulting artifact of work in SILVER. A silversmith makes silverwork. In pre-Contact times, silverwork, although typical of MESOAMERICAN INDIANS and SOUTH AMERICAN INDIANS, was rare north of Mexico, although some nuggets and silver-plaited objects have been found in MOUNDBUILDER sites. Since Contact, various North American tribes have taken up the art, originally taught to the NAVAJOS in the mid-1800s by the Spanish and passed to the PUEBLO INDIANS. The IROQUOIS also are known for their silverwork.

Sinagua Culture A cultural tradition of the American Southwest, lasting from about A.D. 500 to 1350, reaching a peak in about 1100. The Sinagua Indians, or Sinaguans, were centered along the Verde River of present-day central Arizona, where the soil had been enriched by ash from the eruption at Sunset Crater. They are considered a hybrid culture, learning their farming techniques from peoples of the HOHOKAM CULTURE and ADOBE building techniques from peoples of the ANASAZI CULTURE. Montezuma Castle and Tuzigoot are Sinagua CLIFF-DWELLINGS. The soil eventually became depleted and Sinagua groups left the Verde Valley. Those who migrated to Hohokam territory established the SALADO CULTURE.

sinew (tendon) The fibrous tissue that connects a muscle to bone in mammals. Indians used the tendons, especially from both sides of the backbone of the BUFFALO, DEER, or other large mammals, for sewing material or to make cord and fishing line. It was dried, then shaped and softened by pounding, chewing, shredding, and twisting. Because of its strength and elasticity, it was added to BOWS.

sinew twister A tool for twisting and tightening SINEW when adding it to the backs of BOWS.

sing A rite in which one or several SONGS are performed; or, more commonly, in the verb from, making music with the voice. A singer among the NAVAJOS is a specialized PRACTITIONER whose knowledge of songs and chants is applied in HEALING.

single pole ball-game A sport of the CREEKS and SEMINOLES, in which one must hit a cow's skull or a fish effigy figure placed at the top of a pole with a ball. Using two sticks to drive the ball, men play against women, who use their hands to throw the ball.

Sinkaietk See SALISHAN.

Sinkakaius See SALISHAN.

sinker A weight added to a line or NET in fishing. Indians drilled holes and cut notches or grooves in small stones for attachment to cords. Larger versions of the same are classified as PLUMMETS or ANCHOR STONES.

Sinkiuse See COLUMBIA.

Sinkyone See ATHAPASCAN.

Siouan A language family and subdivision of the MACRO-SIOUAN phylum comprising dialects spoken by Indians of the GREAT PLAINS CULTURE AREA, among them the ASSINIBOINE, CROW (ABSAROKEE), HIDATSA, IOWA, KAW, MANDAN, MISSOURI, OMAHA, OSAGE, OTO, PONCA, QUAPAW, and SIOUX tribes; and of the SOUTHEAST CULTURE AREA, among them the BILOXI, Cape Fear, CATAWBA, Cheraw, Congaree, Eno, Keyauwee (probably Siouan), Manahoac, MONACAN, Moneton, Nahyssan, Occaneechi, Ofo, PEE DEE, SANTEE (Issati), SAPONI, Sewee, Shakori, Sissipahaw, Sugeree, Tutelo, WACCAMAW, Watereee, Waxhaw, Winyaw, Woccon, and Yadkin tribes. The WINNEBAGO tribe of the NORTHEAST CULTURE AREA also spoke a Siouan dialect.

Sioux (Dakota, Lakota, Nakota) A SIOUAN-speaking tribe of the GREAT PLAINS CULTURE AREA. The original homeland of the Sioux was on the upper Mississippi River in present-day Minnesota. In the 1600s, Sioux Indians held territory in what is now the southern two-thirds of that state as well as neighboring parts of present-day Wisconsin, Iowa, and North and South Dakota. By the mid-1700s, some bands were migrating westward across the Missouri River. The SANTEE Sioux (Dakota) stayed along the

Minnesota River in present-day Minnesota. They include the MDEWAKANTON, SISSETON, WAHPEKUTE, and WAHPETON bands. The YANKTON Sioux (Nakota) settled along the Missouri River in present-day southeastern South Dakota, southwestern Minnesota, and southwestern Iowa. They include the Yankton band. The YANKTONAI Sioux (Nakota) settled along the Missouri in present-day eastern North and South Dakota. They include the HUNKPATINA and Yanktonai bands as well as the ASSINIBOINES, who split off from other Yanktonais in the 1600s. The TETON Sioux (Lakota) made their new home in the Black Hills region of present-day western South Dakota, eastern Wyoming, and eastern Montana. They include the BRULE (Sicangu), HUNKPAPA, SANS ARCS (Itazipco), MINICONJOU, OGLALA, OOHENONPA, and SIHASAPA bands. In Minnesota, Sioux Indians now make up the Lower Sioux Indian Community near Morton (Santee); Prairie Island Reservation near Welch (Santee); and Shakopee Mdewakanton Sioux Community near Prior Lake (Santee). In Montana, tribal members (Teton and Yanktonai) share the Fort Peck Reservation near Poplar, Montana with Assiniboines. In Nebraska, Sioux hold the Santee Sioux Reservation near Niobrara (Santee). In North Dakota, Sioux hold the Devil's Lake Sioux Reservation near Fort Totten (Santee and Yanktonai). In North Dakota and South Dakota, Sioux hold the Standing Rock Reservation near Fort Yates (Teton, Yankton, and Yanktonai). In South Dakota, tribal members hold the Cheyenne River Reservation near Eagle Butte (Teton); Crow Creek Reservation near Fort Thompson (Yanktonai); Flandreau Santee Sioux Reservation near Flandreau (Santee); Lower Brule Reservation near Lower Brule (Teton); Pine Ridge Reservation near Pine Ridge (Teton); Rosebud Reservation near Rosebud (Teton); Sisseton-Wahpeton Reservation near Agency Village (Santee); and Yankton Sioux Reservation near Marty (Yankton). The Little Shell Band of the North Dakota Tribe operates out of Dunseith, North Dakota. In

Alberta, Sioux belong to the Alexis, Paul (with the CREES), and Stoney bands. In Manitoba, Sioux belong to the Birdtail Sioux, Dakota Plains, Dakota Tipi, Oak Lake Sioux, and Sioux Valley bands. In Saskatchewan, Sioux belong to the Carry the Kettle, Moosewoods, Standing Buffalo, Wahpeton, and Wood Mountain bands. *Sioux* is the shortened form of *Nadouessioux*, a CHIPPEWA word in ALGONQUIAN for "adders" or "snakes," i.e., "enemies." The native names *Dakota* (Santee dialect), *Lakota* (Teton dialect), and *Nakota* (Yankton and Yanktonai dialects) translate as "allies." The Sioux also refer to themselves as *Ocheti shakowin*, meaning "the seven council fires" or the "seven fireplaces."

sipapu (shipapu, sipapuni, shipapulima) A small round, shallow hole in the floor of early PITHOUSES and later KIVAS, located between the FIREPIT and the wall. In PUEBLO INDIAN tradition, the opening symbolizes the center of the universe, leading to and from the SPIRIT WORLD, through which the first humans emerged, deceased people pass, and legendary beings come and go.

sisal See AGAVE.

Sishiatl See SEECHELT.

Sisseton A subtribe of the SANTEE (Dakota) division of the SIOUX Indians, located on Mille Lacs in present-day central Minnesota and later in what is now southern Minnesota and eastern South Dakota. *Sisseton* means "lake village" in SIOUAN.

Sissipahaw See SIOUAN.

Siuslaw A YAKONAN-speaking tribe of the NORTHWEST COAST CULTURE AREA, located on the Siuslaw River in present-day Oregon. Surviving tribal members were settled on the Siletz Reservation near Siletz, Oregon, with the SILETZ and other tribes. The Confederated Tribes of Coos, Lower Umpqua and Siuslaw Indians operates out of Coos Bay, Oregon. (See also COOS; KUITSH.)

Six Nations See IROQUOIS LEAGUE.

Skagit A SALISHAN-speaking tribe of the NORTHWEST COAST CULTURE AREA, located on the Skagit and Stillaguamish rivers in present-day Washington. Skagits live on the Swinomish Reservation in Skagit County, Washington, and the Tulalip Reservation in Snohomish County with SWINOMISH Indians and other Salishans; another group has rights to the Upper Skagit Indian Reservation, also in Skagit County; the SAUK-SUIATTLE subtribe holds the Sauk-Suiattle Indian Reservation.

Skidi See PAWNEE.

Skilloot See CHINOOKAN.

skin For American Indians, any skin large enough to be stripped from an animal's carcass was a natural resource valued for numerous technologies, among them the making of clothing, boats, houses, shields, masks, containers, and harnesses. The terms skin and HIDE often are used interchangeably, but "skin" is considered the more general term, with "hide" limited to the skins of larger animals, such as BUFFALO and DEER. (See also FUR; LEATHER; PELT; RAWHIDE; SKIN-DRESSING.)

Skin See SAHAPTIN.

skin-dressing The process of preparing the SKIN or HIDE of an animal for use. Different tribes had different tools and methods for fleshing (removing flesh) and dehairing (removing the hair in those instances when not preparing a FUR); different formulas and methods for soaking (soaking in grease, cooked brains, and livers is referred to as braining, brain tanning, or Indian tanning, and soaking in tannin from plant sources is called tanning); different tools and methods for stripping (squeezing out excess moisture); and different tools and methods for working (rendering the skin pliable).

skinwalker In NAVAJO tradition, a sorcerer who transforms into a werewolf; or a man who dresses as a wolf and is believed to practice WITCHCRAFT. (See also SHAPE SHIFTER.)

skirt Skirts are traditional clothing of women from some Indian tribes, rather than full DRESSES. SOUTHEAST INDIAN women fashioned wrap-around skirts that reached from the waist to the knees out of deerskin, woven animal hair, or woven inner bark. MESOAMERICAN INDIAN women fashioned wrap-around skirts of woven cotton cloth, or beaten pieces of inner bark, that reached from the waist to the calf (known as a *cueitl*). In post-Contact times, SEMINOLE women began fashioning brightly colored skirts out of RIBBONWORK. (See also APRON; DRESS.)

Skitswish See COEUR D'ALENE.

Skittagetan See HAIDA.

Sklallam See CLALLAM.

Skokomish A subtribe of the TWANA Indian, located on the Skokomish River and Annas Bay in present-day Washington. Tribal members hold the Skokomish Reservation in Mason County; Washington. *Skokomish* means "river people" in SALISHAN.

skraeling The Viking (Norse) name for Native Americans, as found in the text *Saga of the Greenlanders*, and referring probably to INUITS, but possibly to MICMACS, BEOTHUKS, or other Atlantic coastal peoples the Vikings encountered in northeastern North America from about A.D. 1000 to 1010.

Skwawksnamish See SQUAXIN.

slash-and-burn A type of farming, typical of MESOAMERICAN INDIANS, in which the ground is cleared by cutting and burning trees and undergrowth. The resulting ashes help enrich the soil. When the fields lose their fertility, they are allowed to lie fallow for a number of years.

slate A dense, fine-grained rock, metamorphosed from clay, shale, and other rocks; varying in color, but often gray to black, with a blue, purple, or green cast. Slate has the property of cleavage, breaking into thin, smooth layers. Native Americans, especially EASTERN INDIANS, used it in making tools and ornaments. One variety is known as argillite; it is quarried by the HAIDA Indians on the Queen Charlotte Islands of British Columbia. Although soft enough to carve with woodworking tools, it hardens with exposure to air and takes a polish.

Slave (Slavey, Awokanek, Etchaottine) An ATHAPASCAN-speaking tribe of the SUBARCTIC CULTURE AREA, located west of the Great Slave Lake and Mackenzie River to the Rocky Mountains, including the lower Liard River, in present-day Northwest Territories, Alberta, and British Columbia. Tribal members include the Dene Tha' Tribe in Alberta; the Fort Nelson and Prophet River bands in British Columbia; and the Fort Liard, Fort Norman, Fort Providence, Fort Simpson, Fort Wrigley, and Hay River bands in the Northwest Territories. *Etchaottine*, the CHIPEWYAN name for the tribe, means "people sheltered by willows" in Athapascan; *Awokanek*, the CREE name, means "slaves" in ALGONQUIAN.

slave killer A club, typical of the TLINGITS and other NORTHWEST COAST INDIANS, with the designated purpose of killing slaves.

slavery Slaveholding was practiced by a number of tribes in pre-Contact times, especially among MESOAMERICAN INDIANS and NORTHWEST COAST INDIANS, who carried out slave raids on other tribes. Among Northwest Coast tribes, slaves were not essential to the economy; rather, they were status symbols and might more appropri-

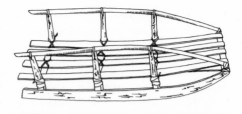

Inuit sled

ately be called CAPTIVES. ADOPTION of prisoners was a more widespread practice than slavery. In post-Contact times, some among the wealthier SOUTHEAST INDIANS kept black slaves, as their white neighbors did. The taking of slaves was a major economic impetus for the European exploration and development of the Americas, starting with the voyages of Christopher Columbus. Some tribes, such as the SEMINOLES, adopted runaway slaves into their families.

sled (sledge) A vehicle for carrying people or possessions over snow and ice; drawn by people or dogs. A sled has runners and a raised platform, as distinguished from a TOBOGGAN, the platform of which touches the frozen surface. The use of sleds was widespread among the INUITS and some SUBARCTIC INDIANS. There were many different designs; a fully equipped sled consists of runners, shoes (SLEDGE SHOES), crossbars, handles, braces, webbing, lashings, lines, traces, toggles, and packing. Many contemporary Inuits have given up the dog sled in favor of the snowmobile. (See also HUSKY.)

sledge See SLED.

sledge shoe A replaceable strip of bone, antler, or wood attached with pegs to the wooden runner of a SLED.

sling A weapon consisting of a looped strap, usually of hide, in which a small projectile, usually a stone, is whirled and thrown. Slings were also made of wood. They were used for hunting small game, especially among MESOAMERICAN INDIANS and SOUTH AMERICAN INDIANS, and by some North American tribes, such as the APACHES. The AZTECS used slings in war. "Sling" also is applied to a device strapped over the shoulder and used to carry children; the INUITS had a hide variety of this type of sling.

slip   A thin mixture of fine clay and water, and sometimes other materials, applied to the surface of POTTERY before FIRING, usually of a different color than the rest of the clay. The slip can be left as a matte finish or given a high polish. (See also GLAZE).

slit drum   See *TEPONATZLI*.

smallpox   See DISEASE.

smoke flap   The movable part of a TEPEE covering, attached to an outer pole (typically two flaps and two poles). The smoke flap is opened to control drafts and smoke through the SMOKEHOLE and closed to seal out rain.

smokehole   A hole in the top of a dwelling to allow for the escape of smoke from an open fire. TEPEES, EARTHLODGES, LONG-HOUSES, WIGWAMS, and other Indian dwellings had smokeholes.

smoke house   A name applied to the ceremonial house of the SALISHANS of the NORTHWEST COAST CULTURE AREA (Coast Salish). A long PLANK HOUSE, lined with rows of benches, it can be referred to as a big house or longhouse. The ceremonial *VAHKI*, or "rain house," of the PAPAGOS sometimes is called a smoking house.

smoke signal   The use of smoke as a long-distance SIGNAL. A person would build a fire of dry wood and add slow-burning material, such as damp grass, to create smoke. After letting the fire burn long enough to attract attention, the signaler would use a blanket to block the smoke, then remove it to create puffs. The number of puffs and length of time between them would communicate messages. Typical of PLAINS INDIANS.

smoking   The inhaling and exhaling of TOBACCO, *KINNIKINNICK*, or other dried plant matter in PIPES. Certain tribes also smoked tobacco in cigars (wrapped in tobacco leaves) or in cigarettes (wrapped in some other material, such as cane). Smoking for Indians served a ceremonial purpose and was a shared act in many COUNCILS. "Smoking" also refers to one means of FOOD PREPARATION AND PRESERVATION, in which meat and fish held on racks is exposed for a period of time to smoke from a fire.

snake (serpent)   Any of various reptiles of the suborder Serpentes, having long, legless, scaly bodies. Some Indians, such as those of the GREAT BASIN CULTURE AREA, hunted snakes for food. Snakes have been a prevalent symbol among native peoples. The Indians of the ADENA CULTURE built the effigy MOUND known as the Great Serpent Mound in the shape of a snake. Among SOUTHWEST INDIANS, the serpent is an emblem of fertility and HEALING and is associated with lightning. (See also QUETZALCOATL; SNAKE DANCE; SNOW-SNAKE.)

Snake Dance (Snake-Antelope Ceremony, Chutiva)   A RAINMAKING ceremony of the HOPI INDIANS, traditionally held every two years by each pueblo and lasting 16 days, alternating with the FLUTE CEREMONY. The preliminary ritual is held secretly inside the KIVAS. Different species of SNAKES — bull snakes, whip snakes, and rattlesnakes — are housed in a KISI. In the public part of the ceremony, participants dance with snakes in their mouths. After songs and other rites, the snakes are released at sacred locations on the edge of the village as messengers to rain gods. Other PUEBLO INDIANS also probably practiced the ceremony. The YOKUTS of California held a similar ceremony with rattlesnakes, known as *Tatu-lowis*.

Snake Indians   A name used by whites for the BANNOOKS, COMANCHES, Northern

SHOSHONES, and especially the Walpapi and Yahuskin bands of Northern PAIUTES.

snare A device to trap game, mostly small mammals and birds, usually with a rope or leather noose. Snares were common throughout the Americas, except in the GREAT PLAINS CULTURE AREA. (See also BLIND; TRAP.)

Snohomish A SALISHAN-speaking tribe of the NORTHWEST COAST CULTURE AREA, located on the lower Snohomish River and on Whidbey Island in present-day Washington. Tribal members share the Tulalip Reservation in Snohomish County, Washington, with other Salishans; others make up the Snohomish Tribe of Indians, with headquarters at Snohomish.

Snoqualmie (Snoqualmu, Snuqualmi) A SALISHAN-speaking tribe of the NORTH-WEST COAST CULTURE AREA, located on the Snoqualmie and Skykomish rivers in present-day Washington. Some descendants share the Tulalip Reservation in Snohomish County, Washington, with other Salishans; a group known as the Snoqualmie Tribe operates out of Redmond, Washington.

snow INUIT bands have many different words for snow and ice, defining all the variations and gradations from new to old and from wet to crusty. Among the Inuits of western Alaska, the Bering Sea islands, and coastal Siberia, for example, *siku* is "ice," *sallek* is "new snow," *genu* is "slush," and *duvaq* is "shore-fast ice."

"snowgo" An INUIT expression for a snowmobile.

snow goggles See GOGGLES.

snowhouse See IGLOO.

snow knife A knife having a bone or ivory blade two to three feet long, curved and wide at the end; used by INUITS to cut blocks of ice in the making of IGLOOS.

snow-pit A hole dug in the snow for hiding in order to surprise game.

snowshoe A device, typical of SUBARCTIC INDIANS and ARCTIC PEOPLES, for walking on top of deep snow; made from a racket-shaped wooden frame, BABICHE webbing, and thongs to attach the foot. Snowshoes vary significantly in shape from tribe to tribe: round, oval, elliptical, pointed, or irregular.

snow snake A game, typical of the IRO-QUOIS, in which players attempt to throw a wooden staff the greatest distance over ice, snow, or frozen ground, usually along a prepared trough. The staff, sometimes carved to represent a snake, is called snow snake as is the game itself.

soapstone (steatite) A kind of stone with a soapy texture, a variety of talc; gray, green, or brown in color; soft enough to be carved with stone tools, but hardening with exposure to air and is resistant to fire; and darkening with polishing and handling. Soapstone has been used to make BOWLS, PIPES, ornaments, and ceremonial objects throughout the Americas. Contemporary Native American sculptors, especially IRO-QUOIS, work in the material.

Sobaipuri A UTO-AZTECAN-speaking tribe of the SOUTHWEST CULTURE AREA, located on the San Pedro and Santa Cruz rivers and their tributaries in present-day Arizona. The Sobaipuris eventually merged with the PAPAGOS, of whom they originally may have been an offshoot.

social organization The structure and systems of a community. Under this general heading are grouped both political and familial relationships. (See also BAND; CASTE SYSTEM; CHIEFDOM; CITY-STATE; CLAN; CULTURE; FAMILY; KINSHIP; SOCIETY; TOWN; TRIBE; TRIBELET; VILLAGE.)

society A group or community of human beings. "Society" also can indicate the totality of social relationships. Another meaning is that of a club or SODALITY. (See also CULTURE; MEDICINE SOCIETY; MILITARY SOCIETY; SECRET SOCIETY; SOCIAL ORGANIZATION.)

sociology The study of the origin, development, organization, and function of human social groups; a branch of ANTHROPOLOGY.

sodality A club, association, or organization, often with closed membership and secret rites. (See also MEDICINE SOCIETY; MILITARY SOCIETY; SECRET SOCIETY.)

sod house (turf house) A dwelling of either stones and sod or logs and sod, depending on availability of materials. INUITS in Alaska and Greenland built permanent sod houses rather than IGLOOS, sometimes in a dome shape like the snow houses but more often rectangular. Whale ribs also were used in construction, with the guts of sea mammals as windows. (See also QARMAQ.)

sofki (sofk, sofkee, sofkey) A thin, sour corn gruel, prepared by cooking CORNMEAL in hot water and adding lye, i.e., water poured through wood ashes. Flavoring, such as hickory nuts or bone marrow, sometimes is added. Typical of the CREEKS, SEMINOLES, YUCHIS, and other SOUTHEAST INDIANS. The vessel used for cooking sofki is called a sofki dish; the large wooden spoon, usually of cypress, used for dipping in the cooking vessel and passing it communally is called a sofki spoon.

soldier An individual who serves in an army; the AZTECS and INCAS fielded large armies and had a special soldier class. "Soldier" is rarely applied to North American Indians, except in the case of "soldier society," an equivalent term for MILITARY SOCIETY, and in the case of SOLDIERS' LODGE. Because of the individualistic nature of most Indian WARFARE, WARRIOR is more often used. (See also "BLUECOAT.")

soldiers' lodge The residence of men of MILITARY SOCIETIES; used in reference to PLAINS INDIANS.

soldier society See MILITARY SOCIETY.

solstice Either of the times of year when the sun is at its greatest distance from the equator, on December 21 or 22 (winter solstice), the shortest day of the year; or June 21 or 22 (summer solstice), the longest day of the year. Many native peoples have solstice ceremonies in their religions, with the theme of renewal.

song A vocal expression using musical tones or inflections; the terms song and CHANT can be used synonymously, since chanting has musical elements as well. When there is accompaniment from MUSICAL INSTRUMENTS, however, "song" is more appropriate. Songs are an important part of Native American ritual, with words regarding many activities: hunting, farming, making tools, playing games, sleeping, courtship, healing (curative song), war, death, etc. Not all songs have words, however; some merely have vocal sounds. Some songs are sung only by an individual, such as a SHAMAN; others are performed in unison or as rounds, the entire tribe sometimes participating. Octave harmonies sometimes are used. Many songs have accompanying DANCES. The rhythm of the song can differ from the rhythm of the drum. Some songs are considered the property of CLANS, SODALITIES, or individuals; they might even be purchased. Clans and sodalities have officers whose task is to assure the proper rendition of their songs. (See also DEATH SONG; MONOPHONY; PENTATONIC SCALE; SING.)

song fight (song duel) Grudges settled by opponents singing sarcastic and satirical songs at each other. The purpose is to elicit the greatest amount of laughter from the audience. Indians also had song fights with contestants from different bands trying to remember the greater number of songs, or repeating a new song after hearing it once. (See also NITH-SONG.)

Songish (Songhees)   A SALISHAN-speaking tribe of the NORTHWEST COAST CULTURE AREA, located at the southern end of Vancouver Island in present-day British Columbia and on San Juan Island in present-day Washington. The three principal subdivisions are the Songish proper, Sanetch, and Sooke. The following contemporary bands are of Songish ancestry: Beecher Bay, Esquimault, Pauquachin, Songhees, Sooke, Tsartlip, Tsawout, and Tseycum.

soospuk   INUIT word for a stupid person or nitwit in the ESKIMO-ALEUT language.

sorcerer   A person who practices WITCHCRAFT. The name sometimes is applied to MEDICINE MEN and SHAMANS among GREAT LAKES INDIANS who practice "good medicine"; they also are called jugglers. The POTAWATOMI word in ALGONQUIAN is *chasgied.*

sorcery   See WITCHCRAFT.

sotol   Any of several tall, woody desert plants of the genus *Dasylirion,* especially *D. wheeleri,* having prickly leaves and a cluster of white flowers. The leaves were used in WEAVING and the sap for an ALCOHOLIC BEVERAGE by MESOAMERICAN INDIANS and SOUTHWEST INDIANS. "Sotol" derives from the NAHUATL word *tzotolli,* via Spanish.

soul   In discussions of Indian RELIGION, the term soul is used most often in refer to the disembodied SPIRIT of a deceased human, whereas GHOST is used for a spirit in human form. Some tribes, such as the SIOUX, believed that humans have four souls. The HIDATSAS believed that the loss of any of the souls causes sickness. Some among the INUITS believed in three souls: an immortal spirit that returns to the Spirit World at death; the life force, or BREATH OF LIFE, that expires with the person; and a "name-soul" that can be passed to others with a name. They also speak of the *INUA,* the soul shared by species. The NOOTKAS believed that the soul of a person is a tiny man. The MONTAGNAIS and NASKAPIS believed that a person's soul, the *mistapeo,* reveals itself in dreams. Some tribes associated the human soul with OWLS. (See also DOUBLE; GHOST; SOUL CATCHER.)

soul catcher   (spirit catcher, soul case)   A ceremonial object, typical of NORTHWEST COAST INDIANS, used by a SHAMAN to trap a patient's spirit or soul to aid in HEALING. Soul catchers often were carved from the femurs of bears, with abalone shell inlaid.

South American Indians   The native peoples of South America often are treated as a separate sphere of study from North American Indians. They might be touched upon in North American Indian studies because of linguistic and cultural similarities to MESOAMERICAN INDIANS and CIRCUM-CARIBBEAN INDIANS. INCA culture, for example, often is compared to that of the OLMECS, MAYAS, TOLTECS, and AZTECS. Or contemporary issues, such as those pertaining to the Brazilian rain forest, might

Haida soul catcher

bring a particular people to the public's attention. Such is the case with the Yanomani (Yanoama, Yanoamo, Shirishani) Indians of southern Venezuela and northern Brazil; nothing was known of them until mining began depleting their rain forest homeland in the 1970s; now their struggle is seen as relevant to all of humankind since the rain forest is vital to the world's oxygen supply. But, for the most part, other than at the college level, South American Indian history and culture are excluded from Native American studies. The stories of all native peoples of the Americas are, of course, interrelated. The pathway to South America for PREHISTORIC INDIANS was through North America. The complex societies of the Andes and MESOAMERICA had much in common not only among themselves, but also with North American societies, such as ANASAZI CULTURE, HOHOKAM CULTURE, ADENA CULTURE, HOPEWELL CULTURE, and MISSISSIPPIAN CULTURE. Lifeways of South American tribes shed light on lifeways of North American tribes, and vice-versa. The political and economic injustices to which peoples of both continents have been and continue to be subjected and their ongoing challenges have much in common. As for CULTURE AREAS of South American tribes, the following categories are applied: irrigation civilizations of the Central Andes; farmers and pastoralists of the Southern Andes; tropical forest village farmers; nomadic hunters and gatherers; and chiefdoms of Central America and the Caribbean. Different South American Indian language families are listed under the ANDEAN-EQUATORIAL, GE-PANO-CARIB, and MACRO-CHIBCHAN language phyla (or superstocks), with a number of particular tribes mentioned.

Southeast Culture Area The geographical and cultural region bordered on the east by the Atlantic Ocean; on the south by the Gulf of Mexico; on the west approximately by the Trinity, Arkansas, and Mississippi rivers; and on the north approximately by the Tennessee and Potomac rivers. It includes all of the following present-day states: Florida, Georgia, Alabama, Louisiana, and South Carolina; most of Mississippi, Tennessee, North Carolina, and Virginia; and parts of Texas, Oklahoma, Arkansas, Illinois, Kentucky, West Virginia, and Maryland. Since this part of North America is largely forested, the CULTURE AREA is sometimes called the Southeast Woodland Culture Area. Yet the varied physiography and vegetation includes coastal plains with saltwater marshes, grasses, and stands of cypress trees; the subtropical Everglades with jungle and swampland; the sandy soil of river valleys, plus the Mississippi floodplain; the fertile soil of the Black Belt; and the forested highlands of the Piedmont Plateau, Blue Ridge, Smoky Mountains, and Cumberland Mountains, all part of the southern Appalachian chain. SOUTHEAST INDIANS hunted and fished the abundant fauna and gathered wild plant foods, but farmed as well, growing enough crops to support sizable populations in villages along river valleys. Their mostly WATTLE-AND-DAUB houses were both rectangular and circular.

Southeast Indians Inhabitants of the SOUTHEAST CULTURE AREA, including tribes of the widespread MUSKOGEAN language family as well as ALGONQUIAN, CADDOAN, IROQUOIAN, SIOUAN, TIMUCUAN, and TUNICAN peoples. (See also CATEGORICAL APPENDIX, "TRIBES, BANDS, PEOPLES, LANGUAGES, AND CULTURES.")

Southern Cult (Southern Death Cult, Death Cult, Buzzard Cult) A tradition of the MISSISSIPPIAN CULTURE, especially in the Gulf Coast region, after about A.D. 1000 until about 1500. Death was celebrated in jewelry and other artifacts with symbols representing human SACRIFICE, including skulls, bones, buzzards, and weeping eyes.

Southwest Culture Area A geographical and cultural region in what is now the American Southwest, including most of Arizona and New Mexico, and small parts of

California, Utah, Colorado, and Texas; plus much of northern Mexico as well. This CULTURE AREA has varied topography: the rugged high country of the Colorado Plateau in the northern part, with its tablelands of flat-topped mesas separated by steep-walled canyons (the Grand Canyon, cut by the long and winding Colorado River, among them); mountain country, such as the Mogollon Mountains in New Mexico; and desert lands, including the Painted Desert along the Little Colorado River in Arizona. These different landscapes have aridity in common; the rainfall for the region ranges from less than four inches a year to less than 20. Most precipitation occurs within a six-week period in summer. Because of the extreme dryness, flora is sparse. There are three patterns of dominant growth in the Southwest, depending, on altitude and rainfall: western pine trees; PIÑON and JUNIPER trees; and MESQUITE trees; plus varying species of cactus and desert shrubs. The fauna is also scarce: mostly small mammals and reptiles, such as deer, rabbits, squirrels, mice, and lizards; and some large birds, such as eagles, hawks, and vultures. Two main ways of life evolved among SOUTHWEST INDIANS: sedentary farming and nomadic hunting and raiding. Those peoples who practiced agriculture managed to support sizable populations in permanent villages. Most Indian villages in the Southwest had what is known as PUEBLO architecture, ADOBE structures generally located on mesa tops. Some villages were located in the desert lowlands, however, or along rivers, with other types of houses, such as small pole-framed huts covered with plant matter or earth. Those who did not farm — the nomadic hunters-and-gatherers, the APACHES and NAVAJOS — supplemented their diet by raiding the PUEBLO INDIANS and other peoples for their crops. The two main kinds of houses among the nomadic peoples were brush-covered WICKIUPS and earth-covered HOGANS.

Southwest Indians Inhabitants of the SOUTHWEST CULTURE AREA. The tribes of the region can be grouped according to their different life-styles: the agricultural PUEBLO INDIANS speaking KIOWA-TANOAN, UTO-AZTECAN, KERES, and ZUNI; the agricultural desert and river peoples speaking UTO-AZTECAN, YUMAN, and KARANKAWA; and the nomadic hunting-and-raiding peoples speaking ATHAPASCAN. Other Southwest peoples include the HOKAN-speaking COAHUILTECAN Indians on the present U.S.-Mexican border plus many other Mexican Indians, such as the Concho, Huichol, Jonaz, Jumano, Opata, Pame, Seri, Suma, Tarahumare, Tepecan, Tepehuan, and Zacatec tribes. (See also CATEGORICAL APPENDIX, "TRIBES, BANDS, PEOPLES, LANGUAGES, AND CULTURES.")

sovereignty Independent authority. The issue of tribal sovereignty with regard to federal, state, or provincial governments has been in contention throughout post-Contact history. Defeat in war and displacement has led to what in effect is limited sovereignty. (See also NATION; SELF-DETERMINATION.)

spade (shovel, spud) A flat tool for turning soil. Native Americans attached wooden handles to rough-chipped blades for use as spades and HOES in farming.

spade-stone A prehistoric stone artifact, typical of MOUNDBUILDERS, with a broad, thick symmetrical blade and a stem, resembling a SPADE. Since these objects are highly polished and show little wear, they probably served a ceremonial purpose. Some have holes and can be classified as PERFORATED STONES.

spall See CHIP.

spalling A technique of architecture in which CHIPS of stones are inserted between large wall stones to fill gaps.

speaker Tribes chose those who would represent them in negotiations based on merit. Among the IROQUOIS, speakers are those who deliver ritual addresses, such as the thanksgiving address and tobacco invocation, before and during ceremonies. "Spokesman" and "talker" also are used as translations of the various tribal titles for their speakers. (See also ORATORY; STORYTELLING.)

speaker's staff See TALKING STICK.

spear A weapon with a wooden staff and a sharp POINT, usually of stone (and in post-Contact times, of iron). A spear's blade is typically larger than that of an ARROW. HARPOONS, JAVELINS, and LANCES are kinds of spears.

spear-thrower See ATLATL.

specialization The existence of full-time occupations within a society other than food gathering. AZTECS, for example, had a specialized society.

specimen A sample representative of a whole or a class of items. More specifically, a material object under study in archaeology.

spider See GRANDMOTHER SPIDER.

spindle A notched stick used in hand SPINNING onto which the thread or yarn is wound as it is spun from fibers. A spindle whorl is a perforated disk-shaped weight attached to a hand spindle to help keep it in motion; made of stone, clay, wood, or some other material.

spine-back stone A prehistoric flat stone artifact, generally of polished slate, having one end pointed and the other blunted and sloping, with a spine or knob on top, about four to six inches in length. Although the shape of whales, spine-back stones typically are found at MOUNDBUILDER sites. Sometimes they are classified with BOATSTONES.

spinning The act or process of making fiber from plants (COTTON) or animals (wool) into thread. American Indians used hand SPINDLES in pre-Contact times.

spirit A general term for many different concepts of the unseen world. A spirit can be a GHOST, a SOUL, a SPIRITUAL BEING, or the mysterious force of nature and life. Names for the all-pervasive spirit include *coen* (ATHAPASCAN); MANITOU (ALGONQUIAN); *naualak* (KWAKIUTL) ORENDA (IROQUOIS); pokunk (SHOSHONE); SILA (INUIT); *sulia* (FLATHEAD); *tirawa* (PAWNEE); WAKANDA (SIOUX); and ZEMI (ARAWAKAN). (See also ANIMISM; BREATH OF LIFE; CATEGORICAL APPENDIX, "SPIRITS AND LEGENDARY BEINGS"; DOUBLE; GREAT SPIRIT; GUARDIAN SPIRIT; SPIRIT HELPER; SPIRIT WORLD.)

spirit break (ceremonial break, line break, spirit path) In POTTERY, an interruption in the design circling the pot. Some PUEBLO INDIAN and NAVAJO pottery have such breaks in the pattern.

spirit helper SPIRITS called upon by SHAMANS to aid in HEALING and other ceremonies. (See also GUARDIAN SPIRIT.)

spirit rattle See RATTLE.

spiritual being Different terms are used when discussing the nonhuman beings that are part of the beliefs of differing peoples, including god, deity, mythological figure, mythical ancestor, supernatural being, and LEGENDARY BEING. (See also CATEGORICAL APPENDIX, "SPIRITS AND LEGENDARY BEINGS"; GHOST; SOUL; SPIRIT.)

Spirit World (Spirit Land) The place of abode after death; afterlife. Also, the place where supernatural beings dwell, a parallel dimension above, below, or beyond this one. Other terms include AFTERWORLD, other world, sky world, underworld, and first world.

splint A strip of split wood or other vegetable fiber, used in the making of BASKETS. A favored wood is the black ash tree (*Fraxinus nigra*), tough and elastic and suitable for splitting; sometimes called basket ash.

Mohawk ash-splint and sweet grass basket

IROQUOIS women make ash-splint baskets with interwoven SWEET GRASS.

Spokane (Spokan) A SALISHAN-speaking tribe of the PLATEAU CULTURE AREA, located on the Spokane and Little Spokane rivers in present-day Washington and the border area of western Idaho, and ranging into present-day western Montana. Spokanes hold the Spokane Reservation in Stevens County, Washington.

spokeshave A stone tool with a concave cutting edge used to shape and smooth wooden pieces of round diameter, such as poles and shafts. The term was first applied to the iron tool used for rounding wagon spokes.

sponsor The person who requests and provides a ceremonial event, such as a POTLATCH. It also can refer to a non-Indian individual who provides for the education of a Native American.

spool A small prehistoric object cylindrical in shape with a hole through the center like a spool, but thought to have a ceremonial purpose; usually carved out of sandstone, but sometimes crafted from baked clay, with irregular incised lines.

spoon A utensil consisting of a bowl and handle, generally larger than present-day spoons. American Indians made spoons from stone, wood, bark, gourd, shell, bone, horn, antler, ivory, basketry, and pottery. Some were simple in design; others were elaborately carved. A ladle is a deep-bowled, long-handled spoon; dippers are closer in shape to cups. In many tribes, individuals used their own spoons to eat from a communal kettle or cooking vessel. (See also SOFKI.)

sport (athletics) A GAME or contest involving athletic skill. Many sports played by children, such as ARCHERY, served as training for adult life. Many 20th-century Indians have made their mark on competitive athletics. The most famous is the SAC Indian (with FOX and POTAWATOMI ancestry, too) Jim Thorpe, who won the 1912 Olympics pentathlon and decathlon and was a baseball and football star. (See also BALL-GAME; RACING; WRESTLING.)

Squamish (Squawmish, Squawmisht) A SALISHAN-speaking tribe of the NORTHWEST COAST CULTURE AREA, located on Howe Sound and Burrard Inlet, north of the mouth of the Fraser River, and on Squawmisht River in present-day British Columbia. Contemporary bands living in their ancestral homelands use the names Burrard and Squamish.

squash Any plant of the genus *Cucurbita*, part of the GOURD family, having fleshy edible fruit protected by a hard rind; also, the fruit itself. Indians cultivated squash such as pumpkins in pre-Contact times and passed their knowledge to Europeans. The word squash derives from the NARRAGANSET word *askutasquatch* and the MASSACHUSET *askoot-asquash*, meaning "vegetables eaten green" in ALGONQUIAN. Squash was a staple of the IROQUOIS and, along with CORN and BEANS, one of the THREE SISTERS.

squash-blossom hairdo A HAIRSTYLE of HOPI girls, showing their maturity and readiness for marriage. The whorl on each side of the head represents the flower of the SQUASH, a TOTEM of the tribe.

squaw A North American Indian woman. An ALGONQUIAN-derived word: in the NARRAGANSET dialect, it is *eshqua*; in MASSACHUSET, *squa*; in DELAWARE, *ochqueu*; in CHIPPEWA, *ikwe*; in CREE, *iskwew*. The term spread via whites to Indians of other tribes. It came to be used for an Indian wife, especially a hard-working one, in servitude to her husband. Sometimes used derogatorily.

"squaw man" An expression for a non-Indian man who marries an Indian woman, or for an Indian man doing woman's work.

Squaxin (Squaxon, Squakson, Skwawksnamish) A SALISHAN-speaking tribe of the NORTHWEST COAST CULTURE AREA, located on North Bay in Puget Sound, Washington. Squaxins hold the Squaxin Island Reservation in Mason County, Washington; another band, using the Skwawksnamish version of the tribal name, shares the Puyallup Reservation with PUYALLUPS and other Salishans.

staff A pole, rod, or stick carried for a variety of purposes, such as a weapon (cudgel) or as a symbol of authority (baton). The staff of a SHAMAN also might be referred to as a wand. Staffs were made from wood, stone, bone, horn, and ivory and usually were carved and decorated. (See also CLUB; COUP STICK; HUNTING CLUB; PRAYER STICK; QUIRT; TALKING STICK; WARCLUB.)

Stalo See COWICHAN.

stamp A tool with a design on its end, used to impress a pattern on wood, leather, pottery, or metal. A dentate stamp is a comblike tool with teeth used to impress designs in clay's surface before the FIRING of pottery. (See also ROCKER STAMPING.)

staple A basic food, essential to survival. Acorns, corn, buffalo meat, deer meat, salmon, and sea mammals are examples of dietary staples for various Indian peoples.

star American Indians used the stars to determine directions and tell time. They were also an important part of Native American cosmology and mythology, personified individually and in constellations as Star People and other beings. The PAWNEES performed the MORNING STAR CEREMONY in honor of their god of vegetation. (See also STARGAZING.)

stargazing A method of diagnosing or divining illness among the NAVAJOS. The stargazer reads the sun, moon, and stars to help determine the cause of sickness and to select a series of rituals and a PRACTITIONER to cure it. (See also HAND-TREMBLING.)

steatite See SOAPSTONE.

Steilacoom (Steilacoomamish) A subtribe of the PUYALLUP Indians, located on the Steilacoom Creek in present-day Washington. The Steilacoom Tribe has its headquarters at Spanaway, Washington; some Steilacooms live on the Puyallup Reservation in Pierce County, Washington; others share the Squaxin Island Reservation with SQUAXINS and other SALISHANS.

stela (pl., stelae; stele) An upright MONOLITH or wooden slab serving as a monument, marker, or column, typically with reliefs or inscriptions; also a tablet set in the face of a building, bearing an inscription. Typical of the OLMECS, MAYAS, and other MESOAMERICAN INDIANS as well as INCAS.

stickball See LACROSSE.

stick game See GUESSING GAME.

stick dice game See DICE.

stilts Long poles with raised platforms used for walking above the ground in a game. Typical of the HOPIS, SHOSHONES, and MESOAMERICAN INDIANS.

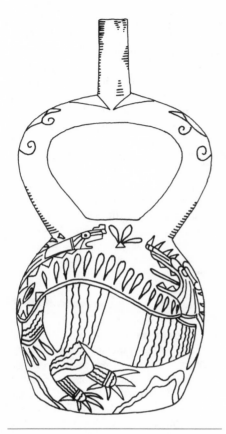

Pre-Inca stirrup spout pottery

stimulant See PSYCHOTROPIC SUB-STANCE.

stirrup spout A type of spout on POT-TERY, typical of pre-INCA Peruvian Indians, in which two ends of a semicircular tube are attached to the top of the otherwise closed container, with an opening that protrudes from the hollow loop. The spout has the shape of a stirrup.

stockade See PALISADE.

Stockbridge Indians (Housatonic) A sub-tribe of the MAHICAN Indians, located on the Housatonic River in present-day Massachusetts. Westenhook, the principal village of the Housatonic band, became the loca-

tion of the Mahican Confederacy's council fire, after it was moved from Schodac on the Hudson River in New York. Whites moved into the Housatonic Valley and established a Calvinist mission in 1736; they called the village Stockbridge and the inhabitants Stockbridge Indians. This band moved to New York among the ONEIDAS in 1785. In 1833, they relocated to Wisconsin, where, in 1856, they were granted reservation lands among the MUNSEE band of LENNI LENAPES. The Stockbridge-Munsee Reservation is in Shawano County, Wisconsin.

Stomp Dance A dance of the CREEKS and SEMINOLES, held on various ceremonial occasions in the spring and summer. The name derives from the stomping motion of the male dancers; "shell-shaker girls," wearing rattles on their legs, provide rhythmic accompaniment.

Stone Age The period of human culture marked by the use of stone tools. The Stone Age in the Americas is generally divided into the PALEOLITHIC PERIOD and ARCHAIC PERIOD. (For the rest of the world, the Stone Age is defined as the Paleolithic, Mesolithic, and Neolithic periods.) Nor did Native Americans go through a "Bronze Age" or an "Iron Age" as such; during their FORMATIVE PERIOD (or CLASSIC PERIOD), they manifested many cultural traits similar to these Bronze or Iron Age peoples.

stone-boiling A type of food preparation in which stones, known as BOILING STONES, are heated and placed in containers holding water in order to cook food, or in liquid food itself. Clay cooking balls also are used.

stonework The act, process, or resulting artifact of work in stone. American Indians, starting with PALEO-INDIANS of the STONE AGE who made tools, through contemporary artists who make SCULPTURES, have been master stoneworkers. The basic processes for shaping stone are fracturing, such as breaking and FLAKING; crumbling, such as battering and PECKING; abrading, such as scraping, grinding, drilling, and sawing; and polishing. Stonework in the building of houses and walls is known as masonry. (See also CATEGORICAL APPENDIX, "TOOLS, UTENSILS AND WEAPONS.")

Stoney See ASSINIBOINE.

story A story can be an account of an actual event, such as a battle, or a supernatural event, such as a LEGEND. STORYTELLING was ritualized by Native Americans. The terms tale and folk tale are used as synonyms.

storytelling (narrative) The spoken history, mythology, and anecdotal wisdom of a people, as ritual, entertainment, and education; part of the ORAL TRADITION of a tribe. Among the INUITS, storytelling was a way to pass long winter days. As illustration for their tales, the storytellers used story knives—usually of ivory with etched designs—to draw scenes in the snow. (See also DRAMA.)

Straight Dance (Straight-Up) A subtle, dignified style of dancing, which has evolved among PLAINS INDIANS from a number of traditional dances, and usually is performed by chiefs and elders. The opposite of FANCY DANCE.

strap drill See DRILL.

stratigraphy The branch of GEOLOGY dealing with the arrangement and succession of rock strata or layers. Or, in ARCHAEOLOGY, the method of determining the time sequence of a culture by studying the superposition and stratification of artifacts and refuse, typically with the earliest events indicated at the bottom stratum and the most recent at the top.

stroud (strud cloth, strouding) A coarse woolen cloth or blanket from England, often red or blue. Euroamericans used stroud cloth in trade with PLAINS INDIANS.

structuralism An anthropological theory that attempts to define the workings of a society in terms of the underlying principles of the workings of the human mind.

stucco A finish for walls applied wet, or a fine plaster to shape moldings or sculptures. For their stuccowork, the MAYAS used a lime plaster.

Stuwihamuk See ATHAPASCAN.

Subarctic Culture Area The geographical and cultural region stretching across northern latitudes from the Pacific Ocean to the Atlantic Ocean. The CULTURE AREA covers a vast region, including most of Alaska's and Canada's interior. What is known as the Northern Forest, or TAIGA, filled mostly with evergreen trees—pine, spruce, fir, and some birch, aspen, and willow—grows in the Subarctic. Since there is relatively little topsoil for deep root systems, the trees of the taiga generally are scraggy and short. The northern edge of the taiga borders the treeless TUNDRA of the ARCTIC CULTURE AREA. Subarctic woodlands are broken up by a network of inland waterways: large lakes, such as the Great Bear Lake, Great Slave Lake, and Lake Winnipeg; large rivers, such as the Yukon, Mackenzie, Peace, Saskatchewan, Red River of the North, and La Grande; and thousands of smaller lakes, rivers, ponds, streams, and swamps. In the western part of the Subarctic, the rolling taiga and swamplands give way to the northern Rocky Mountain chain, the Yukon Plateau, and the British Columbia Plateau. The Subarctic has long, harsh winters, during which snow covers the forests and ice covers the lakes. During the short summers, mosquitoes and black flies breed in the swamplands. Large mammals include CARIBOU, moose, musk oxen, bear, and deer; small mammals include beaver, mink, otter, porcupine, rabbits, and squirrels. There are many species of birds, especially waterfowl, and fish. SUBARCTIC INDIANS were nomadic hunter-gatherers who traveled in small bands. The most common type of house was a small cone-shape TENT covered with animal hides. LEAN-TOS of brush and leaves also were fairly common, especially in the west. Subarctic Indians did not farm.

Subarctic Indians   Inhabitants of the SUB-ARCTIC CULTURE AREA, including the ATH-APASCAN-speaking peoples to the west and the ALGONQUIAN-speaking peoples to the east. The Churchill River, flowing north-eastward into Hudson Bay, separated the peoples of these two different language families. The BEOTHUKS of Newfoundland spoke a unique language called Beothukan. (See also CATEGORICAL APPENDIX, "TRIBES, BANDS, PEOPLES, LANGUAGES, AND CULTURES.")

subtribe   A social grouping of people with language and customs in common with the larger TRIBE, but politically and geographically autonomous from it. "Subtribe" is sometimes used synonymously with "BAND." The term subdivision also is used.

succotash   A prepared dish of CORN and green BEANS, in particular string beans or lima beans, cooked together; sometimes meat is added. A corruption of the NARRA-GANSET word *msickquatash*, meaning "ear of corn" in ALGONQUIAN.

sucking doctor   (tube-sucking shaman, bone-sucking shaman)   A SHAMAN who heals the sick by sucking out the evil or illness with the mouth or with a SUCKING TUBE and by blowing onto affected areas. CHIPPEWA for "sucking doctor" in ALGON-QUIAN is *nanandawi iwe winini*.

sucking tube   (bone tube)   A bone TUBE used by a SHAMAN to suck out disease or pain in HEALING ceremonies and to blow on relief; often made from the wing bone of an EAGLE.

Sugeree   See SIOUAN.

Suiattle   See SAUK-SUIATTLE.

Sun Dance   (Medicine Dance, Medicine Lodge, Mystery Dance, New Life Dance, New Life Lodge, Offerings Lodge, Sacred Dance, Sacrifice Dance, Thirsting Dance)   An annual renewal ceremony among PLAINS INDIANS, as well as some PLATEAU INDIANS and GREAT BASIN INDIANS, in which a vow was fulfilled to a sun deity. Tribes held their annual Sun Dance—the most important of summer ceremonies—usually during a full moon in June or in late summer when berries were ripe. The bands set up their tepees in a great circle. Men and women socialized together and courted one another. They held horse races and other games. Band leaders smoked tobacco together and re-established tribal unity. The entire ceremony lasted from eight to 12 days. The numerous Sun Dance rituals are complex, many of them involving drumming, singing, and dancing. In the course of the ceremony, the Indians found and erected a sacred tree trunk—often a cottonwood, as much as 30 feet high—in the center of a sacred lodge of poles and branches. On top of the tree, they placed a figure, usually made of raw-hide. One particular ritual, coming near the end of the Sun Dance, has come to be associated with the entire ceremony above all others. Some young men had skewers implanted in their chest muscles, which were tied to the sacred pole with ropes. Blowing eagle-bone whistles and dancing to the drumbeat, they danced backwards for hours until the skewers ripped through their flesh. Others dragged BUFFALO SKULLS about the camp with similar skewers. The self-mutilation induced visions and suppos-edly brought good fortune for the entire tribe. The name Sun Dance derives from the SIOUAN *Wiwanyag Wachipi* or *wi wany-ang wacipi*, for "dance looking at the sun." Other tribes have different names. For ex-ample, the ARAPAHOS call it Offerings Lodge; CHEYENNES, New Life Lodge; the Plains CREE, Thirsting Dance; and the PON-CAS, Mystery Dance. Moreover, different tribes had different rituals. But for all those tribes who held the ceremony, the overall purposes were the same: to come into contact with the SPIRIT WORLD; to renew nature, including the sun, the sky, and the earth; to keep buffalo plentiful, thereby assuring future prosperity; to bring victory in battle; to make marriages successful; to heal the sick; and to settle old quarrels. In 1910, the federal government outlawed the Sun Dance in a policy of ACCULTURATION, giving the use of self-torture as the reason.

sunka wakan A SIOUX name for "horse" in SIOUAN (Dakota), literally "mystery dog."

Sun Watcher An individual among the HOPIS who advised his people on the yearly cycle of planting, based on the location of the sun on the horizon.

superintendent See INDIAN SUPERINTENDENT.

supernatural being See LEGENDARY BEING; SPIRITUAL BEING.

supreme being See CREATOR; GREAT SPIRIT.

Suquamish A SALISHAN-speaking tribe of the NORTHWEST COAST CULTURE AREA, located on the west end of Puget Sound. Descendants have rights to the Port Madison Reservation in Kitsap County, Washington.

surround A method of group hunting in which a herd of prey, such as BUFFALO, is encircled. Surrounds often were used to drive animals off a cliff or into a CORRAL.

Surruque See TIMUCUA.

Susquehannock (Susquehanna, Andaste, Conestoga, White Minqua) An IROQUOIAN-speaking tribe of the NORTHEAST CULTURE AREA, located on the Susquehanna River in present-day Pennsylvania and ranging up and down the river into present-day New York to the north and present-day Maryland to the south. Begin-

ning in the late 1600s, because of pressure by both the IROQUOIS and white settlers, Susquehannocks settled in both New York and Maryland before returning to the area of Paxton, Pennsylvania. They now are considered extinct.

Sutaio See CHEYENNE.

Swallah See SALISHAN.

swanneken An ALGONQUIAN name for Dutch fur traders; commonly used in the 17th century.

swastika A CROSS with the arms bent at right angles, all extended in the same direction, with each extension the same length as the parallel arm of the cross. A design and symbol common to many tribes; found in the SANDPAINTINGS of NAVAJOS. The symbolism of the swastika involves cosmological themes, such as the cyclical nature of time. In the American Indian and Asian versions, the extensions typically are counterclockwise; Germany's Nazi party made the clockwise version its symbol. The word derives from the Sanskrit word *svasti*, for "good luck."

sweat-bath See SWEATING.

sweathouse (sweat lodge, bathhouse) A structure used for SWEATING. Sweathouses generally are a dome shape and made of a variety of materials, such as saplings, branches, bark, hide, or earth. Heat can be generated with a fire in an open FIREPIT or by pouring water onto hot stones and making steam. The pits often are located just outside the sweathouse door. "Sweat lodge," used interchangeably with "sweathouse," sometimes indicates a large version that doubles as a clubhouse. Many tribes have a Sweat Lodge Ceremony, for which they have varying names.

sweating (sweat, sweat-bath) Purposeful perspiration through heat exposure. Sweating was a widespread practice among North Americans Indians as a form of ritual PURIFICATION; as a technique of HEALING; for personal hygiene and relaxation; or, in the case of communal sweats, for socialization.

sweet grass Any of various sweet-smelling grasses of the genus *Glyceria* or *Hierochloe*, used in BASKETRY, especially by the IROQUOIS, and as INCENSE.

Sweet Medicine A spiritual being and CULTURE HERO in CHEYENNE tradition. He reportedly met with Maheo, the CREATOR, on Sacred Mountain (Noaha-vose), and was given the MEDICINE ARROWS for the people.

sweet potato A tropical vine, *Ipomoea batatas*, with a thick tuberous edible root. The sweet potato was cultivated for food by SOUTH AMERICAN INDIANS, MESOAMERICAN INDIANS, and CIRCUM-CARIBBEAN INDIANS, then passed to the rest of the world in post-Contact times. In pre-Contact times, the sweet potato probably was passed from South America to Polynesia, where it became a staple crop, evidence of early transpacific voyages in an east-to-west direction.

Swinomish A SALISHAN-speaking tribe of the NORTHWEST COAST CULTURE AREA, located on Whidbey Island and at the mouth of the Skagit River in present-day Washington. Some researchers consider the Swinomish Indians a subtribe of the SKAGITS. Some tribal members settled on the Tulalip Reservation in Snohomish County with other Salishans. The Swinomish Indian Tribal Community has a reservation in Skagit County, Washington, with headquarters at La Conner. The Aboriginal Swinomish band has tribal headquarters at Friday Harbor.

syllabary A list of symbols, each one representing a syllable and not a single sound, as in the case of a true alphabet. (See also CHEROKEE ALPHABET.)

symbol That which stands for something else; a design or mark representing an object or idea. "Symbolism" is the use of symbols, as occurring in art, ritual, and communication. (See also PICTOGRAPH.)

T

Tabeguache (Uncompahgre) A subtribe of the UTE Indians, located in present-day southwestern Colorado. Descendants, known as the Ouray band after their 19th-century leader, hold the Uintah and Ouray Reservation near Fort Duquesne, Utah, along with descendants of the UINTAHS and other Ute bands. *Tabeguache* derives from the UTO-AZTECAN phrase for "people living on the warm side of the mountain."

tablita (tableta) A headdress of the PUEBLO INDIANS, sometimes attached to a mask, consisting of an upright board that is symbolically carved and painted with sky designs and decorated with feathers. In the Tablita Dance (also called the Corn Dance or Feast Dance), women wear tablitas; men wear white kilts and tasseled sashes symbolizing rain. A ceremonial pole is waved over the dancers. The dance usually is commonly held on a FEAST DAY to celebrate the corn crop. "Tablita" is Spanish-derived, meaning "tablet."

Hopi tablita

taboo A prohibition or restriction from an act or use of an object because of its sacred nature. The violation of taboos is thought to bring about misfortune and necessitates action to restore harmony. Taboos varied from tribe to tribe. Many involved reproduction and the gathering and eating of food. From the Polynesian term *tabu* or *tapu*. (See also INCEST TABOO.)

Tacatacura See TIMUCUA.

Tachi (Tache) A subtribe of the YOKUTS Indians, located north of Tulare Lake in present-day south-central California. The Tachis hold the Santa Rosa Rancheria in Kings County, California.

Tachuktu A SECRET SOCIETY of sacred CLOWNS of the HOPI Indians, the equivalent of the KOYEMSHI of the Hopis and, like them, popularly known as MUDHEADS because of the earth-colored masks worn in ceremonies.

Taensa See NATCHEZ.

Tagish A subtribe of the NAHANE Indians, located on Tagish Lake in present-day northern British Columbia and on Marsh Lake in present-day southern Yukon Territory. The Atlin band holds reserve lands in British Columbia; the Carcross-Tagish and Teslin bands in the Yukon Territory.

Tahltan An ATHAPASCAN-speaking tribe of the SUBARCTIC CULTURE AREA, located in present-day northwestern British Columbia and southeastern Alaska, especially on parts of the Stikine, Tahltan, Nass, and Taku rivers. Some scholars classify the Tahltans as a subtribe of the NAHANES. The Tahltan band holds reserve lands in its ancestral homeland in Canada.

Taidnapam   See COWLITZ; SAHAPTIN.

taiga   The coniferous forests and swamplands of the SUBARCTIC region, south of the treeless TUNDRA. The evergreen woodlands of the taiga can be referred to as BOREAL forests.

Taimé (Tai-may)   A sacred object or PALLADIUM of the KIOWA Indians, a small stone image resembling the head, shoulders, and chest of a man, adorned with feathers and painting of the sun and crescent moon. Kept in a PARFLECHE, the Taimé was taken out once a year at the tribe's annual SUN DANCE.

Taino   See ARAWAK.

Takelma (Takilma, Rogue River)   A PENUTIAN-speaking (Takelma or Takilman isolate) tribe of the NORTHWEST COAST CULTURE AREA, located on the Rogue River in present-day Oregon. The LATGAWA Indians spoke the same dialect. Takelmas share the Siltz Reservation near Siletz, Oregon, with the TUTUTNIS and other tribes. *Takelma* means "those who live on the river" in Penutian.

Takilman   See TAKELMA.

tale   See STORYTELLING.

talisman   Any object believed to contain supernatural powers and offer protection. "Talisman" can be used interchangeably with AMULET and "charm," but it generally connotes wider powers. (See also CHARMSTONE; FETISH; MEDICINE.)

Talking God   See HOLY PEOPLE.

talking stick (speaker's staff)   A staff with carvings representing family origins and tribal legends that is held as a symbol of authority and prestige during speeches; typical of the KWAKIUTLS.

Taltushtuntude (Galice Creek)   An ATHAPASCAN-tribe of the NORTHWEST COAST CULTURE AREA, located on Galice Creek in present-day Oregon. The neighboring Dakubetedes spoke a similar dialect. Both tribes were placed on the Siletz Reservation near Siletz, Oregon. Descendants of the Taltushtuntudes use the tribal name Galice Creek.

talus   Rock debris at the base of a cliff or slope; used specifically for the rocks that separate from the roofs of CLIFF-DWELLINGS and form slopes in front of them.

tamanous (tamanoas, tamanawas)   CHINOOK JARGON for anything relating to the spiritual realm, including SECRET SOCIETIES and dances.

Tamathli   See MUSKOGEAN.

Tanaina (Kaniakhotana, Kenaitze)   An ATHAPASCAN-speaking tribe of the SUBARCTIC CULTURE AREA, located north of Cook Inlet in present-day Alaska. Descendants living in their ancestral homelands use the Eklutna, Kenaitze, Knik, Iliama, Ninilchik, and Tyonek band names. *Tanaina* means "people" in Athapascan.

Tanana   An ATHAPASCAN-speaking tribe of the SUBARCTIC CULTURE AREA, located on the lower Tanana River in present-day central Alaska. The Tanana Native Village is located near Tanana, Alaska. *Tanana* means "people" in Athapascan.

tangakwunu   The HOPI word for "rainbow" in UTO-AZTECAN.

Tanoan   See KIOWA-TANOAN.

Taos Pueblo   See TIWA.

Taovayas   See TAWEHASH.

tapestry   A type of WEAVING in which threads of different colors are woven by hand across the WARP, creating a design.

tapioca   See CASSAVA.

tapir Any of the hoofed, herbivorous mammals of the genus *Tapirus*, having large heavy bodies, short legs, and a long flexible snout, found in Central and South America and in Asia. Mostly nocturnal, they spend much of their time in water. "Tapir" is from the TUPI-GUARANI word *tapira*.

Taposa See MUSKOGEAN.

Tatsanottine (Copper, Yellowknife) An ATHAPASCAN-speaking tribe of the SUBARCTIC CULTURE AREA, located on north and east Great Slave Lake in the present-day Northwest Territories. The Yellowknife band presently lives in its ancestral homeland. Like the Tatsanottines, the AHTENAS have been referred to as Yellowknife Indians and Copper Indians. *Tatsanottine* means "people of the scum of water" in Athapascan, referring to copper.

tattoo A permanent mark made on the skin by means of pricking and ingraining a pigment or by means of SCARIFICATION. A common method of tattooing was to run needles under the skin, followed by leather threads dipped in water and pigment, often charcoal; another was to cut the skin surface, then rub pigment on with a stone. Some tribes, especially in the SOUTHEAST CULTURE AREA, wore tattoos from head to foot. ARCTIC PEOPLES, SUBARCTIC INDIANS, and CALIFORNIA INDIANS also widely practiced this art, as did the MOJAVES and YUMAS of the SOUTHWEST CULTURE AREA. The purposes varied: Tattoos were used to indicate TRIBE, CLAN, FAMILY, or SODALITY; to indicate a marital relationship (as in the case of women); to show rank or deeds; to ward off sickness or injury; to frighten an enemy; or as personal adornment. "Tattoo" derives from the Polynesian word *tautau*; it can be a verb or a noun.

Tawakoni A CADDOAN-speaking tribe of the GREAT PLAINS CULTURE AREA, located on the Canadian River north of the upper Washita in present-day Oklahoma. The Tawkonis were part of the Wichita Confed-

eracy. In the 1770s, some among them moved to the Brazos and Trinity rivers in present-day Texas. In 1855, the Tawakonis were placed on a reservation near Fort Belknap on the Brazos, but, four years later, they were forced northward back into present-day Oklahoma, whereupon they merged with the WICHITAS. *Tawakoni* probably means "a river bend among red hills" in Caddoan.

Tawasa See CREEK; MUSKOGEAN.

Tawehash (Taovayas) A CADDOAN-speaking tribe of the GREAT PLAINS CULTURE AREA, located on the Canadian River north of the headwaters of the Washita in present-day Oklahoma and later on the upper Red River in present-day Texas. Some researchers consider the Tawehash Indians a subtribe of the WICHITAS (or a tribe in the Wichita Confederacy), with whom they eventually merged. The alternate name, Taovayas, has been applied more generally to both WICHITAS and CADDOS, who traded furs with the French in the mid-1700s. The name Tawehash also applies to the JUMANO Indians.

Tawiskaron (Tawiskaro, Tawiskara, Taweskare, Tawiscara) A legendary being in IROQUOIS tradition, who supposedly makes and controls the winter; the Dark One; the twin brother of TEHARONHIAWAGON. To other IROQUOIAN-speaking peoples, such as the CHEROKEES (who knew him as Tawiskala), he was associated with FLINT.

technology The body of knowledge surrounding the use of tools and making of artifacts within a society.

Tegua See TEWA.

Teharonhiawagon A LEGENDARY BEING in IROQUOIS tradition; the Master of Life and all that is good; the twin brother of TAWISKARON.

Tehua See TEWA.

Tekesta See MUSKOGEAN.

temper In POTTERY, an agent added to clay to counteract shrinkage and assure uniform drying. Sand, volcanic rock, shell, and POTSHERDS are typical additives, leading to terms such as grit-tempered and shell-tempered pottery. "Fiber temper" refers to the addition of fibrous material, such as grass, to the clay. In METALWORK, "temper" refers to a metal or combination of metals added to another metal to form an alloy. Also used as a verb to mean "modify," "moderate," or "harden" materials.

temple A building or place of worship, dedicated to one or more gods. The INCAS and some among the MESOAMERICAN INDIANS built stone temples to their deities; Indians of the MISSISSIPPIAN CULTURE built WATTLE-AND-DAUB temples with THATCH roofs on top of earthen MOUNDS.

temple mound See MOUND.

Temple Mound Culture See MISSISSIPPIAN CULTURE.

Tenino (Warm Springs) A SAHAPTIN-speaking tribe of the PLATEAU CULTURE AREA, located at the junction of the Deschutes and Columbia rivers in present-day Oregon. In 1855, the Teninos were placed on the Warm Springs Reservation near Warm Springs, Oregon, where their descendants now live under the Warm Springs tribal name; others settled among the YAKIMAS on the Yakima Reservation near Toppenish, Washington.

tent A portable dwelling made of skins or cloth supported by poles. The TEPEE of the PLAINS INDIANS is a kind of tent. The INUITS made a tent of driftwood poles and caribou hide, known as a *tupik*.

tepee (teepee, tipi) A conical TENT, typical of PLAINS INDIANS, having a pole frame

Blackfoot tepee

and covered with buffalo hides. A tepee has 13 to 20 poles, averaging 25 feet in length. Three or four main poles hold up the others. The poles are placed firmly in the ground at one end and tied together about four feet from the top at the other. The resulting circular base is about 15 feet in diameter. The covering consists of about 14 to 20 (and even 30) dressed buffalo hides (and in post-Contact times, canvas), sewn together with SINEW. About 20 wooden pegs hold the base in the ground. Stones also hold the covering in place. At the top, there is a SMOKEHOLE; adjustable SMOKE FLAPS attached to two outer poles allow the smoke from a central FIREPIT to escape. The door, a piece of hide—often from some other animal with the fur still attached, stretched on a pole or on a hoop—traditionally faces east. The ground serves as the floor; in the winter, grass is added around the bottom for insulation. A DEW CLOTH or tepee liner also provides insulation. Three or four beds are situated along the wall on either side of the door and opposite. Tepees often are painted or decorated with ornaments. The word consists of the SIOUAN roots *ti*, "to dwell," and *pi*, "used for." (See also LODGE; TEPEE RING; TRAVOIS.)

tepee circle See CAMP CIRCLE.

tepee liner See DEW CLOTH.

tepee ring A circle of stones, formerly used to weigh down a TEPEE covering and left behind after a tepee is removed.

teponaztli (slit drum) A wooden drum of the AZTECS, barrel shape with slits, creating two to five tongues of different pitch; played with rubber-tipped mallets.

Tequistlatecan A language family and subdivision of the HOKAN phylum comprising dialects spoken by Indians of the MESOAMERICAN CULTURE AREA, among them the Tluamelula and Mountain Tequistlatec (Chontal) tribes of what is now southern Mexico.

termination A policy of the U.S. federal government practiced from the late 1940s to the early 1960s, that sought to end the special protective relationship (TRUST STATUS) between the government and Indian tribes, transfer much of the responsibility for Indian programs to states, and induce RELOCATION to urban areas. Policies of SELF-DETERMINATION replaced termination. (See also URBAN INDIANS.)

terraglyph An image carved into or built upon the earth. Effigy MOUNDS are a type of terraglyph.

territory In a general sense, LAND. More specifically, a defined region that is not yet admitted as a state (or in the case of Canada, not yet admitted as a province). Historically the president appointed and the Senate confirmed the governors and other officials of territories, while their inhabitants elected their legislatures. (See also INDIAN TERRITORY.)

tesguino (tesvino, tiswin) A corn beer, typical of the Tarahumare Indians of Mexico and the APACHES, made of juices pressed from corn stalks or green corn sprouts and heated. The Apache variety in ATHAPASCAN is *tulipai*, although the words *tesguino* and

tiswin appear in writings.

Tesuque Pueblo See TEWA.

Tête de Boule See CREE.

Teton (Lakota) A subtribe of the SIOUX Indians, located in the Black Hills region of present-day western South Dakota, eastern Wyoming, and eastern Montana, and ranging throughout other parts of the Northern Plains, including present-day North Dakota and Nebraska. Teton bands include the BRULE (Sicangu), HUNKPAPA, MINICONJOU, OGLALA, OOHENONPA, SANS ARCS (Itazipco) and SIHASAPA. The Tetons can be referred to as the Western Sioux to distinguish them from the SANTEES (Dakotas), YANKTONS (Nakotas), and YANKTONAIS (Nakotas). *Teton* means "dwellers on the prairie" in Siouan. The Tetons call themselves *Lakota*, meaning "allies."

Tewa (Tegua, Tehua) A KIOWA-TANOAN-speaking tribe of the SOUTHWEST CULTURE AREA, located on the upper Rio Grande in present-day northern New Mexico. Tewa peoples lived in politically distinct PUEBLOS and are classified as PUEBLO INDIANS. One pueblo, Hano, was located in present-day eastern Arizona near the HOPIS. Tewa Indians hold the following pueblos: Nambe, Pojoaque, San Ildefonso, San Juan, Santa Clara, and Tesuque, all to the north of Santa Fe, New Mexico. Their name derives from a KERES word for "moccasins" in Keresan.

textile Any woven material. Although used to refer to cloth and clothing, the so-called textile arts broadly include WEAVING, BASKETRY, BEADWORK, EMBROIDERY, FEATHERWORK, and QUILLWORK.

Tezcatlipoca (Yoalli Ehecatl) The AZTEC god of night and darkness as well as of OBSIDIAN and the SACRIFICIAL KNIFE. A warrior god symbolized by a JAGUAR, he supposedly observed the deeds of men through a MIRROR. His name means "smoking mirror."

thanksgiving The ritual expression of gratitude, often for a successful harvest, hunt, or catch. Many tribes had special thanksgiving ceremonies or thanksgiving rituals during other ceremonies; feasting typified such celebrations. In 1621, the Pilgrims shared a thanksgiving feast with the WAMPANOAGS, who had enabled them to survive by teaching them how to plant corn and use fish as a fertilizer. The custom was adopted as a U.S. national holiday. (See also FIRST FOOD CEREMONY; HARVEST FESTIVAL; NATIVE AMERICAN DAY.)

thatch Straw, reeds, rushes, grasses, or palm fronds used to cover a DWELLING. "Thatched" is the adjective form. (See also GRASS HOUSE.)

theocracy A government in which a god or gods are considered to have supreme authority, with a powerful PRIESTHOOD. INCA, MAYA, TOLTEC, and AZTEC societies were theocratic.

Thlingchadinne See DOGRIB.

Thompson See NTLAKYAPAMUK.

Three Sisters In IROQUOIS mythology, CORN, BEANS, and SQUASH. Iroquois farmers planted the Three Sisters together on earthen hills: The corn stalks on each hill supported the vines of bean plants while the large-leafed squash plants served to block weed growth. The nonedible parts of the plants were returned to the soil as compost.

throwing board See ATLATL.

throwing stick See ATLATL; RABBIT STICK.

Thunder Beings (Thunder People, Thunder Spirits, wakinya) In SIOUX tradition, powerful spirits living in the West responsible for thunder and LIGHTNING. The SI-

OUAN name is *wakinya*. Many other tribes personified thunder in their religions. (See also HEYOKA; KETTLE DANCE.)

Thunderbird A legendary being especially in the traditions of NORTHWEST COAST INDIANS and PLAINS INDIANS, but also found in other traditions, sometimes represented as an EAGLE. When the Thunderbird flies, the flapping of its wings creates thunder; the opening and closing of its eyes create lightning; and the lake it carries on its back creates rain. A prevalent symbol in Native American design.

tie-dye A method of coloring textiles in which the material is folded, with parts tied off with a string; when DYE is applied, it does not penetrate the folded areas, but forms a pattern of the cloth's natural color against the background, which absorbs color. Typical of SOUTHWEST INDIANS, MESOAMERICAN INDIANS, and SOUTH AMERICAN INDIANS.

Tigua See TIWA.

tihu A painted representation of a KACHINA on cottonwood, given to HOPI children; considered the earliest kachina dolls.

Tihua See TIWA.

Tillamook See SALISHAN.

time cycle A repeated sequence of events. Many Native American peoples, such as the MAYAS and other MESOAMERICAN INDIANS, believed that time was cyclical rather than linear, as revealed in the movements of the sun, moon, and stars. (See also CALENDAR.)

Timotean A language family and subdivision of the ANDEAN-EQUATORIAL phylum comprising dialects spoken by SOUTH AMERICAN INDIANS, in particular the Timote tribe of present-day Venezuela.

Timucua A TIMUCUAN-speaking tribe of the SOUTHEAST CULTURE AREA, located in present-day northern and central Florida and extending into present-day Georgia and possibly Alabama. The Timucua proper can be referred to as the Utinas. The Timucuan-speaking subtribes—Acuera, Fresh Water, Icafui, Mococo, Mosquito, Ocale, Pohoy, Potano, Saturiwa, Surruque, Tacatacura, Tocobaga, and Yui—are classified by some scholars as distinct tribes. They are all extinct. The tribal name, Timucua, can be applied to all tribes of the Timucuan language family. *Utina*, meaning "powerful" in Timucuan, probably refers to a chief.

Timucuan A language family of undetermined language phylum affiliation comprising dialects spoken by the TIMUCUA tribe of the SOUTHEAST CULTURE AREA.

tinkler A small metal cone, typical of SOUTHWEST INDIANS in post-Contact times. When attached to the fringes of clothing, tinklers serve as noise makers ("jinglers") as well as ornaments. Also used as clasps on jewelry.

Tionontati See TOBACCO (Petun).

Tiou See TUNICAN.

tipi See TEPEE.

tiponi A FETISH of the SECRET SOCIETIES of the PUEBLO INDIANS, consisting of an ear of corn, piñon seeds (or seeds of other vegetables), and feathers.

Tiwa (Tigua, Tiguex, Tihua) A KIOWA-TANOAN-speaking tribe of the SOUTHWEST CULTURE AREA, located on the upper Rio Grande in present-day New Mexico. Tiwa peoples lived in politically distinct PUEBLOS and are classified as PUEBLO INDIANS. Some Tiwas inhabited northern Mexico. Tribal members hold the following pueblos: Picuris and Taos north of Santa Fe, New Mexico, and Isleta and Sandia near Albuquerque.

tlachtli (tlatchli, hip ball) A ritualized BALL-GAME of the AZTECS, developed by the OLMECS and refined by the TOLTECS, in which players tried to put a heavy rubber ball of about four pounds through a stone ring affixed to a stone projection high on a wall. They could touch the ball only with their backs, hips, and knees, and wore padding as protection. The winners won the clothing of the losers; the latter also might be sacrificed. (See also BALL-COURT.)

Tlallam See CLALLAM.

Tlaloc The TOLTEC and AZTEC god of rain, thunder, and lightning, the equivalent of the MAYA god CHAC MOOL, the Huastec god Tajin, and the Zapotec god Cocijo. The color green and JADE are associated with Tlaloc. Among the peoples of the city of Teotihuacan, he was considered the guardian of water.

Tlapanecan A language family and subdivision of the HOKAN phylum comprising dialects spoken by Indians of the MESOAMERICAN CULTURE AREA, including the Tlapanec tribe of what is now south-central Mexico; the Subtiaba tribe of what is now Nicaragua; and the Maribichicoa tribe of what is now El Salvador.

Tlingit A NADENE-speaking (Tlingit isolate) tribe of the NORTHWEST COAST CULTURE AREA, located on coastal regions and adjacent islands of present-day southern Alaska and northern British Columbia. Subdivisions include the Auk, CHILKAT, Gonaho, Hehl, Henya, Huna, Hutsnuwu, Kake, Kuiu, Sanya, Sitka, Stikine, Sumdum, Taku, Tongass, and Yakutat bands. Tlingits are united with the HAIDA Indians in the Sealaska Corporation, comprising 11 native villages and operating out of Juneau, Alaska. *Tlingit* means "people" in Nadene. The language of the Tlingits formerly was referred to as Koluschan after their Russian name, *Kolusch* or *Kolush*.

Tloque Nahuague An AZTEC god, referred to as the God of Surroundings or He Who Has Everything. Tloque Nahuague was known to the priesthood; he was not worshipped by commoners since no image was allowed of him.

tobacco Any of various plants of the genus *Nicotiana*, especially *N. tabacum* and *N. rustica*. Native Americans consider tobacco sacred and use it in many rituals and for healing purposes. It is smoked, eaten, and snuffed; burned ceremonially as INCENSE; sprinkled in the air; and tied in a small bundle and placed on an altar (tobacco tie or prayer tie). Some tribes consider tobacco the first plant passed to the people from the CREATOR and a channel to the SPIRIT WORLD. In less than a century after first contacts with whites, the use of tobacco had circled the globe, making its way to Alaska via Europe and Asia. "Tobacco" is derived from the ARAWAKAN word *tabaco*, meaning a cigarlike roll of tobacco leaves. (See also *KINNIKINNICK*; OFFERING PIPE; SMOKING.)

Tobacco (Petun, Tionontati) An IRO-QUOIAN-speaking tribe of the NORTHEAST CULTURE AREA, located south of Georgian Bay in present-day Grey and Simcoe counties, Ontario. The Tobaccos suffered attacks by tribes of the IROQUOIS LEAGUE in 1649 and afterward merged with the HURONS, the descendants of both peoples using the name Wyandot. The French referred to the tribe as *Gens du Petun* for "Tobacco Nation" because of their tobacco farming. Their native name, Tionontati, means "there the mountain stands" in Iroquoian.

tobacco bag A pouch for holding TO-BACCO.

tobacco flask (miniature canteen) A small silver container, made by SOUTHWEST INDIANS in post-Contact times for trade.

toboggan A vehicle, typical of SUBARCTIC INDIANS, for transporting people or possessions over snow or ice. Toboggans, unlike true SLEDS, have no runners; their platforms are directly on the snow. An ALGONQUIAN-derived word, passed first to the French, probably from the MICMAC *tobakan*, meaning "what is used for dragging."

Tocobaga See TIMUCUA.

Tohome See MUSKOGEAN.

Tohono O'odham See PAPAGO.

toka A Sioux word for "enemy" in SIOUAN (Lakota). It also signifies "disease"; i.e., to remove the *toka* means to "cure."

toloache See JIMSONWEED.

Tolowa An ATHAPASCAN-speaking tribe of the CALIFORNIA CULTURE AREA, located on Crescent Bay, Lake Earl, and Smith River in northwestern California. Tribal

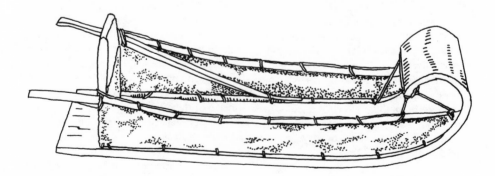

Athapascan toboggan

members hold the Big Lagoon Rancheria near Trinidad, California, with the YUROK Indians. The Melochundum Band of Tolowa Indians and the Tolowa-Tututni Tribe of Indians operate out of Fort Dick, California. (See also TUTUTNI.)

Toltec (Tolteca) A NAHUATL-speaking people of the MESOAMERICAN CULTURE AREA, located in the Valley of Mexico of present-day central Mexico. A nomadic hunting tribe, sometimes referred to as Chichimecs, they migrated from the north into the Valley of Mexico in about A.D. 900. They possibly had ties to the Mixtecs and Zapotecs. After a prolonged power struggle, the Toltecs became the most dominant tribe of the region. Adapting cultural traits of the OLMECS, MAYAS, and peoples of Teotihuacan, they developed a highly organized civilization. Tula was their central city. They erected tall PYRAMIDS, beautiful palaces with colonnaded and frescoed halls, BALLCOURTS, and other elegant stone structures; developed new strains of corn, squash, and cotton; crafted exquisite objects in gold and silver; shaped new designs in pottery; made beautiful clothing in textiles, decorated with feathers; and used PICTOGRAPHS in writing. At its peak, the Toltec Empire stretched from the Gulf of Mexico to the Pacific Ocean. A branch of Toltecs invaded the Yucatan Peninsula to the east, interbred with the Mayas, and brought about their Postclassic renaissance. Those who stayed in power in Tula and the Valley of Mexico gradually fell into a state of decline, plagued by a series of droughts, famines, fires, and invasions from northern tribes. Tula was destroyed in 1160. After a period of tribal rivalries and power struggles, the AZTECS rose to dominance.

tomahawk A type of WARCLUB. "Tomahawk" is ALGONQUIAN-derived for a number of stone and wooden clubs, used as tools or weapons (both hand weapons and missiles). The CREE word for "hammer" is *ootommoheggun*. Early English spellings were *tomahack, tomahog, tommahick, tamahake* and *tamahaac*. In popular usage, "tomahawk" refers to an axlike weapon with an iron head, made by Europeans (sometimes called trade tomahawks). Those that doubled as pipes are called PIPE-TOMAHAWKS.

tomato A plant, *Lycopersicon esculentum*, with edible fleshy fruit; native to Central and South America. Like CORN and the POTATO, the tomato was first cultivated by SOUTH AMERICAN INDIANS and passed to the rest of the world. The English word derives from the NAHUATL *tomatl* via the Spanish *tomate*.

tom-tom A popular term for a hand drum. Although used for Native American drums, "tom-tom" probably derives from the Hindu word *tamtam* and more accurately applies to Asian drums.

Tonacacihuatl (Omecihuatl) The AZTEC goddess of creation and wife of TONACATECUHTLI; the Wife of Duality.

Tonacatecuhtli (Ometecuhtli, Ometecutli) The AZTEC god of creation, the Ruler of Duality. He and his wife, TONACACIHUATL, were considered the supreme deities who created the universe and all other gods.

Tonikan See TUNICAN.

Tonkawa A MACRO-ALGONQUIAN-speaking (Tonkawa or Tonkawan isolate) tribe of the GREAT PLAINS CULTURE AREA, located between Cibola Creek and Trinity River in present-day Texas. The name applies to a number of linguistically related subtribes in addition to the Tonkawa proper. Tonkawa descendants live in Kay County, Oklahoma. Their name may mean "they all stay together" in CADDOAN.

Tonto A subtribe of the SAN CARLOS division of the APACHE Indians, located on and near the upper Verde River in present-day central Arizona. The Northern Tontos consist of the Bald Mountain, Fossil Creek, Mormon Lake, and Oak Creek bands; the

Southern Tontos consist of the Mazatzal band and six neighboring loosely organized bands. *Tonto* is Spanish for "fool"; the Spanish applied it to other Apache groups as well.

tool (implement) Any device for performing a particular task or work, especially if hand-held. The term utensil often is applied to tools used for specific purposes, such as in cooking and eating. (See also CATEGORICAL APPENDIX, "TOOLS, UTENSILS AND WEAPONS"; CONTAINER; WEAPON.)

tool kit The set of tools carried and used by a prehistoric individual.

top A spinning toy, usually cylindrical in shape, tapering to a point, made of wood, bone, horn, or stone.

torch A portable source of light with an open flame. American Indians made sources of light from a variety of flammable materials, including pine knots and other resinous woods, rolls of bark, grass bundles, and plant material dipped in wax or oil. (See also LAMP.)

Tornit A mythical race of giants in INUIT tradition. They supposedly carry stone lamps under deerskin coats, with which they cook seals after having killed them; knowing how to work in no material other than stone, they steal KAYAKS and tools from people. Tornit is the Central Inuit name; Labrador and Greenland Inuits had other names for legendary giants.

tortilla A round, flat, unleavened bread made by baking corn-meal on a pottery grill. Typical of MESOAMERICAN INDIANS and SOUTHWEST INDIANS. The word is of Spanish derivation. (See also COMAL.)

torture Some tribes, especially among EASTERN INDIANS, ritually inflicted pain on captives following warfare as a means of catharsis; in many cases women participated to a greater extent than men. Indian captives

from other tribes sometimes played their part in the ritual by trying not to show pain. Some ceremonies, such as the SUN DANCE, involved self-torture or self-mutilation. (See also RUNNING THE GAUNTLET; SCARIFICATION.)

totem An animal, plant, natural object, natural phenomenon, or legendary being serving as the symbol of a TRIBE, CLAN, FAMILY, SECRET SOCIETY, or individual. "Totemic" is the adjective form. The totem is regarded as an individual's GUARDIAN SPIRIT; if an animal, it is not to be hunted by that individual. The ALGONQUIAN word is from the CHIPPEWA *ototeman* or CREE *ototema*, meaning "his brother-sister kin" or "his relations." "Totemism" is the belief in totems and totemic relationships, i.e., a mystical connection between humans and other living, creatures or natural objects; "totemistic" is the adjective form. (See also CLAN ANIMAL; CLAN EMBLEM; CREST; TOTEM POLE.)

totem pole A wooden post, carved and painted with a series of figures and symbols, i.e., TOTEMS, relating to tribal legends and history and totemic relationships. Some totem poles are structurally part of a PLANK HOUSE; others stand alone. Typical of NORTHWEST COAST INDIANS, who carved totem poles from cedar. Some EASTERN INDIANS, in particular the DELAWARES, CREEKS, IROQUOIS, and SHAWNEES, erected smaller poles with a similar purpose, usually in MEDICINE LODGES. Some doubled as HOUSEPOSTS. Mortuary poles (or grave markers), erected near the grave of a deceased chief, also are types of totem poles.

Totonacan A language family and subdivision of the PENUTIAN phylum comprising dialects spoken by Indians of the MESOAMERICAN CULTURE AREA, including the Totonac and Tepehua tribes on the Gulf Coast of what is now central Mexico.

tourist A visitor to tribal lands or ancient sites. Tourists are appreciated for the in-

come they bring, with some tribes actively promoting tourism. Yet tourists sometimes are resented for their disrespectful behavior, and the term occasionally is used derogatorily.

tourist pot Low-priced nontraditional POTTERY or TRADEWARE; crafted as curios or souvenirs for TOURISTS.

Towa (Jemez)   A KIOWA-TANOAN-speaking tribe of the SOUTHWEST CULTURE AREA, located on the Jemez River, a tributary of the Rio Grande in present-day New Mexico. Towa peoples lived in politically distinct PUEBLOS and are classified as PUEBLO INDIANS. Towa Indians hold the Jemez Pueblo in Sandoval County, New Mexico.

town   A permanent abode with a number of structures; applied especially to tribes of the SOUTHEAST CULTURE AREA, such as the CREEKS, where a town was a political unit with a hierarchy. Indian towns typically had COUNCIL HOUSES and CEREMONIAL HOUSES as well as a public square. (See also CITY-STATE; *ITALWA*; VILLAGE.)

toy   An Indian object for play might be a miniature version of adult artifacts and serve

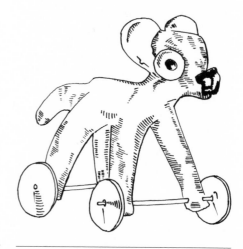

Haida totem pole

Mesoamerican ceramic toy deer with wheels

an educational, as well as a leisure purpose, such as a miniature BOW and ARROW; or it might be designed specifically for GAMES, such as a TOP. (See also DOLL.)

tracking (trailing)   Indians are famous for tracking humans and games, i.e., reading their SIGN and following them. A tracker relied on changes in the environment, such as broken vegetation, moved stones, foot and animal prints, and droppings, as well as knowledge of the countryside and intuition to follow their enemy or prey. White armies often hired Indians as SCOUTS and trackers.

trade (commerce)   An exchange of one object for another. Evidence of widespread commerce in pre-Contact times has been found in archaeological sites, with resources of one region, such as stone, shell, animal teeth, and copper, preserved far away in another. A number of rules governed intertribal commerce, with traders guaranteed safe passage over TRADE ROUTES, which included well-beaten paths, rivers, and lakes. In post-Contact times, the introduction of domestic animals to North America, especially the HORSE, as well as other TRADE GOODS, especially IRON tools, GUNS, and ALCOHOLIC BEVERAGES, had immediate impact on Indian lives. Commerce was also central to the course of white settlement, i.e., as determined by the FUR TRADE. (See also MEDIUM OF EXCHANGE; TRADE LANGUAGE.)

trade ax   See AX; HATCHET.

trade goods   Items made or gathered for TRADE. The term applies to Native American goods used in intertribal trade or to barter with or sell to whites, as well as to goods obtained or manufactured in Europe to exchange with Indians, especially in the FUR TRADE. (See also MEDIUM OF EXCHANGE; TRADEWARE.)

trade language (trading language)   A language used among Indians of different tribes or among Indians and non-Indians for the purpose of trade. (See also CHINOOK JARGON; MOBILIAN TRADE LANGUAGE; SIGN LANGUAGE.)

trade route   An established course of travel for purposes of commerce. Many such routes involved a combination of land and waterways. (See also PORTAGE.)

tradeware   POTTERY made for the purpose of commerce. Tradeware was produced by ancient as well as post-Contact peoples. Some contemporary Native American potters earn a living through the sale of their pottery, whether low-priced TOURIST POTS or highly valued traditional pottery. The term tradeware can be used in a general sense as a synonym of "trade goods."

trading post (trading fort)   A settlement established in a sparsely settled region by non-Indians for commerce with native peoples, as in the FUR TRADE. In most regions of North America, trading posts were the first non-Indian settlements; many evolved into contemporary cities. "Trading post" applies to general stores run by non-Indians and Indians on or near Indian lands. Some trading posts sell Native American arts or crafts (or copies) to tourists.

tradition   In a general sense, the lifeways and beliefs that have root in a family, tribe, or people and are passed down from generation to generation. In archaeology, the term is used for a continuous record of a prehistoric culture, i.e., a distinct way of life lasting a defined period of time and usually restricted to a particular region. (See also CULTURE.)

trail   A blazed path or beaten track through the wilderness. HUNTING PARTIES, WAR PARTIES, and traders used well-established trails. White trappers and explorers later used them in their travel through the wilderness. Many of these trails evolved into the wagon roads of white settlers and eventually present-day roads, highways, and railways. "Trail" also can refer to the SIGN of a person or animal. A SIOUX word for "trail" or "road" in SIOUAN is *chanku*. (See also PORTAGE.)

trailer (streamer) A piece of narrow cloth or leather, attached to a headdress or belt; often decorated with beads, feathers, or brooches.

Trail of Tears The death march of the CHEROKEE Indians from their homelands in the East to the INDIAN TERRITORY. In 1830, President Andrew Jackson signed the Indian Removal Act to relocate eastern tribes west of the Mississippi River. The principal chief of the Cherokees, John Ross, argued against force REMOVAL before the Supreme Court of the United States and won, but the decision was ignored. The state of Georgia began forcing the Cherokees to sell their lands at low prices; Cherokee homes and possessions were plundered. Whites destroyed the printing press of the *Cherokee Phoenix* because it published articles opposing Indian removal. Soldiers began rounding up Cherokee families and taking them to internment camps in preparation for the journey westward. Some escaped to the mountains of North Carolina, where they successfully hid out from the troops. The first forced 800-mile journey began in the spring of 1838 and lasted into the heat of summer; the second mass exodus took place in the fall rainy season—when the wagons bogged down in the mud—carrying over to the winter of 1839, during freezing temperatures and snow. The Cherokees suffered from exposure, inadequate food supplies, disease, and attacks by bandits. During the period of confinement and the two trips, about 4,000 Cherokees died, a quarter of those relocated. More Cherokees died after arrival in the Indian Territory because of epidemics and continuing food shortages. Other tribes endured similar experiences, including the CHICKASAWS, CHOCTAWS, CREEKS, and SEMINOLES. The "Trail of Tears" has come to symbolize the forced removal of all Indian peoples. (See also LONG WALK.)

transportation Means of travel from one place to another. (See also CATEGORICAL APPENDIX, "TRANSPORTATION.")

trap A device for or method of catching or killing animals. Some traps were designed to hold animals upon capture, as in a pen, cage, or pit. Others were weapons that sprung automatically, launching a heavy object or impaling device. Traps also were used in warfare, and the term is used in a general sense for a tactic. (See also CORRAL; DEADFALL; NET; PITFALL; SEINE; SNARE; WEIR.)

travois A device for transporting possessions behind dogs (dog travois) or horses (horse travois). People also were carried, especially the sick and elderly. A travois consists of a wooden frame shaped like a V, the closed end over the animal's shoulders

Sioux travois

and the open end dragging on the ground, with hide, basketry, webbing, or a plank serving as a litter in the middle. TEPEE poles could double as the travois frame and the tepee covering as the litter. *Travois* is French, probably from *travail,* meaning "work," and also applies to a type of frame used to restrain horses while shoeing them.

treaty   A formal agreement, pact, or contract negotiated between two or more political authorities, i.e., between the federal government (or state, provincial, or territorial governments) and Indian tribes as sovereign nations. Treaties define terms of peace, including issues such as political control, boundaries, land sale, restitution, and trade. (See also BROKEN PROMISES; LAND CESSION; RESERVATION.)

tree burial   A type of BURIAL in which the body is placed in a tree. Typical of NORTHEAST INDIANS and those Indians who practiced SCAFFOLD BURIALS.

Tree of Life   According to SIOUX tradition, all the people and their interaction with creation. The Tree of Knowledge, i.e., all knowledge of nature, is one aspect of the Tree of Life.

tree-ring dating   See DENDROCHRONOLOGY.

tribal entity   A term used by the federal government for Indian tribes or bands having special TRUST STATUS.

tribal government   The leadership of a tribe, sometimes hereditary and sometimes elected. Tribal governments might consist of a traditional CHIEF (or chiefs) and/or CHAIRMAN, as well as a tribal COUNCIL.

tribal headquarters   The location where a tribal government meets, or in some cases simply the post office address of a tribe. A modern term commonly appearing with reservation names.

tribal restoration   See RESTORATION.

tribe   A general term applied to different kinds and degrees of SOCIAL ORGANIZATION. Tribes usually have language, culture, kinship, territory, and history in common, resulting in a common purpose, and are comprised of a number of BANDS (SUBTRIBES) or TOWNS. The term tribe also generally implies political and economic equality among tribal members, as opposed to a CHIEFDOM. In the modern legal sense, a distinction is made among tribes that are federally recognized, state-recognized, or self-recognized. Some tribes are organized as corporations, as in the regional and village corporations of Alaska. Some refer to themselves as NATIONS; others, as communities. "Band" is used in Canada for tribal entities. "Tribe" derives from the Latin word *tribus,* a division of the Roman people. (See also CLAN; CONFEDERACY; FEDERAL RECOGNITION; PUEBLO; TRIBAL ENTITY; TRIBELET.)

tribelet   A grouping of Indians who have one main permanent village and a number of temporary satellite villages. A single chief presided over each tribelet; applied to CALIFORNIA INDIANS.

tributary tribe   A conquered tribe forced to pay tribute in the form of agricultural products or other resources to another tribe. In return, the tributary tribe might receive protection against enemies.

Trickster   A name for a recurring CULTURE HERO among various tribes, who symbolizes the unpredictable and absurd nature of reality and fate. A Trickster figure represents both the sacred and the profane, a creator and a destroyer. Humor is central to his behavior. Trickster is commonly depicted as a COYOTE or a MAGPIE. The ABENAKI version, *Azaban,* translates as "raccoon." (See also SHAPE SHIFTER.)

trophy   Indians preserved parts of animals, such as bear claws, to indicate triumph over an animal in a hunt; or they kept an enemy's weapon to indicate victory. Some tribes also practiced SCALPING, in some cases preserving the scalps. Trophies were kept as ORNAMENTS as well as AMULETS. (See also PRESTIGE ITEM.)

trust land Indian land that is protected by the federal government and state government, although not a true RESERVATION; applied especially to the allotted lands of Oklahoma tribes.

trust status A tribe's special relationship, called a trust relationship, with the U.S. government, unlike that between the government and any other political or economic group, resulting from FEDERAL RECOGNITION. When a tribe has trust status, the government has assumed trust responsibility, based on treaties, statutes, and court cases to recognize, protect, and preserve tribal SOVEREIGNTY and guarantee the transfer of resources.

tsanahwit The NEZ PERCE word for "equal justice" in SAHAPTIN.

Tsattine See BEAVER (Tsattine).

Tsetsaut An ATHAPASCAN-speaking tribe of the SUBARCTIC CULTURE AREA, located from the Chunah River to Observatory Inlet and north to the watershed of the Iskut River in present-day British Columbia. In the late 1800s, the few surviving tribal members merged with the NISGA'A Indians. *Tsetsaut*, in the Nisga'a dialect of PENUTIAN, means "people of the interior."

Tsimshian (Chimmesyan) A PENUTIAN-speaking (Tsimshian or Chimmesyan isolate) tribe of the NORTHWEST COAST CULTURE AREA, located on the Skeena River and along the Pacific Coast to the south in present-day British Columbia. The Tsimshians are related linguistically to the NISGA'A Indians. In 1887, many moved to Annette Island, Alaska, where descendants live on the Annette Island Reserve. Tsimshi-

ans in Canada include the Hartley Bay, Kitasoo, Kitkatla, Kitselas, Kitsumkalum, Metlakatla, and Port Simpson bands. *Tsimshian* means "people of the Skeena River" in Penutian.

Tsistsistas See CHEYENNE.

Tubatulabal (Kern River) A UTO-AZTECAN-speaking tribe of the CALIFORNIA CULTURE AREA, located on the upper Kern River in present-day California. Subtribes include the Tubatulabal proper, the Bankalachi, and the Palagewan. The Kern Valley Indian Community operates out of Weldon, California. *Tubatulabal* means "pine-nut eaters" in Uto-Aztecan.

tube A hollow cylinder, made of bone, horn, stone, clay, wood, and reed. A variety of tubes have been found, the use of which is uncertain. Some are tapered at one end; some are shaped like hourglasses. The smaller ones may have been used as BEADS; the larger ones, as PIPES or pipestems. Some tubes are identifiable as SUCKING TUBES.

tuckahoe A number of plants and plant parts eaten by Native Americans, especially among eastern ALGONQUIANS, from whom the word derives. The term, meaning "it is globe-shaped," sometimes is used specifically for the edible roots of certain arums or the edible sclerotium of certain fungi. Also known as Indian bread, Indian loaf, or Virginia truffle. In the South, "Tuckahoe" is also used as a slang word for a "poor person."

tug-of-war A game of strength common to many tribes in which two teams on either end of a rope try to pull each other across a dividing rope. Some tribes also played a push-of-war in which the purpose was to push opponents across a line.

tule Any of several bulrushes or reeds of the genus *Scirpus*, with long flat leaves. SOUTHWEST INDIANS, CALIFORNIA INDIANS, and MESOAMERICAN INDIANS used tule to make rafts, baskets, sandals, mats, decoys, and other items. The terms tule and CAT-TAIL sometimes are interchangeable; but "cattail" more commonly refers to plants of the genus *Typha*. Tule also was chewed as a QUID. From the NAHUATL word *tollin* or *tullin* via Spanish. (See also BALSA.)

tuma A type of INCA headdress, with splayed feathers, worn by nobility.

tumbaga An alloy of gold and copper, usually with a small percentage of silver. Typical of the Indians of Colombia and Central America, who were skilled in GOLDWORK in pre-Contact times. (See also MISE EN COULEUR.)

tumpline (carrying strap, forehead strap) A piece of animal skin or cloth slung across the forehead or chest to support a load on the back. Tumplines were used to carry packs or game. From an ALGONQUIAN word (*madumbi* in the ABENAKI dialect and *tampam* in the MASSACHUSET dialect), meaning "burden strap," with the English word "line" added.

tumulus See MOUND.

tundra The treeless plain of the Arctic region, frozen in winter and marshy in summer, with a permanently frozen subsoil (PERMAFROST) and low-growing vegetation, such as mosses, lichens, and dwarf shrubs. To the south of the tundra lies the BOREAL forests of the TAIGA.

Tunica (Tonika) A TUNICAN-speaking tribe of the SOUTHEAST CULTURE AREA, located on the lower Yazoo River in present-day Mississippi. By 1803, the Tunicas had settled on the Red River near present-day Marksville, Louisiana. Tribal members share the Tunica-Biloxi Indian Reservation at that location with BILOXI Indians. *Tunica* means "people" in Tunican.

Tunican (Tonikan) A language family (or, according to some, isolate) and subdivision

of the MACRO-ALGONQUIAN phylum spoken by the Bidai (probably Tunican), Chawasha, Grigra, Koroa, Tiou, TUNICA, Washa, and YAZOO tribes of the SOUTH-EAST CULTURE AREA.

Tupi-Guarani A language family and subdivision of the ANDEAN-EQUATORIAL phylum comprising dialects spoken by SOUTH AMERICAN INDIANS, among them the Camayura, Munduruca, and Parintintin tribes in the Amazon Basin of present-day Brazil; the Tupinamba tribe of the Brazilian coast; the Guarani tribe of present-day Paraguay; the Chiriguano and Siriono tribes in present-day Bolivia; and others. Tupi serves as the lingua franca among Indians in Brazil. Guarani is co-official with Spanish in Paraguay and is spoken by about 1 million Indians in Paraguay and Brazil.

turban A type of headdress, resembling the turbans of Asia. A SASH was wrapped around the head. Typical of SOUTHEAST INDIANS, such as the SEMINOLES, and some NORTHEAST INDIANS as well, such as the SACS.

turf house See SOD HOUSE.

turkey The North American species of this bird is *Meleagris gallopavo*; in Mexico and Central America is a related bird, *Agriocharis ocellata*. Turkey feathers were valued by many different peoples. SOUTHWEST INDIANS domesticated turkeys for their feathers; MESOAMERICAN INDIANS bred them in captivity for food. The NAVAJOS accredit the mythological figure known as Turkey with the gift of seeds for domesticated plants. In 1621, WAMPANOAG Indians provided the Pilgrims with wild turkeys and other food for a THANKSGIVING feast, beginning a tradition in the United States.

turquoise A blue, bluish-green, or greenish-gray mineral of aluminum phosphate with some copper, which takes a high polish and is valued for its beauty. In pre-Contact times, turquoise was mined extensively by

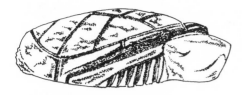

Iroquois soapstone turtle

SOUTHWEST INDIANS. Beginning in the 19th century, it was combined with SILVER-WORK in JEWELRY-making. Contemporary Indians, especially the NAVAJOS and PUEBLO INDIANS, have continued this tradition. Treated turquoise is darkened by means of a chemical hardener.

turtle An order of reptiles known as *Chelonia*, having bodies enclosed in bony or leathery shells. "Tortoise" refers to terrestrial turtles, especially of the family Testudinidae. Indian peoples used turtle shells as bowls and RATTLES. The IROQUOIS are known for their turtle-shell rattles, as are PUEBLO INDIANS. According to Iroquois tradition, the earth sits on the back of the Great Turtle. Turtle occurs in the legends of many other tribes as well, symbolizing endurance and persistence. (See also TURTLE CONTINENT.)

Turtle Continent Reference to North America in many Native American legends, such as those of the IROQUOIS, who believed that the Great Turtle carries the earth on its back. According to the SIOUX and other tribes, "Turtle Island" is both North and South America, or the entire earth.

Tuscarora An IROQUOIAN-speaking tribe of the NORTHEAST CULTURE AREA, located on the Roanoke, Tar, Pamlico, and Neuse rivers in present-day North Carolina. After 1712, tribal members migrated northward to present-day New York, settling among the IROQUOIS Indians, and becoming formally recognized as part of the IROQUOIS LEAGUE in 1722. Tribal members hold the

Tuscarora Reservation in Niagara County, New York. Tuscaroras also are part of the Six Nations of the Grand River band near Oshweken, Ontario. A group known as the Hatteras Tuscarora Tribe is centered in Maxton, North Carolina, as is the Tuscarora Indian Tribe of the Drowning Creek Reservation. *Tuscarora* may mean "hemp gatherers" or "shirt-wearers" in Iroquoian.

tusk An elongated tooth, usually found in pairs, on certain animals, such as the walrus, wild boar, or elephant. (The narwhal, however, has a single tusk.) INUITS traditionally have used tusks in carving. PREHISTORIC INDIANS used the tusks of MAMMOTHS and MASTODONS for artifacts. (See also IVORY WORK.)

Tuskegee See CREEK; MUSKOGEAN.

Tutchone (Caribou, Mountain) An ATHAPASCAN-speaking tribe of the SUBARCTIC CULTURE AREA, located on the Yukon River to the east of present-day Fort Selkirk, Yukon Territory. The Tutchones were formerly known as Tutchone-kutchin, but they are no longer considered a subtribe of the KUTCHINS. Descendants live among other Athapascans. *Tutchone* means "crow people" in Athapascan.

tutelar See GUARDIAN SPIRIT.

Tutelo See SAPONI; SIOUAN.

Tututni (Rogue River) An ATHAPASCAN-speaking tribe of the NORTHWEST COAST CULTURE AREA, located on the lower Rogue River and neighboring parts of the Pacific Coast in present-day Oregon. Tututnis share the Siletz Reservation near Siletz, Oregon, with the TAKELMAS and other tribes. The Tolowa-Tututni Tribe of Indians operates out of Fort Dick, California. (See also TOLOWA.)

Twana (Toanho, Tuwa'duxq) A SALISHAN-speaking tribe of the NORTHWEST

COAST CULTURE AREA, located on the Hoods Canal in present-day Washington. The Twanas live on the Skokomish Reservation in Mason County, Washington, named after a subtribe. *Twana* may mean "portage" in Salishan. (See also SKOKOMISH.)

twilling A type of WEAVING in which the WEFT (woof) is carried over one or two threads of the WARP, then under two or more, creating diagonal lines; used in BASKETRY and TEXTILES.

twining A type of WEAVING in which splints or threads are intertwined, then wrapped around a foundation of rods or threads.

Two Kettles See OOHENONPA.

Tyigh See SAHAPTIN.

type site An ARCHAEOLOGICAL SITE considered as the first or most typical example of a culture or tradition, the name of which often is applied to that culture and to artifacts from other sites as well. For example, the FOLSOM CULTURE and Folsom POINT are named after a particular site in New Mexico. Geological formations also have type sites.

Uchean See YUCHI.

Uintah (Uinta, Yoovte) A subtribe of the UTE Indians, located in present-day northeastern Colorado. Descendants of the Uintahs, TABEGUACHES, and other Ute bands hold the Uintah and Ouray Reservation near Fort Duquesne, Utah.

ulu (uluk, ulon) The knife of an INUIT woman, with a semicircular, crescent-shape stone blade and a slotted handle, usually wood or ivory. The blades evolved from stone to steel in post-Contact times. Used especially in SKIN-DRESSING and food preparation.

Umatilla A SAHAPTIN-speaking tribe of the PLATEAU CULTURE AREA, located on the Umatilla River and on the Columbia River near the mouth of the Umatilla in present-day Oregon. Tribal members share the Umatilla Reservation in Umatilla County, Oregon, with CAYUSE and WALLA-WALLA Indians.

umelik (umialik, umealiq, omalik) An IN-UIT term for "boat owner" or "boat captain" in the ESKIMO-ALEUT language that also has the broader meaning of "chief."

umiak (omiak) A large, open, flat-bottomed boat, made by stretching hide, usually walrus or seal, over a wooden or whale-rib frame; used by INUIT women as well as men, usually eight to 10 at a time, especially in the summer. A beached umiak sometimes was turned on its side for shelter. *Umiat* is the plural form, although "umiaks" is also used.

Umpqua (Upper Umpqua) An ATHAPAS-CAN-speaking tribe of the NORTHWEST COAST CULTURE AREA, located on the upper Umpqua River in present-day Oregon. The Umpquas are not to be confused with Lower Umpquas, or KUITSH Indians. Descendants are part of the Grande Ronde Indian Community near Grande Ronde, Oregon.

Unalachtigo A subtribe of the LENNI LENAPE (Delaware) Indians, located in present-day northern Delaware, southeastern Pennsylvania, and southern New Jersey. The Natuxents and Passayonks are two of the 17 known Unalachtigo bands. *Unalachtigo* derives from *Nentego*, meaning "tidewater people" or "people who live near the ocean" in ALGONQUIAN, referring to Delaware Bay.

Unami A subtribe of the LENNI LENAPE (Delaware) Indians, located on the Delaware River in present-day Pennsylvania and New Jersey and on the lower Hudson and on western Long Island in present-day New York. The Canarsees, Hackensacks, Haverstraws, Manhattans (possibly WAP-PINGER), Navasinks, Raritans, and Reckgawawancs are among the 14 known Unami bands.

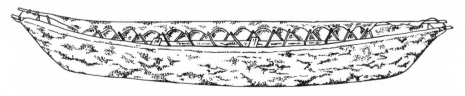

Inuit *umiak*

"Uncle Tomahawk" A derogatory expression among Native Americans for an Indian who parrots non-Indians in positions of authority for his own personal gain. A take-off of the similar expression, "Uncle Tom," referring to an African-American who emulates whites.

unilineal descent See DESCENT.

unilocal residence See MATRILOCAL; PATRILOCAL.

urban Indians It is estimated that one-third to one-half of Native Americans now live in cities in the United States. Some Indians also commute from reservations to cities for work. Since the 1920s, HIGH-STEEL workers among the MOHAWKS, e.g., have lived in Brooklyn, New York; others travel from the reservation to any number of cities, depending on union contracts. Urbanization began to accelerate during World War II, when Native Americans began working off-reservation jobs. During the ensuing period of the federal government's TERMINATION policy and the related Voluntary Relocation Program of 1952, Indians were encouraged to seek economic opportunities in cities. Various political organizations, such as the American Indian Movement (AIM) founded in Minneapolis in 1968, began in cities.

urn burial A type of BURIAL in which the remains, either CREMATED or noncremated, are placed in vessels. The urns usually were of POTTERY, but stone, shells, and BASKETRY also were used. Burial urns have been found throughout North America, covered, uncovered, or inverted over the remains.

Ute A UTO-AZTECAN-speaking tribe of the GREAT BASIN CULTURE AREA, located in present-day central and western Colorado, eastern Utah, northern New Mexico, and ranging into eastern Nevada and southern Wyoming. Subdivisions include the CAPOTE, Elk Mountain, Kosunats, MOUACHE, Pahvant, Pavogowunsin, Pikakwanarats, Sampits (Sanpet), Seuvarits (Sheberetch), TABEGUACHE (Uncompahgre), Tumpanogots (Timpaiavats), UINTAH, and WIMINUCHE bands. Utes hold the Southern Ute Reservation in La Plata, Archuleta, and Montezuma counties, Colorado; the Ute Mountain Reservation in Montezuma and La Plata counties (Colorado), San Juan County (New Mexico), and San Juan County (Utah); and the Uintah and Ouray Reservation in Uintah, Duchesne, and Grand counties, Utah. The Allen Canyon Ute Tribe is centered in Blanding, Utah. *Ute* derives from the Spanish *Yuta*, the meaning of which is unknown. The Ute native name is *Nu Ci*, meaning "person."

utensil See CONTAINER; TOOL.

utility ware POTTERY made for a practical purpose, such as cooking, eating, or storing, as opposed to an esthetic or ceremonial purpose. Archaeologists often consider pottery with little decoration to be utility ware.

Utina See TIMUCUA.

Uto-Aztecan (Utaztecan) A language family and subdivision of the AZTEC-TANOAN language phylum comprising dialects spoken by Indians of the CALIFORNIA CULTURE AREA, among them the Alliklik, CAHUILLA, Cupeno, Fernandeno, Gabrilino, Kitanemuk, LUISENO, Nicoleno, SERRANO, TUBATULABAL and Vanyume tribes; of the GREAT BASIN CULTURE AREA, among them the BANNOCK, CHEMEHUEVI, GOSHUTE, Kawaiisu, MONO, PAIUTE, Panamint, SHOSHONE, and UTE tribes; of the SOUTHWEST CULTURE AREA, among them the HOPI, Jumano (probably Uto-Aztecan), PAPAGO, PIMA, SOBAIPURI, and YAQUI tribes; and of the GREAT PLAINS CULTURE AREA, the COMANCHE tribe. Some peoples of the MESOAMERICAN CULTURE AREA, such as the AZTECS (NAHUATL), as well as of the CIRCUM-CARIBBEAN CULTURE AREA, also are part of this language family.

uxorilocal See MATRILOCAL.

▲ V ▲

vahki (rain house, round house, smoking house) A ceremonial structure of the PA-PAGO Indians, made of WATTLE-AND DAUB; used to store the fermenting pulp of the SAGUARO cactus, to prepare sacred saguaro wine, and for ceremonies before and during the Saguaro Festival.

vanilla Any of various tropical orchids of the genus *Vanilla*, especially *V. planifolia*. Native Americans cultivated the plants for the long seed pods. To make a flavoring, they picked the pods before they were ripe, dried them, and removed the crystals from the outside. The word is from the Spanish *vainilla*.

Vanyume See UTO-AZTECAN.

vicuña See LLAMA.

viga A heavy rafter, often a log, support-ing the roof and projecting beyond the exte-rior wall of a building in both PUEBLO INDIAN and Mexican architecture. A Span-ish word.

vigesimal system See COUNTING.

village A permanent place of abode with a number of dwellings and community buildings. "Village" applies to small Indian population centers, some of them even tem-porary, whereas "settlement" is applied to those of whites. TOWN is more often used than "village" in reference to SOUTHEAST INDIAN population centers. (See also CAMP; CITY-STATE.)

Viracocha The INCA god of creation and founder of civilization. In pre-Inca cultures, he was known as Pachacamac.

Virgin of Guadalupe A manifestation of Christianity's Virgin Mary or Madonna, the mother of Jesus. In 1531, a Nahua (NAHU-ATL-speaking) Indian known as Juan Diego reportedly encountered the Virgin Mary at the ruins of the Temple of Tonantzin on a hill outside Mexico City, where she be-stowed her patronage to native peoples.

virilocal See PATRILOCAL.

vision The seeing of mental images; a mystical or prophetic experience or revela-tion. In many different Indian religions, it is believed that images seen with the eyes closed—in wakefulness, half-sleep, or DREAMS—are glimpses of and messages from the SPIRIT WORLD, relevant to individ-uals or to an entire tribe. Certain rituals and deprivations have been traditionally under-taken in order to enhance visions, as in the VISION QUEST typical of PLAINS INDIANS. PSYCHOTROPIC SUBSTANCES, such as PEY-OTE, also have been taken as a means of producing visions. From visions, Indians re-ceive guidance in choosing a name, a TO-TEM, and a path of life as well as methods of HEALING. (See also HIEROPHANY.)

Vision Quest The PLAINS INDIAN ritual seeking of VISIONS through isolation, expo-sure to the elements, and FASTING; a vigil undertaken by youths, typically male, but sometimes female as well, in the hope of receiving a sign from a supernatural being, as well as power or MEDICINE. The quest usually occurs around some important event, such as passage from childhood into adulthood or preparation for war. In order to achieve visions, an individual normally first purifies him- or herself through SWEATING in a sweat lodge, strips naked, paints him- or herself with white clay, re-treats to an isolated place, and fasts for days. The vision usually comes in the form of an animal, but it can be a plant, place, object, ancestor, or some natural phenomenon, such as a storm. After the experience, a SHAMAN helps interpret the vision. What was seen in the vision henceforth symbolizes the individual's TOTEM or GUARDIAN SPIRIT. The individual also prepares a MEDICINE BUNDLE with sacred objects somehow relating to his or her vision. (See also HANBLECHEYAPI; LAMENTING.)

voyageur French for "traveler." A fur trader and paddler of canoes who traveled the rivers and backwoods for the large fur companies, such as the North West Company and Hudson's Bay Company. Many of the voyageurs were of mixed descent, especially French Canadian and CREE Indian. (See also COUREUR DE BOIS; FUR TRADE; METIS.)

.W.

Wabanaki See ABENAKI.

Waccamaw A SIOUAN-speaking tribe of the SOUTHEAST CULTURE AREA, located on the Waccamaw River and the lower Pee Dee River in present-day South Carolina and North Carolina. A group known as the Waccamaw Siouan Tribe operates out of Bolton, North Carolina.

Waco See CADDOAN; WICHITA.

Wahpekute A subtribe of the SANTEE (Dakota) division of the SIOUX Indians, located on Mille Lacs in present-day central Minnesota and later between the Minnesota and Missouri rivers in present-day southern Minnesota and eastern South Dakota. *Wahpekute* means "shooters among the leaves" in SIOUAN.

Wahpeton A subtribe of the SANTEE (Dakota) division of the SIOUX Indians, located on Mille Lacs in present-day central Minnesota and later near the confluence of the Minnesota and Mississippi rivers. *Wahpeton* means "dwellers (or village) among the leaves" in SIOUAN.

Waiilatpuan See CAYUSE.

Wailaki An ATHAPASCAN-speaking tribe of the CALIFORNIA CULTURE AREA, located on the Eel River and its tributaries in present-day California. Wailakis share the Round Valley Reservation in Mendocino County, California, with other tribes and the Grindstone Creek Rancheria in Glenn County with the WINTUNS. *Wailaki* is Wintun for "northern language" in PENUTIAN.

wakan The SIOUAN word for "sacred," "mysterious," or "holy."

wakanda (wakonda) The SIOUAN word for the SPIRIT and power inherent in living creatures and objects; divine essence. Sometimes capitalized. (See also MANITOU; ORENDA.)

Wakan Tanka (Wakontonka, Great Spirit, Great Mystery) The CREATOR, Great Wakan, Great Mystery or GREAT SPIRIT in SIOUX tradition. *Wakantanka Tunkasina* translates as "god grandfather" in the Nakota dialect of SIOUAN. (See also GITCHEE MANITOU.)

Wakashan A language family of undetermined language phylum affiliation comprising dialects spoken by the BELLA BELLA, HAISLA, HEILTSUK, KWAKIUTL, MAKAH, and NOOTKA tribes of the NORTHWEST COAST CULTURE AREA. The Wakashan and SALISHAN language families sometimes are grouped as part of a combined Mosan language family. *Wakashan* possibly means "good."

Walapai See HUALAPAI.

Wallawalla (Walla Walla, Walula) A SAHAPTIN-speaking tribe of the PLATEAU CULTURE AREA, located on the lower Wallawalla River in present-day Washington. Tribal members share the Umatilla Reservation in Umatilla County, Oregon, with CAYUSE and UMATILLA Indians. *Wallawalla* means "little river" in Sahaptin.

Walpapi See SNAKE INDIANS.

Walum Olum (*Wallum Olum, Walam Olum*) The tribal chronicle of the LENNI LENAPES (Delawares), first printed in 1836. Considered sacred, its original form consisted of PICTOGRAPHS carved in wood, relating in meter tribal migrations and legends. *Walum*

Olum translates from ALGONQUIAN as "red score" or "painted tally."

Wampanoag An ALGONQUIAN-speaking tribe of the NORTHEAST CULTURE AREA, located in present-day Bristol County, southern Plymouth County, and western Barnstable County, Massachussets, and on Cape Cod and Martha's Vineyard in Massachusetts; as well as east of Narragansett Bay in present-day Rhode Island. The various Wampanoag bands, such as Pocasset, Pokanoket, and Sakonnet, sometimes are referred to as members of the Wampanoag Confederacy because the various bands, united under a GRAND SACHEM, had political independence and their own leaders. The Nausets, who lived east of the Bass River on Cape Cod, generally are considered a distinct group. Contemporary bands include the Gay Head Wampanoag Tribe, centered in Gay Head, Massachusetts, and the Mashpee Wampanoag Tribe, in Mashpee. *Wampanoag* means "easterners" in Algonquian.

wampum (wampumpeage, wampumpeag) Beads made from shells, or the strings, belts, and sashes of small beads made from shells, especially the dark purple (or black) and white quahog clam shells. ALGONQUIAN and IROQUOIAN tribes used the shell-beads as ornaments. They also used wampum belts as tribal records and to communicate messages of peace or war to other tribes in PICTOGRAPHS. The IROQUOIS still use their wampum belts in religious ceremonies. In post-Contact times, Native Americans began making wampum out of glass beads. Europeans also made wampum for trade purposes; it became a MEDIUM OF EXCHANGE. "Wampum" is a shortened version of *wampumpeag*, Algonquian for "strings of white beads." Early colonists also used "peag" or "peak" to refer to the shell-beads. *SEWAN* was the Dutch word, also Algonquian-derived.

Wanapam See SAHAPTIN.

wand See STAFF.

wapiti See ELK.

Wappinger An ALGONQUIAN-speaking tribe of the NORTHEAST CULTURE AREA, located on the east bank of the Hudson River in present-day New York, from Poughkeepsie to Manhattan Island, as far east as the Connecticut River in present-day Connecticut. Among the 17 subtribes in what often is referred to as the Wappinger Confederacy are the Wappinger proper, located near present-day Poughkeepsie, New

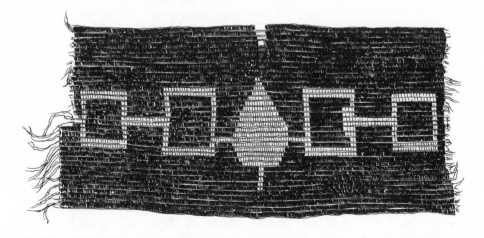

Iroquois wampum

York, as well as the PAUGUSSETT, Podunk, and Quinnipiac bands. Many of the Wappinger bands merged with the LENNI LENAPES (Delawares), MAHICANS, NANTICOKES, and PEQUOTS. (The Manhattan band of Lenni Lenapes are thought by some to have been part of the Wappinger Confederacy.) The Golden Hill Paugussett Tribe has its headquarters at Colchester, Connecticut. *Wappinger* means "easterners" in Algonquian. (See also BROTHERTON INDIANS; MORAVIAN INDIANS.)

Wappo See YUKIAN.

war A state or period of conflict between peoples or nations. Wars also are called rebellions, revolts, and uprisings. Battles, many of them formerly called MASSACRES, are engagements during a war. (See also RESISTANCE; WARFARE; WARRIOR.)

warbonnet A type of HEADDRESS with different FEATHERS, usually golden EAGLE feathers, representing feats in battle. The making of warbonnets was a ceremonial event. The eagle-feather headdress, more commonly known as warbonnet, is the most recognizable of all American Indian clothing. At modern-day POWWOWS, Indians from all over North America wear warbonnets, although they originated among the PLAINS INDIANS. Warbonnets traditionally were worn only by those few men who had earned the honor to do so in warfare. The number of black-tipped tail feathers of the male golden eagle represented the wearer's exploits, thus the term EXPLOIT FEATHERS. The feathers were attached to a skullcap of buffalo skin or deerskin, with a brow-band decorated with quillwork or beadwork and dangling strips of fur or ribbons. Additional downy feathers were tied to the base of the eagle feathers and tufts of dyed horsehair to their tips.

warclub A CLUB designed as a striking weapon. Some are single pieces of wood,

Sioux warbonnet

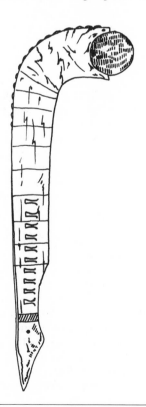

Menominee "ball-head" warclub

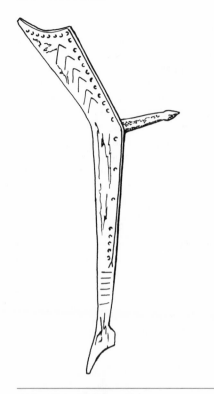

Miami "gunstock" warclub

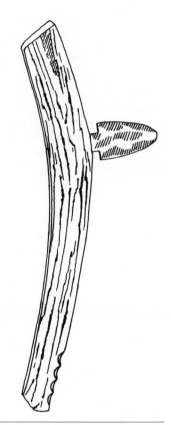

Chippewa "rabbit's hind leg" warclub

such as the ball-headed club, or pieces of bone or antler; others have heads attached to handles. In post-Contact times, iron also was used for one or more pointed heads. There were numerous other designs besides the ball-head; some had handles shaped in the gunstock style; others in the rabbit's hind leg style. (See also *POGAMOGGAN*; TOMAHAWK.)

War Dance A dance performed before WARFARE. What was originally called the War Dance is thought to have been a misnomer for the GRASS DANCE. In one variety of a PLAINS INDIAN "war dance," men who intended to go into battle would circle a post or tree in the center of camp, striking it with a weapon or COUP STICK. Non-Indians have used the term to apply to a number of other different Indian dances with war symbolism, such as the SCALP DANCE.

warfare Native Americans fought defensive WAR to protect families, homes, and lands as well as aggressive war to take spoils and seek revenge. Warfare generally was a man's activity, as when WAR PARTIES were sent out, but women often fought side by side with men in defensive war. For most Indian peoples, warfare was ritualized, with special ceremonies, songs, and dances surrounding the event. Dreams played a part in decisions about the waging of war. The armies of the AZTECS and INCAS were organized and regimented, with what might be called professional SOLDIERS. Other native peoples were for the most part individualistic in their approach to war. The themes of warfare have become a form of stereotyping of Indians. The logos of sports teams and the use of such names as warriors and braves emphasize this one aspect of Indian history. (See also CAPTIVE; CATEGORICAL APPENDIX, "TOOLS, UTENSILS, AND WEAPONS"; COUP; MILITARY SOCIETY; WARRIOR.)

Warm Springs See TENINO.

Warm Springs (Ojo Caliente) A subtribe of the GILENOS division of APACHE Indians, located at the head of the Gila River in present-day southwestern New Mexico. Some of their descendants live among the MESCALERO Apaches on the Mescalero Reservation in Otero County, New Mexico. The name Warm Springs is the translation of the Spanish *Ojo Caliente*, the band's traditional residence.

warp In WEAVING, a vertical thread, or one extended lengthwise. Warp threads are attached to the top and bottom of a LOOM and serve as the foundation before WEFT threads are added at right angles, over and under.

war paint See PAINTING.

war party A group of men who leave a camp or village for the purpose of waging WAR. Participation in war parties was for the most part voluntary. They varied in size from half a dozen men to more than 100. Assigned hunters sometimes accompanied the larger parties, as did women to help make camp. (See also HUNTING PARTY; WAR WOMAN.)

"warpath" A path to WAR or a state of war. The phrase on the warpath applied to Native Americans is a cliché.

war pony See HORSE.

warrior One who wages WAR. Among many Indian tribes, there were grades and ranks of warriors. But in battle, WARFARE was largely individualistic without strictly defined roles. As a result, "warrior" is more appropriate than SOLDIER, except in the case of the regimented armies of MESOAM-

ERICAN INDIANS, especially the AZTECS and INCAS. In contemporary usage, the term capitalized is applied to an organization of Native Americans, the Warrior Society, made up mostly of MOHAWKS, who are prepared to use armed self-defense for political and economic goals, such as protecting reservation lands from development.

war society See MILITARY SOCIETY.

War Woman A CHEROKEE woman who traveled with raiding parties and performed such tasks as setting up camp, cooking, and administering to captives.

Wasco See CHINOOKAN.

Washa See TUNICAN.

Washani Religion A religion of the PLATEAU INDIANS, emphasizing traditional beliefs and customs. Its origin is uncertain, but it is thought to be associated with the arrival of whites or an epidemic in the early 19th century and the teachings of a PROPHET or "dreamer-prophet" who had experienced an apocalyptic vision. It is not known when Christianity came to influence its aboriginal form. One of the Washani rituals is the WASHAT DANCE. The WANAPAM Indian Smohalla used Washani doctrine as the basis for what has become known as the DREAMER RELIGION. The Washani Religion also has been referred to as the Prophet Dance, Seven Drum Religion, Indian Religion, and Longhouse Religion (not to be confused with the LONGHOUSE RELIGION of the IROQUOIS). *Washani* is SAHAPTIN for "dancers" or "worship." (See also FEATHER RELIGION.)

Washat Dance A ceremony of PLATEAU INDIANS, involving a dance with seven drummers, a feast of salmon, the ritual use of eagle and swan feathers, and a sacred song to be sung every seventh day. The Washat Dance still is practiced today as a religion unto itself and also is a part of the

WASHANI RELIGION, which evolved into the DREAMER RELIGION.

Washoe (Washo) A HOKAN-speaking (Washo or Washoan isolate) tribe of the GREAT BASIN CULTURE AREA, located on the Truckee River and on Carson Lake and Lake Tahoe in present-day western Nevada. Washoes hold the Alpine Colony and Woodsford Colony in Alpine County, California; Carson Colony in Ormsby County, Nevada; Dresslerville Colony in Douglas County, Nevada; and the Washoe Reservation near Gardnerville, Nevada; they also share the Reno-Sparks Colony in Washoe County, Nevada, with the PAIUTES. *Washoe* derives from *washiu*, meaning "person" in Hokan.

watap (watape, watapeh) The stringy roots of coniferous trees, especially pine, spruce, and tamarack, used to sew BIRCH-BARK canoes and other artifacts. An ALGON-QUIAN-derived word from the CREE wataply for the root of the tamarack, adopted first into French.

water In the Native American worldview, water, as found in oceans, lakes, ponds, rivers, streams, and rain, is considered a mysterious force that has to be respected and used properly for continuing survival. In a modern ecological sense, that means water cannot be polluted. Many tribes have legends of "Great Floods" in which the earth is purified by the power of water, much like the Bible's story of the flood in which only the worthy survive. As water is essential to life and farming, many tribes, especially in the arid regions, had RAINMAKING ceremonies. (See also IRRIGATION; WATER RIGHTS.)

water drum A type of DRUM, made of tightly fitted wood sections with a skin head, and shaped like a small pot. Water is added to vary the tones, usually through a hole on the side that can be plugged.

Wateree See SIOUAN.

water rights The rights of Indian tribes to ancestral waterways. Although water rights are protected by treaties or by federal enactments, they have been weakened in a number of ways. Both the United States and Canada have used the policy of eminent domain to build dams on Indian waterways, changing the ecology and flooding lands. Moreover, with TERMINATION, those tribes whose TRUST STATUS was abolished became subject to state laws, which stipulate constructive use or development of waterways in order to retain them. Without money for investment, some tribes have been unable to prove constructive use. Industry also has taken advantage of Indian poverty to build factories near reservation lands, polluting their lakes, rivers, and streams. In western states where water is scarce, water rights often are central to a tribe's economic survival. In Canada, a current dispute surrounds Hydro-Quebec's ongoing development of the James Bay region for hydroelectric power. The plan will lead to the eventual flooding of 6,000 square miles of wilderness area, creating ecological destruc-

Chippewa Midewiwin water drum

tion and forever changing the way of life of the region's CREE Indians. Mineral rights and grazing rights are similar to water rights in their importance to tribal economic development. (See also FISH-IN.)

Watershed Age   The transitional period between the PALEOLITHIC PERIOD and the ARCHAIC PERIOD. The late PLEISTOCENE was a time of great climatic change in North America. From about 10,000 to 8000 B.C., the climate warmed and the great glaciers retreated northward once and for all. The melting ice created numerous lakes and swamplands, many of which gradually evaporated. North America gradually evolved to its present form with regional variations of terrain and plant life by about 5000 B.C. The Watershed Age is dated from about 8000 B.C. to 5000 B.C. Other terms applied to the same stage are Paleotransitional period, Pluvial period, postglacial period, and protoarchaic period.

wathonwisas   One of the IROQUOIAN names for "woman," literally translating as "she sways or rocks," referring to the woman's style of dance as opposed to the stomping of men.

Watlala   See CHINOOKAN.

wattle   A number of poles or stakes intertwined with twigs, branches, or vines, used in building houses.

wattle-and-daub   A type of construction using a pole framework interwoven with saplings and vines and filled with mud or clay; found especially among SOUTHEAST INDIANS but also among SOUTHWEST INDIANS. (See also ASI; JACAL.)

Wauyukma   See SAHAPTIN.

Waxhaw   See SIOUAN.

Way   The term way, which can mean "path" as well as "method," is used in NAVAJO religion, implying a tribal myth and a series of rituals derived from that myth, for purposes of purification, healing, and renewal. Some among the more than 50 Navajo Ways, past and present, are the Bead Way; Beauty Way; Blessing Way; Bluejay Way; Enemy Way (*Enteh*); Evil Way (also called Evil-Chasing Way and Squaw Dance, and countering the effects of WITCHES and GHOSTS); Feather Way; Flint Way; Holy Way (invoking the HOLY PEOPLE); Life Way; Mountaintop Way; Moving Up Way; Night Way (also called Night Chant or Yeibichai Ceremony); Water Way; and Wind Way. Sometimes the words are combined into one, as in "Blessingway." The rituals of the various Ways include singing, dancing, storytelling, and SANDPAINTING. (See also YEIBICHAI MASK.)

Wea   A subtribe of the MIAMI Indians, located in present-day eastern Wisconsin and later on the St. Joseph River in present-day Indiana; and, in present-day Illinois, on the site of present-day Chicago and on the Wabash River below the mouth of Wea Creek. Weas later lived in Kansas, then in the INDIAN TERRITORY. Their descendants live in Oklahoma, with tribal headquarters at Miami. Wea is possibly a contraction of the ALGONQUIAN word *wawiaqtenang*, meaning "place of the curved channel"; or of *wayahtonuki*, meaning "eddy people."

Weapemeoc   See ALGONQUIAN.

weapon   A tool used in HUNTING and WARFARE. (See also CATEGORICAL APPENDIX, "TOOLS, UTENSILS, AND WEAPONS.")

weaving   The making of artifacts, in particular TEXTILES or BASKETS, through the interlacing of flexible materials, from plants as well as animal hair. Some tribes practiced only hand weaving (finger weaving); others suspended the materials from trees, staked them on the ground, or used frames. MESOAMERICAN INDIANS and SOUTHWEST INDIANS used true LOOMS. ("Weaving" is generally differentiated from BASKETRY by the use of support of some kind during the process.) In post-Contact times, the European hand loom became widespread. (See also   BAYETA;   BLANKET;   BRAIDWORK; CHECKERBOARD;   PLAITING;   TAPESTRY; TWILLING;   TWINING;   WARP;   WEFT; WICKER.)

wedding jar (wedding vase) A POTTERY container made by PUEBLO INDIANS, having two spouts for husband and wife and a handle connecting them.

wedge A tool tapered at one end, used primarily for splitting and cutting wood in WOODWORK. Wedges were used for the most part in conjunction with HAMMERS. Indians made them from stone, wood, antler, bone, copper, and, in post-Contact times, iron and steel. Early wedges resemble CELTS and CHISELS in shape, but are not as carefully crafted and show signs of pounding with hammers. (See also PIÈCE ESQUILLE.)

weft (woof) In WEAVING, a horizontal thread woven at right angles, over and under the WARP.

weir A fenced-in enclosure, placed in water to trap fish; typically a wooden or brush fence or rock wall forming a narrow channel.

Weitspekan See YUROK.

"Welsh Indian" See WHITE INDIAN.

Wenatchee See SALISHAN.

Wenro See IROQUOIAN.

Westo See YUCHI.

"wet head" A PUEBLO INDIAN name for a missionary practicing the Christian rite of baptism.

whale Any sea mammal of the order Cetacea. Native peoples who practiced WHAL-

ING used every part of the whale: They ate the meat and skin; they used the bones for building and carving; they shaped the intestines into containers; they braided the tendons into rope; they extracted oil from the blubber; and they used the BALEEN for tools and ceremonial objects.

whalebone See BALEEN.

whaling ARCTIC PEOPLES, especially the INUITS of central Canada and Alaska, hunted whales in boats. Along the Arctic Coast, Inuits used their KAYAKS to frighten small whales near the shore. Along the Alaskan coast, hunters went after whales in UMIAKS. Some NORTHWEST COAST INDIANS, in particular the MAKAHS and NOOTKAS, hunted whales in DUGOUTS. Other tribes used only beached whales as a resource. Some NORTHEAST INDIANS living along the sea, such as the MONTAUKS, also hunted whales. In post-Contact times, Native Americans have participated in the Euroamerican whaling industry.

wheel-and-stick See CHUNKEY.

whetstone A stone for sharpening tools, a type of ABRADER. The term applies to small hand-held GRINDSTONES.

Whilkut See ATHAPASCAN.

whistle A wind instrument that makes a single tone by means of blowing. Sometimes two whistles were tied together to produce two notes. American Indians made whistles out of bone, wood, cane, reed, or pottery; the hollow wingbones of birds often were used. "Eagle-bone whistles" were used in the SUN DANCE of the PLAINS INDIANS. In the PEYOTE RELIGION, a bird-bone whistle

Miwok cane whistle

is blown at midnight in all four directions to summon the winds. (See also FLAGEOLET.)

whistling jar (whistling bottle)   A POT-TERY container, often in the shape of a bird or animal, with two openings (or two connected pots) arranged so that when liquid is poured from one, the onrushing air makes a whistling noise in the other. Typical of the INCAS and SOUTH AMERICAN INDIANS.

white   One of several terms applied to Caucasians to distinguish them from Indians; a shortened form of "white man." "White," "non-Indian," or EUROAMERICAN are more commonly used nowadays, being genderless. Different tribes had different names for whites, some of them similar to PALEFACE, such as the ARAPAHO term "yellow hide." Most were descriptive in one way or another: the colonial Indian "long knives" (for the Americans) or "coat men" (for the British). The KIOWA word *bedalpago* translates from the KIOWA-TANOAN as "hairy mouths." The ACHOMAWI word *inallaaduwi* translates from the PALAIHNIHAN as "people not connected to anything." The Navajo term *Belagana* is a mispronunciation of the Spanish word *Americano*.

white buffalo   See BUFFALO.

White Buffalo Woman (White Buffalo Calf Woman, White Buffalo Calf Maiden, White Buffalo Cow Woman, Ptehincalasan-win)   A spiritual being in SIOUX (Lakota) tradition who supposedly passed the BUFFALO CALF PIPE to the people along with sacred rites. The COMANCHES and KIOWAS also have a White Buffalo Woman in their mythology.

White Deerskin Dance   A ceremony of the HOOPA, KAROK, and YUROK Indians, held in autumn during the World Renewal Ceremonial Cycle. The dancers wear animal skin aprons, dentalium shell necklaces, and feather headdresses. They carry poles draped with deer hides, the heads of which are decorated with the red-feathered scalps of woodpeckers. White deerskins are thought to cast the greatest powers of renewal and provide the dancer and the dancer's sponsor with great prestige.

"white Indian"   A phrase used historically for an Indian of light skin, often with blue eyes and beards. Early scholars used reports of "white Indians" to try to confirm erroneous theories of lost peoples. "Welsh Indians," supposed descendants of an unconfirmed Welsh colony of 1170, were identified with the MANDANS. Mormon tradition maintains that all Indians were descendants of one of the Lost Ten Tribes of Israel. "White Indians" also have been associated with the lost Roanoke Colony of North Carolina.

"white man"   See WHITE.

White Mountain (Sierra Blanca, Coyotera)   A subtribe of the SAN CARLOS division of the APACHE Indians, consisting of the Eastern White Mountain and Western White Mountain bands, located in the area of the upper Gila and Salt rivers in present-day southeastern Arizona. Other Apache bands also placed on the White Mountain Reservation, established in 1871, came under the general heading White Mountain. In 1897, the White Mountain Reservation was divided into the San Carlos and Fort Apache reservations. Most of the descendants of the White Mountain Apache proper are on the Fort Apache Reservation near Whiteriver, Arizona. The alternate name *Coyotera*, applied to more than one Apache band, means "wolf-men" in Spanish.

White Stick   A term applied by whites to the CREEK bands who allied themselves with the army against the militant bands known as RED STICKS.

Wichita (Pani Piqué, Pict)   A CADDOAN-speaking tribe of the GREAT PLAINS CUL-

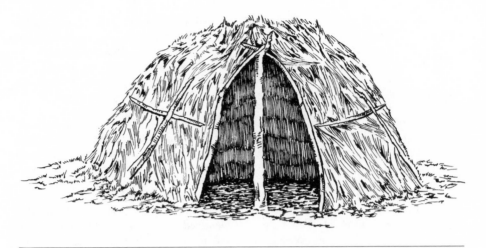

Apache wickiup

TURE AREA, located on the Canadian River north of the headwaters of the Washita River in present-day Oklahoma and later on the Red River in present-day Texas. A number of tribes—Kichai, TAWAKONI, TAWEHASH, Waco, and Yscani—were united with the Wichitas in the Wichita Confederacy. The Wichitas hold trust lands in Caddo, Canadian, and Grady counties, Oklahoma. Their name derives from *wits*, meaning "man" in Caddoan.

wicker   A type of WEAVING in which slender, pliant WEFT strands, especially willow, are interwoven with thicker, less flexible WARP strands in a simple over-and-under pattern. The term has come to refer to a variety of slender, pliant shoots, woven into baskets or furniture (wickerwork).

wickiup (wikiup)   A domed or cone-shape dwelling, typical of the APACHES and PAIUTES, with a pole frame covered with brush, grass, reeds, or mats. Probably ALGONQUIAN, from the same root as WIGWAM. The term sometimes applies to any brush shelter, as those constructed by PLAINS INDIANS to be used as SWEATHOUSES, and also to the domed winter dwellings of the KICKAPOOS.

wife-lending   The sharing of a wife with a friend or guest, as a demonstration of public generosity. In some instances, a mate was shared with another individual because of a couple's inability to have children. Typical of the INUITS.

wigwam   A domed or cone-shape dwelling, with a pole frame (BENT-FRAME construction) overlaid with bark (especially BIRCHBARK and ELM BARK), reed mats, or hide. Wigwams usually were built over a shallow pit, with earth piled around the base. Some wigwams were rectangular with an arched top, similar to the LONGHOUSES of the IROQUOIS. Wigwams have holes in the top to let out smoke. The coverings could be transported and used again. Typical of ALGONQUIAN tribes of the NORTHEAST CULTURE AREA from whom the word is derived. (The ABENAKI version is *wetuom*, for "dwelling.") "Wigwam" also has been applied by early writers to dwellings of non-Algonquians, as an equivalent of LODGE.

wild rice   A tall plant of the grass family (*Zizania aquatica*), with an edible grain, growing especially along the western Great Lakes; not a true rice. (The British called it "wild oats.") ALGONQUIAN peoples gathered wild rice. The MENOMINEE Indians are

Kickapoo wigwam

named after the plant, from the CHIPPEWA word *manomin*, meaning "good berry" or "spirit delicacy." The traditional method of gathering is floating in a canoe through the shallow water where the wild rice grows, bending the grain heads over the side of the canoe, and knocking them with a stick inside the boat.

willow Any of several trees or shrubs of the genus *Salix*. The strong but pliable shoots are used in BASKETRY and the saplings in BENT-FRAME construction.

Wiminuche A subtribe of the UTE Indians, located on the San Juan River and its northern tributaries in present-day southwestern Colorado. Wiminuches hold the Ute Mountain Reservation near Towaoc, Colorado.

wind See BREATH OF LIFE; WIND PEOPLE.

Windigo A monster in the mythology of the eastern SUBARCTIC INDIANS, including the MONTAGNAIS, CREES and CHIPPEWAS.

According to legend, the Windigos were cannibals of the northern woods. Sometimes called "ice giants," they were as tall as 30 feet with lipless mouths and long jagged teeth, steeped in blood, as were their eyes; they hissed when they breathed; they had claws for hands. They would eat animals or other Windigos, but preferred human flesh. Hunters and children who disappeared were thought to have been taken by the Windigos. Windigos could take possession of human bodies; people with Windigo souls would crave human flesh. The Windigo legend may have evolved out of incidents of humans resorting to CANNIBALISM when faced with starvation; the legend created a TABOO surrounding the act. The NASKAPI equivalent of Windigo is Atsan.

Wind People The NAVAJOS and other tribes refer to the wind as "Wind People," one of the many personifications of nature in Native American cosmology.

wine See ALCOHOLIC BEVERAGE.

Winnebago A SIOUAN-speaking tribe of the NORTHEAST CULTURE AREA, located on the south side of Green Bay, as far inland as Lake Winnebago in present-day Wisconsin. (Ancestors of the IOWA, MISSOURI, and OTO Indians probably separated from the Winnebagos.) In the 1700s, Winnebago bands also lived on the Fox, Wisconsin, and Rock rivers. In the mid-1800s, bands lived for a time in present-day Iowa and Minnesota before returning to Wisconsin. Others settled near the OMAHAS in present-day Nebraska. Tribal members hold the Winnebago Reservation near Tomah, Wisconsin and the Winnebago Reservation near Winnebago, Nebraska (with some adjoining nonreservation homes in Iowa). *Winnebago* derives from the FOX and SAC term in ALGONQUIAN for "people of the dirty water." Their native name is *Hotcangara*, meaning "people of the big speech."

winnowing basket A shallow BASKET used to separate the chaff from the grain by means of tossing the grain in a breeze.

winter count A CALENDAR of PICTOGRAPHS, recording a tribal event for each "winter" or, more accurately, the period from spring to spring, or one year. PLAINS INDIANS, especially the KIOWAS and SIOUX, drew winter counts with pigments and dyes on buffalo and deer hides and, in post-Contact times, on pieces of canvas, cotton, or muslin. Some winter counts spiral outward from the center; others wind irregularly; some read left to right or right to left. (See also KIOWA CALENDAR.)

Wintu See WINTUN.

Wintun A PENUTIAN speaking tribe of the CALIFORNIA CULTURE AREA, located from the west side of the Sacramento River to the Coast Range in present-day northern California. (The Wintu Indians on the upper Sacramento and upper Trinity rivers are considered by some researchers as a subtribe of the Wintuns; others do not distinguish between the names.) Descendants hold the Colusa Rancheria near Colusa, California; Cortina Indian Rancheria near Sacramento; Grindstone Creek Rancheria near Elk Creek (with WAILAKIS); and the Rumsey Indian Rancheria near Brooks. The NOMELACKI subtribe shares the Round Valley Reservation in Mendocino County, California with other tribes. *Wintun* or *Wintu* means "people" in Penutian. Some scholars group the various dialects spoken by the Wintun and PATWIN bands us a distinct language family, Wintun, a subdivision of the Penutian phylum; it was formerly known as Copehan.

Winyaw See SIOUAN.

Wishoskan See WIYOT.

Wishram See CHINOOKAN.

witch A person who practices WITCHCRAFT. "Witch" is usually applied to woman, with "SORCERER," "wizard," or "warlock" applied to men. There is a tradition of both male and female "witches" among SOUTHWEST INDIANS, however. They are believed to be SHAPE SHIFTERS, assuming the shapes of animals. The NAVAJOS have complex rituals to ward off the power of witches. (See also BRUJO; WAY.)

witchcraft (sorcery) Manipulating another person's will or well-being through use of supernatural power. Some reported methods of sorcery were attaining hair, nails, partially eaten food, clothing that had absorbed perspiration, or some other possession, then stuffing them in a corpse's mouth, or making an EFFIGY figure with them, which would be penetrated with an arrow. Most tribes had TABOOS against witchcraft, blaming those known to practice it for sickness and death and severely punishing them. (See also SHAMAN.)

Wiyot (Wiyat, Waiyat, Wishosk) A MACRO-ALGONQUIAN-speaking (Wiyot or Wishoskan isolate) tribe of the CALIFORNIA CULTURE AREA, located on lower Mad

River, Humboldt Bay, and lower Eel River in present-day northern California. The Wiyots are now extinct. The Wiyot language formerly was classified as a distinct stock, Wishoskan.

Woccon See SIOUAN.

wokas (wocas) A yellow water lily (*Nuphar polysepalum*), found in the American West. The roasted seeds were a staple of the KLAMATH Indians. A Klamath word in PENUTIAN.

wolf Either of two carnivorous mammals of the genus *Canis: C. lupus* in northern parts of North America or *C. rufus* (also called *C. niger*) in the Southwest. Since wolves hunt in packs, wolf is likely to be considered dependable in Indian legends, unlike the COYOTE. To the NAVAJOS, Wolf is the leader of the hunting animals.

wood carving See WOODWORK.

wooden Indian A carved wooden sculpture of an American Indian, originally placed outside of TOBACCO stores for advertising. The custom began in England as early as 1600, because of the association of tobacco with Indians, who had first cultivated the plant. Such statues began appearing in North America by the 1700s.

Woodland Indians A term sometimes applied to EASTERN INDIANS; for example the NORTHEAST CULTURE AREA and SOUTHEAST CULTURE AREA are sometimes referred to as Northeast Woodland and Southeast Woodland. Since there were many other Indians living in North American forests—in the SUBARCTIC CULTURE AREA, NORTHWEST COAST CULTURE AREA, and PLATEAU CULTURE AREA—the term woodland can be confusing when limited to Eastern Indians. (See also WOODLAND PERIOD.)

Woodland period A cultural period of eastern PREHISTORIC INDIANS living in for-

ested areas. The cultural traits specifically referred to as the Woodland tradition are thought to have originated in the Great Lakes region in about 1000 B.C. and have spread as far east as Nova Scotia and as far west as the Great Plains. Some scholars refer to the ADENA CULTURE as "Early Woodland" and the HOPEWELL CULTURE as "Late Woodland." For others "Early Woodland" refers to the transitional stage between the ARCHAIC PERIOD and FORMATIVE PERIOD. In any case, the Woodland period as a whole can be viewed as the equivalent of the Formative period in the East. (See also WOODLAND INDIANS.)

woodwork (wood carving, woodcraft) The act, process, or resulting artifact of work in wood; or the carved wooden objects themselves. For American Indians, wood was a valuable resource, used in the making of houses, boats, tools, utensils, weapons, containers, and ceremonial objects. In pre-Contact times, a variety of stone tools were used in woodworking, many of these replaced after Contact by iron tools. Among NORTHWEST COAST INDIANS, wood carving became highly intricate and detailed, as evidenced in their PLANK HOUSES, TOTEM POLES, MASKS, and CHESTS. (See also BARK CRAFT; DRIFTWOOD; ROOT CRAFT.)

woof See WEFT.

world renewal (cosmic rejuvenation) Native American ceremonies traditionally have celebrated the cycle of seasons and renewal of life and food resources. Modern-day activists speak of a need for an "ecological world renewal."

World Tree See COSMIC TREE.

worldview A modern-day term for a people's philosophy and religion, i.e., a view of themselves in relation to the rest of reality. Different tribes and cultures had different worldviews. But it can be said that in a generalized sense, the Native American worldview, as it has been passed down through the ages, is more reverent of nature, the land, and the spiritual world than the Western (European) tradition that came to dominate the Americas. Humankind is considered on an equal footing with fellow life forms; interconnectedness is assumed; and spirituality is more important than material goals. (See also COSMOLOGY.)

Wounded Knee The name of a creek in South Dakota and an event of December 29, 1890 that has come to symbolize the end of the Indian wars, the cruelty to native peoples, and the continuing struggle for justice. The events of Wounded Knee evolved out of the GHOST DANCE RELIGION. White officials became alarmed at renewed Indian militancy and banned the Ghost Dance on SIOUX reservations. When troops rode in to the Pine Ridge and Rosebud reservations in South Dakota to enforce the ban, Ghost Dancers planned a huge gathering on the Pine Ridge Reservation and sent word to the Hunkpapa chief Sitting Bull, then on the Standing Rock Reservation in North Dakota, to join them. The army, fearing Sitting Bull's powers to unite the bands, ordered his arrest, during which Sitting Bull and seven warriors were killed. The army also ordered the arrest of a Miniconjou chief named Big Foot, who formerly had advocated the .Ghost Dance but now sought peace. Big Foot led his band to Pine Ridge to join up with the Oglala chief Red Cloud, not with the Ghost Dancers. A detachment of the army intercepted Big Foot's band and ordered them to set up camp at Wounded Knee Creek. The following morning, the army attempted to collect all Indian firearms. When the soldiers tried to disarm a deaf Indian named Black Coyote, his rifle discharged in the air. The soldiers shot back in response. At first the fighting was at close quarters, but heavy artillery soon cut down men, women, and children alike. At least 175 Indians died unnecessarily at Wounded Knee, with many more injured. In honor of their ancestors and in protest of the broken treaties by the federal government, members of the American Indian Movement (AIM) staged an occupation at Wounded Knee in 1973. The incident ended in violence, with two Native Americans killed by federal agents.

wound plug A tapered plug made from wood or ivory, used for insertion in the wound of a harpooned sea mammal to stop the flow of blood. Seal float mouthpieces were variations of wound plugs, designed to be inserted into special cuts in the skin; air could be blown through the mouthpiece's perforation to create air pockets between the animal's blubber and muscle layers so that the carcass would remain buoyant during towing. Typical of the INUITS.

wrestling A sport in which unarmed contestants attempt to throw each other to the ground and pin each other down or to force each other from a delineated area. Native peoples wrestled for exercise and entertainment, but also as a DISPUTE SETTLEMENT. Among the INUITS, an individual who sought revenge against a person for a murder might challenge the offender to a wrestling match, with the loser forfeiting his life.

writing Language symbols drawn or carved on a surface. In pre-Contact times, Native Americans used PICTOGRAPHS, also called glyph writing or hieroglyphics, to record events and CALENDAR systems. (See also LITERATURE; POETRY.)

Wyandot See HURON.

Wynoochee See SALISHAN.

X

Xipe Totek (Xipe, Yopi) The AZTEC god of spring, growth, and vegetation. The Flayed Lord, he obtained his power from the skin of humans sacrificed to him. He was the patron deity of goldsmiths.

Xolotl The TOLTEC and AZTEC god of lightning and the evening star (the planet Venus), who accompanies the setting sun and the dead to the nether world. He also is god of the ball-game TLACHTLI. The twin brother of QUETZALCOATL, he was represented as dog-headed and had semi-mythical status as a ruler of Chichimec peoples, probable ancestors of the Toltecs and Aztecs.

Y

Yadkin   See SIOUAN.

yage (ahuahuaso, ayahuasca, caapi, kaahi) A hallucinogenic substance made from a number of vines of the genus *Banisteriopsis*. SOUTH AMERICAN INDIANS prepare it as a liquid, which they drink for religious experience. Among some peoples, its use is restricted to SHAMANS.

Yahi   A YANAN-speaking tribe of the CALIFORNIA CULTURE AREA, located on Mill and Deer creeks in present-day northern California. The Yahis are related linguistically to the YANA Indians. The Yahis are extinct, the last Yahi, Ishi, having died in 1916. *Yahi* means "person" in Yanan.

Yahuskin   See SNAKE INDIANS.

Yakima   A SAHAPTIN-speaking tribe of the PLATEAU CULTURE AREA, located on the lower Yakima River in present-day Washington. The Sahaptin-speaking Pshwanwapams are known as the Upper Yakimas. Yakimas hold the Yakima Reservation in Yakima and Klickitat counties, Washington. *Yakima* means "runaway" in Sahaptin. Their native name is *Waptailmin*, meaning "people of the narrow river."

Yakonan   A language family and subdivision of the PENUTIAN phylum comprising dialects spoken by the ALSEA, KUITSH, SIUSLAW, and YAQUINA tribes of the NORTHWEST COAST CULTURE AREA.

Yamasee   A MUSKOGEAN-speaking tribe of the SOUTHEAST CULTURE AREA, located on the Ocmulgee River near the mouth of the Oconee River in present-day Georgia and, after 1687, across the Savannah River in present-day South Carolina. Starting in 1715, most Yamasees settled in Florida,

eventually merging with the SEMINOLES. Others merged with the APALACHEES, living for a time on Mobile Bay in present-day Alabama. They are extinct as a tribal entity. *Yamasee* may mean "gentle" in Muskogean.

Yamel   See KALAPUYAN.

yampa (yamp)   A plant *(Atenia gairdneri)* of the family Ammiaceae. Its roots were used by PLATEAU INDIANS and GREAT BASIN INDIANS for food. The term derives from the UTE name for the plant in UTO-AZTECAN; a subtribe of the Utes living in eastern Utah became known as the Yampa Indians. The plant has been referred to, along with other plants with edible tuberous roots, as the Indian potato.

Yana   A YANAN-speaking tribe of the CALIFORNIA CULTURE AREA, located in Shasta and Tehama counties in present-day northern California. The now-extinct Yanas are subdivided into the Northern, Central, and Southern Divisions, the various bands linguistic relatives of the YAHI Indians. *Yana* means "person" in Yanan.

Yanan   A language family and subdivision of the HOKAN phylum comprising dialects spoken by the YANA and YAHI tribes of the CALIFORNIA CULTURE AREA.

Yankton (Nakota)   A subtribe of the SIOUX Indians, located on the Missouri River in present-day southeastern South Dakota, southwestern Minnesota, and southwestern Iowa. The Yankton proper are a band in the Yankton division. Along with the YANKTONAIS, the Yanktons sometimes are referred to as the Middle Sioux, to distinguish them from the SANTEES (Dakotas) and TETONS (Lakotas). *Yankton* means "end village" in SIOUAN. The Yanktons call themselves *Nakota*, meaning "allies."

Yanktonai (Nakota) A subtribe of the SIOUX Indians, located on the Missouri River in present-day eastern North Dakota and South Dakota. They include the Yanktonai proper (Upper Yanktonai) in the vicinity of the upper James River, and the HUNKPATINA (Lower Yanktonai) band around the lower James River. The ASSINIBOINES split off from the Yanktonais in the 1600s. Along with the YANKTONS, the Yanktonais are sometimes referred to as the Middle Sioux to distinguish them from the SANTEES (Dakotas) and TETONS (Lakotas). *Yanktonai* means "little end village" in SIOUAN. Yanktonais call themselves *Nakota*, meaning "allies."

Yanomani See SOUTH AMERICAN INDIANS.

Yaqui A UTO-AZTECAN-speaking tribe of the SOUTHWEST CULTURE AREA, located on the Rio Yaqui in the present-day state of Sonora in northern Mexico. In the late 1800s and early 1900s, many Yaquis crossed the border into Arizona, where their descendants live in communities at Eloy, Marana, Pascua, Scottsdale, Tempe, and Tucson.

Yaquina A YAKONAN-speaking tribe of the NORTHWEST COAST CULTURE AREA, located on the Yaquina River and Yaquina Bay in present-day Oregon. The Yaquinas are related linguistically to the ALSEAS. Descendants live on the Siletz Reservation near Siletz, Oregon, with other Yakonen-speaking and KUSAN-speaking tribes.

yaupon See BLACK DRINK.

Yavapai (Yavepe, Mojave-Apache) A YUMAN-speaking tribe of the SOUTHWEST CULTURE AREA, located in present-day western Arizona, from the Pinal and Mazatzal mountains in the east to the Colorado River in the west, and from the Williams and Santa Maria rivers in the north to the

Gila River in the south. Tribal members hold the Yavapai-Prescott Reservation in Yavapai County, Arizona. Other Yavapais share the Camp Verde Reservation in Yavapai County with APACHES and the Fort McDowell Reservation in Maricopa County in Yavapai County with the Apaches and MOJAVES. *Yavapai* may possibly mean "people of the sun" or "crooked-mouth people" in Yuman.

Yazoo A TUNICAN-speaking tribe of the SOUTHEAST CULTURE AREA, located on the Yazoo River in present-day Mississippi. The Yazoos probably merged with the CHICKASAWS and CHOCTAWS.

yei Spiritual beings in NAVAJO tradition, some among the HOLY PEOPLE, who came to the earth before humans and have stayed to offer assistance. In rituals, sacred YEIBICHAI MASKS are worn to impersonate the *yei*. The *yei* are the equivalent of the GANS of the APACHES.

Yeibichai mask A mask worn by the NAVAJOS to impersonate the YEI. Ritually made of buckskin, they are painted black, white, red, or blue, with added feathers. POLLEN is sprinkled over the eyes and mouth. (See also WAY.)

Yellowknife See AHTENA; TATSANOTTINE.

Yeponi A SECRET SOCIETY of the MAIDU Indians. Any male tribal member could earn his way into the Yeponi through deeds. Old men instructed young men in Yeponi rituals and tribal mythology. Different villages or groups of villages had branches of this sodality under a leader known as *Huku*.

Yokuts (Mariposa) A PENUTIAN-speaking tribe of the CALIFORNIA CULTURE AREA, located on the San Joaquin River and to the east in the foothills of the Sierra Nevada. Along with the MIWOKS, the Yokuts have been referred to as the Chowchilla Indians. Tribal members hold the Santa Rosa

Rancheria in Kings County, California, and share the Tule River Reservation in Tulare County with other tribes. *Yokuts* means "person" or "people" in Penutian. Some scholars group the various dialects spoken by the Yokuts bands as a distinct language family called Yokuts and a subdivision of the Penutian phylum; it was formerly known as Mariposan. (See also TACHI.)

Yoncalla See KALAPUYAN.

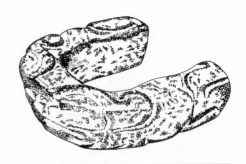

Mesoamerican yugo

yopo (nopo, vilca, aiuku) A hallucinogenic snuff made from a large leguminous tree (*Anadenanthera perigrina*). Typical of SOUTH AMERICAN INDIANS of the rain forest.

Yscani See CADDOAN; WICHITA.

yucca (yuca) A genus of plants of the lily family (Liliaceae), having long, pointed, fibrous leaves and a large cluster of white blossoms. The fruit of certain varieties were eaten by SOUTHWEST INDIANS, and the flowers of other varieties were eaten by some SOUTHEAST INDIANS. These peoples and GREAT BASIN INDIANS made use of other parts of the plants as well: Leaf, stalk, and root fiber was used in crafting sandals, baskets, mats, nets, cordage, hairbrushes, and paintbrushes; roots also were used as soap and as an ingredient in SKIN-DRESSING; juices were used in DYES; the dried flower stalk was used in making FIRE-DRILLS and also for ceremonial wands and whips. Other names for some of the varieties of yucca include soapweed and Spanish bayonet. The alternate spelling, yuca, more often applies to the CASSAVA plant. The HOPI word for "yucca" in UTO-AZTECAN is *sowungwa*.

Yuchi (Westo) A MACRO-SIOUAN-speaking (Yuchi isolate) of the SOUTHEAST CULTURE AREA, located in present-day eastern Tennessee and northern Georgia. Over the years, the Yuchis also lived in present-day coastal Georgia, southern Kentucky, western North and South Carolina, eastern Alabama, and western Florida. They merged with the CREEK Indians and were relocated with them to the INDIAN TERRITORY (present-day Oklahoma). They are extinct as a tribal entity. *Yuchi* possibly derives from "those far away" in MUSKOGEAN. The Yuchi language was formerly classified as a distinct stock, Uchean.

yugo A stone sculpture in the shape of a large horseshoe; often made of green granite with carvings in BAS-RELIEF. Typical of the Totonacs of the Gulf Coast of present-day central Mexico. As with HACHAS and PALMAS, the purpose of *yugos* was probably ceremonial; they are possibly representations of the belts worn by players in BALL-GAMES. *Yugo* means "yoke" in Spanish.

Yui See TIMUCUA.

Yuki A YUKIAN-speaking tribe of the CALIFORNIA CULTURE AREA, located on the Eel River in present-day California. The Yukis are subdivided into the Yuki proper and Coast Yuki (or Ukhotno'em) on the Pacific Coast. The neighboring Huchnoms sometimes are classified as a subtribe. Yuki descendants share the Round Valley Reservation near Covelo, California, with the POMOS and other tribes. *Yuki* means "stranger" or "foe" in PENUTIAN.

Yukian A language family of undetermined language phylum affiliation comprising dialects spoken by the Huchnom,

Wappo, and YUKI tribes of the CALIFORNIA CULTURE AREA.

Yuma (Quechan, Kwichana, Kwitchiana) A YUMAN-speaking tribe of the SOUTHWEST CULTURE AREA, located on both sides of the Colorado River near the junction of the Gila River in present-day western Arizona and southeastern California. Yumas hold the Fort Yuma Reservation in Imperial County, California, and Mohave County, Arizona. Others hold the Cocopah Reservation in Yuma County, Arizona. *Yuma* possibly means "people of the river" in Yuman. Their native name, *Quechan*, probably means "people." (See also COCOPAH.)

Yuman A language family and subdivision of the HOKAN phylum comprising dialects spoken by Indians of the SOUTHWEST CULTURE AREA, among them the COCOPAH, Halchidhoma, Halyikwamai, HAVASUPAI, HUALAPAI, Kohuana, MARICOPA, MOJAVE, YAVAPAI, and YUMA tribes; as well as by

Indians of the CALIFORNIA CULTURE AREA, among them the Akwaala, DIEGUENO, and Kamia (Tipai) tribes.

Yurok A MACRO-ALGONQUIAN-speaking (Yurok isolate) tribe of the CALIFORNIA CULTURE AREA, located on the lower Klamath River and nearby Pacific Coast in present-day California. Yuroks hold the Big Lagoon Rancheria (with the TOLOWAS) near Trinidad, California, the Trinidad Rancheria near Trinidad, and the Hoopa Extension Reservation near Weitchpec. *Yurok* means "downstream" in the KAROK dialect of HOKAN. The Yurok language was formerly classified as a distinct stock, Weitspekan.

Yuwipi (Yuwipi lowanpi) A HEALING ceremony of the SIOUX Indians. Spirits are called upon to aid the *Yuwipi wicasa*, a SHAMAN who has been bound up in a blanket; he is released by the spirits during their visitation. *Yuwi* translates from the SIOUAN (Lakota) as "to tie up."

.Z.

Zamucoan A language family and subdivision of the ANDEAN-EQUATORIAL phylum comprising dialects spoken by SOUTH AMERICAN INDIANS, in particular, the Zamuco tribe of present-day Paraguay.

Zaparoan A language family and subdivision of the ANDEAN-EQUATORIAL phylum comprising dialects spoken by SOUTH AMERICAN INDIANS, in particular, the Zaparo tribe of present-day Peru and Ecuador.

Zapotecan A language family and subdivision of the OTO-MANGUEAN phylum comprising dialects spoken by Indians of the MESOAMERICAN CULTURE AREA, including the Chatino and Zapotec tribes of what is now southwest Mexico.

zemi The ARAWAKAN name for an all-pervasive spirit, or the power found in objects.

Zia Pueblo See KERES.

zoomorphism The use of animal forms and traits in artwork. "Zoomorphic" is the adjective form. "Theriomorphism" is the use of part-animal and part-human forms in art; as representing legendary beings. (See also ANTHROPOMORPHISM.)

Zuni A PENUTIAN-speaking (Zuni or Zunian isolate) tribe of the SOUTHWEST CULTURE AREA, located on the north side of the upper Zuni River in present-day western New Mexico. The Zunis are classified as PUEBLO INDIANS. Tribal members hold the Zuni Pueblo in McKinley and Valencia counties, New Mexico. *Zuni* derives from a KERES word of unknown meaning. The Zuni native name, *Ashiwi*, means "the flesh."

CATEGORICAL APPENDIX

ANIMALS
Appaloosa
bear
beaver
bird
buffalo
caribou
coati
coyote
crow
deer
dog
eagle
elk
fish
hawk
horse
husky
hutia
jaguar
llama
magpie
malamute
mammoth
mastodon
moose
owl
parrot
peccary

porcupine
pronghorn
puma
quetzal
rabbit
raven
saber-toothed tiger
salmon
sea mammal
sheep
shellfish
snake
tapir
turkey
turtle
whale
wolf

ANTHROPOLOGY AND SOCIOLOGY
See also ARCHAEOLOGY; ARTS
AND CRAFTS; COMMUNICA-
TION AND LINGUISTICS; FOOD
PRODUCTION; MUSIC; POLITI-
CAL AND HISTORICAL CON-
CEPTS; RELIGION AND RITUAL;
TRIBES, BANDS, PEOPLES, LAN-
GUAGES, AND CULTURES.

aboriginal

adaptation
adoption
affinal
agamous
ancestor
anthropology
band
basic culture
berdache
bilocal
cache
cacique
camp
carrying capacity
caste system
category
chief
chiefdom
childbirth
child life
city-state
civilization
clan
cognate
composite tribe
consanguinity
courtship
couvade
cultural diffusion

cultural evolutionism
cultural relativism
cultural trait
culture
culture area
culture sequence
culture stage
demography
descent
dispute settlement
endogamous
ethnobotany
ethnography
ethnology
exogamous
family
fieldwork
fire-making
gens
grand sachem
Great Sun
headman
hereditary title
historic period
horizon
humor
incest taboo
indigenous
informant
joking relative
kinship
life history
marriage
material culture
matrilineal
matrilocal
medium of exchange
migration
moiety
monogamy
nativism
neolocal
nomadic
papoose
patrilineal
patrilocal
phratry
polygamy
population
pre-Columbian

prehistory
primogeniture
property
protohistory
rank
sachem
sagamore
scarification
sedentary
sib
slavery
social organization
society
sociology
sodality
soldier
sovereignty
specialization
structuralism
subtribe
technology
town
trade
tradition
tribe
tribelet
tributary tribe
village
warfare
war party
warrior
wife-lending

ARCHAEOLOGY

See also ANTHROPOLOGY AND
SOCIOLOGY; NATURAL PHE-
NOMENA; TOOLS, UTENSILS,
AND WEAPONS.

absolute dating
archaeological site
archaeology
Archaic period
artifact
artifact density
ashpile
assemblage
bundle burial
burial
cairn

cairn burial
canoe burial
catastrophe
chullpa
cist
Classic period
complex
continuity
cross dating
dendrochronology
earthwork
excavation
Formative period
fossil
geology
grave
grave goods
house burial
house mound
in situ
kill site
midden
mound
mummy
necropolis
ossuary
Paleolithic period
paleontology
palynology
phase
pit
Pleistocene
Pleistocene Overkill
post mold
potsherd
pre-ceramic
provenance
provenience
quarry site
radiocarbon dating
relative dating
scaffold burial
shell-heap
specimen
Stone Age
stratigraphy
tool kit
tree burial
type site
urn burial

Watershed Age
Woodland period

ARTS AND CRAFTS

See also CLOTHING, COV-
ERINGS, AND ADORNMENT;
CONTAINERS; HOUSES AND AR-
CHITECTURE; MUSIC; TOOLS,
UTENSILS, AND WEAPONS;
TRANSPORTATION. (Possible
tools whose exact purpose is
unknown also are listed here.)

alabaster
amber
annealing
anthropomorphism
appliqué
articulate mask
arts and crafts
babiche
baleen
bark craft
basalt
basketry
bas-relief
bast
bayeta
bead
beadwork
birchbark
blackware
blade and core
blank
boatstone
bonework
braidwork
ceramic
chalcedony
checkerboard
chert
chip
cire perdue
coiling
cold-hammering
cone
copper
cordage
cord-marked pottery
core
corn cob

cornhusk
crazing
cross
danzantes
deerskin
dentalium
discoid
driftwood
duck tablet
dye
effigy
elm bark
embroidery
engraving
etching
excising
fair
featherwork
fiber craft
figurine
fine art
firing
flake
flaking
flint
flint disk
float
fluting
footprint sculpture
fresco
fur
galena
German silver
glaze
glue
gold
goldwork
gourd
grasswork
hacha
hair pipe
hairwork
heartline
hematite
hemisphere
heshi
hide
high-steel
hocker
hook-stone

horn and antler work
icon
iron
ironwork
ivory work
jade
kiln
leather
ledger art
mat
metalwork
mica
mining
mise en couleur
mosaic
mound ware
negative painting
netting
notched plate
obsidian
ocher
ornament
paddle-and-anvil
paddling
paint
painting
palma
parfleche
pearl
pecking
pelt
perforated stone
pierced tablet
pigment
pipestone
pitch
plaiting
plummet
polishing implement
polychrome ware
pony beads
positive painting
pottery
punctation
pyrite
quarrying
quartz
quillwork
rawhide
redware

repoussé
reserve decoration
resin
ribbonwork
ringstone
rock art
rocker stamping
root craft
rubber
runtee
sandpainting
scrimshaw
sculpture
sewan
shaganappi
shellwork
silver
silverwork
sinew
skin
skin-dressing
slate
slip
soapstone
spade-stone
spine-back stone
spinning
spirit break
splint
spool
stirrup spout
stonework
stucco
swastika
tapestry
temper
textile
tie-dye
tourist pot
trade goods
tradeware
tumbaga
turquoise
tusk
twilling
twining
utility ware
wampum
warp
watap

wattle
weaving
weft
wicker
wooden Indians
woodwork
yugo
zoomorphism

CLOTHING, COVERINGS, AND ADORNMENT

See also ARTS AND CRAFTS.

anklet
apron
armor
bandolier
bar-gorget
bear-claw necklace
belt
blanket
boot
breastplate
breechcloth
buffalo robe
bustle
button
button blanket
chief's blanket
Chilkat blanket
cloak
concha
dance apron
dress
earspool
exploit feather
Eye Dazzler
frontlet
goggles
gorgerin
gorget
hairstyle
head deformation
headgear
helmet
Hudson's Bay blanket
jewelry
labret
legging

mask
matchcoat
medal
mitten
moccasin
mukluk
naja
Navajo blanket
Nootka hat
parka
pendant
poncho
rebozo
roach
robe
sandal
sash
scalplock
serape
shirt
skirt
squash-blossom hairdo
stroud
tattoo
tinkler
trailer
tuma
turban
warbonnet

COMMUNICATION AND LINGUISTICS

See also MUSIC; TRIBES, BANDS, PEOPLES, LANGUAGES, AND CULTURES.

calendar
calendar stick
calendar stone
camp crier
Cherokee alphabet
childhood name
Chinook Jargon
chronology
code talker
codex
counting
dialect
dream name
glottochronology

glyph
inscription
invitation stick
Kiowa calendar
language
language family
language isolate
language phylum
linguistics
literature
Mobilian trade language
morpheme
oral tradition
oratory
petroglyph
phoneme
phonology
pictograph
place name
poetry
polysynthesism
protolanguage
quipu
signal
sign language
smoke signal
speaker
story
storytelling
syllabary
symbol
talking stick
terraglyph
trade language
Walum Olum
winter count
writing

CONTAINERS
See also ARTS AND CRAFTS.

aryballos
bag
bandolier bag
basket
bowl
box
chest
comal
container

cradleboard
cupstone
degikup
dish
head pot
jar
kero
kiaha
killed pottery
mealing bin
metate
mocuck
moss-bag
olla
patojo
pipe bag
pouch
quiver
rain god
seed jar
tobacco bag
tobacco flask
wedding jar
whistling jar
winnowing basket

EXPRESSIONS AND SLANG
"apple"
"Blanket Indian"
"bluecoat"
"Boston"
"brave"
"broken promises"
"bury the hatchet"
"cayuse pony"
"Great White Father"
"half-breed"
"happy hunting ground"
hootchenoo
"how"
"Indian file"
"Indian giver"
"iron horse"
mahala
"massacre"
"New World"
"paleface"
"redskin"
"savage"

"schmoehawk"
skraeling
"snowgo"
squaw
"squaw man"
"Uncle Tomahawk"
"warpath"
"wet head"
"white Indian"

FOOD PRODUCTION
See also ANIMALS; CONTAINERS; PLANTS; TOOLS, UTENSILS, AND WEAPONS.

alcoholic beverage
baking stone
balche
berry
big-game hunting
blind
boiling stone
cannibalism
chicha
chinampa
chocolate
cooking
cornmeal
corral
crusting
curare
curing
deadfall
decoy
domestication of animals
drying
farming
fire-drive
fishing
food preparation and preservation
foraging
fry bread
granary
hominy
horno
hunting
hunting-gathering
hunting ground
hunting party

Indian bread
Indian market
irrigation
jerky
leaf bread
maple sugar
meal
mescal
milpa
mortar and pestle
oven
pemmican
piki
pinole
pitfall
pit oven
poison
pulque
quid
rockahominy
sagamite
salt
samp
seine
setline
sign
slash-and-burn
snare
snow-pit
sofki
staple
stone-boiling
succotash
Sun Watcher
surround
tesguino
tortilla
tracking
trap
tuckahoe
whaling

GAMES, SPORTS, AND TOYS
archery
arrow game
ball-court
ball-game
bingo
cat's cradle
chunkey

chunkey stone
cornhusk doll
dice
doll
double-ball
football
gambling
game
gaming piece
guessing game
handball
hoop-and-pole
juggling
kickball
lacrosse
nugluktag
patolli
pillma
puppet
quoits
racing
ring-and-pin
Seminole doll
sham battle
shinny
single pole ball-game
snow snake
sport
stilts
tlachtli
top
toy
tug-of-war
wrestling

HOUSES AND ARCHITECTURE
adobe
aqueduct
arbor
architecture
asi
atlantes
banco
barabara
bent-frame
camp circle
cave
ceremonial house
chickee
chinking

cliff-dwelling
compression shell
corbeled arch
Cosmic Tree
council house
cry house
deflector
dew cloth
dwelling
earthlodge
firepit
furniture
grass house
gravehouse
Great House
hammock
hogan
house
housepost
igloo
jacal
karmak
kashim
ki
kihus
kisi
kiva
lean-to
lintel
lodge
log cabin
longhouse
medicine lodge
monolith
obelisk
palisade
pilaster
pisé
pithouse
plank house
plaza
post-and-beam
protokiva
pueblo
pyramid
qarmaq
ramada
shaking tent
shelter
sipapu
smoke flap

smokehole
smoke house
sod house
soldiers' lodge
spalling
stela
sweathouse
temple
tent
tepee
tepee ring
thatch
vahki
viga
wattle-and-daub
wickiup
wigwam

INDIAN WORDS AND PHRASES

(Not commonly used in English.) See also FOOD PRODUCTION; HOUSES AND ARCHITECTURE; RELIGION AND RITUAL.

ayorama
bacheeitch
bani
copalli
da neho
degyagomga
elke
eyayeye
hageota
hau kola
hecetu
hoka hey
ila
italwa
kinnikinnick
maka
minototak
mitakuye oyasin
nanuk
nistsistanowan
nyaweh gowah
ohwachira
okey
oleohneh
pila'mayan
posah-tai-vo

sannup
soospuk
sunka wakan
swanneken
tangakwunu
toka
tsanahwit
umelik
wathonwisas

MUSIC

See also RELIGION AND RITUAL.

Apache fiddle
bullroarer
bell
chant
clapper
dance
drum
flageolet
foot drum
monophony
music
musical bow
musical instrument
nith-song
notched stick
ocarina
panpipe
pentatonic scale
rattle
shell trumpet
sing
song
teponaztli
tom-tom
water drum
whistle

NATURAL PHENOMENA

See also ANIMALS; ARTS AND CRAFTS (for rock types and other natural resources); PLANTS.

bayou
Beringia
boreal
caliche
cardinal points

cenote
chinook wind
disease
drought
fire
hurricane
Indian summer
lightning
moon
muskeg
permafrost
pogonip
sierra
snow
solstice
star
taiga
talus
tundra
water

PLACES

(Historical and Cultural Classifications)

Arctic Culture Area
California Culture Area
Circum-Caribbean Culture Area
Great Basin Culture Area
Great Plains Culture Area
Mesoamerica
Mesoamerican Culture Area
Middle America
Northeast Culture Area
Northwest Coast Culture Area
Nuclear America
Paha Sapa
Pipestone Quarry
Plateau Culture Area
Southeast Culture Area
Southwest Culture Area
Subarctic Culture Area

PLANTS

acorn
agave
bean
camas
cassava

cattail
cedar
chili
coca
coontie
corn
cotton
guava
herb
jimsonweed
juniper
lichen
mesquite
moss
mushroom
ololiuqui
palmetto
pecan
persimmon
peyote
piñon
pod corn
pollen
popcorn
potato
puccoon
quinoa
saguaro
sotol
squash
sweet grass
sweet potato
tobacco
tomato
tule
vanilla
wild rice
willow
wokas
yampa
yucca

POLITICAL AND HISTORICAL CONCEPTS

See also ANTHROPOLOGY AND
SOCIOLOGY; PLACES; TRIBES,
BANDS, PEOPLES, LANGUAGES,
AND CULTURES.

acculturation

activism
allotment
annuity
assimilation
boarding school
Bureau of Indian Affairs
   (BIA)
captive
captivity narrative
chairman
Columbian exchange
comanchero
confederacy
conquistador
Contact
council
coureur de bois
cowboy
cultural dispossession
Department of Indian Af-
   fairs and Northern De-
   partment (DIAND)
detribalization
displacement
drift voyage
encomienda
ethnocentric
explorer
federal Indian policy
federal recognition
fish-in
frontier
frontier painter
frontier photographer
fur trade
gold rush
guide
hacienda
Indian affairs
Indian agent
Indian college
Indian Country
Indian police
Indian rights
Indian school
Indian superintendent
Indian Territory
indigenismo
interpreter
Iroquois League

land
land cession
land claim
land tenure
Little Bighorn
Long Walk
mountain man
nation
Native American Day
organization
pan-Indian
Pine Tree
powwow
presidio
promyshlenniki
rancheria
Red Stick
reformer
relocation
removal
repartimiento
repatriation
requerimiento
reservation
reservation state
reserve
resistance
restoration
revitalization movement
Sand Creek
scout
self-determination
sovereignty
termination
territory
tourist
trading post
Trail of Tears
treaty
tribal entity
tribal government
tribal headquarters
trust land
trust status
voyageur
war
water rights
White Stick
Wounded Knee

RELIGION AND RITUAL

See also ARTS AND CRAFTS; COMMUNICATION AND LINGUISTICS; HOUSES AND ARCHITECTURE; MUSIC; SPIRITS AND LEGENDARY BEINGS.

afterworld
akuhua
altar
amulet
angakok
animism
Bear Doctor
Begging Dance
Bighouse Ceremony
Black Drink
Black Legs Dance
Bladder Festival
bloodletting
Bole-Maru Religion
booger mask
brujo
Buffalo Calf Pipe
buffalo skull
calumet
Calumet Dance
ceremonial center
ceremonial runner
ceremony
charmstone
Chelkona
Chungichnish Religion
circle
clan animal
clan emblem
Clan Mother
clown
contrary warrior
Corn Dance
cosmology
coup
creation story
Creator
cremation
crest
culture hero
death song
diagnostician
Dog Soldiers

double
dream
Dream Catcher
Dream Dance
Dreamer Religion
Drum Religion
Eagle Dance
Earth Lodge Religion
elder
Faithkeeper
False Face
Fancy Dance
fast
feast
Feast Day
Feast to the Dead
Feather Dance
Feather Religion
festival
fetish
fiesta
first food ceremonies
First Laugh
Flat Pipe
Flute Ceremony
Galaxy Society
ghost
Ghost Dance
Ghost Dance Religion
Ghost Keeping Ceremony
giveaway
Gourd Dance
grandfather
grandmother
Grass Dance
Green Corn Ceremony
Hako Ceremony
hanblecheyapi
hand-trembling
harvest festival
head-shrinking
healing
heyoka
hierohistory
hierophany
holism
Hoop Dance
hozhoni
huaca
huskanaw

Husk Face Society
idol
impersonator
incense
Indian Shaker Religion
Indian Two Step
inipi
initiation
I'n-Lon-Schka
Iruska Dance
Jump Dance
keeper
Kettle Dance
Koshare
Kotikilli
Koyemshi
Kuksu Religion
Kwerana
lamenting
land
legend
legendary being
Longhouse Religion
magic
masquette
Massaum Ceremony
medicine
Medicine Arrows
medicine bag
medicine bundle
medicine man
medicine society
medicine wheel
Messenger Feast
messiah
mide
Midewiwin Society
Midwinter Ceremony
military society
mission
missionary
monotheism
Morning Star Ceremony
Mosquito Dance
Mountain Spirit Dance
mourning
mourning mask
mudhead
myth
mythical ancestor

mythology
naming ceremony
Native American Church
offering
Okipa
ordeal
Otter Society
Pahko
paho
palladium
pantheism
pantheon
Pascola
peyote fan
Peyote Religion
pipe-tomahawk
polytheism
potlatch
practitioner
prayer
prayer feather
prayer stick
preacher
prestige item
priest
priesthood
Priesthood of the Bow
prophet
psychotropic substance
puberty rite
purification
puskita
Quillworker Society
Rabbit Dance
rainmaking
Rain Priesthood
religion
rite
rite of passage
ritual
ritual drama
roadman
running the gauntlet
Sacred Buffalo Hat
Sacred Hoop
sacred object
Sacred Pipe
Sacred Pole
sacred site
sacrifice

sandpainting
Scalp Dance
scalping
secret society
Shalako Festival
shaman
shamanism
shape shifter
Shield and Spear Dance
shrine
skinwalker
smoking
Snake Dance
song fight
sorcerer
soul
soul catcher
Southern Cult
Spirit World
sponsor
stargazing
Stomp Dance
Straight Dance
sucking doctor
sucking tube
Sun Dance
sweating
tablita
taboo
Tachuktu
Taimé
talisman
tamanous
thanksgiving
theocracy
tihu
time cycle
tiponi
torture
totem
totem pole
Tree of Life
trophy
Turtle Continent
vision
Vision Quest
wakan
War Dance
War Woman
Washani Religion

Washat Dance
Way
White Deerskin Dance
witch
witchcraft
world renewal
worldview
yage
Yeibichai mask
Yeponi
yopo
Yuwipi

SPIRITS AND LEGENDARY BEINGS
See also RELIGION AND RITUAL.

Animal People
Annikadel
Avanyu
Breath of Life
Chac Mool
chapayeka
Creator
djibai
Faces of the Forest
gan
Gitchee Manitou
Gluskap
Grandmother Spider
Great Spirit
guardian spirit
Holy People
Holy Wind
Huitzilopochtli
Hunab-Ku
inua
kachina
Kalopaling
Kokopelli
Kukulkan
Little People
Manebozho
manitou
Michabo
Mictlantecuhtli
Monster
nagual
orenda

Otkon
Oyaron
Pacarina
Poshayanki
Quetzalcoatl
sila
spirit
spirit helper
spiritual being
Sweet Medicine
Tawiskaron
Teharonhiawagon
Tezcatlipoca
Three Sisters
Thunder Beings
Thunderbird
Tlaloc
Tloque Nahuague
Tonacacihuatl
Tonacatecuhtli
Tornit
Trickster
Viracocha
Virgin of Guadalupe
wakanda
Wakan Tanka
White Buffalo Woman
Windigo
Wind People
Xipe Totec
Xolotl
yei
zemi

TOOLS, UTENSILS, AND WEAPONS

See also ARTS AND CRAFTS; CONTAINERS; FOOD PRODUCTION; TRANSPORTATION.

abrader
adz
anchor stone
anvil
arrow
arrow feather
arrowhead
arrow release
arrow shaft
atlatl

awl
ax
bannerstone
bladder dart
blade
blowgun
bola
bow
bowguard
bowstring
burin
celt
chisel
club
coup stick
dart
digging stick
drill
firearm
fire drill
fishhook
flaked tool
flaker
flesher
flintstone
float
fluted point
gouge
grindstone
haft
hammer
hammerstone
harpoon
hatchet
hoe
hunting club
husking pin
javelin
knife
lamp
lance
leister
loom
mano
mattock
mirror
needle
net
paddle
pellet-bow

pick
pièce esquille
pipe
pogamoggan
point
polishing implement
projectile point
quirt
rabbit stick
rake
rope
sacrificial knife
saddle
saw
scraper
sealing dart
seal killer
seal scratcher
shield
sinew twister
sinker
slave killer
sling
snow knife
spade
spear
spindle
spokeshave
spoon
staff
stamp
tomahawk
tool
torch
tube
ulu
warclub
weapon
wedge
whetstone
wound plug

TRANSPORTATION

See also ANIMALS.

baidarka
balsa
bullboat
canoe
dugout

ice creeper
kayak
plank boat
portage
raft
sled
sledge shoe
snowshoe
toboggan
trade route
trail
transportation
travois
tumpline
umiak

TRIBES, BANDS, PEOPLES, LANGUAGES, AND CULTURES

General Groupings
See also PREHISTORIC INDIANS

American Indian
Amerind
Anglo-American
Arctic Peoples
Brotherton Indians
California Indians
Circum-Caribbean Indians
Digger Indians
Eastern Indians
Euroamerican
Five Civilized Tribes
French Indians
genizaro
Great Basin Indians
Great Lakes Indians
Indian
Mesoamerican Indians
mestizo
Metis
Mexican-American
mixed-blood
Mission Indians
Mohican
Moravian Indians
native

Native American
native peoples
Northeast Indians
Northwest Coast Indians
people
Plains Indians
Plateau Indians
Prairie Indians
Praying Indians
Pueblo Indians
Sheepeater
Snake Indians
South American Indians
Southeast Indians
Southwest Indians
Stockbridge Indians
Subarctic Indians
urban Indians
white
Woodland Indians

Prehistoric Indians
See also PEOPLES IN CENTRAL AND SOUTH AMERICA.

Adena Culture
Anasazi Culture
Archaic Indians
Clovis Culture
Cochise Culture
Desert Culture
Folsom Culture
Formative Indians
Fremont Culture
Hohokam Culture
Hopewell Culture
Mississippian Culture
Mogollon Culture
moundbuilders
Old Copper Culture
Old Cordilleran Culture
Paleo-Indians
Paleo-Siberians
Patayan Culture
Plano Culture
Prehistoric Indians
Red Paint Culture
Salado Culture
Sandia Culture
Sinagua Culture

Language Phyla
(Language groupings are based on ongoing research and are theoretical.)

American Arctic-Paleo-Siberian
Andean-Equatorial
Aztec-Tanoan
Ge-Pano-Carib
Hokan
Macro-Algonquian
Macro-Chibchan
Macro-Siouan
Nadene
Oto-Manguean
Penutian

Language Families
Algonquian
Araucanian-Chon
Arawakan
Athapascan
Caddoan
Cariban
Chibchan
Chinantecan
Chinookan
Chipaya-Uru
Chukchi-Kamchatkan
Chumashan
Eskimo-Aleut
Ge
Guaycuruan
Iroquoian
Jivaroan
Kalapuyan
Kiowa-Tanoan
Kusan
Manguean
Mayan
Miwok-Costonoan
Mixe-Zoquean
Mixtecan
Muskogean
Nahuatl
Otomian
Paezan
Palaihnihan

Panoan
Popolocan
Quechua
Quechuamaran
Sahaptin
Salinan
Salishan
Shastan
Shoshonean
Siouan
Tequistlatecan
Timotean
Timucuan
Tlapanecan
Totonacan
Tunican
Tupi-Guarani
Uto-Aztecan
Wakashan
Yakonan
Yanan
Yukian
Yuman
Zamucoan
Zaparoan
Zapatecan

Peoples in Central and South America

CIRCUM-CARIBBEAN
CULTURE AREA
See also LANGUAGE FAMILIES.

Arawak
Carib

MESOAMERICAN
CULTURE AREA
See also LANGUAGE FAMILIES.

Aztec
Maya
Olmec
Toltec

SOUTH AMERICAN
PEOPLES
See also LANGUAGE FAMILIES.

Inca

Tribes and Bands in What Is Now United States and Canada
(Listed by culture area, with bands under parent tribes.)

ARCTIC CULTURE AREA
Aleut
Inuit

CALIFORNIA CULTURE
AREA
Achomawi
Cahto
Cahuilla
Chumash
Costanoan
Diegueno
Hoopa
Juaneno
Karok
Luiseno
Maidu
    Konkau
Miwok
Patwin
Pomo
Salinas
Serrano
Shasta
Tolowa
Tubatulabal
Wailaki
Wintun
    Nomelacki
Wiyot
Yahi
Yana
Yokuts
    Tachi
Yuki
Yurok

GREAT BASIN CULTURE
AREA
Bannock
Chemehuevi
Mono
Paiute

Shoshone
    Goshute
Ute
    Capote
    Mouache
    Uintah
    Wiminuche
Washoe

GREAT PLAINS CULTURE
AREA
Arapaho
Arikara
Assiniboine
Blackfoot
    Blood
    Piegan
Cheyenne
Comanche
Crow
Gros Ventre
Hidatsa
Iowa
Kaw
Kiowa
Kiowa-Apache
Mandan
Missouri
Omaha
Osage
Oto
Pawnee
Ponca
Quapaw
Sarcee
Sioux
    Santee
        Mdewakanton
        Sisseton
        Wahpekute
        Wahpeton
    Teton
        Brule
        Hunkpapa
        Miniconjou
        Oglala
        Oohenonpa
        Sans Arcs
        Sihasapa

Yankton
Yanktonai
  Hunkpatina
Tawakoni
Tawehash
Tonkawa
Wichita

NORTHEAST CULTURE AREA
Abenaki
Algonkin
  Abitibi
Chippewa
  Missisauga
  Nipissing
Conoy
Erie
Fox
Hatteras
  Croatan
Huron
Illinois
  Kaskaskia
  Peoria
Iroquois
  Cayuga
  Mingo
  Mohawk
  Oneida
  Onondaga
  Seneca
  Tuscarora
Kickapoo
Lenni Lenape
  Munsee
  Unalachtigo
  Unami
Mahican
Malecite
Massachuset
Meherrin
Menominee
Miami
  Piankashaw
  Wea
Micmac
Mohegan
Montauk
  Poospatuck
  Shinnecock

Nanticoke
Narraganset
Neutral
Niantic
Nipmuc
Ottawa
Passamaquoddy
Pennacook
Penobscot
Pequot
  Schaghticoke
Potawatomi
Powhatan
  Chickahominy
  Mattaponi
  Pamunkey
  Rappahannock
Sac
Secotan
Shawnee
Susquehannock
Tobacco
Wampanoag
Wappinger
  Paugussett
Winnebago

NORTHWEST COAST
CULTURE AREA
Alsea
Bella Coola
Chastacosta
Chehalis
Chetco
Chimakum
Chinook
Clallam
Comox
Coos
Cowichan
Cowlitz
Duwamish
Gitksan
Haida
Haisla
Heiltsuk
  Bella Bella
Kalapuya
Kuitsh
Kwakiutl

Latgawa
Lumni
Makah
Muckleshoot
Nanaimo
Nisga'a
Nisqually
Nooksack
Nootka
  Clayoquot
Puntlatch
Puyallup
  Steilacoom
Quileute
  Hoh
Quinault
Samish
Seechelt
Semiahmoo
Siletz
Siuslaw
Skagit
  Sauk-Suiattle
Snohomish
Snoqualmie
Songish
Squamish
Squaxin
Suquamish
Swinomish
Takelma
Taltushtuntude
Tlingit
  Chilkat
Tsimshian
Tututni
Twana
  Skokomish
Umpqua
Yaquina

PLATEAU CULTURE AREA
Cayuse
Coeur d'Alene
Columbia
Colville
Flathead
Kalispel
Klamath
Klickitat

Kootenay
Lake
Lillooet
Methow
Modoc
Nez Perce
Ntlakyapamuk
Okanagan
Palouse
Sanpoil
Shuswap
Spokane
Tenino
Umatilla
Wallawalla
Yakima

SOUTHEAST CULTURE AREA
Alabama
Apalachee
Atakapa
Biloxi
Caddo
Calusa
Catawba
Cherokee
Chiaha
Chickasaw
Chitimacha
Choctaw
Coosa
Coushatta
Creek
  Eufaula
Cusabo
  Edisto
Hitchiti
Houma
Lumbee
Mobile
Monacan

Natchez
Oconee
Pee Dee
Santee
Saponi
Seminole
  Miccosukee
Timucua
Tunica
Waccamaw
Yamasee
Yazoo
Yuchi

SOUTHWEST CULTURE
AREA
Apache
  Apache Peaks
  Aravaipa
  Chiricahua
  Cibecue
  Gilenos
  Jicarilla
  Lipan
  Mescalero
  Mimbreno
  Mogollon
  Pinal
  San Carlos
  Tonto
  Warm Springs
  White Mountain
Coahuiltecan
Cocopah
Havasupai
Hopi
Hualapai
Karankawa
Keres
Maricopa
Mojave

Navajo
Papago
Pima
Sobaipuri
Tewa
Tiwa
Towa
Yaqui
Yavapai
Yuma
Zuni

SUBARCTIC CULTURE AREA
Ahtena
Beaver
Beothuk
Carrier
Chilcotin
Chipewyan
  Athabasca
Cree
  Mistassini
Dogrib
Han
Hare
Ingalik
Koyukon
Kutchin
Montagnais
Nabesna
Nahane
  Tagish
Naskapi
Sekani
Slave
Tahltan
Tanaina
Tanana
Tatsanottine
Tsetsaut
Tutchone

BIBLIOGRAPHY

Word Dance: The Language of Native American Culture is designed as a companion to wide-ranging Native American cultural studies. The following short list of resources is designed to give the same scope, with general titles selected rather than specific. A section on language is included for those readers who intend to pursue that area of study. A listing of bibliographies also is given to aid in specialized studies.

General Culture

Baity, Elizabeth Chesley. *Americans Before Columbus.* New York: Viking, 1961.

Berkhofer, Robert E. *White Man's Indians: Images of the American Indian from Columbus to the Present.* New York: Random House, 1979.

Bierhorst, John. *The Mythology of North America.* New York: William Morrow, 1985.

Bierhorst, John, ed. *The Sacred Path: Spells, Prayers, and Power Songs of the American Indian.* New York: William Morrow, 1983.

Billard, Jules B., ed. *The World of the American Indian.* Washington, D.C.: National Geographic Society, 1979.

Brandon, William. *Indians.* New York: American Heritage, 1985.

Bushnell, G. H. S. *Ancient Arts of the Americas.* New York: Frederick A. Praeger, 1965.

Caduto, Michael J., and Joseph Bruchac. *Keepers of the Animals: Native American Stories and Wildlife Activities for Children.* Golden, CO: Fulcrum, 1991.

Ceram, C. W. *The First American: A Story of North American Archaeology.* New York: Harcourt Brace Jovanovich, 1971.

Coe, Michael, Dean Snow, and Elizabeth Benson. *Atlas of Ancient America.* New York: Facts On File, 1986.

Collins, Richard, ed. *The Native Americans: The Indigenous People of North America.* New York: Smithmark, 1992.

Dictionary of Daily Life of Indians of the Americas. 2 vols. Newport Beach, CA: American Indian Publishers, 1981.

Dockstader, Frederick J. *Indian Art of the Americas.* New York: Museum of the American Indian, Heye Foundation, 1973.

Driver, Harold E. *Indians of North America.* Chicago: University of Chicago Press, 1969.

Edmonds, Margot, and Ella E. Clark. *Voices of the Winds: Native American Legends.* New York: Facts On File, 1989.

Embree, Edwin R. *Indians of the Americas.* Boston: Houghton Mifflin, 1939; rpt. New York: Macmillan, 1970.

Fagan, Brian. *The Great Journey: The Peopling of Ancient America.* New York: Thames and Hudson, 1987.

Feest, Christian F. *Native Arts of North America.* New York: Oxford University Press, 1980.

Fey, Harold E., and D'Arcy McNickle. *Indians and Other Americans: Two Ways of Life Meet.* New York: Harper & Row, 1970.

Fiedel, Stuart J. *Prehistory of the Americas.* Cambridge: Cambridge University Press, 1987.

Gonzalez, Ray. *Without Discovery: A Native Response to Columbus.* Seattle: Broken Moon Press, 1992.

Hausman, Gerald. *Turtle Island Alphabet: A Lexicon of Native American Symbols and Culture.* New York: St. Martin's, 1992.

Highwater, Jamake. *Arts of the Indian Americas: Leaves from the Sacred Tree.* New York: Harper & Row, 1983.

———. *The Primal Mind: Vision and Reality in Indian America.* New York: New American Library, 1981.

———. *Ritual of the Wind: North American Ceremonies, Music, and Dance.* New York: Van Der Marck, 1984.

Highwater, Jamake, ed. *Words in the Blood: Contemporary Indian Writers of North and South America.* New York: New American Library, 1984.

Hirschfelder, Arlene, and Paulette Molin. *The Encyclopedia of Native American Religions.* New York: Facts On File, 1992.

Hirschfelder, Arlene, and Martha Kreipe de Montano. *The Native American Almanac: A Portrait of Native America Today.* New York: Prentice-Hall General Reference, 1993.

Hodge, Frederick Webb, ed. *Handbook of American Indians North of Mexico.* 2 vols. Washington, D.C.: Bureau of American Ethnology, 1907–1910; rpt. Westport, CT: Greenwood Press, 1971.

Jaimes, M. Annette, ed. *The State of Native America: Genocide, Colonization, and Resistance.* Boston: South End Press, 1992.

Jenness, Diamond. *The Indians of Canada.* Ottawa: National Museum of Canada, 1932; rpt. Toronto: University of Toronto Press, 1982.

Jennings, J. D., and Edward Norbeck, eds. *Prehistoric Man in the New World.* Chicago: University of Chicago Press, 1964.

Josephy, Alvin, Jr. *The Indian Heritage of America.* New York: Knopf, 1970.

Josephy, Alvin, Jr., ed. *The American Heritage Book of Indians.* New York: Simon & Schuster, 1961.

Klein, Barry T., ed. *Reference Encyclopedia of the American Indian.* 2 vols. 6th ed. West Nyack, NY: Todd Publications, 1992.

Kroeber, Alfred L. *Cultural and Natural Areas of Native North America.* University of California Publications in American Archaeology and Ethnology, 1939; rpt. Berkeley, CA: University of California Press, 1963.

Hultkrantz, Ake. *The Religions of the American Indian.* Berkeley, CA: University of California Press, 1967.

Leitch, Barbara A. *A Concise Dictionary of Indian Tribes of North America.* Algonac, MI: Reference Publications, 1979.

Lesley, Craig, ed. *Talking Leaves: Contemporary Native American Short Stories.* New York: Dell, 1991.

Lincoln, Kenneth. *Native American Renaissance.* Berkeley, CA: University of California Press, 1983.

Mason, John Alden. *The Ancient Civilizations of Peru.* Harmondsworth: Pelican, 1957.

Maxwell, James A., ed. *America's Fascinating Indian Heritage.* Pleasantville, NY: The Reader's Digest, 1978.

McNickle, D'Arcy. *The Indian Tribes of the United States.* New York: Oxford University Press, 1962.

———. *Native American Tribalism: Indian Survivals and Renewals.* New York: Oxford University Press, 1973.

Nabokov, Peter, ed. *Native American Testimony: A Chronicle of Indian-White Relations from Prophecy to the Present, 1492–1992.* New York: Penguin, 1992.

Nabokov, Peter, and Robert Easton. *Native American Architecture.* New York: Oxford University Press, 1989.

Peterson, Frederick. *Ancient Mexico: An Introduction to the Pre-Hispanic Cultures.* New York: Capricorn, 1962.

Sauer, Carl. *Man in Nature: America Before the Days of the White Man.* New York: Charles Scribner's Sons, 1939; rpt. Berkeley, CA: Turtle Island Foundation, 1975.

Sejourne, Laurette. *Burning Water: Thought and Religion in Ancient Mexico.* New York: Grove, 1960.

Snow, Dean R., and Werner Forman. *The Archaeology of North America.* New York: Viking, 1976.

Spencer, Robert F., et al. *The Native Americans: Prehistory and Ethnology of North American Indians.* New York: Harper & Row, 1965.

Steward, Julian H., ed. *Handbook of South American Indians.* Bureau of American Ethnology Bulletin 143. Washington, D.C.: Smithsonian Institution, 1946–50.

Swanton, John R. *The Indian Tribes of North America.* Bureau of American Ethnology Bulletin 145. Washington, D.C.: Smithsonian Institution, 1952.

Tax, Sol, ed. *The Civilizations of Ancient America.* Chicago: University of Chicago Press, 1951.

Turner, Geoffrey. *Indians of North America.* Poole, Dorset: Blandford Press, 1979.

Underhill, Ruth M. *Red Man's America: A History of Indians in the United States.* Chicago: University of Chicago Press, 1953.

———. *Red Man's Religion: Beliefs and Practices of the Indians North of Mexico.* Chicago: University of Chicago Press, 1965.

Versluis, Arthur. *The Elements of Native American Traditions.* Rockport, MA: Element, 1993.

Wax, Murray L. *Indian Americans: Unity and Diversity.* Englewood Cliffs, NJ: Prentice-Hall, 1971.

Weatherford, Jack. *Native Givers: How the Indians of the Americas Transformed the World.* New York: Crown, 1989.

———. *Native Roots: How the Indians Enriched America.* New York: Crown, 1991.

Willey, Gordon R., ed. *Prehistoric Settlement Patterns in the New World.* New York: Viking Fund Publications in Anthropology, 1956.

Wissler, Clark. *Indians of the United States: Four Centuries of Their History and Culture.* 1940; rpt. Garden City, NY: Doubleday, 1966.